Pam Richards

UNDERSTANDING TAROT

A detailed guide to the Rider Waite Smith Tarot cards, for both the new and experienced Tarot student

AUSTIN MACAULEY PUBLISHERS™
LONDON • CAMBRIDGE • NEW YORK • SHARJAH

Copyright © Pam Richards 2022

The right of Pam Richards to be identified as author of this work has been asserted in accordance with section 77 and 78 of the Copyright, Designs and Patents Act 1988.

All rights reserved. No part of this publication may be reproduced, stored in a retrieval system, or transmitted in any form or by any means, electronic, mechanical, photocopying, recording, or otherwise, without the prior permission of the publishers.

Any person who commits any unauthorised act in relation to this publication may be liable to criminal prosecution and civil claims for damages.

A CIP catalogue record for this title is available from the British Library.

ISBN 9781398431485 (Paperback)
ISBN 9781398431492 (ePub e-book)

www.austinmacauley.com

First Published 2022
Austin Macauley Publishers Ltd
1 Canada Square
Canary Wharf
London E14 5AA

To Debbie for introducing me to Tarot all those years ago.

To Robin, Martin George, Suzi for your input and wisdom.

To Saskia for the wonderful and rare 78 Rose and Lilies images.

CONTENTS

Introduction 11
    New Tarot Students and the Rider Waite Smith Tarot Deck 12
    A Brief History of The Rider Waite Smith Tarot Deck 13

The Tarot Deck 17
    The Tarot Deck 18
        The Major Arcana 19
        The Minor Arcana 19
        To Reverse or Not to Reverse 20

The Tarot Cards 21
    The Major Arcana 22
        The Fool - 0 23
        The Magician - 1 28
        The High Priestess - 2 32
        The Empress - 3 37
        The Emperor - 4 42
        The Hierophant - 5 47
        The Lovers - 6 52
        The Chariot - 7 56
        Strength - 8 61
        The Hermit - 9 65
        Wheel of Fortune - 10 69
        Justice - 11 73
        The Hanged Man - 12 78
        Death - 13 83
        Temperance - 14 89
        The Devil - 15 94
        The Tower - 16 100
        The Star - 17 105
        The Moon - 18 109
        The Sun - 19 114
        Judgement - 20 119
        The World - 21 125
    The Minor Arcana 129
        The Suit of Wands 130
            Ace of Wands 131
            Two of Wands 135
            Three of Wands 139
            Four of Wands 143
            Five of Wands 147
            Six of Wands 150
            Seven of Wands 154

- Eight of Wands ... 157
- Nine of Wands ... 160
- Ten of Wands ... 163
- The Wand Family ... 167
  - Page of Wands ... 168
  - Knight of Wands ... 172
  - Queen of Wands ... 176
  - King of Wands ... 181
- The Suit of Cups ... 185
  - Ace of Cups ... 186
  - Two of Cups ... 190
  - Three of Cups ... 194
  - Four of Cups ... 198
  - Five of Cups ... 202
  - Six of Cups ... 206
  - Seven of Cups ... 210
  - Eight of Cups ... 213
  - Nine of Cups ... 217
  - Ten of Cups ... 221
- The Cup Family ... 224
  - Page of Cups ... 225
  - Knight of Cups ... 229
  - Queen of Cups ... 233
  - King of Cups ... 238
- The Suit of Swords ... 243
  - Ace of Swords ... 244
  - Two of Swords ... 248
  - Three of Swords ... 252
  - Four of Swords ... 255
  - Five of Swords ... 259
  - Six of Swords ... 263
  - Seven of Swords ... 267
  - Eight of Swords ... 272
  - Nine of Swords ... 276
  - Ten of Swords ... 280
- Sword Family ... 284
  - Page of Swords ... 285
  - Knight of Swords ... 290
  - Queen of Swords ... 295
  - King of Swords ... 300
- The Suit of Pentacles ... 305
  - Ace of Pentacles ... 306
  - Two of Pentacles ... 310
  - Three of Pentacles ... 314
  - Four of Pentacles ... 318
  - Five of Pentacles ... 323

    Six of Pentacles 328
    Seven of Pentacles 333
    Eight of Pentacles 337
    Nine of Pentacles 341
    Ten of Pentacles 346
    Page of Pentacles 352
    Knight of Pentacles 356
    Queen of Pentacles 360
    King of Pentacles 365

Using Your Tarot Deck 369

Choosing and Using Your Tarot Deck 370
    Choosing Your Tarot Deck 370
    Using Your Tarot Deck 371

Preparing for a Reading 374
    My ritual or routine 374

1 Your Question 376
    Timing in Questions 377

2 Your Spread 378

3 Preparing your Deck 378
    Chaos Method 379

4 Significators 379
    Court Cards as Significators and within Readings 380
    Traditional Court Card Depictions 381
    Astrological Signs and Colouring 382

5 Shuffling 383
    How to Shuffle your Tarot Deck 383
    Reversed Cards 384
    Jumper Cards 385

6 Laying Your Cards 385

Putting Your Cards Away 385
    Storage of Your Tarot Deck When Not in Use 385

Traditional Tarot Spreads 387

Using and Creating Tarot Spreads 388
    Can I create my own spreads? 388
    Do I lay my cards face down or face up? 388
    Clarifier cards 389

Spreads: Some General Timing Insights 390
    One Card Reading 392
    Three Card Spread 393
    Six Card Spread 394
    Six Card Spread 1 394
    Six Card Spread 2 395

The Celtic Cross..396
The Traditional Celtic Cross 397
The Cross 397
The Column (starting from the base upwards)....................................397
The Traditional Rider Waite Celtic Cross 1 398
Alternate Celtic Cross 2 399
Alternate Celtic Cross 3 400
Alternate Celtic Cross 4 401
The 26 Card Celtic Cross, or the Super-Duper Celtic Cross! 402

Tarot Superstitions and Hearsay..403

Superstitions, Hearsay and Negative Presumptions on the Tarot 404

Some Common Superstitions and Myths..405
'You should not read Tarot for yourself.'...405
'You are not allowed to buy your own Tarot deck.' 405
'You are not allowed to let others touch your Tarot deck.' 405
'You cannot use the Tarot unless you know how to.' 406
'You need to sleep with the deck under your pillow.'........................ 406
'You must interview a new Tarot deck.'... 406
'You must not cross your legs when you read Tarot.'........................ 406
'Tarot cards are evil and attract negative energies.'...........................407
'Pregnant women should not use Tarot.'...407
'It is a gift from God, so you should not charge to read for another.' 407
'Tarot must be tapped three times before you use your Tarot cards.'.. 408
Smudging, Moonlight, and Crystals... 408

Reading for Other People 409

Reading for Others 410

Readings for or about Others without Their Knowledge or Permission .412

The Future..413

The Future? 414
Probable Outcomes...414
Free Will..415

Tarot Meditations for Psychic Development or Subconscious Connection 417

Stepping into Tarot 418
Stepping into Tarot - Getting to Know a Card................................421
Stepping into Tarot - Personal Answers..424
How Often Should I Meditate upon a Card? 426

Enjoy Your Tarot Journey 427

*Clear your mind – and welcome in The Sun
Clear your mind – and welcome in the dawning
Clear your mind – connect with The One
In the light of The Sun – in the light of the morning*

~ *'The Telling' by Davey Dodds*

Introduction

Welcome to *Understanding Tarot* and the wonderful world of Tarot. This book has been written as a guide, a resource and a friend to help you on your journey.

If this is your first introduction to the Tarot, you will find you are entering a fascinating field of study containing all of life's possibilities. Within the pages of this book, you will meet with most facets of human existence and learn a lot about both yourself and others along the way.

Understanding Tarot is aimed at those completely new to Tarot as well as the more advanced student. If you have already been introduced to the Tarot, then I hope that this book is helpful, interesting and inspiring. You may have found out from previous study that the Tarot is a complex subject and not one best suited to conventional teaching. You can, however, be guided and hopefully this book will help you achieve that aim.

For those of you who are new to the study of the Tarot, the words in ***bold italics*** are to help you understand each card more quickly and to help bring the card's main points to the beginner's eye. The 'In a Nutshell' descriptions fulfil a similar function by offering a brief summing up of each card.

Tarot is an endless subject, branching into many others such as Astrology, Alchemy, Numerology, Chakras, Occultism, the Kabbalah, dreams, psychology and many, many more. Each author and deck designer have added their perspective of the Tarot, which gives us all a personal Tarot niche to settle into. However, when Tarot cards were created, those equally deep subjects were not an aspect for the tarot student or tarot reader to consider, nor were reversed cards. If you're not drawn to any of these complex subjects, do not worry they are not needed to be able to learn and read Tarot, as the imagery holds all you need to know. We will touch on the subjects of Numerology *(the study of numbers and how they affect life, personalities and events)*, Chakras *(energy centres within the body, based on eastern spiritual practices)* and Astrology *(how the stars and planets affect the world about us, personalities and life)*; however, with just a passing interest in these subjects, I'm not qualified or knowledgeable enough to go into deep detail in these areas. This shows you need only go to what you're drawn to with Tarot to make it work for you. Don't expect to have a grasp of the Tarot overnight: it's best approached as a long and pleasant journey, so keep it simple.

This book is here to guide you towards an understanding of the Tarot and its symbolic nature, especially the Rider Waite Smith deck, with both upright and reversed meanings (the latter you can take or leave as befits your study). You can also use this book to aid your psychic development by learning how to use Tarot as a steppingstone to clairvoyant development, or subconscious growth, via the meditation exercises which utilise the Tarot in a less traditional way. Yet do understand: you do not have to be spiritual, clairvoyant, or mystical in any way to use the Tarot, as they are a subconscious tool first and foremost.

I wish to give, as far as I can, an uncomplicated approach to the Tarot. My aim is to show you as much of its magic as possible from the images of the Rider Waite Smith Tarot Deck, with the book also being of use to all Tarot users and any deck they wish to work with.

New Tarot Students and the Rider Waite Smith Tarot Deck

Understanding Tarot goes in-depth, showing the symbolic meanings behind as much as the imagery as possible in each card within the Rider Waite Smith deck (traditionally called the Rider Waite tarot deck). There are countless variations of this deck in print by new artists, as well as the deck itself, which is what I recommend to those new to or struggling with their Tarot journey to use. The reason this deck is so great to learn from is due to the amount of symbolism each card has drawn within it. Tarot stems from its symbolism, and learning the intricacies of each card is easier when they are in front of you.

To have your first Tarot deck as one which is pretty, yet has none of the symbolism, can make it harder for you to develop an understanding of them, as the subconscious mind will not be able to pick up on the universal symbolism which you already have within yourself if it is not present within the cards. The amount of resource material for this deck is also outstanding, from books such as this one to thousands of others and websites dedicated to them, so you will always be able to find a teacher or resource which you can gel with.

Understanding Tarot is a journey, one which can take time to grasp, and one where you never really stop developing your understanding of the cards' meanings and symbolism. I know I haven't. There are no shortcuts to learning such a complex system, so go for a deck that is fit for that purpose - the Rider Waite Smith.

I don't have a Rider Waite Smith Tarot Deck; can I still learn from this book?

Yes! While this book investigates the symbolism, the imagery of each card within the RWS deck, the card meanings and all the other pages of information will still help you with your Tarot study and practice, as it is universal information.

Your own journey with the Tarot is individual to you and I hope this book will introduce you to your own inner guide.

Grab your cards and let your journey begin!

A Brief History of The Rider Waite Smith Tarot Deck
(with contributions from Saskia Jansen)

Tarot is said to have been born in Italy around the 14th century. The Major deck was used to play a card game called Tarocchi, which is like Bridge and is still played today, mainly in France. These decks were often highly decorated works of art, having been hand-painted and some decorated with gold leaf.

Later in the 14th century, the French introduced playing cards to the Tarocchi deck, and these two decks were paired together to create Tarot, although this still would most likely have been used as a parlour game, as opposed to divination.

Major changes came with Antoine Court de Gébelin, who held the opinion that Tarot held the secrets of the Egyptians. Without producing any historical evidence, he developed a reconstruction of Tarot history, stating that Egyptian priests had distilled the ancient Book of Thoth into these images. These they brought to Rome and secretly shown to the popes, who brought them to Avignon in the 14th century, whence they were introduced into France. In 1788 Court de Gébelin introduced Tarot for divination purposes in his compendium series, Volume VIII in an essay called 'Le Monde primitif, analysé et comparé avec le monde modern'. Within two years the fortune-teller known as 'Etteilla' (Jean-Baptiste Alliette) published a technique for reading the Tarot, and the practice of Tarot reading was born with the first deck specifically printed and designed for divination.

The Rider Waite Tarot deck was first published in 1909. Its name derived from the name of the publisher, William Rider and Son, and Arthur Edward Waite who designed the deck. The Rider Waite name only appeared in 1971. Before that, they were merely called Tarot cards.

Arthur Edward Waite (2 October 1857 - 19 May 1942) was born in Brooklyn, New York to an American father and British mother. Arthur's father died when he was very young, which prompted his family to move back to England, where he lived for the rest of his life. As he grew, he became interested in the occult; this may have, in part, been due to the death of his sister. Christian Spiritualism and its belief in proof of survival of the Spirit after death were on the rise within the UK at that time, which no doubt stirred his interests.

In January 1891, aged 34, he joined the Hermetic Order of the Golden Dawn, a secret society dedicated to the study of the occult, paranormal and metaphysical, which disbanded in 1914, after which Waite started the Fellowship of the Rosy Cross. He also became a Freemason and belonged to the *Societas Rosicruciana in Anglia*. These groups had a Christian basis to them, particularly Christian Mysticism, the Kabbalah, ceremonial magic, and even the Holy Grail. He authored many books and publications but is best known for his Tarot deck, the Rider Waite.

Pamela Colman Smith, known also as 'Pixie', was born in London on 16 February 1878. Her father, like Arthur, was born in Brooklyn; her mother was Jamaican-born. As a child, she lived in Manchester before moving to Jamaica and the West Indies then to Brooklyn as a teenager. Her uncle was the artist Samuel Colman, and she studied art at the Pratt Institute herself but left without qualifications. Her father died when she was 21, which saw a move back to England in 1900. There she joined the Lyceum Theatre Company and toured with the group. She undertook various jobs: a publisher of small books, designer of theatre costumes and sets, an illustrator, yet an artist by nature. She worked on a few books such as Bram Stoker's *The Lair of the White Worm*, which was published after the Rider Waite Tarot deck.

She joined the Order of the Golden Dawn at the same time as Arthur. With his idea and her artistic ability to bring it to life, they created this much-loved Tarot deck after Waite commissioned her services as an artist.

What may have prompted Arthur to create a Tarot deck was a museum display of a Tarot deck dating back to the 15th century, the Sola Busca. Yet it is widely assumed that Pixie was the one more influenced by this deck. While Waite is credited for 'designing' the cards, if one reads his descriptions of the cards and then looks at the artwork, it seems clear that most of the imagery originated from Pixie, not Arthur Waite. She didn't follow his instructions. It is also thought that what prompted Arthur more to create a tarot deck was his membership to the Golden Dawn and his need for a more comprehensive deck that didn't 'veil the secrets' of the Golden Dawn Tarot.

Sadly, she was paid badly for her artwork. Waite's name and the Rider company took precedence in the title, and Pamela herself said that *'it was little money for a lot of work'*, or words to that effect. When she died on 18 September 1951, it is said she was buried in an unmarked pauper's grave and all her goods were sold to pay her debts.

Today, a lot of people recognise that Pamela Colman Smith was an artist but was poorly paid due to being female, a sign of the times she lived in. She never received the rewards which Waite did. In respect of that, the deck is now often referred to as the Rider Waite Smith, Waite Smith, or RWS to honour her massive contribution.

The Tarot deck, first sold in November 1909, is referred to today as the Rose and Lilies. There are only a handful of these decks left in existence: five at the time of writing. The cards from one of those five decks illustrate this book. This deck's rarity has resulted from the publisher's dissatisfaction with the quality of the deck: they were recalled the following year with the promise of the deck, which collectors call the 'Pam A', as a free replacement, and so most were returned. In the years 1910-1920 William Rider & Sons published the Pam A in both a book and deck version and just a deck version in a slipcase. Presumably, when they ran out, they published other, newer versions of the deck, resulting in the Pam B, C and D. These decks were printed with different print techniques from the original ones. The Roses and Lilies deck and the Pam A were printed by the time-consuming chromolithography process, resulting in lines to produce colours on the cards. The subsequent decks were also printed lithographically, but as with modern 'offset' printing the images were screened, which rendered them as a series of tiny dots.

Also, even though the logical order would be B, then C, then D, it appears that the C and D were released in the 1920s, while the B was printed and released from 1931 till 1939.

Of note is also the change in the artwork. For the Pam C, it seems they hired new copyists, which changed the line art of the original. This changed artwork has been used for both the C and B decks.

Sadly, the printing plates were lost in the bombing of Plymouth in 1942; these were probably the print plates from the Pam B, as the chromolithography decks would have used different plates. What happened to the original artwork and print plates of the Roses and Lilies and Pam A is unfortunately unknown. The print plates were likely destroyed or reused.

Rider did not publish the deck between 1939 and 1971. In that year, Rider joined with US Games to obtain a license from the heiress of Arthur E. Waite and published the deck again. It was at this point that the deck was named Rider Tarot; later this would be changed to Rider Waite Tarot. There have been Rider Waite-like decks printed in the meantime, by the US companies University Books and Merrimack Publishing, but these had neither a proper licence nor the Rider Waite name. The Rider Waite Smith Tarot deck and its symbolism is the basis for most decks which have come since, with many being 'Rideresque' or near-clones of the original. There are, of course, many decks that are completely independent – the array of Tarot decks available today is amazing, even if the Rider Waite Smith is still the most popular deck in print.

Saskia Jansen
www.waitesmith.org

THE TAROT DECK

The Tarot Deck

Tarot cards are made from card stock, plastic, or linen. Like most things published nowadays, they are mass-produced in printing factories; this can help dispel some of the superstitious mysticism that surrounds them. They contain symbolic drawings and imagery, so at their heart, they are simply seventy-eight pieces of paper with pictures on them. Yet they are images which can take us to many places within our minds, as the images are universal and recognised by our subconscious. In all the questions we have, most of the answers are inside us, but for whatever reason, we cannot find them. The Tarot act as a key to bringing those answers out, putting the jigsaw together for us to see the bigger picture and those things we wish to hide from ourselves, reflecting our own truths. In this book, they are not presented as a mystical object, but more a practical tool and a means to link you to your subconscious mind and psychic self, depending on which route you, the reader, wish to take.

A Tarot deck is made up of seventy-eight cards but is in fact made up of two separate decks, which consist of twenty-two Major Arcana and fifty-six Minor, or Lesser, Arcana. These minor cards are sometimes referred to as 'Pips,' though this term strictly refers to cards one to ten that have no imagery: for example, only five swords are depicted in the Tarot de Marseilles.

The word Arcana is taken from the Latin word *arca* which means *'a chest in which secrets are stored'*. This alone gives us an idea of the many possibilities that the Tarot holds. Each individual card represents the possible forces that have influenced, are influencing or will influence one's life.

A lot of Tarot decks have seventy-eight cards that are pictorial or show a scene relevant to the emotion, thought or situation that the card represents. Being archetypal images, they represent those things in life that recur through the generations and are subconsciously understood by most, even if we see them differently at different life stages, levels of understanding and experience. In short, Tarot are you and me.

Within this book, the 1909 original edition of the deck, now long out of print, is pictured. You will find many more versions available if you have a liking for the symbolism. I favour the deck recoloured by *Mary Hanson-Roberts,* the so-called 'Universal Waite', as its pastel colouring makes the symbolism easy to see. My references in this book often go between this version and the original.

The Major Arcana

The Major Arcana are numbered from 0 to 21 and they are titled as follows.

0 The Fool - 1 The Magician - 2 The High Priestess - 3 The Empress - 4 The Emperor - 5 The Hierophant - 6 The Lovers - 7 The Chariot - 8 Strength - 9 The Hermit - 10 Wheel of Fortune - 11 Justice - 12 The Hanged Man - 13 Death - 14 Temperance - 15 The Devil - 16 The Tower - 17 The Star - 18 The Moon - 19 The Sun - 20 Judgement - 21 The World.

These twenty-two Major cards represent the principal forces that guide and mould the paths of a person's life, and all of them at one stage or another will be present within our lives to influence us. The energies that the Majors bring to us are of paramount importance and hard to hide from. They inform us of the power that we should use and of what energy governs us at any time; they represent the core, or area of focus, within any given situation.

The Minor Arcana

The Minor Arcana consists of fifty-six cards. This, sometimes called Lesser Deck, Lesser Arcana or Pip cards, is comprised of four suits titled Cups, Wands, Swords and Pentacles. Each suit contains fourteen cards, while a conventional deck of playing cards has thirteen. This difference arrives due to the Tarot deck having a Page and a Knight, whereas the playing deck has a Jack. The numbering of the Minor deck goes from Ace to Ten, followed by Page, Knight, Queen and King. In some Tarot decks, you will find the Page and Knight called Prince and Princess, making them the children of the King and Queen.

The journey through the Minor Arcana from Wands, Cups, Swords, and Pentacles can be viewed as a microcosm of the Major Arcana from Fool to World, which is mirrored in the Minor Arcana from the Ace of Wands to the Ten of Pentacles, some say the King of Pentacles, in which The Fool navigates from innocence to experience and youth to old age, often called *The Fool's Journey*.

The Pages and Knights represent not only individual characters and personalities but are also messengers and bringers, or representatives of events. The Queens and Kings of the suits also represent personality types but they, as well as the other court cards, can indicate our emotional, mental and physical responses to events or certain situations, which leaves gender fluid between all the court cards.

In a reading, i.e., when consulting the Tarot, the Minor Arcana will add clarity and depth to the question asked, with each Minor suit representing a different element.

CUPS = **WATER** represent emotions. They tell of feelings, relationships and the effects that they have on us.

SWORDS = **AIR** bring difficulties and strife, and they show intellectual action and mental force.

WANDS = **FIRE** bring us creativity, putting ideas into action and the creation of energy.

PENTACLES = **EARTH** deal with the practical, physical and mundane areas of life, especially money.

To Reverse or Not to Reverse

I feel it best to place this aspect of the book before the cards meaning are discussed in case you are new to Tarot, as opposed to at the back where all the other Tarot information can be found.

When you are learning Tarot, you have seventy-eight complex cards to learn, which can be a daunting process. Seventy-eight relationships to forge. With the reversed meanings, that is one hundred and fifty-six, which can be too much information to study in one go. It can take years, decades, to truly understand the Tarot; reversed meanings are not needed unless wished for.

You can approach the issue of reversed cards three ways.

1: Ignore them.
Nothing will be missing from your readings as other cards will fill in the insights. If you're new to the study of Tarot, or confused by it, this is the method which I recommend wholeheartedly. I didn't study reversed cards for at least a decade. There is nothing to be gained by confusing your study.

2: Learn both the Upright and Reversed.
Jump in and study both at the same time. If you find yourself confused, stop, then go back to it at a later date.

3: Use just upright cards BUT view them as Well-Defined or Ill-Defined.
To view cards as ill- or well-defined, keep them upright, and just mentally change the word 'reversed' to' ill-defined' and 'upright' to 'well-defined', and then study both aspects as one. Treat them as flipsides, the yin and yang of an upright card. How any card would be read would be relevant to the other cards within the spread: a positive card may lean more towards its ill-defined aspect, as equal as if it were an ill-defined card placed amongst optimistic cards. This takes you into Comparative Tarot reading which encompasses every aspect of a reading, from question to placement, to the other cards and how they all link together. As with all things Tarot, try them all and see what you're drawn to most.

THE TAROT CARDS

THE MAJOR ARCANA

THE FOOL - 0

The Fool is unnumbered, and so he can be placed at the start or end of the Major deck. He is placed where the Major Arcana starts, before The Magician, and ends, after The World, representing a cycle of life, area of life, or experience. Zero, 'o', represents nothing, chaos, potential, and it is from nothing that anything is possible. He is instinct, possibility, and no limitations, which brings us the formation and the onset of new and sudden events. The Fool is the leap of faith we may need between each card as we travel through life and situations.

The Fool is ruled by Uranus and associated with Aquarius, yet some say he has no sign attributed to him, as he can be placed anywhere within the deck as he travels through it experiencing life.

The Fool shows us the image of a man looking to the sunny sky, seemingly unaware of the cliff edge.

The Fool's youthful appearance represents positivity and enthusiasm and a childlike, playful, innocent outlook on life. He wears colourful clothes, indicating he has a lack of insight or thought concerning his actions as he acts on pure impulse. His tunic has a ripe pomegranate pattern symbolising abundance, yet most are not in full seed leaving him full of potential, readiness and enthusiasm. The lining of his tunic is orange, a colour that brings optimism, fun and enthusiasm. His tunic represents productive energy which wants to rush towards what is desired, especially if it's new, enticing and waiting to be experienced or attempted. Together, the pomegranates and orange show indulgent and enjoyable energy.

Under his tunic, he wears a white shirt, which shows his innocence as it is closest to his body. At heart, this card is pure in its nature, driven more by instinct than anything else.

Around his waist, he wears a yellow belt made of seven small balls. Some authors say these are bells, which playfully announce his arrival, while others see them as planets. They may represent the seventh planet, Uranus, which The Fool is ruled by and is a sign of his unpredictable, imaginative, and original personality.

His shoes are also yellow like the sky, and so he walks confidently; even though he is not looking where he is going, he trusts the faith he has that the experience will be worth it. The Fool is surrounded by magnetic energy that, as yet, has no real concrete definition. The excitement of new possibilities being within his grasp means that he is willing to suffer the unknown just to see them implemented instead of wasted. He brings a time to leave the past behind, to take a deep breath and move forward.

The Fool's black hat is surrounded by a laurel wreath showing his presumption that he will succeed, and the red feather shows desire as well as representing his mental desire to create something new. It is this desire fuelled by instincts and a willingness to explore that pushes him forward. Being black, the hat itself shows his mind holds potential as black absorbs all other colours, so therefore holds all the possibilities available in life. You may notice in this original image shown that his laurel crown is blue. Blue about the head shows a mind which is serene, meditative, calm and lost in the moment.

In his right hand, the side of our emotions and dreams, he holds a black magician's wand that shows he has power; latent and unknown, maybe - but present. The colour, like his hat, symbolises potential and here carries his past experiences which he wishes to take with him as he finds somewhere new to explore. He may have given little thought as to the way ahead as he is working from a need to discover and experience. He hopes his journey will enable him to add to the bag he carries, as The Fool aims to enjoy and learn, as that is where success lies for him.

On the bag facing left is the head of an eagle, symbolising the ascending spirit. His bag sits under the sun, firing his imagination, burning him from within to move and gravitate towards something new. It looks like a satchel, which suggests a student of life, learning and soaking up experiences. Eagles soar, giving The Fool a burning desire to make changes, as he wants to see and do it all. Eagles, along with the scorpion and phoenix, are linked to the sign of Scorpio, an aspect of The Fool that acts, strikes and dives into something in an instant from its panoramic view, yet even he cannot guarantee the outcome should The Fool jump as he faces in the opposite direction and sits under the glare of the sun.

In his left, logical, hand, he gently holds a white rose between his thumb and finger in a position called the Gyan Mudra, a traditional eastern meditation hand gesture that focuses the mind. Together, these tell of The Fool's intentions which are pure and from the heart; even though they have no founding in actual experience or maturity, it shows simplicity and trust in the unknown. He does not wish to think too deeply but flows with the energy he feels propelled by, preferring to be mindful and to live in the moment.

The Fool's dog also symbolises his instincts, some could say his ego, which urges him towards the dangerous edge of the rocks. Yet dogs are companions, friends to be trusted, loyal and faithful, lending feelings of safety to The Fool's actions and desires. The dog jumps up at him and might be trying to warn him of the fall ahead and to look before he leaps, but The Fool gazes upwards into the expense of the sky, oblivious to any danger.

His upwards gaze is to the heavens, telling us he is full of dreams and high aspirations. He is not considering failure nor concerned at the height of the cliff, nor the ground he will land upon; it's the idea and the inspiration which lead him into this impulsive action. The Fool states that when you are without the relevant experience you can only gain by jumping in at the deep end and at least trying.

The mountains behind him warn of the possible dangers his situation might bring, but he ignores the signs, just feeling the positive sun on his back, happy, enthusiastic, and willing to try. The rocky cliff he is about to jump over tells of the unknown, and although anything might greet him once over the edge, The Fool is still happy to walk or jump over, seemingly without fear. The Fool is going to enter the thrill of the cliff drop, armed simply with an incurable desire to understand, and learn with his innocent outlook.

Behind him is a stone hut; we can only see a portion, yet there seems to be just a door. He has emerged from a womb-like place, dark, safe, and secure. In a way, born and inexperienced into the world, ready for change and the chance to lead him to what is new.

I don't feel that The Fool is particularly brave, nor stupid, but innocent and naïve about the possibility of fear and failure. To The Fool, the cliff doesn't represent panic, danger or the unknown; instead, it is merely a way to somewhere else. So surely only a fool would jump and risk failure? Or could it be that The Fool has a strong desire to take the risk, feel the adventure and see what is past the obstacle that, to others, the cliff would represent? He may also feel that he has nothing to lose and everything to gain just from the experience alone.

The Fool's card is instinctual, impulsive, and spirited. His essence is both inspirational and explosive. He has been offered an opportunity, or discovered one, and is bold enough to leave where he is to go and explore it. His ideas and desires may not be totally clear to him, and he may also be unaware of where they will lead him, as once he jumps as he has no idea if he will have a soft or hard landing, but he is going to do it anyway. The Fool does not give us time to think about things, he is pure enthusiasm. Acting, not thinking.

Suddenly, anything is possible. He is like a bubble of excitement!

IN A NUTSHELL

Hold your nose and jump in, be brave, throw caution to the wind and take a chance for the sake of it. This is not a time to think, but to grab opportunities or ideas and run with them, allow actions to take you to where they will lead.

Leave the past behind, allowing excitement to lead you forwards. Be impulsive! Start afresh.

The Fool – 0: Upright

The Fool brings a time to enjoy life for the moment, to dive into **new circumstances and opportunities without consideration or apprehension** for what the future may or may not bring.

Spontaneous and **unpremeditated actions** will be called for to bring about desired results. The Fool's arrival tells us that dreams should be tested, and any desires should be made a goal; **new pathways** will require **faith and action** to make them happen.

This card can also be an indication that **free will** is needed and should be implemented rather than waiting for 'something' to happen! If no opening is present, make one.

The Fool offers **new probabilities and new beginnings,** the type that brings fresh **new challenges** as The Fool brings **originality**.

When The Fool appears in a Tarot spread, situations will change suddenly and events will take on new directions as ideas and opportunities come to light seemingly out of nowhere, out of the blue, and when **unexpected influences** come into one's life or situations.

The Fool brings **major choices** and avenues of change for those who are brave enough to take them. He brings situations where thinking is not an option, or where we need to grasp an opportunity and worry about the outcome later.

The Fool manifests a strong desire and **an instinctual need to accept any change,** and you will know that whatever the outcome those changes just must be made. This card shows the energy is there along with the **enthusiasm** and drive to make such decisions and changes. All that one has to do and will feel naturally impelled to do is **make that vital and exciting next step**.

There is a need to **take risks and abandon old restricting views** even though it means putting your trust in the unknown and following your destiny. A time to just jump in!

Children and those young at heart are represented by The Fool and the card could show the influence of a younger person affecting your decisions. The young have an innocent excitement and a desire to learn by moving forward without restrictions presented by the past, or from present fears. They possess an innocent **curiosity** about life, as they **live in the moment**.

The Fool – 0: Reversed

Reversed, this card points to **acting the fool,** as it can indicate that you are acting in an **irresponsible** manner and not listening to the views of others. This will result in **recklessness, making rash or even dangerous or stupid decisions**; there will be **impatience and daydreaming** when facing reality is called for.

Yet, it can also show someone who is being **overcautious** and **missing opportunities** due to a fear of responsibility or the outcome, leaving you overshadowed by your inability to rise to a challenge.

Opportunities that arise will cause concern and worry. You may be left *feeling unprepared*, stupid and superficial when new chances for change present themselves, or when you wish to make changes for yourself.

If opportunities make you feel this way, then it is not the time to act, and one should look deeper into the situation with thought and consideration for what the change will really bring. Your *fears* show that you are **not ready or brave enough to accept the outcome** and that looking at your fears will reveal a lot about yourself.

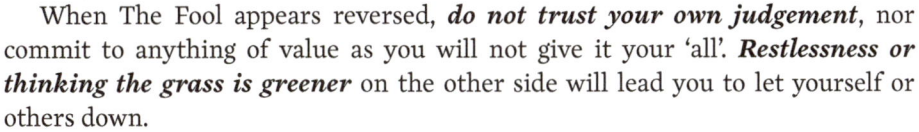

When The Fool appears reversed, ***do not trust your own judgement***, nor commit to anything of value as you will not give it your 'all'. ***Restlessness or thinking the grass is greener*** on the other side will lead you to let yourself or others down.

On a simpler note, the reversed Fool can mean ***silly, rash, impulsive and immature actions*** being taken.

THE MAGICIAN - 1

The Magician is the first numbered card of the Tarot deck, number one, representing wholeness and ambition. One is a masculine number and the basis for all proceeding numbers. New beginnings are possible and given the power not only to exist but also to grow from the number One. It shows us the possibility of future creativity, making it an extremely powerful number. One represents a starting point, the point of originality. From this number, everything else will naturally follow. It represents Divine power and the ability to mould and create our desires, bringing ambition for power and movement. It represents unity as its drive to create is single-minded. The Magician is like the casting of the die, symbolising events, and magic set into motion.

The Magician is linked to the planet Mercury which rules both Gemini and Virgo.

We see a man wearing a long white tunic and a red robe. He stands behind a wooden table, which grounds his wishes and abilities. On the table are the symbols of the Minor Arcana: Sword, Cup, Pentacle, and Wand, showing he is in possession of all he needs to create his desires from.

He wears a white headband which covers his third eye, indicating that he respects his ability to see potential and creation, showing us his focus and his ability to direct his visions. It represents his pure thought, clarity and directed ideas, as you cannot create positive magic with a messy, wandering mind. Inspiration, divine or practical, needs control to truly manifest.

His red cloak shows us his ability to add movement and action into his life, and his white tunic shows his purity and spirituality, his intent. While his white tunic shows he is pure and uncontaminated within himself, the red cloak tells us that he can fuel his basic higher nature to create, manipulate and bring forward what he sees within his mind's eye when he is ready, governed by his own will and passion, leaving his desire untarnished by lust, ego, or greed.

Above his head is the symbol of infinity, called a lemniscate, which represents unending spiritual energy, and so lessons, once learnt, cannot be forgotten. It is a higher link to draw inspiration and power from, be that spiritual or from the subconscious mind. Being above his head, the infinity loop shows that mentally he can access the wisdom, knowledge, and deep understanding of matters about him as his mind is infinite.

About his waist, he wears a snake belt, which represents Ouroboros. Ouroboros can also be depicted as a dragon, yet with both, they eat their own tail. Like the infinity loop, Ouroboros symbolises life, death, and the harmony of opposites. A symbol of wisdom and strength which is earthy and physical, and the cycle of life. Wrapped about his body, this shows The Magician to be grounded in the physical world and equally open to the mental and spiritual. It shows his creativity, confidence, and self-awareness, indicating he uses his passion and determination to bring forwards the best energy and innovation that he can. He has both a clear spiritual and subconscious link, a solid grounding force linking both heaven and earth. This link is echoed by the positioning of his hands. One, pointing to heaven, pulls down spiritual energy and combines it with energy being drawn up from the earth by the other hand - *As above, So below*. This reflects The Magician's ability to transmute ideas, intuition, and knowledge into something solid, as he combines inspiration or spiritual wisdom with physical skills and knowledge.

Unlike The Fool, The Magician understands and recognises his true potential, and, more importantly, he knows how to use his potential and energy rather than rushing into chance pursuits. The Magician's hands effectively channel positive spiritual and creative energy that is not going to be squandered; he will use the energy created for real and concrete purposes. By becoming The Magician, you can direct his energy so that you can move positively within your life or towards your chosen goals.

The flowers at his feet show a firm grounding in solid reality, with his actions not filled with fantasy and illusion. The white lilies represent innocence and purity, being symbolic of rebirth and renewal, while the red roses connect to passion and beauty. Mixed in are some snowdrops, bringing us a change from winter to spring and new growth, all showing us that he represents potential, growth, and life. He is filled with a purpose that is to fulfil and create something tangible. He is our link between God and reality, or our inspirational mind and ideas, or from idea to creation. There is no neatness to his garden, as it grows as it wishes, like raw organic energy at his feet and hanging about his head, allowing him to create on the wonderfully fertilised ground; as with the flowers being in bloom, he is ready to blossom.

Carved on the front of his table are three small images. The mountains represent reality, the bird his inspiration. The middle image in newer decks depicts waves representing emotions, and here in the original image, could be waves, or a lion. If the latter, we see his courage and fortitude in controlling his ego and talents. All of these are set into a wooden table grounding him in reality, acting as his foundation.

The Magician's force is felt on a mental level by a sudden drive of ambition and recognition of future success, as the intellectual side of our nature is prodded, bringing inspiration and dreams to the forefront. This is shown by The Magician's active mind being symbolised by the yellow light that surrounds him, as yellow represents the free will, intellect, and the power of self. He is surrounded by a white aura in some versions of the deck, indicating his pure and charged nature.

The Magician's card lets us know that we can and should turn our dreams and creative ideas into realities and he will offer us the possibility to do so. He tells us that anything is possible! The Magician shows that life is not a spectator sport but for actively taking part in and that we have full control over our situations and lives via action.

IN A NUTSHELL

Just do it! You have the passion, the knowledge, the drive, so what will you create? Now is not the time to talk about things, but to take direct action. Be single-minded in your goals and get moving.

Make firm decisions, take new opportunities – this is a time for progress and success, not for sitting on your laurels. What you want can be yours – create it and go out and grab it.

The Magician – 1: Upright

The Magician is full of positive energy as he encompasses all the power of the Minor Arcana and therefore the universe – **anything is possible** from the direct results of your own actions. He represents **positive creative energy, activity and the use of free will**: leaving you positively grounded in reality and feeling a strong sense of personal identity.

The Magician guides you when you are so full of **inner confidence** and **single-mindedness** that you know that you can achieve your aim. You are using energy from within to mould your future pathways and are governed by a strong sense of direction, leaving you feeling very constructive in your aims and ideas. **You know that success is possible, and you reach out to grab it.**

The Magician always brings with him opportunities for movement and growth, such as **an important new beginning or opportunity and a time to put ideas into action.**

When he appears, it is an ideal time to start new stimulating projects or to put anything into action that will benefit your future. The energy that surrounds you when this card is present is directed and full of purpose, you will feel driven to succeed.

Opportunities may well be offered to you resulting in the need to make **important decisions**, so make those positive changes or **make use of the creative energy presented.**

This card brings satisfaction regarding questions about work and money or anything of a mentally creative nature. **Grab opportunities** that come your way with both hands when presented under this card, as this is not a card of dreaming but of doing.

A card of action!

The Magician - 1: Reversed

Reversed, The Magician shows us **apathy** - a **can't be bothered** attitude. This shows that creative energy is wasted due to a lack of ability to make the most of what life has to offer at the given time.

There will be shyness, panic, hesitation, irrational thoughts, and feelings over events, all of which will lead to missing opportunities, and which represents **a lack of confidence** in abilities.

Quick results will be wanted, pointing to no dedication. While in this state, there will be a lack of thought for others, and **selfishness** may repel those whom you would wish to support you during this **self-centred** time.

When reversed, The Magician shows that his energy is being held onto and not being realised. Magic or energy needs to be used to fulfil its potential and here it is being squandered or ignored.

Emotional or intellectual power is used wrongly when this card is laid reversed, which can point to **lying, blackmail, tricking, conning and a general lack of honesty** all born from feelings of inadequacy, a lack of mastery and ability; with some, **laziness** is thrown in.

Do not trust your own judgement and motives, or that of others. Friendships and relationships about you may be **superficial** in nature, leaving opinions or desires to be shallow.

Here you can be quick to take an easy route, cut corners, listen to false promises and rush to create your future - all of which will not be beneficial in the long run.

THE HIGH PRIESTESS - 2

The High Priestess is numbered Two, which governs inner thoughts and brings wisdom, expectancy, and balance. With the Two, we are given interaction and balance along with duality, making the Two a number which acts as a uniting force. Two is a passive number, resulting in all action being projected inwards towards the self to be able to move forwards.

The Magician's masculine number One has been doubled to produce its feminine counterpart. The arising Two is its opposite number and shows the other side to The Magician's powerful active number and asks for understanding through quiet contemplation of the mind and the inner self.

The High Priestess is linked to the Moon which rules Cancer.

The High Priestess pictures a woman wearing a white tunic with a blue draped shawl, sitting between two pillars with a curtain draped behind her.

The white of her dress informs us that The High Priestess is a spiritually evolved, pure and spiritually motivated individual, with her intent linked to higher values. The blue shawl acts like flowing water, linking her to the moon and acts to represent flowing intuition. Blue is associated with spiritual aspirations and faith, showing a calm, truthful flow of insights. Her blue shawl also represents inner realisations and awareness which are born from spirit, the higher spiritual mind or from within the subconscious. Unlike The Magician, she is not showy and shouting her skills from the rooftops. Instead, she sits and waits for the time to be right before gently delivering her wisdom, as ears need to be ready with The High Priestess to hear her words; she is not one to speak simply because you have asked.

She wears an equal-sided cross which represents the elements of air, water, earth, and fire, and of the north, south, east, and west. The cross is worn over the heart, symbolising a link between nature, God, the self and inner knowledge, showing her in tune with all aspects of who she is.

Her veil under her triple goddess crown represents hidden qualities and abilities, and her personal ability to separate the conscious from the unconscious. Her crown symbolises the maiden, mother, and crone, representing all stages of female life, hormones and cycles, the waxing, waning and full moon, birth, love and death, all subjects associated with psychic abilities and the divine female. The maiden represents youth, new beginnings, excitement, birth, sexuality, purity, and enchantment. The mother is a symbol of fertility, birth, fulfilment, compassion, and security. The crone, of life experience, wisdom, and knowledge, and ultimately of death or transition. The sphere within the crown is a pearl symbolising wisdom and is placed on the Crown Chakra, bringing her spiritual wisdom via her spiritual self, and a direct link to her subconscious mind. Pearls also represent purity and virginity, representing dedication to spiritual pursuits over the physical. Due to her link with feminine cycles and changes, she can arise with pregnancy or female health changes, informing you that the information is there if you're ready to hear it, and any insights or potential you seek may be developing about you waiting to be revealed.

The crescent moon at her feet symbolises the passive, changing and mysterious nature of the feminine moon, ebb and flow, natural cycles and brings inner awareness of the connected nature of existence. Her gown drapes over the crescent moon showing her gentle control over the mysteries of the mind and spirit. She is in tune with the changes which naturally flow about her and shows that the unconscious self is the foundation of this card, so what is unknown to others, she sees clearly.

The scroll she holds is the Torah (the h is hidden), which contains writings relevant to Jewish law containing the law of God, where God offers the intent and purpose of all of creation to humanity. It is hidden as her hands are restricting our view of it, indicating she will protect the contents from those who are not prepared or not aware of how to use its energy proficiently or justly. Her insights will only be openly given to those pupils who share the same depth of respect for her knowledge.

On each side of the High Priestess, there are two pillars. One is black showing the letter B and the other pillar is white showing the letter J. The black pillar symbolises the subconscious mind, while the white our conscious. The B stands for Boaz, meaning *'completion'* and the J for Jachin, meaning *'begin'*. These two pillars represent two temples found in King Solomon's Temple, representing inner and outer, passive, direct, conscious, and subconscious, masculine and feminine. Combined with the black J being in the white column and the white B being in the black, it brings a balance to all things represented.

Behind her, a curtain blocks the view to what is behind, hiding from us those things she wishes to keep secret. The curtain or veil is decorated with ripe seeding pomegranates, a feminine symbol of potential, abundance, and growth. She is the potential before creation, showing the time is right to start focusing on what you wish, but first, you need to be shown the way forwards and that lies within your intuition, at times you may even realise that you have what you need already. The pomegranates with The Fool were ripe but not open; here they are ready to be sown and utilised, with her bringing a push towards realising potential. With The High Priestess, their latent abilities are grasped as she creates on a spiritual and psychic level. She is a reminder that our bodies, mind or life may be telling us all we need to know in relation to issues and so we need to listen to our intuition. The palms are the Sago Palm, a masculine image next to the ripeness of the pomegranates, and its ripe red fruits which symbolise ovaries showing a plant with both female and male energies. This adds to The High Priestess's energy of potential; she is complete as she is, balanced, full of wisdom.

Behind the veiled curtain is a river representing hidden depths. The water tells of subconscious thoughts and deep emotions, a pool of subconscious wisdom.

The High Priestess's lessons, as well as her answers, are not always apparent to the questing mind, and so the curtain is closed to us until we cease to be hindered by our physical needs, and by our emotional and mental ramblings. She will only show you what is beyond the veil when you are ready, and not before.

The High Priestess is a guide to our inner life, she is a Spiritual Mother. She is representative of Psychics and Mediums who are also a bridge to the knowledge she holds. She may be a person, or even a pack of Tarot cards, meditation, Runes, Psychometry (touching an object to feel the energy of the owner) or any other means of reaching her energy. These are all tools, stepping stones to our unconscious self and to spiritual growth. The High Priestess's energy is present when one has visions or flashes of insight, and she tells us that these special abilities should be cultivated and used effectively. She is the truth that rises within us, a light bulb shining insights onto an issue we have sought answers to, truths we can only see when we are ready to see them. She shows that we can move out of our own way and see past our wishes and desires to be open enough to see our inner wisdom. She is the gateway to our own inner guide.

IN A NUTSHELL

Sometimes you need to look within yourself for answers, your intuition is key; your inner voice needs to be listened to. We are all Spiritual Beings; therefore, we are all psychic to one degree or another. That aspect of you holds the answers, and yet they will only be given to you when you are ready to hear your own truths.

Look beyond what is obvious; allow events to unravel naturally. What is not known yet is for a reason and often knowing would not benefit you at this stage. Situations are evolving, so answers will come. Whatever your question, deep down you may well already know the answer.

The High Priestess – 2: Upright

The High Priestess **is our inner voice and intuition**, the guiding voice that we hear trying to tell us which path is right for us. As a result, this card often arises when we have a feeling, a suspicion of something and a sign we need to **listen to our inner voice and insights**. Sometimes she is a gentle and knowing nudge from the mind or Spirit, and at other times, a loud voice from within which cannot be ignored. She is about when, suddenly, we find the guidance or direction that we need.

The High Priestess indicates that the truth can be hidden, hard to find or simply not to be seen and may well change soon as **facts come to light**. Information will be made accessible making a situation a lot clearer and easier to understand.

Due to the **secretive nature** of the High Priestess, secrets will naturally be withheld, not in the form of deception, but as it's not yet time for you to know, or you're not able to listen to the truth at present. Yet things will be revealed when the time is right. If you do not know which way to turn, then you should **be quiet and patient, as the situation is developing behind the scenes,** and realisation will arrive as events naturally unfold. You will get the insights you need, although maybe not when you demand them.

The High Priestess can show an unrealised ability for development which is not acknowledged, felt, or seen, and not just on a psychic and spiritual level, but within any area unbalanced in your life or where you find yourself avoiding flow. **Intuition is the answer** to being able to see your capabilities.

She brings the potential for growth. At times, we can feel the ebb and flow of the changing energies about us, yet not understand them, which can lead to frustration within situations, as we try to force things to gain information which is not available. We can feel that something is not right, yet not be able to put our finger on what that is, which can lead to uncertainty.

Faith is needed when she appears; **trust the workings of the universe to bring you what you need rather than what you want.** Being ruled by the number two, decisions will be hard to make at times as she shows the duality of the mind. Intuition and patience should be followed with The High Priestess. She tells us to **be submissive** and **allow events to evolve without interference.** While waiting, you should **follow your intuition**, as when you cannot find your way without it, it can usually be found within.

The High Priestess represents **psychic** matters and intuitive awareness, she represents positive spirituality, and she brings a period of **psychic growth or increased spiritual awareness.** Her wisdom can come in many ways, from dreams, flashes of insight during waking hours and coincidences. All you have to do is listen; the more you listen, the more you will develop.

Linked to the feminine spirit and the moon, the High Priestess can represent **the female cycle, gynaecology and female sexual health**, showing now is a positive time to investigate the potential you have as a woman. Whilst this is not a pregnancy card, she can show that now a spark of life is possible if it hasn't already happened. She can also arise for a man when they need to connect with their feminine side.

The High Priestess – 2: Reversed

The Reversed High Priestess represents you when you *ignore your intuition* and avoid listening to your inner voice of reasoning. You are *thinking too much* and not letting her patient and intuitive nature shine through as *impatience and misunderstanding take hold.*

She can show that we *dislike the truth* shown to us and are *trying to force the revealing of information which we do like instead* or pushing her away to avoid the truth. Instead of seeing solutions, we see roadblocks and *unwanted answers,* and we are *blind to our connection to our higher selves.*

Reversed, she can leave you feeling very out of sorts, *disconnected from yourself, causing answers and reasoning* to leave you feeling envious, moody and even defeated. All of this is a sign that *grounding and faith are needed.* To be open to your subconscious wisdom or that of spirit, you need to be balanced, open and grounded in equal quantities. Often reversed, this card shows you stuck in the physical with a need to lighten up and stop demanding answers. Inner peace is lost and taking some time to gather that back is needed.

This card brings us *confusion* and *jumping to conclusions* – you may only have half of the facts or misinformation as the veil has not yet been lifted. Find out facts first and where facts are not possible, *let go of what cannot be grasped and accept that now is not the time for you to understand* or have that outcome which is dwelling in your mind, as it is destroying your calm and mindfulness.

Another aspect is *being kept in the dark* concerning matters that involve you. *Secrets are being held* for various reasons making situations seem indistinct and uncertain. At times, this may well be due to the selfish or deceitful needs of others, or those wishing to keep their own truths hidden, yet also maybe to save you from feeling hurt. If you feel *mistrust for another,* then you are probably justified in that thought, and we are warned not to trust implicitly when The High Priestess appears reversed.

On a spiritual level, The High Priestess shows that psychic abilities are not being used productively, if at all, and can occur during times when it is *hard to hear your spiritual self.* This can also show fear or a superstition-based approach to spiritual development. With psychic or spiritual events, she shows that experiences are not understood which leads to *irrational fears concerning the unknown.*

Female problems with unbalanced hormones, fertility or conception issues may be hindering a situation causing confusion and a lack of trust in the body and mind.

The potential you wish for is not available in any area of life with this card reversed.

THE EMPRESS - 3

The Empress's number is Three, the number that is born from the feminine Two and the masculine One. Three brings creation and productivity which stimulates growth and offers understanding with unconditional compassion. The One had the drive to succeed and the Two the ability to nurture. When combined, they are optimistic and productive, with a drive to create with love and kindness.

The Empress is ruled by Venus and astrologically to both Libra and Taurus.

Within the Empress's card, the picture is of a crowned woman sitting on a luxuriously cushioned seat, giving us feelings of indulgence.

The bright colours of orange and yellow within the card represent optimism, happiness and positivity. Within the original card image shown, these are the colours of her cushions, yet in others, they are pink, red and golden. In orange, they show energy, drive, enthusiasm, a need for playfulness, yet the other colours depict her well too: feminine, passionate and opulent. With her body sitting on the plush throw, leaning against the soft cushions, we are shown comfort and luxury. The cushion at the back is filled with the feminine Venus symbol, also found on her crest, showing her femininity to be her source of strength, her backbone, her support. Beneath all the soft cushions there's a solid stone seat, showing that the comforts she offers have a firm grounding in reality and not just a whim of erratic emotion.

She wears a flowing gown decorated with pomegranates, symbolic of her flowing abundance and full of the seeds of possibility; being worn, it shows that these seeds are ripe and ready to be used, rather than viewed as a latent potential as within The High Priestess' card. Where The High Priestess tells of the inner intuitive virginal aspects of the female, a passive nature, The Empress tells of the outer, sensual, maternal, passionate and emotionally mature female, a crowned ruler, a Goddess. Here the seeds can be planted, be that an idea, a new life, or a new creation. Pointing to her fertility, natural life cycles and optimism for the gestation and the birth of those things we wish to bring into the world.

One red shoe can be seen poking out from her gown, which represents that each step she takes is with a passion for creating. Her feet rest on the sand from the riverbank of the stream by her side, symbolic of comfort and relaxation.

Her body is curvy and feminine, representing physical pleasure and comfort and of course her fertility. Her voluptuous persona shows us emotional fulfilment and emotional satisfaction within relationships, especially within family arrangements. She shows the purity and simplicity of emotions and of their earthy and sensual realism. The Empress's nature is to nurture and protect in an unconditional and soft, loving manner. She symbolises sexual love and desire, while at the same time these sexual desires are contained by The Empress within the confines of a deep, loving and committed attachment, which is both emotionally fulfilling and physically responsive. This is echoed by her sitting with her ankles together, but knees apart showing that she is both sexually mature, yet demure in her approach as sex needs to have emotional substance. Her nature demands that love and sex are a joined force, as for her, they go together hand in hand.

Placed against her seat is a heart-shaped shield. The sign on the shield represents the planet Venus, so she protects with love and compassion. Within the sign is a green circle representing the earth, meaning that her tenderness and growth are aimed at creativity on a physical level as an earthly mother.

Her crown contains the twelve stars of the zodiac, showing her reign to cover all the twelve months of the year. Each star has six points: a hexagram, a combination of male and female, thought and compassion interlocked. The crown has a victory wreath wrapped about it, showing her control of her feelings, emotions and creativity.

Her hair is not long, as would be a traditional representation of someone young and inexperienced in life. Blonde hair symbolises attraction, beauty, procreation and fertility like Aphrodite the Greek Goddess. Blonde hair tends to darken with age, so her blonde hair represents a woman, or anyone, in their reproductive or creative prime.

Her necklace represents the nine planets in our solar system, indicating her connection to the seasons, her ability to ebb and flow and a transcendence of time. All nine pearls can be seen clearly in the original RWS, yet some are missing in later decks. Each planet evokes different energies, and she brings them all together with her reign of compassion. The nine planets also show the nine months of gestation needed for a foetus to grow. This can link her to the Goddess Diana, who rules over childbirth and fertility. Pearls are also symbolic of fertility and femininity, as well as a hidden knowledge, here of creation, yet here she shares her knowledge and love openly.

Her orb, which is also associated with earthly power, as well as the wreath around her crown, demonstrates her control over the senses and pleasure. She is relaxed, at ease and there is no rush in this card, just enjoyment and the time to go slowly, to be generous, to overflow and to create.

In front of the Empress are stalks of wheat symbolising fertility, harvest and the cycles of growth and renewal. The Empress is representative of Mother Earth as she brings forward life, ripeness and the power to create. They represent the rhythms of nature and the basic driving forces present within all of us, two of which are to procreate and to be accepted unconditionally. Seeds planted with the Empress thrive, be that pregnancy or a creative idea. The Empress knows her power; she gives life, love and emotional intelligence. She is the Queen of the Queens, the Mother of the Tarot Deck, and her ability to rule over nurture and creation is immense.

The card's background has a waterfall which gently falls into a flowing river, indicating to us that her emotions are not static, but moving and constantly changing, flowing, and easily expressed. She is truly in the flow of life, in tune with her emotions, at ease within her skin, at peace with all that she is. A sign also that her emotional wisdom gives life to the land about her, creating an abundant life.

The forest at the back shows mature energy, stability and long-term growth. Forests are connected to the feminine and the subconscious and are a symbol of the mother.

The Empress when truly felt and understood will give immense satisfaction and pleasure to our senses. We feel loved, cared for, cherished and encouraged. Remember the first time that you fell in love, held your child for the first time, found out that you could create what you desired, and it came into being - didn't the whole world seem brighter and clearer? She heightens senses and awakes emotions.

The Empress is non-rational, nor is she an intellectual; instead, she rules the heart and sensuality, our desire to create. The Empress allows us to wallow in luxurious emotions and warm feelings of security. She is loving emotion in its purest form. This is a card of enjoyment, being spoiled and feeling at peace emotionally.

IN A NUTSHELL

Nurture yourself as well as those you love. What you have created needs love and support. Be generous and unconditional with your affections. Use your intuition if it speaks. Listen to your heart and follow it to be happy.

Now is a fertile time, so plant the seeds of the future. A positive pregnancy card! Have some fun enjoying the good things in your life with those you love and care for. A time to be happy and feel nourished by your surroundings.

The Empress - 3: Upright

The Empress represents **abundance, good health, and a relaxed mind.** Within any area of life, she is a good sign for positive emotional investments and commitments. She does not just show us committed relationships or happy family life, as her **emotional abundance** can flow into any area where your heart takes you, such as work or other areas where you're passionate and wishing to grow.

She brings a time to **be in touch with emotions**, to flow with feelings, and listen to your **intuition and emotional wisdom** - if not your own then to another's. **A time to connect with who and what you care about,** to support and protect what you love, and a time to get in touch with your surroundings and nature.

She embodies **unconditional love** and emotional growth. Not only does she bring us love and tenderness, but she also generates sensual pleasure and represents marriage, domestic bliss, and general happiness regarding all manner of relationships, especially romantic and loving family ones. The Empress represents **stability and contentment within a specific relationship or within any situation that brings fulfilment.**

This card gives us a time to eat, drink and be merry, to indulge in sensory delights that are to be shared with others. She is relevant to one's **home and family** life and would point to the importance of family when she appears.

One major aspect of The Empress is **fertility**, her maternal nature. If you wish to investigate pregnancy issues, this is an important card, as she embodies both the creation and birth and a positive card to have in such matters. Yet, she does not always have to refer to **pregnancy or the birth of a child**, as she can also refer to **the birth of a creative idea or venture** that will need gentle care and consideration to grow. You have probably heard of people **nurturing a new idea** as if it were a baby, which can also bring financial growth.

The Empress also represents **women** who play active roles in your life such as your **mother or wife.** She is a strong but gentle, influential, feminine figure within your life, someone wise and non-judgemental who will build you up rather than breaking you down.

She can link up to your childhood, to returning to your roots, to being with family and creating your own home and enjoying home comforts. If you are ever in doubt as to where the heart lies, this card tells that it is at home where your family are and often where your roots are.

The Empress – 3: Reversed

Reversed, the Empress is a card of **sadness** as she tells of **emotions and desires being suppressed.** You will be afraid of showing emotions for fear of failure and/or rejection. **Flow and abundance have been lost,** which can also bring financial and other security issues, leading to us **feeling trapped emotionally, vulnerable and insecure.**

Now may not be the time to create or to grow the things you wish in life, and you may be surrounded by 'conditional love', or even the conditions you may place upon yourself.

There is **unhappiness within personal relationships**, and domestic life will not be running smoothly. This unhappiness could spill out into other areas of your life such as work. Now is a time to **listen to your heart** rather than your mind; do not be afraid of your dreams and do what is best for yourself.

The feelings and needs of others can be seen to be more important than your own, leading to **over-protection** and this can drain you as you give your power and energy away. **Wrapping people in cotton wool** is not beneficial to you or them. Reversed, she can lead us to hold onto things and cling to the past, however unhealthy that may be.

She can also show an abuse of pleasures such as comfort eating or excessive drinking, as we try to fill an emotional void.

When reversed, she also points to ***difficulties with fertility matters.*** She can show difficulties or unhappiness with pregnancies, problems with conception, sexual difficulties and gynaecological problems, anything connected to this area of life especially in connection to the female body.

If The Empress reversed appears in a man's reading, it can refer to ***fear or dislike of women***, either as a whole or show of a particular and problematic female who is in his life, or who has influenced him. For females, this can represent a clingy and deeply unhappy woman in their lives.

As a mother card, reversed she can foretell difficulties in families, particularly ***problems between mothers and children.***

THE EMPEROR - 4

The Emperor is governed by the number Four, a rigid number which is both organised and methodical; it has logic, is active and creative. Four shows stability and control of the head over the heart. It is a number representing strength of will, which allows its energy at times to be restricting and somewhat stubborn. Four is the number for security and dependability, being organised and equitable. This number brings loyalty; a concrete, no-nonsense number, whose security can be as restricting, as it can be comforting.

The Emperor is ruled by the planet Mars, and astrologically connected to Aries.

You have met the Mother of the Tarot deck, The Empress; now to the Father of the deck. The Emperor is a strong, masculine, mature and bold figure who holds a position in, and who represents, authority and action. This card shows us a mature bearded man wearing rich, luxuriant robes and armour seated on a throne. His hair and beard are white to show us his maturity and wisdom, he is a seasoned soldier, a lifelong warrior, a commander, and a leader who has gained his sense of fairness through action and direct experience.

His eyes face front, looking at the reader, a direct gaze, showing his confidence, his forceful nature which demands to be seen and taken seriously. In some versions of the RWS deck, you will see his line of sight being taken to the left of the card, showing his looking to the side of action, movement and logic, on guard, and never relaxed as he serves and protects his kingdom. As he looks to the card's left, it means he looks to his right, so while not devoid of feeling, he may not trust emotions and rises above them as they do not serve his situations well, as to him, the rational mind is more productive, certain and valuable. His red tunic represents his desire to succeed in all that he does and to bring achievement to all his endeavours. The colour is a sign of achievement, status, wealth and of his social standing. He is not one to hide his light under a bushel; he is proud of his battles, his victories, and his gains. His cloak has a ram emblem, his sign of Aries, as he sports his colours showing him to be ready for action. Underneath we can see his blue sleeves which show his integrity, calmness, devotion and stability. In some decks, his sleeves are indigo which also shows his sense of justice and impartiality.

His armour shows us a warrior. He is willing to be and has been front-line in battle, his strength and courage have been tested, he has truly gained his throne and crown through action and experience. He can and will fight for what he is aiming for to achieve his desires, with his mind dominating his emotions.

The throne is solid stone, representing stability and permanence, with four rams' heads, one at each corner, again representing Aries, signalling his power and strength. Aries as the first sign of the astrological calendar begins the zodiac year, so any new beginnings that fall under this card's energy are going to be full of direction and a forthright, determined influence. Aries, or Ares, was the son of Zeus and Hera, and was the God of War, representing physical battles; this Emperor influences our practical lives. Rams symbolise striving energy, positivity and strength, and for The Emperor, the rams' energy is his grounding force. The Emperor is secure in his knowledge on how to implement his energy to its best advantage.

His crown indicates the Emperor's standing in society as well as his financial and material success. On the top are a pair of rams' horns, for his sign of Aries, showing a set mind, someone firm in their view of the world, and stubborn in their opinions. The crown, in this original image, has five stones, two orange and three white, in other versions they can be red and blue. The orange gemstones represent his mental power, lively mind, drive and enthusiasm. Having two indicates a mind full of enthusiasm, balanced and having them being placed over his eyes, shows that he sees things optimistically. Yet, like the sky, the orange can also act as a warning to others, like traffic lights to be on your guard and get ready to act. The white stones show The Emperor's sincerity; there are three of them, a number which likes to create, so he wishes to spread balance with a genuine outlook on life. When these are seen as red and blue, they show his power and ambition, along with his communicative wise nature. Overall, these gemstones temper each other in whichever combination, leaving him doing everything for a solid reason.

In his left hand, his orb symbolises law and responsibility, rules and regulations. Emperors hold supreme power and have a no-nonsense, direct insight into situations. As the King of Kings, the buck stops here; there is little flexibility in this card. As it is in his left hand, he takes this seriously, as he views the world, and the law, logically.

In his right hand, he has an ankh, the Egyptian sign for life. The Ankh is symbolic of the physical life, being a representation of the spiritual, what is gained within physical life can be carried to the afterlife, and so representing everlasting power, a God in human form. Being in his creative hand, his emotional self is linked to the power he holds, which will make him very profound in all he does. He is powerful, independent and precise; he never attacks blindly, everything is weighed up and considered. Right is right and wrong is wrong.

The mountains behind The Emperor symbolise his triumph over difficulties, success in overcoming their challenge, and in tackling the sharp cutting harshness of truths - as most of his truths are neither reassuring nor pleasant, but factual and logical. This demonstrates that he uses rational thought as a means of controlling the harsher side of nature. This man hides from nothing in his pursuits. He may not always be popular in his drive for success as he has confidence in his abilities and in implementing his laws. He is a dominant force which those of a lesser disposition may find unsettling or intimidating as he strives for the goals that others may only think of attaining.

The sun is setting, turning the sky into brilliant orange, showing us his creative nature, and ability to be optimistic as well as powerful. The aspect of the setting sun can be seen in other decks' depictions of this card more than this original. He takes responsibility for his choices made at the end of the day, and his duty to see things through is taken seriously. The orange sky, as mentioned, can also be a warning sign, as it is a colour which draws attention to an action needed to be taken or avoided.

At the base of the mountains is a stream hugging the mountains, so here is a man not devoid of emotions, yet they lay at the base of his logic flowing round the corners of his facts. They will be noted but they are overshadowed by reality.

The Emperor is strict but compassionate as he uses fairness as his measure; his energy is used with careful thought and consideration for what all his actions may bring. He has his own laws which stop him from taking wild actions, with rules and regulations at his heart. You will find him immovable in his thoughts, views and beliefs, with a tendency to be persistent and unbending, but strong and direct in what he knows to be true.

The Emperor is wise and experienced, one who serves and protects without illusions or emotions and is a positive driving force.

IN A NUTSHELL

A masculine card of mind over emotions, a time for focusing on facts and taking direct action. The buck stops here, honesty is called for and an attitude of force in the face of problems as strong leadership is needed. Be confident.

Success and security are with you; being stubborn can have its benefits. Roll up those sleeves for some hard work, fight for what you want, as what you wish to gain will have to be worked towards, yet your foundations are solid. A disciplined mature mind will be of value, be that yours or another's.

The Emperor - 4: Upright

This King of Kings represents a strong, **assertive** masculine and mature force, and **a father figure**. When he appears, there is a need to **take control** of life and events. He shows us **a strong and determined attitude** along with a desire to build for the future so that there is concrete matter to hold onto. **Hard work is shown here as is steadfast, resolute effort.**

With his card, we are told that now is an ideal time to move forward with ideas and desires and to put plans into action. **If starting a new project, then you are reassured that you are starting from a secure and solid base**; all added responsibility will be greeted appropriately and maturely. Building for the future is possible, but use proper planning as your guideline and be correct in all that you do to achieve what it is you have set out to do. Be disciplined with thoughts and emotions.

As a man among men, he represents another who possesses rational thought and intellect that presents itself in a fair, law-abiding and responsible manner, so this card may represent **a person in authority over you**. The Emperor indicates that **long-term success is possible**, and realisations of goals are most definitely achievable.

Taking full responsibility is called for as this card brings the accountability and owning of actions which have been made or need to be taken; there is an 'in-charge' energy and responsibilities should be welcomed with open arms.

The Emperor as the father figure may represent your father or a person who plays a similar role in your life, such as a male relative or friend, even a boss or mentor. Someone who can teach you a lot about how life works, how to navigate the everyday real world rather than the emotional side of life. **Someone who can guide you in a practical manner**, using logic, strategy and who understands that life comes with rules which we all need to understand to succeed.

The Emperor - 4: Reversed

Reversed, the Emperor tells us that **responsibilities are an unwanted burden;** life will be filled with **drudgery and frustration,** leaving **an inability to cope** with what life is throwing at you. There will be an underlying feeling of inconsistency along with deep feelings of **insecurity** at your ability to succeed. A card of **failure**. One will be suffering from either **not taking responsibility** when it was needed or from cutting corners and being slapdash.

Immaturity is present and shown in the form of **hostility and boldness**. Due to **a lack of confidence,** there will be an inability to get close to others and one will feel isolated and inadequate.

There are still drives and desires present but they either fail or are given up on. Nothing is going to be achieved, as at any hurdles, there will be sulking and apathy if things do not go right. **Hard work is simply seen as too much effort.**

As an individual, a reversed Emperor will *usually* be male, yet whatever gender this card represents reversed they will be **corrupt,** and wish to find the route of least resistance, be **unreliable,** sexist, prejudiced, ignorant of the wishes of others for their own selfish gain, and often be **a bully** when all else fails.

If this card is laid when you are dealing with authority, then **you are not going to be treated fairly**. Due to dishonesty, ignorance or laziness, **your needs or views will be belittled** and seen as an obstacle or of holding no importance. A **dominant person**, probably male, will misuse power, or be so **rigid in his thinking** that you simply cannot have your say or your way. You can try to stand up to this person, but it may not end as you wish.

Father issues can also be highlighted with this card reversed. For both men and women, this can show dominant fathers or problematic relationships with a man who has influenced their lives negatively.

The reversed Emperor can also show ***someone who may wish to give bad advice*** as it makes them feel better and is based on their limited views of success and life.

THE HIEROPHANT - 5

The Hierophant's number is Five, which corresponds to uncertainty and criticism, and which then leads us to communication. Hard work and an amount of personal striving are always needed to satisfy the Five's energy due to it being a mentally active number bringing mental expansion. Five is a number that requires thought to be used in action; it rules the senses and governs our mental and intellectual selves. It strives to move forwards and learn, bringing communication, exchanges of ideas and opportunities to pass on information. This number needs to interact, analyse and argue, if necessary, to be able to create and move forwards. Five searches for the truth in all situations, even if that brings a need to strive for what is sought.

The Hierophant is ruled by Venus and the sign Taurus.

The Hierophant's card depicts the inside of a church or temple, with The Hierophant dressed in ceremonial robes standing in front of two pillars, delivering his sermon or wisdom to two men below.

The Hierophant, like The High Priestess, concerns itself with spirituality and knowledge. We could view The Emperor and The Empress as our physical parents, and The Hierophant and The High Priestess as our subconscious or spiritual ones. The Hierophant is the conscious to The High Priestess's subconscious. The High Priestess shows that all is not revealed and to listen to your inner self, while The Hierophant offers a more conventional or 'outer' approach towards gaining information and wisdom.

The church or temple represents religion, which is another difference between the High Priestess and the Hierophant. Organised religion shows organised thought and procedures, which can be static in its approach and avoids change when absolutely possible, whereas The High Priestess's approach tends to be flexible and open to more eventualities via the flow of intuition. Both cards are equally important, as different situations obviously require different solutions. What is hidden with The Hierophant is not that which is not yet known as with The High Priestess, but that which has not yet been found, learnt, studied, or mentally digested. The religious or conservative aspect of this card tells that The Hierophant directs his energies toward tradition, to tried and tested conventional methods and to the teaching and understanding of known truth or accepted beliefs. The Hierophant is a moral crusader with strong ethics and beliefs which he steadfastly adheres to. He expects others to follow him if they wish to succeed under his guidance; his way is traditional, laid down in history, and because of this, he states that he would like us to approach events and situations in an appropriate manner. He expects the correct thing for the situation to be done, and for doing what is right rather than what we wish, or an expression of the self and personality.

The two grey pillars that stand behind The Hierophant indicate, unlike The High Priestess, that his knowledge is easier to obtain, as there is no veil, yet still not readily at hand to be taken at will. To receive The Hierophant's help, you first have to know you want or need it, yet the pillars show he holds no secrets. Grey is a colour of wisdom in contemplation. It is the merging of the white and the black of The High Priestess's pillars to produce a whole inner and outer force that allows the subconscious mind to work with the conscious, so what we seek has substance. The pillars, inside of a church, represent protection and safety from what is beyond. This gives us somewhere to turn in times of trouble, a point of safety. Both pillars have an undefined emblem engraved at their tops. In some images, they look like vine leaves, in others a uterus, yet what they are I have not been able to determine, as neither connect with The Hierophant, except that the pillars give a safe place to learn a new idea or concept right from the start. Instead, I believe them to be a gourd and leaves. The bottle gourd symbolises the world in two halves: heaven and earth. Over his head, they could also represent Jonah's Gourd. God was said to have grown one above Jonah's head, to then send him a wife who was meant to cut it down, yet instead helped him cultivate it, which can represent The Hierophant's desire to help others cultivate themselves. Yet, they could just be squiggles for decoration - which is unlikely, as Waite designed/Smith drew the cards down to their last detail.

His stone chair has two symbols representing the solar system or sun on each side, circles with a dot in the middle. These highlight his wisdom, representing the light which he shines onto issues, and his wisdom and clarity to all those who seek him. The sun brings life and hope, it shines the way forwards. In some, faith's deities are represented by the sun, as it is an emblem of power. The symbol represents the sum of all we can be. Together they bring an energy to The Hierophant, which is optimistic, as, often with this card, once we take an active part in those things which he leads us to learn, we are able to start a new page in our lives; he is simply the key.

Like The Magician, The Hierophant wears red, a robe which covers a white shirt. The red shows his desire, potential and determination, with the white his purity and integrity. The three crosses down the front show the Holy Trinity, the father (mind), son (body) and the holy ghost (spirit) = all is one in God. An indication of the strict beliefs held by this teacher: rules are never bent or gone around. At the bottom is a diamond shape, an alchemy symbol symbolic of the journey our souls make in life, or when seeking enlightenment. Diamonds also reflect light, which shows him acting as a guide, as with the symbols of the sun. Underneath, he wears a blue tunic or gown, slightly darker than The High Priestess's, which shows his spiritual element. It drapes onto the floor showing his connection to the realities of his teachings, that he is governed by doctrine and firm beliefs which are delivered from a place of sincerity. With a cross on both his shoes, he walks a pathway full of conviction.

He wears a triple crown, again a sign of the Holy Trinity, governing his thoughts. At the top of his crown is what looks like a W: this has been reported to be three nails, as were used in Christ's crucifixion, with W being a Hebrew word for nail. This can show a sign that we need to sacrifice ignorance to grow, as it rules the crown and beliefs. He also holds a triple cross, which is a sign of the Pope, which in a lot of Tarot decks he is called. Both are gold representing the outer side of our search for answers, the conscious.

Placed in front of him, at his feet, are two golden keys. If they were silver, they would guide you through an inner journey or a subconscious path, such as with The High Priestess. Being gold, they show an outer approach to life, a more physical, realistic approach to issues. The Hierophant offers a gateway to knowledge and resolution, the keys the means of unlocking that guidance so that you can arrive at a solution and gain the wisdom needed. The Hierophant also requires us to play an active role in our own salvation and in our own personal quest for the truth in any situation. You will have to use the keys yourself, which places The Hierophant in the position of teacher, mediator and guidance counsellor. This card shows outside energy being bought in to help with an issue via teaching, instruction and guidance.

The Hierophant has two fingers raised as if to initiate or anoint and bless the two men in front. This action of his hand acts as a messenger, as in The Magician's card, to pull down spiritual energy and truth to the men before him. With The Hierophant, this also includes teachings and guidance of a practical nature. The Hierophant has total faith in his beliefs and teachings and in our ability to receive them.

The two men in front are robed, and so shown to be actively in search of the answers they seek. Both wear gold, so both are aware they are on a conscious learning journey. They have shaved heads, showing them to be monks and slaves to Christ, and can often mean they have renounced all worldly goods, yet here they are dressed in decorative robes. One wears red roses showing a desire for knowledge and the other white lilies, symbolising life and rebirth, so he wishes for a new start. Their flowered garments show them grounded, open and willing to learn; they have invested time into their endeavours and are taking their lesson seriously.

As monks before a pope, they symbolise submission to a more powerful or knowledgeable force or person. The Hierophant is initiating or welcoming them into his circle, and with the keys and communion wafers placed by their sides, a literal digesting of his teachings. There are four wafers in total, showing security and structure, with two each, bringing balance. The black and white checks beside the wafers and keys show a combination of opposites, and again balance - of good and evil, light and darkness, so you can learn all sides of an issue. The students also know that while they need to learn alone, they are not alone in their search as theirs is a road many have trodden before them.

The title 'Hierophant' stems from the word *hierophany* which means 'manifestation of the sacred', bringing what is within the mind out into our daily, physical lives. The Hierophant lets us know when we need help and advice, and more importantly when we are ready to receive and accept it. When the student is ready, the teacher will appear!

IN A NUTSHELL

Advice coming your way will be honest, take it. Do the right thing, stick to rules and regulations; they are there for a reason. Decisions should be faced from a traditional perspective, an age-old way of doing things will be important. Stand up for what you know is right. Do what is expected of you. Put all your cards on the table and sort things out.

A tried and tested way of doing things teaches well, so if you seek to learn something, follow those qualified to help.

The Hierophant - 5: Upright

The Hierophant is both a spiritual and educational card, representing **a calling, a drive for truth, a thirst for knowledge.** He shows a passion to learn and understand what is sought and represents **moral and ethical matters**.

Whatever our problem or issue, whatever we wish to understand or challenge, this card warns that we should stick to **traditional, tried and tested ways of doing things and methods** of reasoning. Right now is not the time to be independent and original, or to throw tradition to the wind. **Convention** should be adhered to for matters to succeed. With this card, an orthodox and accepted view is required, and one should **do what is socially, morally, spiritually, or practically expected**.

The Hierophant can symbolise **traditional ceremonies** such as marriage and christenings, showing family and intimate relationships are conventional and traditional and **bound by commitment**.

The Hierophant is a teacher, guru and counsellor and as such represents doctors, solicitors, counsellors, priests, teachers and even driving instructors, and even a chance piece of **moral or honest advice**. He is **anyone in a position to pass on organised and recognised information of value** that will assist in your life conducted in an unbiased and fair fashion, or teach you something of importance. He is all about **education**. He may also be a book or study in the conventional sense; either way, this card shows **questions are being asked and direction is being actively sought**. If you are not looking for a teacher or instruction, he may be a sign that now is the time to do so to gain the answers and knowledge you need.

The Hierophant can show tension arising from trying to balance your spirituality, morals, or other beliefs with either what is wanted in life or the views of others - now is the time to follow what is right, not necessarily what is wanted. **Rules are important** and will govern your progress with this card rather than exercising freedom of choice.

If you are asking questions of a philosophical nature, he shows us that the appropriate answers will be found. He gives a need to make sense of life, to understand events, and you will find that this usually accompanies either extreme change or the opposite, stagnation.

If an immediate change of circumstances is wanted, you may just have to wait as there is a need to learn first, and this will result in *a continuation of events* while you do so. You cannot rush this card.

This card often turns up when a heart-to-heart is needed to set things straight, a time to place all facts on the table so that everyone can absorb the truths of everyone else.

The Hierophant – 5: Reversed

Reversed, the Hierophant indicates that tradition and convention are leaving you feeling **restricted and bound by outdated rules.** You may seek to rebel against them with **a need or desire for originality** as the old ways do not fit you.

Relationships and views will be **unconventional** with this card, which may be because of wanting to shock others into recognising your independence, of wanting to be seen as separate from the 'norm', yet also because of beliefs simply not being in line with those imposed. **A traditional way of doing things or acting is rejected** and so here we can find the black or tie-dye sheep of the family.

This card shows an individual avoiding or not wanting to conform to tradition or what is expected of them. This does not mean a lack of commitment or sincerity but a need to **look outside of the box, compromise and come to an agreement**. Relationships can still be committed and secure, family ties can still be full of love, yet old routes fail to entice.

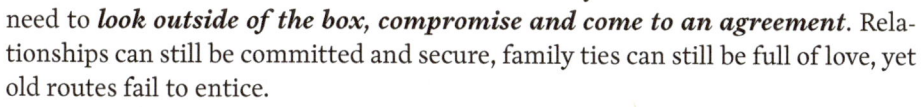

Reversed, he can bring **altering opinions** that will have an impact on the subject at hand. With changes in character and in beliefs, views or opinions that may have taken precedence in one's mind for a long time. **In short, you will change your mind about what you have once held dear, or another will.**

Those that wish to learn tend to avoid traditional ways of learning, not to cut corners, but with a need to **absorb information in a different way than expected**, desired, or achieved by others or available.

Yet by the same token, if you're looking for advice or have been given some, then **get a second opinion**, as any advice given may be from someone who is not able to give you the facts you need, leading to **misleading, judgemental, or even detrimental information**. The teacher or advice-giver in this instance may not be qualified, literally or otherwise, to educate or explain correctly. Give careful thought as to the validity of any claims given.

THE LOVERS - 6

The Lovers card is numbered six, which relates to all that is beautiful and harmonious, being the number of attraction. Like the Two, Six is a number of balance and diplomacy, bringing understanding and ease of tension. Relationships and domesticity are placed under Six, as the energy it creates brings about a desire for continuity. It is a very physical number which needs to be with others to express itself.

The Lovers card is astrologically linked to the sign of Gemini and ruled by Mercury.

The card depicts a naked man and woman, behind them an angel. The human couple represents Adam and Eve in the Garden of Eden, yet they also show opposing energies, two sides of a single coin, yin and yang. The man looks at the woman's body showing intellect, drive, passion and physical desire, whilst the woman gazes upwards to the angel with emotional and spiritual inspiration, seeking a higher route to salvation. They are all elements which when put together raise us up above ourselves, as balance is needed to create a union of whatever kind.

Their nakedness is not just symbolic of temptation and desire but also of their innocence. Nothing is hidden: it shows us they are both pure, seeking their goals driven by nature, urged by an inner calling to become more than they are alone. The Lovers is not just a card that shows the simple presence of a relationship, or sex and intimacy, but can relate to any area of life which the heart can tempt or drive us to. They stand with their arms open: this shows, again, their innocence, their transparency and their desire to accept the gifts given to them.

Behind the woman is a snake coiled around the Tree of Knowledge, the tree which contained *that* apple, and held all the knowledge of heaven and earth, both the good and bad, with the snake representing temptation. There are four apples, all about her head. Four brings us security, a rigid energy which leaves the temptation these apples bring very absorbing; they will feel like a certainty rather than an option. Therefore, she stands in front of a forbidden choice with adamant thoughts and looks above for guidance.

The man stands in front of the biblical Tree of Life, which represents the sum of all we are or can be. Its leaves are flames representing passion, and so he wants to be more than he is, and that is an ingredient he seeks within the woman. Flames also destroy the physical, allowing for rebirth, so he has a desire to change and transform. Each one of the twelve flames is a branch of the Tree of Life. In the bible, each one represented a fruit, or gift: faith, peace, joy, kindness, gentleness, charity, goodness, chastity, self-control, modesty, patience and moderation. Here he stands with it all, alive and wanting to be all that he can.

Above the Lovers is an angel, a divine messenger, there to remind us of the higher nature of desire and love. He sits amongst the clouds, like the Aces a gift of opportunity, yet also in the clouds, just out of reach to those who cannot reach up. The angel is draped in a pale indigo robe, his wings red (also with a touch of indigo), symbolising integrity, spiritual growth, sincerity, wisdom and power. In other versions his robe is violet and his wings red, showing he is bringing desire down to earth, as well as faith and love.

He is lit alight by the sun behind, which is representative of growth and optimism. His hair is aflame; some flames are green which brings an earthly element to this angel's arrival, along with excitement and drive from the orange. The sun brings us happiness, and the colour of the flames shows that this is a chance for positive change, yet it will be driven by a mindset excited by what is on offer, making us feel inextricably drawn to it.

Who is the angel? Maybe Raphael, whose name means God's Healer or God Heals, an archangel who represents air, thus communication? Or maybe Archangel Michael, who is connected to fire with the flaming hair? Or even Uriel, the archangel linked to the sun, the Flame of God. Either way, we are told that love is meant to transcend us and bring harmony, not undermine us with physical gratification and desires alone. Love is a uniting force that can set us free, but the angel tells of the spiritual aspect of love, and to some, that can be out of reach. Through sexual love, or by following the heart's desire in any area of life, we try to have everything, thinking that it can solve our ills and heal us, but unless we let it be more than an act of passion, we can get caught up in the heart-breaking search for satisfaction and acceptance from another, an object or from a situation. This block is shown by the mountain between them, which indicates that difficulties can be bridged with higher love and higher love alone.

A major aspect of The Lovers is choice. The nakedness tells us of desire and temptation, and as we travel along life's path, we will meet with sexual love or some other form of temptation to distract us from our intended goal. It is at these junctures that decisions must be made. Do we follow our heart's desire, or do we allow our passions to envelop us?

The card forms two halves, the bottom showing the physical aspects of love, two people joined together and moving through the passages of a relationship, the difficulties, while above are the spiritual elements, the commitment, ideals and deeper wishes that unions bring.

Above them all is the sun, shining down in rays symbolising happiness. Positivity and hopefulness are brought by the card, leaving it free from deceit, pain or stress. The sun highlights situations and lightens up dark corners, leaving us illuminated and showered with optimism. Yet, in the bottom half is the red mountain, reminding us that harsh realities need to be conquered: acting on a whim with The Lovers can let that sun burn you.

The snake symbolises our wisdom; he warns us to use our discretion, to be careful when faced with heartfelt challenges of choice, especially when the direction of our life is to be changed. Choice can be of any nature, in any area of life, anything of importance. We will be fuelled by passion, desire and inspiration and so any decisions we make can have a hefty response and impact on our lives. So if one makes the wrong decision or choice, it may be a difficult one to rectify.

IN A NUTSHELL

What or who you are attracted to will call for a decision. Choices will need to be made which will direct your future, so think carefully. Your heart will be calling you to action, temptation leading you, so do allow the head a look in. Once you have made a choice, there may be no turning back, so choose wisely.

If you are not sure where a path may take you, think seriously about what you do next.

Lovers - 6: Upright

The most obvious representation of The Lovers is of an *important and intimate relationship*.

Although this card can show **the past or present existence of a relationship in your life,** or that **a new one is arriving**, it can also indicate that a relationship will become more important and be brought to the forefront of the questioner's mind. This will require **an important decision to be made that will affect the relationship's future,** and both people's needs, hopes and ideas need to be taken into consideration.

Relationships which have ended or are current, or even future ones dreamed of, can be affecting choices being made.

Sexual love can be a fragile and often superficial subject, whilst it can also be absorbing, expressive and enlightening, but however **intense feelings** can be, they will not remain constant. For a relationship to deepen, it will have to move forward and only then can the sincerity of any feelings be realised as love will either deepen or fail, so **necessary movement can be shown within a relationship as it develops**, with **communication** an essential.

Yet any area of life can be represented with this card: **what is calling your heart?** What tempts and inspires you to make changes? What has sparked a passion in you? **Decisions need to be made carefully** as due to the emotional nature of choices careful thought is needed, as **once the decision is made, there may be no turning back.**

Overall, The Lovers represent **an emotional choice** and the uncertainty attached to such events. Often decisions where the practical aspects differ from the spiritual or aspirational and **the head and the heart argue, creating a dilemma.**

Lovers – 6 –Reversed

Reversed, this card shows the breakdown of a relationship – *separations, divorce and irreconcilable differences within an established relationship.* It can show that relationship issues are dominating other areas of life.

One partner will be in a state of indecision and change about an important relationship, bringing about *separation, real or needed.* A time has arisen for one of the partners to grow and move away from the present arrangement, as *feelings are no longer mutual.*

Sexual and emotional problems can be shown within an existing relationship that is in a severe state of breakdown but where the two are still together due to the insecurity and fear that separation would bring.

Any problems present within a relationship will come to the surface with The Lovers reversed; there will be *no hiding from any mistakes or secrets* that have been made within the relationship bringing pain and hurt. *Affairs or deceptions will be found out,* and all parties will suffer as temptations would not have been avoided and decisions not well thought out.

The Lovers reversed can also show *unrequited love* that is causing problems for the questioner, and an indication they should try to emotionally move away from the person they are *infatuated* with.

If this card arises when relationships are not relevant, it shows that *an unwise decision* has been made and the consequences are being felt, or that you are in the process of making a terrible choice. Decisions made under this card will be for *instant gratification,* so *bad quick-fix solutions* are found, leading to *rash choices* being made.

THE CHARIOT - 7

Seven rules The Chariot, bringing movement that leads to growth and evolution of the inner self. The number Seven has a strong sense of striving and urges us to proceed despite difficulties. Seven brings us spiritual growth and wisdom through actively seeking answers. It is a number that seeks and pursues the philosophies of life. Through Seven's searching nature, we are given the evolution of the self, as we do not progress through standing still. As with the Five, Seven seeks development via mental activity and action.

The Chariot is ruled by the Moon and is linked astrologically to Cancer.

This card shows a warrior seated in a chariot with two seated sphinxes, and he faces us head-on, showing that this is a card of action.

The Sphinxes show the body of a lion, with the head and breasts of a woman. The female Sphinx was a monster sent to punish and plague people with riddles and destroy those who could not solve them, and so they represent a mentally driven energy full of strength, fierceness and control. Both wear the crown of the Pharaoh, showing their power and influence over the charioteer. Together they are seated on grass which is a grounding force, and with no harnesses or reins holding them to heel, as they are subdued and calmed by the charioteer's will. Their colours, one black and the other white, represent opposing forces and opposites; they would cause chaos and pull the chariot in two directions at once if they were not both controlled. Together, they show opposed forces either within the driver's personality or within his outer life, both of which must be dominated by the charioteer to stay on track. If this were to fail, the sphinxes would repel each other, as they are seated facing slightly different directions away from each other and both would wish to have an equal pull on the vehicle. If that happened, the chariot would be overturned, yet the charioteer is standing strong, calm and poised and directing the differing energies, keeping them together. Regardless of any apparent difficulties, the driver takes his place and prepares to move forward, maybe at great speed; and with no reins, his control must come from his personality, thoughts and desires. Their Pharaohs' headdresses are also black and white, showing that they are dually bound by the actions of the other, and symbolic of the charioteer's efforts to balance the minds of both Sphinxes to his desires.

The chariot itself is a square stone block, cast about the charioteer's body, leaving him stuck and unable to leave his situation; if he changes his mind, this is one ride he cannot depart without causing a crash. The chariot is at rest, which can symbolise achievement and triumph over problems, yet as the town is just behind them, theirs is a journey just starting, even if it's another chapter. The stone square brings unyielding energy; its structure is rigid, harsh, and not designed for comfort but to get the job done. The lines and sharp corners represent a structured ordered foundation to work from.

The winged sun on the front of the chariot may symbolise Helios who rode a chariot of the sun across the sky each day, a sign of control over nature and being able to direct and focus outcomes. The blue wings are a sign of faith in his journey.

The red bolt secured by a pin indicates that the chariot can take the strain, yet even bolts can come loose, so desire alone will not be enough to keep things on the wished-for pathway, he needs to maintain and keep an eye on any potential stones in the road which may shake his resolve loose. The symbol can also represent the Yoni, which symbolises the female sex organ, and the Lingam, representing the male, symbols of a Hindu god and goddess, Shiva and Shakti. Again, opposites which are needed for balance.

The gold of the wheels shows an outer energy and so the practicalities of life, and so this is not a card of wishful thinking but of ideals being balanced with solid direct action.

The Chariot's canopy of stars indicates that he has high expectations and hopes, and the veil behind focuses him on the road ahead, as he is not looking back to what has gone before but to the future and the road ahead.

The river in the background represents his emotions which are calm and flowing as he needs to be flexible to make course changes at any second. There are six trees on either side of his chariot, behind the river, three on either side. This adds to his balanced, grounding nature, which shows he has come from common sense. Being Six they show a desire to progress, to attain and build, separated into threes: this gives him a balanced view of those things he wishes to make for himself. Behind the river is a town, which tells he has driven from a successful place and past accomplishments will not easily be given up, yet the town and its protective wall are behind; without that safety, he is at risk. His yellow sky shows this to be an intellectual card, one where confidence plays a role.

The charioteer wears armour and chain mail which act as his protection; he's a warrior and won't shy away from the difficulties presented. His belt contains signs of the zodiac and his skirt signs of ceremonial magic, so he can take power from many sources. The chariot may be rigid, but the driver is open to the magic of the mind and the universe, from the riddle of the sphinx to the weighing-up of power, he is quick-witted and uses what inspiration comes his way. His belt is hung at an angle, which could show an independent soul who is willing to be unconventional if necessary.

He carries a single-ended wand in his left hand, which points upwards and slightly to the left of the card, showing his mental, inspired, and innovative nature. Logic over emotion. It's blue, like the wings on the chariot, his small belt, undershirt, and his canopy, showing faith and confidence, yet as a soft blue, maybe there is an injection of hope in there too. Its tip is gold, looking like a spear, so he is creating, on an outer physical and practical level, with a spear, not so much a symbol of war, but of power. Unlike The Magician, he has already brought into creation what he wants. Even if it is just a firm mental concept, he is now the driving force behind making more out of it.

His right hand is held in an Adi or Brama mutra, a mutra being a hand position held in yoga; both mentioned are to steady the mind, create calm and energise the body, creating a mindful balance between the emotional, mental and physical self.

The half-moons on his shoulders represent change and confusion: one is upright, the other upside down, so more opposing forces of right and wrong, positive, negative, left and right and so a heavy responsibility to shoulder. He needs to balance the two and will be aware of their presence.

The square on his chest represents earth and the physical side of life, the four seasons and four compass points and so practical matters are dealt with. It can also be a sign of safety; as with the block of the chariot, it can show a situation where change is to be endured or won over due to circumstances. The square isn't central on his chest but placed over his heart, showing a need to control but respect emotions.

Although the chariot is placed on grassy ground, rather than a pathway or road, failure is not a possibility to be entertained, as he will wish to keep his past success, shown by his crown of laurel leaves. The laurel wreath shows his confidence and success at dealing with his situation, as he sees himself as a champion and in charge of his own fate.

His star crown is his inspiration, like his canopy, he has a dream and wishes, and this crown will guide him and keep him true to his path like an inner compass. It is decorated with an eight-pointed star representing the start of a new week, a new phase and eight being a determined number which strives to control, they can also symbolise chaos. Stars are a sign of hope and renewal, and it sits in an arch which represents the moon with the sun's rays at the bottom showing us his mind is driven, yet with that night-time canopy, the sun, star and moons, his mind may be as dual as the Sphinxes.

The charioteer's actions are guided by maturity and inner strength; he has an exploring, intellectual nature that needs to be grounded. He owns a strong sense of direction as well as rationality and without that, his intellect would place his head in the clouds, resulting in the charioteer thinking but not acting. If he could not control his thoughts, he would have no clear sight of his aims and if this were to be the case, the Sphinxes would control the situation, resulting in chaos, destruction, loss and failure. The charioteer knows if he is to keep the Sphinxes under control, he will have to assert effort and willpower, and however hard that may be to maintain, he will have to persevere throughout the entire journey. He knows the victory that he wishes or craves, will and can be his through hard work, determination and keeping his goal in sight.

The chariot is a man-made structure, so the driver may be controlling a conflicting situation not of his making, or a challenge that he has not willingly or knowingly taken on. Either way, the charioteer cannot dismount the chariot for fear of loss or damage, so he is there for the duration of the ride, however long and difficult it may be. Yet he sees the challenge and strives to control the temperamental energies that surround him, facing head-on the problems ahead.

IN A NUTSHELL

You will need to take control of a situation, goal or idea which could easily veer out of control or be derailed. People or beliefs will be at opposite ends of the spectrum, and it will be hard for a situation to stay focused when views disagree. At times, you may not feel totally in the driving seat and struggle to stay on top of issues, leaving situations needing a firm hand to avoid chaos.

Yet this card offers us a safe arrival, so putting effort into a situation to maintain control will make the rewards worth it. If you have been stuck for a while, then this is a time of movement.

The Chariot - 7: Upright

The Chariot brings a time of **progress or changes maybe after a delay**. A time to take up position, act and triumph over difficulties, but warns that **tension, mental effort, and stress will be present**.

There is a need to remain alert and adaptable as **quick decision-making** may be needed to keep a situation under control. You may have to get over **obstacles on your pathway**, but a clear mind and **faith in yourself** and the situation will help you achieve this.

While you may not see them, **you have the reins to a situation** and how you think, feel, act and react will determine where you end up. To reach goals or a place of security, you need to be **determined and focused**, as you direct your intent, motivation and wishes.

The Chariot can also bring **fast-moving situations**, leaving extra care needed to control circumstances if success is to be assured. **Self-discipline** and willpower are needed to stay on track, and any bumps in the journey will strengthen you if you stay focused, as The Chariot does offer **a troubled ride but assures us a safe arrival** if we stay in control.

The Chariot shows that life will proceed regardless of our wishes and when this card appears, at least we have a say in the outcome simply by the amount of energy and hard work we wish to put into **guiding our own future**.

The Chariot tells us to **never give up** and to keep going however hard it may seem at the time, as the energy you need is available and that **now is a good time to progress and succeed**. Stay focused on your efforts and keep momentum and **stay on track with 100% dedication**.

Travel can also be represented by The Chariot and can indicate dealings with vehicles and trips away going well, although other cards will help to support this.

The Chariot – 7: Reversed

Reversed, the Chariot shows **a conflict of interests**; ideals or plans will clash, causing anxiety between either you and another or on an inner personal level.

You may find it hard to gain control of events and situations and you may struggle to get plans started. At other times, however much effort you put into something, it will still crash and burn, leaving **failure** and **lack of fulfilment**.

There will be **the inability to make an important decision, and emotions or ego will get in the way**.

Maybe now is a time to stop what you're doing and review goals and the direction you wish to move in, yet this can often be hard to do as there will be **a feeling that everything is out of control and chaotic**.

The Chariot reversed indicates **your mind will be unfocused, undecided and unsettled**, leaving you with **no clear sense of direction** and a **confusion** which could result in differences becoming irreconcilable. A result of this could even be **emotional and angry outbursts** as compromises cannot be found and the weight of issues can be too much, with the effort needed to succeed feeling insurmountable. This can also allow chances for change to be missed as **you feel too rushed to make a clear or quick choice**.

An awkward situation will veer out of control, leaving the situation to run amuck or have the power handed over to another. Be it big or small, there will be breakdowns of emotions as well as situations. A cycle of good luck will be at an end with feelings that life or a situation is **moving in the wrong direction**.

If things seem 'too good to be true', this card tells you to look closer at expectations and ability. Yet sometimes we need to know that even the most well-planned situations can be overturned.

With the reversed Chariot, we have not only suffered **delays** to personal situations, but also with travel, and can indicate all manner of **vehicle or travel difficulties and accidents**.

STRENGTH - 8

Strength's number is Eight which indicates positivity, challenge and courage combined with effort. It shows honesty and spiritual endurance but, in the process, it brings physical restrictions. Being a multiplication of the Four, it magnifies its earthly values, bringing hard work and rewards, but also the restrictions created by physical or life's realities. Eight has connections to the Spiritual Self as well as the physical and represents a Karmic link, as your physical life reflects your spiritual being and vice versa.

Strength is associated with Leo, which is ruled by the Sun.

The card pictures a young, fair-haired maiden stroking a lion, depicting a calm scene and one which could be very, very different, due to the lion, by nature being a wild and unpredictable creature.

The maiden is dressed in a flowing white gown showing she is pure in thought and motives. As a feminine energy, she links us to the subconscious self which flows out into her life, like an abundance of personal understanding. Her white gown flows into the earth connecting her to its healing, practical energy and allowing her to understand her connection to the lion.

Her crown and garland belt are made from leaves and small, red flowers, all symbolic of growth and abundance. The red flowers show passion and a need for movement. About her head, this shows a grounded desire: she knows what she wants but will not battle to get it as she prefers a more passive, flowing natural way to bring her wishes forward. Her crown is her intellect, showing her to be grounded in reality, relaxed, focused and connected to the moment.

She is not a soul merely full of kindness and calm, as she also has wishes and drives, both physical and mental. Her belt shows her ability to not be ruled by her mind or ego, nor her physical drives, which allows her to be confident and calm, with a positive sense of self-identity. Not blinded by needs, she can see the beauty in the world about her and her creativity. Her belt flows from her waist and down her left side, the side of intellect, to the grass, again, around her legs a sign of grounded energy, this time with her physical self, and logical mind. She is sure of her role in the world or within situations; she is a very gentle feminine energy who uses quiet force. This grounding energy, with her youth, also shows positive health, both mentally and physically.

She does not look above to the heavens for confidence or answers to her concerns as she is aware of her connection to the earth and life. She realises that courage, depth of heart and calmness are the values needed to move a situation forward. Although this card is earthlier in its values, as with The High Priestess, a quiet mind is a productive one. If she can tame the lion, then optimism is felt, as the possibility of what other problems may come can be equally subdued.

Above her is an infinity symbol, a sign of self-mastery, simplicity and balance. Within this card, it shows control over nature, over personality and over continuing life cycles.

Lions are kings, hunters - fierce, brutal, proud, dominant - and here the lion is a representation of the maiden's inner self, her ego and subconscious mind. She gently strokes the lion showing she has no fear of her situation; nor fear of herself or of her own reactions. She does not imply simple innocence in doing this, but rather self-confidence, inner radiating peace and strength. The maiden's touch acts to control and pacify the wild animal or her own emotional, physical and mental urges. The position of her hands on the lion's head indicates the control and acceptance that she has over her emotions, words, and the areas of her personality she wishes to subdue or keep private. By controlling the lion's head, she controls its thoughts and in return, it licks her hand in submission. The lion's tail is between its legs, another sign of submission, yet this can also show stress and fear, feelings she wishes to keep controlled, as she has no desire to be dictated to by her personality or ego. She instead allows her spiritual and rational self to hold control, showing a carefree, strong, outward appearance in response to her circumstances.

She has judged her situation from the basis of her calm inner being, which outwardly projects her to be as fearless on the outside as she is within, so that absolute confidence is felt and shown.

If the maiden were to take away her gentle controlling hand, she would break the physical contact, leaving her fate to an unpredictable force, and she would indeed risk losing control of the situation. This would allow the lion a chance to resume his natural behaviour and turn against the maiden, as he is by far the stronger; he is a king and she a mere girl. Just like our own emotions and instinctual urges when we let them take precedent within our lives. When they rule, we suffer.

In the background is a mountain, pointing to harshness and difficulties. The maiden turns her head from these troubles and past events and looks forward to what she is faced with at present. The past cannot be changed, but she is gently holding the forces present within her life, regardless of what or where they originated from, as she has learnt some harsh lessons in the past. Her body leans towards the logical left of the card and the mountain, but she faces the emotional right of the card, showing she is capable of both action and logic, as well as owning a balanced emotional viewpoint. She is wise to the pain which the mountain represents, and knows it is down to her to keep it at a distance.

Strength's energy is one that is hard to obtain simply out of a desire to be in control of life and circumstances. It is a state of 'being' that you arrive at accompanied by honesty and it arrives merged with a strong logical will. It deals with the subconscious mind, the control of the self and your own reaction to situations via the rationalisation of the conscious mind. It is about living in the moment and not running to the future or the past to hide or find excuses. Strength is about bravery, love and self-compassion and asks us to be courageous and realise how strong we really are.

IN A NUTSHELL

Being calm, focused and connected to life, show respect to yourself and towards others. Nothing should be rushed, and all dangers will be seen, and yet there will be a lack of concern as confidence is your quiet friend.

This is a time for mind over matter, a time to control your instinct and urges so your energy is channelled to a positive end. Strength of mind and heart will accompany you as you conquer your fears. You master your emotional self and react with patience and courage to situations and life in general. Be brave, as you're stronger than you think.

Strength – 8: Upright

Strength indicates that **life will not be problem-free**, as events will try your patience and test your abilities. It's not a card of action, but of **quietly soothing worries and concerns**, both yours and others, and not giving into fears, temptation, curiosities, expectations, or ego trips.

Inner strength will be needed to keep problems from losing control, especially where emotions, wants and needs are concerned. With Strength, there is a need to exercise **self-control** and to get hold of insecurities and be patient rather than poking the beast or upsetting situations to get quick answers.

Strength has **determination, strong will and remains still in the face of problems.** It shows us facing life positively and applying **courage** and optimism to all areas.

It's important to **know yourself** and accept any inner defects that you feel are holding you back. With this card, you can **master your fears** and **control your emotions** with understanding and be given the ability to soothe problems with understanding, gentleness and **true compassion.**

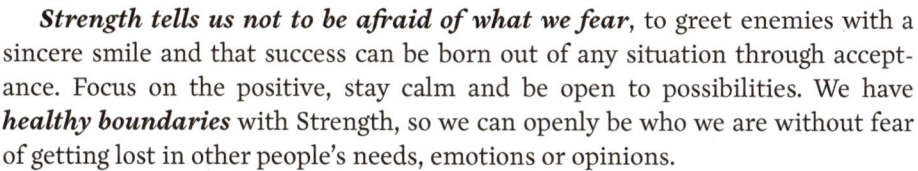

Strength tells us not to be afraid of what we fear, to greet enemies with a sincere smile and that success can be born out of any situation through acceptance. Focus on the positive, stay calm and be open to possibilities. We have **healthy boundaries** with Strength, so we can openly be who we are without fear of getting lost in other people's needs, emotions or opinions.

This card asks us for **self-respect** and to value ourselves; with that, we can cope with an issue and see it through to its end. We do not need to push our views onto others to be heard, just **shine by example**.

Strength is a healthy and positive card to have: if there has been sickness, whether physical, mental or emotional, then **good health** will return. It shows you rising above what has ailed you, determined to regain your health back and not to be beaten by anything which in the past has worn you down.

Strength – 8: Reversed

Reversed, Strength indicates **weakness,** not only of character but also physically, mentally or emotionally. This leads to **feeling vulnerable**, inadequate and even cowardly, as we do not stand up for others or ourselves.

Physically, there will be **illness** or concern for it; **emotions cannot be calmed** or contained, leading to outbursts, while mentally there will be a lack of confidence and **a lack of self-respect**.

Strength reversed shows an individual **controlled by emotions or physical urges**. Saying No may be an issue, as **personal boundaries are lost or weak** leading to **a lack of control over needs and wants**. This is a result of insecurities presenting themselves as **personal problems, irrational thoughts or unhealthy actions and self-indulgence.**

Change will be hard to understand, accept or deal with efficiently, and may lead to **deep anguish and powerlessness** over events. There will be **defeat** in the air as one gives up to a situation which looks like a fearful monster. Maybe this monster is you, maybe it is an object or a person. But vanity, self-image, and a fear of losing out may be driving things, due to **a lack of self-esteem.**

When this card is laid reversed, take the advice that is offered when it is in its correct position - **don't give in,** be firm but calm in all that you do, aim for some balance and boundaries. **Do not doubt yourself** as quite often with this card reversed, there is strength in abundance; it is just not realised, due to feeling **overwhelmed with feelings of failure or loss.**

THE HERMIT - 9

The Hermit's number is Nine, representing understanding, discretion, tolerance and compassion. It is concerned with progress and inspiration, as the road has been travelled with lessons recognised and processed. It brings us closer to the end and shows assimilation. Nine is a springboard for development as it contains all the knowledge of the previous numbers and deeply seeks perfection and finalisation.

The Hermit is astrologically linked to the sign Virgo, and the planet Mercury.

Traditionally, a hermit is a man seeking solitude away from civilisation, either to gain spiritual insight and truth or to simply remove himself from society to gain simplicity and peace. As a result, The Hermit is often viewed as a highly spiritual card, bringing teachers our way. Those who make you think deeply about your own pathway in life, as well as any withdrawal from life to gain clarity and recovery from matters which have caused you to retire from life, other people or situations.

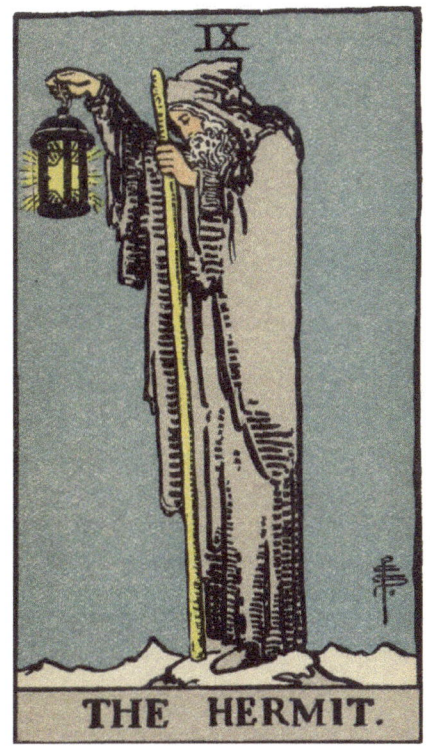

Our Hermit card depicts the lonely figure of an elderly, cloaked man standing alone on top of a mountain at night-time, holding a staff and a lantern.

His head hangs down, symbolising his submission to his situation, as well as to his need to reflect and to give in to his need to look within, as it's understanding he seeks. The Hermit's eyes are closed as he is looking within himself for answers as he seeks to deal with a deeply personal transition. The outer world is not where he will find his answers, so he closes his eyes to the practical, physical world and goes inwards. With our eyes open, our brains try to sift through millions of bits of information per second; when we close our eyes, we block out all the visual elements surrounding us. While this does not free the brain, it does allow for the distraction of our visual selves to be put to one side, which here includes the outside world as a whole. The Hermit is meditating and contemplating his situation; aiming to free his mind from mental ramblings, to clear the constant thunder of thoughts. His aim is to find peace, answers and understanding which can only come from within and which will, in time, bubble up slowly from his unconscious self for him to grasp and heal with. Answers here need not only be of a spiritual nature but also emotional, mental and even practical; anything which places us on a truly intimate and isolating inner search.

The Hermit's lantern shows a glimpse of what lies beyond, yet only as far as the light carries, narrowing his world and forcing him to seek solace and the examination of events, along with the answer to his problem or predicament all in one. Not only did his lantern help him reach his place of solitude, but it will also hold the guiding light for his journey back down the mountain and through the darkness once his inner search is over. It offers hope and light to travel by, yet as only a small light shines from it, it will be a slow journey, made step by step. At that time, he will use the light from the star as a beacon to guide him back to civilisation with his newfound knowledge, understanding and acceptance. The Star's Major Arcana card is placed within his lantern, and if you view it as such then you can see that the lantern offers healing, hope and a time of spring after The Hermit's dark winter.

Inside the lamp is a six-sided star, a hexagram, a Star of David – two triangles placed together representing inner and outer forces, the practical and the spiritual, masculine and feminine, a talisman to protect and shield. The star is a guide: it symbolises hope and offers healing that replaces fear, grief and confusion once a new peace has been found. Held in his right hand, it is a sign of following intuition and feeling over intellect, yet he faces to the left of the card towards logic, action and intellect, all of which can be found within.

The whole look of The Hermit himself represents wisdom, maturity and knowledge through experience. His white, flowing beard shows his maturity, age and knowledge and his grey tunic symbolises contemplation and safety. His grey shoes show that each step is considered, taken slowly with thought and purpose.

The Hermit's staff supports him, and he holds it in his left hand, the hand of reasoning and wisdom, and like the star and the lantern, it has helped get him to this place of solitude and withdrawal and will help him back when the time is right. With both hands holding valuable items of trust and illumination, his energies are fully focused and show us that time is not being wasted. To others, the scene may be still and devoid of hope, yet to The Hermit, his inner self is working its way around issues, coming to terms with life and learning. His staff shows his potential to move onwards, as this is not a place to stay. The colour of his staff is the same yellow as the star in his lantern, showing how much support and direction the light gives when it comes to actual movement, healing and progress in the real world. In some versions of the Rider Waite Smith decks, his staff is wooden, bringing a grounding energy; again, a physical representation of support taken from the strength given by withdrawal and contemplation.

The mountaintop is barren and devoid of life; it is night-time and filled with quiet darkness, surrounding The Hermit with stark reality, in the cold and alone. If it is the truth he searches for, he is in the right place to find it, as the empty darkness of his view allows no extra clutter to fill his head, as all he can see, if he opens his eyes, is his guiding light. The view may be bleak to us on the outside, yet for The Hermit, this is a place he is visiting to heal and gain insights, a respite on life's journey which he cannot avoid.

He may be there through personal choice, as a positive aspect of this card is personal development through acceptance. Yet he may be there due to forced circumstances and mourning the isolation, with a desire to escape life and outside influences, as he cannot cope. He may wish to avoid life while he heals, and those who visit unwillingly may stay longer in this lonely place than the traveller who is seeking acceptance and understanding. He has no sun or warmth, and the darkness within The Hermit card shows suffering, remoteness, a reality that cannot be ignored. It forces us to face our own selves, as, like The Hermit, we will be stuck in place until our minds, or our bodies, have rested enough.

The Hermit either cannot or will not leave his mountaintop until he has been enlightened in the knowledge and truth that he needs, or that which he has been seeking has been found. As such, a certain amount of waiting may have to be done and patience used: time is needed with The Hermit, as he offers no quick solutions.

IN A NUTSHELL

It is okay to be alone. By seeking your own company or solitude, it can help you to recharge and find solutions, as well as to find acceptance and healing. A time to contemplate your life is called for and to depend only on yourself for answers as they lie within you. If another offers you solutions, be cautious to make sure they are true to your experience.

You may feel alone, yet it will not be permanent, just until acceptance and answers from within come to you.

The Hermit - 9: Upright

The Hermit is a card of **withdrawal and solitude**, whether enforced by oneself or by circumstances.

He announces a time of **soul-searching, contemplation and looking deep within oneself to find answers and acceptance of problems.** There will be the need to completely re-evaluate one's life as a whole or within a specific area.

A period of **mourning** is brought about which can be literal, yet which is also due to **feeling alone and striving to accept a situation.** There is **loneliness, sadness and isolation** with this card and a realisation that your problems are yours and yours alone to be dealt with.

If the above does not apply and a decision has to be made, then show **caution**. If you must put your trust in another person, then only do so when you are sure that you will be rewarded with honesty; but mostly **depend upon yourself**. Always **take events slowly** with The Hermit, as he does not like to be rushed. **Hold back plans until it feels right to progress, as all progress should be taken with care.**

The Hermit may also represent a mature and wise person with influence within your life, **someone who will teach you something of value,** be that a direct or indirect lesson in understanding or acceptance. You can learn from the pain and acceptance of another, yet only if you can connect to it.

Remember, however sad you may feel, and however bleak and lonely a situation may be, light is always at the end of the tunnel and peace can always be regained.

It is okay to be alone or to wish to spend time with your own thoughts and can be wise to do so with this card's appearance, as *your answers lie within you.* This card can show *the happy loner and introvert.*

The Hermit – 9: Reversed

Reversed, The Hermit shows *a severe withdrawal from life and a refusal to accept change.* There will be *a need to hide from life or a situation* and to try to leave a problem behind, to make it go away, even though it has control over every thought.

Grief and loss could be indicated with *feelings that one cannot cope with the reality of a situation,* and so the sadness that the reversed Hermit brings is too much to bear.

Events could be at crisis level, leaving no ability to see beyond pain and loss, leading you *to withdraw from those who love you and can help*. However hard it may be to do so, it would be beneficial for others to be allowed near to help with recovery, to reach out and ask for help and guidance.

Life will not be progressing and there will be no forward movement, just sorrow and anguish over dreams which have failed and losses endured.

We can become *reclusive and isolated*, showing a need for horizons to be broadened to avoid stagnation.

Reversed, he can also show *immaturity* that results in one not growing up and *living in a make-believe world,* which can lead to not fitting in with others or even society.

While this can show an *eccentric soul* who does not fit in socially with the 'norm', it can also make you feel as if you are seen as a bit of an oddity by others, leaving you *feeling exiled, or ousted by others.*

WHEEL OF FORTUNE - 10

The Wheel of Fortune is numbered Ten, the first number met so far that is comprised of double digits. Ten is reduced to the number One (1+0=1). As we know, One is the number of The Magician and shows action, drive and new beginnings. While Zero (0), The Fool, is the number of all possibilities and holds infinite potential. Ten indicates change on a large scale that holds plenty of energy for forward movement and progression, while at the same time being complete as it gives a sense of arrival. Optimism and purpose are represented with Ten, showing an abundance of energy and fulfilment. It indicates an end of one cycle with the promise of a new one about to begin, or rather to spread out and grow from the Ten's founding energy, as continued growth is possible with this number.

The Wheel of Fortune is linked to the planet Jupiter and astrologically to all twelve signs of the zodiac.

The card pictures a sphere filled with magical symbols and ancient lettering. The letters around the outer sphere of the wheel are alternate Hebrew and Roman letters. The Hebrew letters spell God's name as it would read in traditional Jewish texts: YHWH or Yahweh. The Roman letters spell Rota/Tora, the Latin name for wheel, and on the scroll held by The High Priestess. These letters are also placed at the cardinal points of north, south, east and west. The inner symbols relate to alchemy - Sulphur (right), Mercury (top), Water (bottom) and Salt (left) - and refer to transformation.

The Wheel of Fortune is symbolic of life's ever-changing evolutionary nature. Life never stays still, and The Wheel of Fortune is at the heart of change, representing every changing tide of energy within our lives. Change which can transform everything for us in the blink of an eye, for good or for bad, like ever-shifting energy beneath and about us. The symbols also indicate that change is everywhere, including the four corners of the earth and even in the stars above us; nothing is static, nothing is certain, and nothing is guaranteed, and change is constant.

In each of the four corners of the card are four creatures that may come from the inaugural visualisation of Ezekiel, a Hebrew prophet, often called The Wheel in Ezekiel 1. These symbols also appear in Revelations, known as the Guardians of Heaven. Yet equally, they may be representative of Matthew, Mark, Luke and John, the Four Evangelists. Matthew is characterised by the human, Mark the lion, Luke the calf and John the eagle. The calf = earth, the lion = fire, the eagle = air and the man = water. They correspond to the four fixed signs of the zodiac

– Scorpio, Leo, Taurus, and Aquarius – as well as the four elements of the four suits of the minor arcana – Swords, Cups, Pentacles and Wands – and so the entire zodiac. All four of these figures are reading or studying texts, showing that lessons are to be learnt and implemented with this card, as change is evolutionary and can teach us much if we welcome it into our lives. Being golden, they show eternal energies in our lives which govern and rule, as well as external, real-life changes needed for growth.

At the top of the wheel is a female Sphinx holding a double-edged sword, casting riddles, and destroying those who fail to answer correctly: bringer of life and death, knowledge and strength, wisdom and truth, resurrection and rebirth. She is blue, representing faith in our success, and faith in getting it right so we can stay secure at the top. Her sword represents logic and brutal honesty which cuts away at our lives, separating us from what is no longer ours to keep. It is double-edged, showing that this wheel can turn equally well in the direction of either good or bad luck. The sword is held at an angle to the right of the card; we may not find it emotionally fair nor welcoming. We all constantly wish to be at the top of the wheel, but we are shown that what we want is not always what will give us the necessary experience to evolve.

To the left of the wheel, a snake travels downwards. It represents Typhon, a monstrous snake who tried to take over the universe but was killed by Zeus. Typhon travelling down the wheel represents a downfall, a loss brought on by ego, desire and excessive pride and confidence. He symbolises the wisdom which can be gained by having your view of who you are, or your world, destroyed. He is coloured yellow, showing intellect and confidence, the destruction of the mind as life falls apart, and the deconstruction of the ego as views and beliefs are shattered, as with The Tower.

Travelling up the wheel is Anubis, who guides dead souls to the afterlife and brings rebirth. He symbolises regeneration and regrowth, as he is the decider of the fates of those he guides. He is red, symbolising desire, passion and drive to get back on top, to find happiness or security, and at times, a new life. Anubis brings a time to accept change, as it will be the issue or energy which created the situation brought about by The Wheel of Fortune or was born from the event, which decides what new life or situation awaits.

Imagine a journey around this wheel. At the top there is satisfaction and happiness, you would feel proud and on top of the world. Good luck would be followed by success and, naturally, you would be intent on enjoying the hand dealt. As luck changes, you fall and slip off the treasured position, filled with fear or dread. You may cling onto the wheel, reluctant to let go and accept losses; but you fall all the same. Beneath the wheel, you have nothing to cling to and you are crushed, having lost hope, with no encouragement to draw from, and feeling defeated. Having reached rock bottom, you finally get up and again start to climb, wiser, full of hope and expectancy. And so, the cycle starts again.

The blue sky mixed with grey clouds echoes this card's dual energy for good or bad, happy or sad, positive or negative, growth or destruction, as while it may bring sunshine into your life it can also bring storms.

This wheel can move painfully slowly or exceptionally fast. Life is a constant cycle of death and birth, both big and small, each of which affects every area of our being. The Wheel of Fortune brings into play the element of luck, destiny, karma or fate into our lives, things which remind us that our presumed control is just an illusion. While such things can appear to be out of the blue, everything has a starting point, a motivation; nothing happens by chance and mistakes do not happen. There is a reason behind everything that occurs in life, every action however minute will add to this cycle as cause and effect react to each other. Wheels do not turn without applied motion; we can set this wheel in motion as equally as we can get caught up in another person's spin of the wheel. These causes and effects can have been set in motion days, weeks, years, decades or even generations ago, with each turn affecting its surroundings. At times, the trigger may be a butterfly flapping its wings in the Amazon, so we are not always privy to the 'whys', and when The Wheel of Fortune appears, changes will present themselves, bringing the ups and downs of life. Sometimes they will be small, and other times life-changing.

IN A NUTSHELL

Life, luck, or a situation will be changing. Change should not be resisted, and you will not be able to avoid the hand you are being given.

You are at a turning point: work with what you are given, use what a situation offers you to achieve the best you can, so go with the flow.

Wheel of Fortune - 10: Upright

This card shows **life's ups and downs** and reminds us that **change is life's only consistency**. Changes are needed, and the wheel brings a time to **roll with changes** and to allow life to move forwards. Everything goes in cycles, taking us from good to bad luck, from one phase to another, as everything evolves.

When using both Upright and Reversed cards, The Wheel of Fortune shows a positive flow of change and good luck. A reminder that **nothing stays the same, everything changes**. As the wheel turns, our luck rises and falls depending on where on the wheel we stand. We are brought to a **turning point** and a time to grow, as even the smallest of events can bring major changes. Yet when using both Upright and Reversed cards, The Upright Wheel of Fortune shows a positive flow of change and good luck.

The Wheel of Fortune tells us *a new phase in life is starting and an old one is ending*; there will be changes within our life as a whole or within individual situations, *from micro-changes to life-altering ones*. It will be a time to **accept change openly**, whether the change is *expected or unexpected*.

As life is continually moving forwards and evolving, we should accept the hand that fate offers us, whether it's to our liking or not, and actively **work with the hand we are dealt**, as however hard we try, we cannot avoid change.

If you feel change is necessary, this card tells you it is **a good time to create change** and follow your dreams; luck will be on your side and you can enjoy the benefits of your efforts as now is a time to win, achieve and succeed.

Wheel of Fortune – 10: Reversed

Reversed, The Wheel of Fortune brings us **bad luck**. **Changes for the worse** are on their way bringing unexpected **setbacks, delays and failure**. A definite card of **misfortune** - fate will not be on your side, and this may also leave you feeling awkward, embarrassed and upset.

If you are involved in a distressing situation, then it is not over yet, as **a continuation of a bad phase** remains and **disappointment is guaranteed**.

If you are trying to move in a certain direction and **obstacles** are in your way, you need to realise that not everything you want can be yours. This can be the Universe's way of saying: go back or turn around and leave what you want alone. Be patient and learn, for whatever trouble The Wheel is providing you with will not last forever.

It can be common to be left *feeling like a victim* when changes occur which are outside of our control, not in our favour and do not go our way. Yet life has a way of balancing out, so **get your thinking cap on** rather than allowing disappointment to take control.

As **all of what we reap we have previously sown**, look at what actions have brought about this rough patch and if you cannot see a link, then acceptance is needed all the same.

Although the changes brought by The Wheel of Fortune reversed may not be desired, it can show that **change is being resisted**, which does not help solve matters. It can show **a need to break away from old cycles** or patterns of behaviour which are not serving you well causing bad luck and problems within your life.

JUSTICE - 11

Justice's number is Eleven. In numerology, the numbers 11, 22, and 33 are considered master numbers, and as such, some numerologists believe they should not be reduced. A master number is said to hold power over our lives. Its negatives can be as powerful as its positives due to the duplication and amplification of the original number, increasing its potency. The Master Intuitive is number 11, the Master Builder is number 22, and the Master Teacher is number 33. 44, 55, 66, 77, 88, 99, and 00 are also master numbers, although they can be called power numbers. 11, 22 and 33 hold more value as they are made up of 1, 2, and 3, respectively, forming the Triangle of Enlightenment, symbolising the three phases of creation: visualising, building and delivery. If we break the rules of numerology and reduce the Eleven (1+1=2), the One shows action and strength, and together they bring us the number Two, the number of The High Priestess, allowing for harmony, balance and resolution. Eleven is a progressive number, half feminine fairness and half masculine action and principle. Yet looked at as two Ones, that brings a lot of drive and commitment to create and pursue with power and absolute confidence, a number which owns its potential. As a master number, it requires a high standard of commitment in fulfilling its aim, which is patience and balance in all things. Eleven, although it seeks independence, also requires harmonious resolution to work effectively, and brings unity, principles and progression. A balance is required by this number between the mental and the spiritual self.

Justice is associated with Libra, ruled by Venus.

Justice gives us a woman sitting on a stone seat in front of a veil and two pillars; in one hand she holds a sword and in the other a set of scales.

The two pillars are grey and represent safety, wisdom, and contemplation with duality. Here they represent right and wrong, innocence and guilt, fair and unfair. The pillars themselves give structure and security, showing a place of safety for those wishing fairness.

The purple veil, which hangs between the pillars, is the colour of wisdom, mixing divinity with intuition, giving us compassion and absolute truths. Purple is a mixture of calm, stable blue and powerful, driven red, and is often associated with power, dignity and commitment. The veil hangs softly draped between the two pillars, hiding information, and yet can also protect and keep us safe. The veil itself fills the gap fully and, with no glimpses around the sides as with The High

Priestess, we focus our minds on justice itself, on facts and truth with no distractions of what may be hidden.

The stone seat is plain and undecorated, indicating solid and direct foundations, as no frills are needed with the truth. It shows a lack of comfort, just cold stone which can bring us uncomfortable truths, as not all truths are warm and fluffy. The seat is earthly, grounding and solid, giving a reliable base from which justice can be delivered with sincerity.

Justice's golden crown is decorated with a blue stone set over her third eye, showing intuition; the blue represents a calm mind and view of the world with a lack of mental clutter. This shows an openness in the search for justice, rather than a rigid black and white outlook. The stone is square, showing organisation, so there is no predominance of her intuition over logic, but balance. The square also represents the earth, symbolising north, south, east and west. Being placed over the mind, it brings mental direction and an ability to navigate situations practically as well as emotionally. The crown is gold, which links to the outer, practical and action side of Justice, the rational seeking out what is real and what is not. The shape of the crown is reminiscent of battlements and can bring mental conflict, as wars are waged with facts and truth.

Justice has blonde hair, which can be a sign of innocence and youth, yet here it's more linked to a higher divine energy, showing her mind to be pure and untarnished by her own experiences, able to see events in their simple truth to be able to give a divine, universal verdict.

She wears a red ceremonial gown with a green cloak and stole, symbolising service, so here we have a card not based on opinion or self-importance, but from an experienced and literal viewpoint. Her clothes show her role is one which is respected and not made up willingly to suit whims. Her gown shows us a sign of authority and superiority, which truth itself is, within our lives. The green cloak symbolises balance, creativity, compassion and growth, while the stole represents a yoke of service. Her red gown flows onto the stone floor, showing that she connects with the hardness of her position, and with the sleeves open you can see she has nothing to hide – just balance and facts.

Her foot sticks out from her gown; it is unclear if it is her right or left, as her ankles are crossed, so I presume it to be her right, showing her emotions to be clear and unhindered by feelings and desire. Yet if it is her left, then it shows her logical mind is steering away from emotion. Either would fit the energy of Justice. Her white shoe shows genuine motives and the importance of correct action. It serves to remind us that all our actions and words need to be at peace with our conscience and spirit; we need to walk hand in hand with ethics and moral values. Her legs are crossed at the ankles, which shows her to be relaxed and confident as the truth simply *is*: a fact which cannot be changed.

Her brooch is a red stone circle, set again in a square, which covers her heart centre, showing inner emotional strength and compassion. The red stone is her passion for truth, the circle is her true self, wholeness and the divine, the square direction and strength. The circle represents the universe, the square the earth, and so God or perfection found within earthly deeds and emotions. A circle within a square is called 'squaring the circle', which is an expression used when two opposites are brought together to create harmony.

She faces forwards, showing action. She looks at everything head-on and sees everything; you cannot hide from this card's energy as it's an honesty that penetrates everything.

The perfectly balanced set of scales is held in her left hand, symbolising balance and equality. Her hand does not grasp the scales, but has a light touch, showing her faith in their ability to be correct. She does not cling to them with force, but with gentleness. They point to her skill at weighing up events and show that order can be reached and maintained. The weighing-up process of the scales shows decisions are well thought out before conclusions are reached. *Libra* is Latin for scales and symbolises the heavens being balanced by both day and night during the autumn equinox. As a Karmic card, all things need to be balanced, so effect follows cause and cause creates effect, everything balancing out with acceptance.

The sword in her right, emotional, hand is logic, thought and reasoning and shows straightforward intellect and powerful action which cuts through emotions. Here it is the same blue as the stone in her crown. This sword slices through illusions so the truth can be exposed and seen in all its glory; it's dual-edged and so cuts both ways as it does not take sides. A sword cuts away fantasies and is a symbol of friction and conflict. It is held upright which indicates there are no opinions, no version of the truth other than that which is factual and evidence-based. Do not attach a personal sense of fairness or right and wrong to this card: to do so would result in disappointment. Universal balance means situations being put right, yet that may not always gel with your sense of fairness. Do not confuse the two.

Justice shows us that to achieve balance and truth in our lives, we all can use our free will; we are given the absolute ability to direct our own futures. We as lone individuals, as well as together, should use this card's energy as we are all ultimately responsible for our own lives simply by the decisions that we make every moment of every day. Justice shows the responsibility that we must take for our own misgivings and choices. If our life is to take the correct path, then we can help achieve that aim by letting truth prevail and by not letting other influences cloud our judgement.

When this card appears, it shows that the situation has taken the pathway that it should and that the outcome has gone according to plan, whether you like the conclusion or not.

IN A NUTSHELL

A time for all facts to be weighed up as truth is the only currency of value. Honesty is called for and if judgement is given, it should be done using facts, not emotions or hearsay, as every action and word has consequences.

If you have done nothing wrong, then you have nothing to fear. Personal responsibility is needed and will yield the best results. Balance will be restored to a situation.

Justice – 11: Upright

Justice brings **law, balance, responsibility and order to situations**. Truth is a vital aspect of this card, as is the act of **taking responsibility** for one's life regarding past, present and future actions or problems, and shows that the situation at hand is often where it's meant to be, and that acceptance and **taking stock** is called for.

Justice accompanies the **making of decisions** that will determine and shape the future, clear and practical thinking is required - **a literal weighing up of a problem**. Decisions need to be made responsibly or else they will weigh down the conscience and show a time when **you need to do the right thing**.

With Justice, there should be **total honesty** with yourself and others. **Truth** is necessary, and shows an honest personality, as well as a strong and determined character that is striving to maintain truth and balance.

Justice could also refer to a legal union such as business partnerships and weddings, or even dealings with the police, solicitors or **legal ventures and dealings**, and would indicate that **all wrongs will be put right**. The **truth will prevail**, whether this is in your favour or not.

Justice brings **fairness** in whatever form it chooses to take, i.e., **equality, rational thought, weighing up pros and cons**, etc.

Justice also points to the laws of **karma** and shows that life is going in the right direction even if it feels like it is not: *as you sow, so shall you reap*. Whether a debt is to society, oneself or another, order and balance are always restored.

If you are thinking of being dishonest, then do not be: it will be a waste of time, as honesty and justice will win through. **Lies and imbalance will be highlighted as equally as truths and clarity.**

Justice – 11: Reversed

Reversed, Justice leads to *injustice*, leaving you feeling *discriminated against* as *unfairness* is aimed at you, or from you to another.

Truth and facts may not be to your liking and ignored, which leads us to the *denial of facts* and *burying your head in the sand*.

Legal dealings or situations regarding authority will not go well or as expected; *red tape* and legal complications can stop situations from going as planned. Yet, it is also a time to watch for *the abuse of power* and *deceit* from an individual or group who are judging or acting against you in some way to serve their own interests.

When reversed, *personal injustices* are felt; something will go against your sense of fairness. If the injustice is from another, then it will involve *dishonesty, prejudice or double standards*. Be warned not to react in the same manner, as it will give them fuel to use against you. Personal boundaries can feel torn down as you are *treated unfairly* in a situation, making it seem that you're *on trial*, leaving you *feeling vulnerable*.

As the nature of this card is *universal justice*, then it may be that the balance in a situation has been restored, however hurt it may have left you feeling.

The balance has been tipped and the status quo altered, causing negative emotions and feelings of despondency concerning events. When this occurs, *personal responsibility is avoided*, often leading to *lying* outright, blaming and *passing the buck* by shifting blame or responsibility. When it comes to misleading or downright dishonest behaviour, lies will be recognised sooner or later.

THE HANGED MAN - 12

The Hanged Man is number Twelve. Ten is the current number of completion but was once Twelve; a year has twelve months, so this is also a number which seeks completion and new starts. The Twelve's One is wholeness, mental action, independence and purpose, while the Two is passive inner thought and anticipation. When the Twelve is reduced (1+2=3), we are given the Three of The Empress, which symbolises growth and expansion. Twelve symbolises understanding and wisdom concerning the lessons that we are presented with throughout life. It shows great depth of understanding, and this wisdom is expressed as inner growth. This number seeks to bring information and understanding together. All that it lets you experience is felt deep within, is educational and is relevant to the procession of life.

The Hanged Man is linked to the planet Neptune which rules Pisces.

The Hanged Man shows a man tied by one leg to a cross, suspended above the ground. The obvious question to ask is why? He is tied only by one leg so he could easily get himself down. His predicament looks physically awkward as well as inconvenient, but his face is calm but thoughtful. So why is he there?

The rope around his ankle may have been placed there by The Hanged Man himself, and upside down he has been removed from his surroundings. This having been done, by choice or circumstance, allows him to be able to concentrate on a greater objective, without distractions in some cases, but also to obtain a fresh perspective. This rope just suspends him; it does not tie him up and could easily be removed, yet he stays willingly to perceive the world differently.

He is suspended from a T-shaped cross, called a Tau which is symbolic of life and resurrection. Our hanged man's cross is made from living wood, symbolising a suspension from life, and a chance of rebirth via a new interpretation of life and events. The symbolic aspect of the living cross arises from trees being symbolic of life - their roots go deep underground, or rather, into the subconscious. Above ground we have the physical tree representing the body and physical world, which is our consciousness with the trunk, and then up to the sky with the leaves and buds into the heavens which is our higher consciousness. This puts our Hanged Man attached to all that he is, aiming for continued growth and full of potential. The cross is The Hanged Man's intellectual and spiritual grounding force that shows he is not suffering any illusions; he is merely going inwards to process information that he has sought to find.

He hangs by his right leg, the side of creativity, inspiration, intuition, with this left, logical, rational thinking leg placed behind. He hangs linked to his imagination and his inner mind, with his conscious self untied and free, placed out of the way yet moveable, showing him seeking spiritual growth from the world about him.

His legs form an inverted triangle, his arms an upright triangle. The upright refers to the masculine and the active, the inverted to female and passive, showing he has surrendered to his situation. Leaving his passive mental and spiritual top half with a masculine energy and his physical driven bottom half passive, literally turning all that he is on its head. His hands are placed behind his back to allow his situation to unfold without interference. He has sacrificed, suspended all aspects of himself to gain something new.

What he turns upside-down are his own, others' or society's beliefs, views and opinions as they are not facts, nor set in stone: they are just rules, expectations, judgements and attitudes. They provide us with pigeon-holes, safety boltholes, as well as excuses, which allow us to limit ourselves. So here they are put to one side as being true to oneself takes on more importance.

He wears a blue shirt, the colour of gentle thought, inspiration, spirituality, healing and grace, covering his top half; like his right leg being tied, he is very aware of his spirituality, his inner self, as that is where his heart really lays. His purple belt symbolises his higher wisdom, showing he is tying his spiritual experience into his physical, and vice versa. His red trousers are a sign of being led by desire, enthusiasm, bravery and curiosity. So, again he seeks an understanding of physical life and how that fits with his spiritual or personal self. His yellow shoes show it's his thoughts, his ideas, his need to grasp and learn which have brought him to this point. He is seeking a way to bring his conscious desires together with his spiritual and imaginative needs.

He is surrounded by grey, a colour for contemplation, and his face is calm and relaxed as he is in no pain or discomfort. Unlike The Hermit, The Hanged Man's eyes are open, so he again seeks answers from the outside world in resolving and developing his own inner being, as his gaze is introspective, curious and questioning what he sees.

His golden yellow halo or nimbus informs us of his aim for higher personal achievement. The yellow tells us he is driven by mental action and questioning thoughts, with the halo itself showing him to be driven firstly by an inner need and awareness. His shoes, hair and halo are all yellow, signalling that all parts of him are in agreement, as his mental force has led him to this place physically, emotionally, mentally and spiritually.

By suspending himself upside down, his grounding physical side and connection to his higher or mental self are inverted; his normal approach has been turned upside down and this is welcomed as he is seeking to see things differently. His suspension indicates removal from a situation, a time to wait and be patient. By placing himself in the air, above the ground, The Hanged Man gains a different view of his surroundings. He can see what those below cannot, which points to a free-thinking individual, someone prepared to go to sometimes unconventional lengths to see things from a different perspective. His removal from life allows new and progressive light to be shone onto a subject or life itself. He wishes to be independent and does not mind if he is noticed for being different, as he doesn't worry about how others perceive him. He is adaptable, with a desire to learn and is willing to sacrifice one part of his life to benefit from another, as while upside down, it will mean that something else needs to be put on hold. Although The Hanged Man is alone, it doesn't mean that he wishes others to not at least ask why he is there, and this can often be quite a communicative card.

The Hanged Man brings mental action and shows us a highly active mind, which is committed to seeking enlightening truths. Maybe it will be from all the extra oxygen-rich blood flooding to his brain and enhancing the pituitary gland (the third eye, or Brow Chakra), showing other dimensions to his search, but his mind will be seeking to expand and learn from a new angle. He represents a real, solid, personal enlightening experience that will bring change especially on an emotional level, but even more so on a mental one. His mind is being used to bring about rational explanations to summarise events, and during that time, his life will be stationary while he puts his ego to one side to seek an alternative view.

This card tells us not to fear a lack of change or even change which needs retrospection, but to view difficulties from all angles and perspectives before trying to reach an understanding, acceptance or a conclusion to a situation or problem. He tells us to follow our own ideas, as the views and solutions of others will not serve us well at this moment in time. The Hanged Man allows time for ideas to sink in before he tries to fully understand them. Sometimes it is better to accept that our lives must pause occasionally, especially if it is to gain acceptance and insights into the current situation, which here would be better achieved by obtaining a different view.

IN A NUTSHELL

Events will be up in the air, often leading you to take time out to think before you act. Take your time in deciding what to do and be independent in how you approach issues.

Find new ways of thinking and approaching matters; do not be afraid to look in places you may normally ignore in your search for understanding. Sacrifice what is not needed, especially old views and ways of doing things. Give yourself as much time as you need to think clearly. Relax into quiet times, as they will offer a valuable contemplating space.

The Hanged Man - 12: Upright

The Hanged Man indicates that *events will be held back and delayed with setbacks*. Matters will be held up while decisions are made, and you will often find yourself *at a crossroads* regarding a situation or even life as a whole. You should use this *time to reflect*, as *life will be at a standstill* while conclusions are deliberated, and beliefs are challenged.

When this card is drawn, decisions should not be made carelessly: there will be the need to use careful consideration, as *events will be up in the air*. This card shows that everything is a process, with one step needed to follow another. As a result, expect progress to be slow.

The Hanged Man gives us *a time to stop and observe situations*, people and views, to be mindful and see how things pan out without our interference. There will be the need to *remove yourself from a situation*, suspend action, stop play. *Give yourself more time* to be able to make sense of what's occurring, gain *a deeper understanding* and see circumstances in a fresh light. *Problems should be viewed from all angles* with no stone left unturned, as this card shows *an active and open problem-solving mindset*.

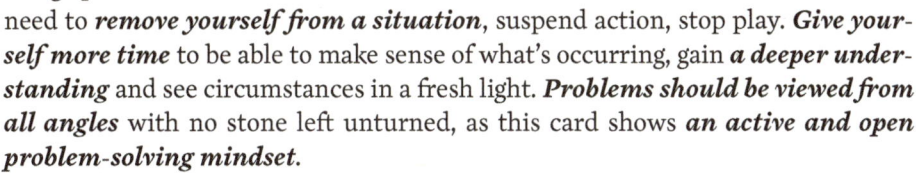

The Hanged Man represents those who are confirmed individualists, so *be independent of other people's views and opinions - even if they object*. Now is a time to do what you feel is right rather than blindly follow other people's suggestions.

The Hanged Man can bring a *personal sacrifice*: one will surrender to change, or lose one area of life to improve or create another, so you will have to *be patient as rewards may not be instantaneous*. For example, you may leave a job to bring up a child, or give up your social life to study every night to create a better career. These instances can lay in any area of life from the small to the life-changing, from choosing not to enter a conversation, or to leave a party, to ending a forty-year relationship, as you challenge on a personal level something which needs a new approach. Whatever the change, *a lot of thought will be instigated* to *make sure that the change will be viable*.

Whatever your sacrifice, put your all into it. *If you are asking if you have made a positive decision, then The Hanged Man would suggest that you have*, if you've been independent in your views and stepped back to evaluate your situation as a whole. However, there may still be some searching to do before taking action.

The Hanged Man – 12: Reversed

Reversed, the Hanged Man would indicate **wasted time and a needless sacrifice**. You have willingly given up your time, dreams, or an area of your life for no real return, if any at all, leaving you **in limbo**. Dreams and ideals have been sacrificed for the needs or wishes of another, or from a fear of breaking free from convention. **Now is the time to make changes** if life is to proceed in a beneficial and positive way.

There can be a lack of confidence and **a strong need to please others** which shows you in a situation of your own making, where **others have taken advantage** by imposing their views and wishes, or where **you simply have not made your needs known**. There is **a lack of independence**, or independent thought and often insecurity in chasing dreams, showing **missed opportunities**.

Views, attitudes and maybe even lifestyle changes are now necessary and it's time to let go of outdated views and often **narrow ideas**. Now is not the time to pass blame as to what or who is at fault, but to simply **let go of what has held you back**, as the responsibility lies with yourself.

Follow your own ideas, not those of another, as to do so will only lead to sadness. You may be **left hanging** by people as they fail to give you what you need as they neglect to fulfil promises. Equally, you can be **hung out to dry,** which means to be left in a difficult or unhappy situation to suit others' needs in order to safeguard their own situations, leaving you abandoned or ignored.

Reversed, this card can also represent being hanged for what you have done wrong, so can indicate **punishment** inflicted by others or yourself, as well as **self-sabotage,** as you do not feel you deserve a new chance or happiness.

DEATH - 13

Death's number is Thirteen, traditionally seen as an unlucky number, yet Thirteen represents a lot more than just plain old-fashioned bad luck. The Thirteen's One points to potential and new beginnings, while the Three to growth. When reduced (1+3=4), we have the methodical number Four which shows an adamant strength and certainty. Thirteen is a powerful number of transformation and transition. It governs rebirth, the unplanned and total change. With the appearance of this number, everything is as it appears to be, as it governs sudden, unplanned changes. Although this may be viewed as unlucky, it is also a necessity. This number brings rebirth, allows growth on whatever level it is felt and is an unavoidable vibration of upheaval. The only consistency that the number Thirteen brings is change.

Death is astrologically ruled by Scorpio, linked to Pluto.

Death shows us a yellow skeleton in black armour, riding a white horse approaching the people before him.

We take it for granted that whooping cough, typhoid, etc., are covered by vaccinations, yet in 1909, when this deck was created, these were new, lifesaving and society-transforming health programmes. Both Waite and Smith, and especially their parents, would have most likely seen Victorian anti-vaccination promotions with yellow skeletons, due to the money which the doctors got paid, yet would have also highlighted the grave cost of contracting an illness. Linking a yellow skeleton to pestilence, a challenge to life, an event that can decimate everything we know. Yellow is also an intellectual colour, and Death is factual: he is not emotional, he simply is, and the colour represents the assurance with which he works, takes, and sculpts those he touches. As a skeleton, we are shown the ultimate symbol of death; the removal of all we know, stripped away down to the bare bones.

His black armour symbolises darkness, night and absorbs all other colours, yet after darkness comes light after night comes day and from black all other colours can spring forth, so black is a colour that shows his potential. Black knights are a symbol of fear and death, yet unlike a traditional black knight, his face is visible, as he has no wish to hide his true nature. The white cross on his chest plate represents a harsh sacrifice with purity, so a cleansing which can feel like punishment is being delivered. His red feather on top of his helmet shows his desire to be successful, his passion and his drive as he charges in, so Death has a purpose.

Death is calm and in control of the horse, who is pawing at the ground wanting to get moving, impatient at staying still, showing the unending cycle of death.

The white horse is a symbol of death in Christianity; his whiteness is clean, pure and untarnished by his surroundings, allowing Death to move forward with pure, incorruptible strength. The horse's neck strap is decorated with swords and skulls, and his red eye is symbolic of action and passion. The horse does not wish to be still, things need to progress, so he is wishing the absolute ending to the scene in front of him, as he desires to move onwards as the deed here is done. The mud he paws at shows a loss of dignity to the king laying in it, yet it brings a grounding reality and a place from where new life can grow.

Death holds a black banner with a white rose, the white represents the integrity of his very existence or essence, while the rose itself symbolises the pure emotions he evokes. The rose is the same as the White Rose of York, an image adopted by Yorkists in England in the fourteenth century, associated with the Virgin Mary, a symbol of purity. It shows innocence, as Death truly is; he is the outcome, the effect, not the cause. Even when we are expecting his arrival and can see his banner over the horizon, we only see him face to face when he finally arrives. His presence is unavoidable in life and, at times, swift and silent. After he has done, we are left with no misunderstandings as he brings the final cut, and he brings us face to face with reality. The ending cycle which this card represents cannot be ignored. Even with the horse's impatience, Death stops to hear the man below. Those in front of Death represent humanity and show all aspects of society. No barriers can be put up to protect against age, race, religion or social standing. Death is generous - he includes us all equally.

The rose consists of two rows of five petals, with ten the number of completion as Death brings things to an end, and five being one of conflict and mental struggles as we try to comprehend him. It has five leaves, which adds to that strain; leaves are symbolic of life and growth, yet here they are drained of colour. I have wondered if the centre of the flower is a representation of the Flower of Life, a symbol of creation.

The dead king lies under the horse, his ego shattered as he has not been able to mentally comprehend or bend to the situation, as shown by his discarded golden crown. His physical and mental worlds are lost. His right fist is clenched on his chest, which is clearer in newer versions of the deck, shows anger and a lost emotional battle, as he tried to hold on to his worldly power, but to no avail. His left logical hand lies lifeless in the mud, as he was unable to beat the situation with logic, power, and strength. His hair is grey, representing that even the wisdom of age could not help him. This king has been dethroned, and with his reign over, he is now powerless and lifeless in the mud. His importance, wealth, and power have been no shield from Death. However plush his robes and ermine furs are, he has lost to something greater than himself.

In front of the horse, a bishop stands with eyes closed, praying to the oncoming transformation. He may be giving last rights to the fallen king, but his crook, representing the Good Shepherd who gave his life for his flock, lays discarded also in the mud. While he would have been preparing for this moment a lifetime, when faced with Death, he wishes mercy, either for his own salvation or that of the two children as he does not know if Death has finished or wishes to take them all. The cross on his hand resembles Christ's wounds and he may be asking to sacrifice himself to save them. He understands, at this moment, that faith will not stop the carnage as faith, ego, wealth and ceremony are not going to save anyone. Faith can only be a strong factor in helping change if it is without ego-driven expectation, and here the priest is not accepting the situation, he has left faith on the floor, and instead reaches forwards with humility, praying to Death rather than to God.

Kneeling on the ground is a young maiden with her head turned away from Death, arms by her side, recognising her own powerlessness. She has innocence and purity with her white dress and flowers in her hair, but she cannot turn to look at Death willingly and be open to her fate. She does not wish to face an experience she is not ready for; she does not wish to lose her naïvety and be forced to witness the change he brings. Yet she cannot keep her eyes closed to the situation forever, eyes open or closed - the king is still laying in the mud, she is in Death's way, and avoidance will not stop her from being trampled if he so chooses. From her hand, she has dropped a pink flower, a sign of her youth and innocence falling and being lost to her as she faces something far beyond her wisdom.

The small boy, however, embodies the simplicity that is needed to help the transition go as smoothly as it can. He welcomes Death with no resistance and with a white posy of flowers, symbolic of funerals and death, and gazes up to welcome him. He also holds the wrist of the girl, trying to get her to look and embrace the nature of the situation. Being very young, he does not comprehend Death's nature, yet he holds a lot of wisdom in his simple acceptance.

Past this scene is a desert with an oasis, which is a part of the pathway back from Death. The surrounding barren desert indicates that growth is not always available in Death's aftermath. Yet there are a few trees along with a couple of graves, so while we travel back from our encounter with Death, we can mourn and rest, however uncomfortable the terrain will be. The oasis offers a chance to recoup and gather strength, yet the journey will not be a fast one. All the mud and sand tell us that the conditions Death works in may not be pleasant but at least there are no hidden extras; he leaves nothing to block the view. The ground that surrounds the four cannot die or be cleared any more than it already has, so new life is the only positive possibility. Death's lack of comforting illusions can either be a stumbling block if the changes that he brings cannot be faced, or relief as all is now apparent.

Further back, a river flows, symbolic of our deep emotions and the continuous flow of change, while the actual river itself represents constancy as it is always present. This tells us that while death may affect us, whatever you lose, you are always in essence - you. The boat although at the mercy of the river is still able to be steered and controlled even though it has no choice but to let the winds of change and currents push it onwards. Its sail is open, showing movement: the journey is being navigated and the only direction to go in is forward. To fight the flow and wind would risk more loss. In this original image, the sail is tinted red, showing a passion to move on from this desolate place. In others, it can be white, showing a simplicity in acceptance, which is needed to heal and move on.

In this original image of Death, the background is blue due to the approaching dawn, leaving the future as an unknown and uncertain journey. In other decks, you can see this in colour. From this point in the card, from the other side of the water, at last, is greenery, a grassy bank which offers a sign of hope in the future, yet it lies at the bottom of a tall vertical cliff, so from the vantage of the people at Death's mercy, the road back to the city at the top may seem impossible and the journey too harsh.

In the distance are two towers, also found within The Moon, with water flowing between them. They are not The Tower but have a duality to them; opposites needed to make a whole. A single window offers a single outlook, and with two, a balance of thought, primarily based on acceptance, is needed to pass through them successfully. Beyond, the rising sun shows the start of a brand-new untarnished day. To reach it, we must pass between these two towers, as they are the gateway to the city, the entrance to a new life. They represent a passageway to travel through, aware of the changes which have occurred to us, however painful they may have been, giving a return to safety and security. Yet, that is all in the shadows and far in the distance as this new day starts. For movement to be made, the ego must be moved aside so the truth can sink in. Death has wiped the slate clean and as we approach this new day, even though we do not know what it will bring, we know that to face it we must accept the change and move forward.

Death is an integral part of life, it's part of the largest cycle that we know - life and death. Both are a constant force and represent different sides of the same revolving door. One naturally follows the other; they exist side by side and we need both to continue our evolutionary path through life and our general existence, both singularly and universally. Every second of every minute of every day, we suffer many tiny little deaths as well as the large, painful ones. The Death card mainly refers to deaths surrounding the ego or sense of self, and you may view Death as bad or negative, but he is neither, as Death simply *is*.

IN A NUTSHELL

Change cannot and will not be ignored. This is a time for forced transformation and cutting of ties. Change will happen regardless of what you want or wish for - so go with the flow, as there is not a lot more you can do, and resistance will just increase unwanted feelings.

Changes will be forced upon you: they may be sudden and unseen or expected, but they will change your life on either an inner or outer level, as what is no longer able to stay within your life leaves.

Death – 13: Upright

A lot of people panic when Death appears in a reading, but he rarely means a physical bereavement, yet if placed next to The Hermit, Ten of Swords and The Tower, or other painful cards, he *could, maybe,* point in that direction.

This brings up an important rule of reading for others: **NEVER TELL A QUESTIONER THAT THEY OR ANYONE CLOSE TO THEM WILL DIE**. *No amount of prejudging can prepare you for how they might react or feel once they have left you. Act responsibly with the knowledge that you have access to, and consider **you may be wrong**.*

Death brings ***major changes*** regardless of whether they are wanted or not. This card brings ***inevitable change*** on a small, as well as a large scale. ***An area of one's life will come to an end or change drastically.*** To struggle against the flow of change or life at the arrival of Death would be futile: Death always wins. These can be small changes, such as the losses we have daily that direct our lives, or an event that creates total upheaval.

The Death card can bring great pain: he can bring a great amount of upset and fear as he leaves us to ***face the unknown***. As with all endings, we are promised a new state of being, and different circumstances to adjust to and that may not be wished for. With Death, you can gain a greater understanding of yourself and others via acceptance. Whether you view this card as positive and welcomed, or negatively and greeted with apprehension and panic, will fully depend on your ability to cope with the particular change or loss brought to you.

Most information written on the Death card portrays it as a card of ***failure, loss, bad luck and setbacks,*** but that point of view entirely depends on how you will greet what it brings. ***If you wish for a positive outcome, this card will often suggest a No.***

It is important to remember that Death is a ***transition*** card - ***a change from one state to another.*** You can only learn from this card if you embrace any changes and accept them, as they will not go away simply by ignoring them.

The effects of this card can be felt with emotions ranging from ***apprehension and nervousness*** to ***outright sorrow and grief***, while the new and probably unknown beginning that it throws us towards will be greeted with an equal mix of emotions.

Death's arrival may be sudden, at times even expected, but his influence can last for as long as it takes for his changes to sink in or be fully worked through.

Death – 13: Reversed

Reversed, Death shows that *change is being resisted* due to the fears already mentioned.

A situation is changing regardless of what you wish or desire to be happening and being ignored while *the past or the present or dreams are desperately clung to* leaving you *living in the past*. This card shows that *acceptance has not been found* and cannot be reached due to the fear of what will be and of what will be lost by accepting a situation, yet the loss has already happened or is in motion.

There will be *feelings of abandonment and isolation*, a loss of faith and trust with anything that promotes the given transformation. Deep down with this card, there is an understanding that change is the only option, but *fear is dominant* and muddles thoughts and shows *an unrealistic determination to defy the impossible*. Sadly, this will only cause additional problems and lead to *emotional and physical stress*.

Even in relation to practical life issues, Death reversed brings dissatisfaction due to *avoiding change* and is often *a sign that areas of life are stagnating and dying*. Situations can be clung to as you continue to go through the motions of maintaining a status quo when, in reality, it's all just dead wood.

TEMPERANCE - 14

Temperance is number Fourteen. The One gives strength, purpose and wholeness, while the Four offers stability and realisation. When Fourteen is reduced (1+4=5), we have Five, the number of The Hierophant, which shows mental action and truth. Fourteen indicates a strong and balanced inner and outer calmness that is mixed with caution and patience to create temperance. Fourteen brings calmness and tranquillity, and within these two forces is found composed concentration and realisation. It is a number of caution, telling us that we need to review and evaluate events so that the inner and the outer selves can be brought together.

Temperance is linked astrologically to Sagittarius and to the planet Jupiter.

The card shows an angel pouring water from one golden chalice to another. The main representations of this card are temperance itself, balance, moderation and restraint.

The angel can be Iris, a Greek goddess, who went to fill her golden cup from the River Styx, said to renew life from within the Mythic Tarot; or the Angel Dokiel, the angel of balance, who restores harmony and brings healing and equilibrium. Or the figure can simply represent an androgynous angel, a messenger from God, here bringing flow into life with connection, balance and hope.

The angel's white dress symbolises pure and passive energy. The white square over the heart with an orange triangle inside connects the element of earth, structure and the physical with the purity of white. The triangle pointing upright is masculine, active and a symbol for fire, with the orange being a fiery colour of enthusiasm and physical energy. With the triangle inside the square, creativity is growing from structure; the spirit and emotional self grows from its interaction with life, evolving with creativity and passion. Above this, which looks like creases within the fabric, is the Hebrew word for God, or YWYW. This symbolises that emotions are raised above desires, and brought into a more spiritual or calming perspective, rather than just drive and cravings.

Within this original card by Pamela Colman Smith the angel's wings are pale pinks and blues, similar to the colours found within the suit of Cups. They bring an element of ease, attraction to balance and a meditative quality. In other decks, they are fiery red, or deep pink with a dark orange representing passion and action, bringing wisdom, flight and freedom, so this isn't a card of unwanted restrictions. It shows a need to reach a higher state of growth and understanding by the taking of opposites, and the combining and calming of them to create something new, as everything needs to balance.

The halo, shown as white space about the head, represents radiance and is also a sign of divinity, spiritual enlightenment and a higher understanding.

The disc on the angel's forehead is gold, masculine, full of power, magic and illumination. It forms a circle with a centre dot representing the solar system and sun, a continuous cycle and a seed or spark of life, the cell and the nucleus. It covers her mind, and her Brow Chakra – her intuition. Gold symbolises understanding of the messages revealed, showing us a developed individual who is following their own true path. Spiritual enlightenment is usually associated with the feminine and with this masculine aspect, visions can be brought to life, as taking in moderation from the two opposites allows for new possibilities to be born, bringing dreams into physical reality. Like the square and triangle, the circle and dot are alchemy symbols, showing we can create, purify and master those things which could unbalance us if allowed. Yet by taking the right amount of each and joining them together, we can create balance.

The angel has one foot in the water pool, providing a link between the subconscious world of watery emotions, and the earthly, conscious, solid world represented by the stone. Water symbolises emotions, here shown calm and clear, with the ripples gently moving representing soothing movement and calmness. The stone represents being grounded. The depth of the pool tells us that emotions are not deep as they would be with a fast-moving river or ocean, but rather gentle and visible. The water and stone connected to the feet show an equal grounding with both the practical and the emotional. The angel coming down to the physical is also a balancing of the spiritual or inspirational with the practical.

The two cups, or chalices, show a merging and mixing of the water. In some instances, this can be symbolic of watering down wine, which tells us not to abstain but to moderate, to dilute something which is unhealthy in excess. The water flowing between them represents emotional balance, action and purpose, combining and reconciling of opposites, calmness and direction. The water gives fluid emotions; flowing feelings lead us to happiness, bringing a much sought-after peaceful and emotional balance after Death's energy. Balance is also shown by two streams of water flowing between the two cups. Opposites are combined into one flow. They are shown as separated by three lines, showing something new being born from opposites. The two cups show co-operation and compromise, indicating that differences can be resolved, with issues being happily merged on an inner and outer level. The angel pours the water at an impossible angle with closed eyes, allowing magic and faith to mix, showing a complete willingness to go with the flow and to simply trust that everything will flow in the right direction, to let the magic of life in to allow life's worries to be simplified. The cups are golden, showing the relevance of the practical side of life. The angel has transcended death, gained wisdom and uses that knowledge to lead her forward, as, without a balanced mind, the water would spill to the water pool, stirring emotions. There can be no tension, forced control or fight here, just acceptance.

The irises symbolise courage, hope and wisdom, with a yellow iris being a sign of passion. In full bloom, they represent happiness, abundance and maturity.

Being two, like the cups, they show balance, with the one still in bud showing future potential.

Behind the angel, a road travels through the green hills, through the two mountains leading us to a golden crown. We have travelled down this road after Death's card and maybe it can even lead us back home: back to life after contemplation, after thought and peaceful inaction, bringing our different torn aspects together.

The sun, in newer versions of this deck, is often shown as a crown, representing our highest spiritual aspirations - to be One with the Divine once again, to be one with ourselves. In the original drawing, we can see the hint of a crown on the inside of the rays, with ten dots, the number of completion - a destination. In small measures, we can gain that sense of oneness if we let go of expectancy, and if we can do it occasionally, then we can achieve it for longer, or at least try. This sun crown represents our ability to unite our own selves, to make something of who we are, and to unify any fractures within ourselves or our surroundings.

The mountains symbolise life's realities, as you cannot avoid life's ups and downs, but here they are accepted and all part of the journey. Like the rest of this scene, the angel's back is turned to it, placing them in the past; and past troubles are not to be dwelt on, instead, the gifts it's given to us are used to create a wise, tempered approach to life.

Temperance can be likened to The Middle Way, an eastern philosophical approach toward life. The aim is to be neither good nor bad. Perfection is unrealistic, neglect damaging, and so to aim for the other end of the spectrum over another is not beneficial. Practitioners of The Middle Way try for somewhere in between the perfect and the imperfect, the good and the bad. The Middle Way is not going to extremes, using self-control, using one's mind before acting, not doing any more than your own personal best and treating others as you wish to be treated. In cases where no way can be found to move forwards, then doing nothing is accepted and opted for. Every action is balanced, nothing is forced, and everything is reconciled.

IN A NUTSHELL

Co-operation and compromise will lead you to solutions and will allow you to be calm in the face of problems. With peaceful contemplation, reconciliations can be reached as we get to a place of calm in our lives after a storm.

Now is the time for a balanced view of life, avoiding extremes of behaviour, thoughts and emotions, and being calm in your outlook. Moderation in all things is called for above all else. Yin and Yang, balance the opposites and iron out the creases.

Temperance – 14: Upright

Temperance is a card of *co-operation and compromise* after difficulties. It brings renewed and refreshed balanced views and emotions. *Getting the right balance* in any situation of concern is needed and can be achieved.

If life has been troublesome, this card shows life's *balance being restored*, as Temperance brings *direction and purpose* when maybe there was none before. It's a healing energy that resolves issues with understanding and peace.

Temperance shows the use of *common sense, staying calm and thinking before making decisions* or dealing with difficult situations. This card tells us to stay in control, be creative but not to force nor *to go to any extremes of behaviour*, but rather to *relax and create balance* in all we do, even if it means doing nothing at all. Exert the energy you need to, rather than over-stretching with meaningless actions.

A card of *good health*, and where health is an issue, *moderation in all things* may be a consideration for improvement.

Temperance can represent someone coping well with problems who has achieved *a calm outlook on life*, even though this life might be filled with problems or the person has suffered many setbacks. If this is someone offering you advice, it will be balanced and worth taking.

The long term is viewed calmly and with clarity, as you know where you are going as *everything falls into place*. This is not a time to resist life, but to *flow, grow and listen* to inspiration as it will be *grounded in realism*. The bigger picture is to be seen in situations rather than narrow hurt feelings.

Where relationships are concerned, temperance brings back together relationships which have suffered difficulties. *Reconciliation and forgiveness* within all manner of situations and relationships are possible when Temperance has been laid upright, as new understandings are reached.

Temperance – 14: Reversed

Reversed, Temperance initially shows **a lack of balance and going to extremes** of actions or emotions. Finding balance in yourself and other areas of your life is important but here it's a missing ingredient in life.

The balance of a situation is lost. The ability to cope within a situation is no longer possible, resulting in *failure and conflict*. Situations will be out of whack; *you will not be able to find solutions* as a natural balance is upset. Difficulties will be aggravated, or new ones will be created, and they will be responded to *irrationally,* leading to *conflicting behaviour or emotions.*

This shows an individual with no commitment or *staying power* who just looks at the short term and with *a lack of patience,* so this is a card which can seek *instant satisfaction. Old habits are repeated*, often showing a deep sense of powerlessness and discontent.

For relationships, there will be no easing of emotional pressure and situations will be irreconcilable; *no healing can be gained from painful situations* and differences will be left unresolved. Opposite views, beliefs, needs or opinions will not be able to be brought together, leaving situations at a standoff with no one seeing the other's perspective.

Relationships are *one-sided* and personality traits will cause conflict within the self or between two people or factions; *understanding each other will not be possible* and *agreements will not be reached.*

Health-wise, this is a card which shows changes are needed to create balance. Our bodies can cope with a lot of abuse; ultimately, they thrive on balance and can show *a battle between the body and mind*. A little bit of what you fancy does you good, a lot does you damage; even a little bit of stress is good, a lot of it - not so good. The wine will not be watered down, and health should be taken seriously.

THE DEVIL - 15

The Devil is numbered Fifteen and can be viewed as one of the most oppressive cards within the Tarot deck. The One represents the desire for achievement, being connected to drive and power, while the Five connects to our mental self and conflict. When the One and Five are reduced (1+5=6), we arrive at Six, the number of The Lovers, which is the number of attraction, choice and adaptability. Fifteen gives us strength in attraction while at the same time reducing our ability to recognise the truth, as it signals a compelling lack of grounded thought. This in turn brings restriction to the mental and the Spiritual Self. This number represents self-deception and fantasy. Fifteen shadows reality by deluding us with magnetism and the possibility, albeit a superficial one, of power and attainment of desires.

The Devil is ruled by Capricorn and the planet Saturn.

This card is dark and shows the image of the devil perched above a man and woman. Regardless of your religious beliefs, you are in no doubt of the presence of good and bad and right and wrong, nor where this character stands between the balance of the two. For positive spirituality or energy to exist, so does an opposing negative force. If there were no devil, we would not know what pain is when it is brought about by mistakes, desire and temptation; and without pain, many of us would fail to learn or progress. Yet, not all of life's problems should be passed onto the shoulders of the devil, however broad they may be, as we make our own decisions; and so disruptions within our life can also be brought about by Karmic means. We are spiritual beings residing within human bodies, which quite unlike our spiritual substance are subject to physical desires and needs from birth to grave. We have a constant battle between our higher spiritual and physical being, and so the devil is always within us, not separate from us. The physical human self is governed by instinct and urges which The Devil represents, and our spiritual aspect tries to control, understand and accept in the pursuit of knowledge and enlightenment. The Devil may not be a positive spiritual energy force, but he is a practical force as he brings into focus that which is earthbound and material.

The Devil's represented here by Baphomet, with the torso, eyes and arms of a man, the feet and wings of a bat and the head and legs of a male goat, symbolising the intellectual thinking man joined and debased by animals and corrupted by their unholy natural urges. Goats are traditionally linked to the devil, unlike sheep who are followers, linked to Christ and quite calm, goats are more unruly and bad-tempered, seemingly only following urges and instinct. In Matthew 25:31-46, sheep are placed on the favoured right side, goats on the left:

When the Son of Man comes in his glory, and all the angels with him, he will sit on his glorious throne. All the nations will be gathered before him, and he will separate the people one from another as a shepherd separates the sheep from the goats. He will put the sheep on his right and the goats on his left.

Pan, the Greek God of Mischief, comes to mind here, who was vilified by early Christians. Pan was the god of mountains, nature, shepherds, and music, and he enjoyed the company of Nymphs, spirits or beings that are derived from or depict nature. Pan's body had hindquarters like that of a goat, making him a bit of a party god. Bats are a symbol of darkness and can be seen in some cultures as bringers of evil and bad luck, as they rise from the darkness of the earth, leaving their caves, linking to death and the underworld.

Baphomet's wings are unfolded to dominate the space, own his situation, and instil terror to the pair below, yet they also help him keep balance while on his perch, so he can swoop down and take what he wants on a whim. The image is meant to portray a perversion of the human condition, the devolution of man, sinking down to the physical rather than rising to the spiritual.

The reversed pentagram above his head symbolises negativity and a perversion of life energy. Upright, a pentagram, a five-pointed star, represents the head and four limbs of the human body. It is used to bring great luck as it unites positive energy, health and achievement, offering the wearer protection from evil spirits with the top of the star representing the head and the spiritual, rational mind. When reversed, that protection is removed and signifies the ruling of matter and desire over the spiritual, as the head now faces down and all positive energies are destroyed, corrupted and distorted. This shows a mental aspect to The Devil, as thoughts drive this card, as the world is seen through this distorted lens, giving permission to any desires felt. The two points (or legs the right way up) are now at the top, representing the horns of the goat attacking heaven; the genitals, now also at the top, indicate sexual energy being placed higher than the spiritual and logical values of the upright.

Both his hands are positioned like The Magician's, yet he is not bringing down creative energy, but a base, crass energy that suits his needs. His right hand is raised with fingers in a position used by Jewish Kohanima, a blessing, a service performed with both hands. To use just one hand and not be a member of that sect is to bring down curses on the self and is where the 'Vulcan Salute' and the quotation *'Live Long and Prosper'* in *Star Trek* stem from. *(According to Wikipedia, the actor Leonard Nimoy, who played Spock in* Star Trek, *was Jewish and took the salute from the positive aspect of the prayer.)* Yet, The Devil here is mocking a faith in something higher, inviting negative judgements down to satisfy his own needs, a sign that we can choose to tempt fate or not.

His open palm shows a cross, suggesting he has nothing hidden: an illusion he draws people in with, using fake sincerity. Placed on his right hand it is a sign which gives false hope and faith to those who need reassurance that all is well, yet it is all just pretence.

His left hand, of logic and action, holds a torch down to the ground, as he is choosing to keep everyone in the dark; he does not wish to illuminate the surroundings and instead he ignites the tail of the man below, fuelling his sexual desire and passion. The man tail shows the bottom five branches of the Tree of Life, more likely from the Kabbalah here, as opposed to The Lovers card, showing those lower branches which connect us to the body and desire. His aim is for physical gratification, lust and to get lost in physical pleasures of whatever kind he desires. The blackness surrounding The Devil is a cloak of deceit which keeps reality at bay and allows only the temptations to be seen, like a comfy, warm blanket telling us that what we wish for is safe. So, the couple are blinded by the nature of their situation, comforted into believing that all is well when they are surrounded by incomplete knowledge and being seduced by illusion.

The block The Devil perches upon is a rectangle and, like a square, shows us its firm boundaries. A square has equal sides, offering security; a rectangle does not. It shows a situation which is not balanced, and which can only support the issue causing the delusion, like a pedestal seating a revered object. This perch holds the anchoring link with chains attached, so it represents a form of imprisonment rather than security, and while we can feel very safe within the confines of a prison's walls, a prison is still a prison.

The man and woman are naked and chained, symbolising enslavement, being owned by a situation, circumstances, values and limitations. This symbolises a restricted set of beliefs along with a warped sense of logic, reasoning and personal confinement, mentally, emotionally and even physically. Their nakedness shows innocence and desire, and so they may not see the trap they are in while they seek to indulge their needs. The pair both have orange hair, showing an impulsive energy.

The man stands as if to suggest he is reaching to the woman for an answer, asking him to join him in his fantasy. She gazes ahead with her arms suggesting she is open to the darkness about her. The woman's tail of grapes shows her desire and greed for abundance, wealth and prosperity. The grapes show a need more for material gains as opposed to the man's sexual and physically gratifying ones. She is desiring comfort, luxury, indulgence and all the material things which can be gained, given or taken.

Note that there are no padlocks or keys, presumably so that there can be no escape, yet the chains are loose and could be lifted and removed if they choose to. Yet the devil makes us feel that we have no power in making positive changes, or that there is even a problem to be feared and so they do not try to escape, as they may feel they have nothing to escape from or feel powerless to try.

The two have chosen the path they wished to take, even if they did so unwittingly, and, unfortunately, it's a pain-filled route which will offer some hard lessons and some manure to grow from. The Devil's card shows events are accumulating to a point of no return, or are already there, and realisations will be forced as the lights go on. Even so, there may be no actual awareness of any pending problems as all might seem calm and jubilant as you ride a high, as he is all about sex, drugs and rock 'n' roll.

Their horns indicate they have taken on the guise of their master in whatever form that takes in their reality. Yet it's all still a mirage, as the devil, although destructive, can be acceptable within our lives because as humans we are highly adaptable. We can get used to the most awful situations and justify them as okay, carrying on as normal, and stop seeing his darkness as a problem, as his energies become a way of life.

The couple represents the ego that begs or waits for The Devil's approval and attention, but he will give none, as the devil does not deal in compassionate, reassuring emotions. With the devil, you are on your own. The pair are seeking reassurance that they are acting appropriately, but all this does is deepen the pathway that they have chosen. They would rather confirm and justify their actions as being harmless than try to leave their current place of entrapment that exists either in their minds, immediate relationships or surroundings, as they cannot see a way out. The Devil shows the mental or emotional being manifest in the physical, bringing us a fear of letting go, of breaking deep ties and of losing perceived power or control or even being left out. Hope is being ignored as they stand surrounded by darkness, lies and desires which feel beyond their control.

The Devil, while negative and destructive, can appear to be extremely attractive and tempting, which is all part of his clever guise. He knows how to call us to him, whether it is by drugs, money, flattery, sex, security, love, popularity, ideals, other people or by many other means as he calls to our vanity. Once we are trapped below him, he does nothing to hold us there; we stay simply through our own misguided desire or by a need to not hear the truth. We lack strength, courage or the initiative to make the relevant changes and we then blame the devil, under whatever name we choose, for our weaknesses and for bringing about our fear and powerlessness. The Devil shows a lack of personal responsibility for our actions, and as adults, we are all responsible for our own conduct and responses, but the arrival of this card shows that none is taken. Everything is someone else's fault or problem.

The Devil has been assigned the job of a universal scapegoat, designed by us to enable a recognised force to be blamed for the suffering that physical desires, a need for power and egos create. We either blame God for not being compassionate enough or the devil for simply being present and calling to us. The Devil is Satan, a fallen angel who desired to share God's status but could not compete on a pure and spiritual level, and so the Earth became his playground and we his playthings. From a philosophical viewpoint, if God is all-powerful, why does he allow the devil to continue to hold a proportion of his spiritual shares? Maybe even God feels we need to be humbled and welcomes the intervention of the devil, even if only for such a reason. But we rarely blame God, or ourselves for the actions of the devil. It is easy to blame the devil, or evil, for humanity's woes rather than admit that it is *us* who commit atrocities or succumb to desires governed by ethics or morality. Humanity finds it's hard to proportion blame - so the devil has his uses. We may view him as an outside force whether real or imagined which we cannot control, but more often than not, he is the destructive force within our own minds which we have created ourselves, and so the devil is simply a man-made entity, a nasty aspect of ourselves that we feel we should be able to control or seek to ignore.

The Devil's card points to an extreme of negative emotions, or even actions and a personal sense of powerlessness. He shows obsessive behaviour, addiction, temptation, hatred, sexual impulses, violence, greed, paranoia, gratification, control, mental issues and fear, to name just a few of the issues in life which take away our power and undermine our sense of self. This card's main energy is destructive and forces us to destroy ourselves with one insecurity or another and can halt progress as we are rooted by our minds and insecurities. The Devil's card warns us of negative excesses being implemented by or against someone.

IN A NUTSHELL

Your prison is self-imposed as you have given your power away. Bad habits, negative views and being attached to what is superficial have not served you well. If you think life is okay, take another look.

You may feel trapped, a victim, or that your fingers have been burnt by an experience. Look at what is destructive and what you fear; and regardless of others' views or actions, seek to free yourself. Others can only abuse and use what you give them to use and abuse.

The Devil - 15: Upright

The Devil indicates **any negative and destructive situation or issue** which makes you **feel powerless** and reluctant to take control. Often, he turns up when we feel that we cannot control issues that leave us **feeling insecure, scared and doubtful.**

Where relationships of any kind are concerned, it shows **individuals who are 'bad' for you**, however powerful, trusting, loving, exciting, sexy and tempting they may appear, and involvement will always **end in tears and these relationships can be abusive, however subtle.** You will well and truly get your fingers burnt!

Any relationship or problem governed by this card will always be hard, **repressive, miserable and difficult to break away from, yet often exciting at the start and enticing.** Blame will often be placed onto an individual, issue or even a substance, turning themselves into a **victim** whilst making the object or person a **scapegoat**.

The Devil shows **a narrow, materialistic view of life**, and single desires will be a focus. Attitudes are **destructive and limiting** and may create an imbalance with the rest of your lifestyle.

Others may force their views onto you, tell you your options are limited as this card brings about bondage: being **tied to a situation**, or rather **being trapped and** *unable to make changes*. Such views stem from *fear, doubt, obsession and envy* – they dislike your happiness as they are a *slave* to what holds them in negativity.

Whatever the circumstances represented by The Devil, it always shows *someone trapped and making excuses to avoid changes*. The opinion here is that it's better to stay with the devil you know...or a problem is just not seen due to *avoidance*, which hands power over to someone or something. This could be because of past events that one cannot or will not let go of or get into perspective, and rather than challenge the situation, it is blindly accepted.

Due to a spiral of negative thoughts, no way is seen out of a problem. The Devil represents *obsessive and impulsive behaviour*, addiction, depression and even deeper mental issues such as paranoia and mental illnesses.

Devil – 15: Reversed

Reversed, The Devil still shows the presence of negativity, except there is an understanding that it is *time to break free. Problems are seen* and it's time to throw down the chains of confinement from whatever has been restricting growth.

It is a card of *escaping old ways of doing things*, getting out of old cycles of negativity, and *freeing your mind* to see new potential.

Decisions of this nature can be hard and long to reach and so *bravery and conviction* will be needed to put the decision into action. There will be a *realisation*, as a way of life, an event or a relationship is seen in reality and put into its proper *perspective* as the lights go on showing you the way out, or the real mess about you.

Decisions are taken to heal, change, reform and challenge negative or harmful behaviours which are causing pain and upset to yourself or others.

Personal power is reclaimed! Small steps are taken, as what is shallow is seen for what it is. Although *the light at the end of the tunnel can be seen,* it still has to be reached. So, to stop from falling back into old habits or negative thoughts, firstly *know your enemy* and then make *self-respect* your motivator through the problems that will lie ahead.

As you *repel and rebel* from what old beliefs, individuals or situations may expect from you, difficulties and barriers to healing may try to get in your way. Yet now *you are finally free to walk away* from what or who has limited you, controlled you or held you back.

THE TOWER - 16

The Tower is Sixteen, a number of bad luck and misfortune brought about by impulsive behaviour. The One brings movement, action, power and beginnings, the Six desire, attraction and change. When the One and Six are reduced (1+6=7), we arrive at Seven, the number of The Chariot: the number of wisdom, honesty, endurance and growth. Sixteen's energy is determined to force the evolution of the self upon us. We often display this response within our lives by the ignorance that we produce while we delude and betray ourselves in the pursuit of attainment. Sixteen is impulsive and forces changes through excessive confidence.

The Tower is astrologically linked to Mars which rules Aries.

The Tower is one of the Tarot's distressing or difficult cards with its black scene of a building being destroyed by lightning. The Tower represents our sense of self and can be seen as the next or progressive step from The Devil. The Tower's image depicts a catastrophe that has dealt a crushing blow to the individuals falling to the rocks below to their fate, both totally overwhelmed by their personal circumstances.

The Tower like The Chariot is a man-made structure built to protect the individual, here built on a mountain peak, far away from the realities of life below, up in the clouds.

Mountains are symbolic of trouble, stress and challenges, and here they have decided to build their tower with expectations that they would be safe up high. Yet they have failed to see that high towers, when they crumble, do so spectacularly.

Their tower was built by the ego to show power, reputation and prestige, and it is the ego which The Tower represents. Up in the clouds, the mind has control, yet without the earth, it cannot ground, and so common sense was not a part of the construction. The three windows represent the trinity of the mind, body and spirit, here representing that this destruction will be felt in all areas of life.

The top of the tower is a golden crown representing the outer self and the conscious mind. It represents our sense of importance, how we see ourselves in the world, how we hope to be seen and how we feel ourselves to be, as well as how we perceive the world about us - our sense of normality. The crown is our mind and thoughts, our beliefs and expectations in life. This is not so much a negative, but more a sign that while you have been decorating your tower, you have missed red flags or simply not seen issues as relevant to you any longer and which are building energy, waiting to explode.

The lightning is The Tower's destructive force. It may be seen as the Hand of God that breaks us free from negativity, even though we may not wish it or know that we even need it. The lightning's shape is linked to the Hebrew letter Shin, which is the initial letter to the name of God, representing Divine power. The arrow focuses the lightning, pinpointing it directly to the crown - shocking us with flashes of enlightenment, breaking through our illusions and separating us from our ego. The lightning has not been expected and, being night-time, they may not have seen the storm clouds brewing. This has been a sudden, explosive energy which has ripped apart the structure of The Tower, or ego, leaving destruction and truth. It is a force that emotionally, mentally and often practically/materially destroys our lives. It pulls the rug out from under us, and yet guides us towards enlightenment and the realisation that life must change. In fact, it leaves us with no other choice, as the truth is left out in the open and very plain to see. The crown being thrown off by the force of this bolt of realisation dislodges our built-up sense of self, safety and security within our lives. The fire acts to cleanse and prepare the way for a new start, even if we will need to start from scratch.

The couple are thrown free from the tower which allows their active minds to no longer be controlled by their ego or dreams. They are forcibly thrown into the cold, dark night to fall to the ground, which is a long way down, and so a very sobering experience. The fall subjects them to the truth, which can give them freedom if they choose, as when they reach the ground, broken and shattered from the physical or emotional upheaval they have suffered, they will have two choices. The first is to rebuild the tower from the rubble and ignore the truth; the other is to move on and grow from the experience and build something more balanced and secure elsewhere.

The woman wears a crown, so as she falls, her ego remains: is this disbelief at the explosion or her thinking she can keep it at the bottom? Either way, she is not looking down and so is blinkered as to the height she is falling from. As the ground advances, she may hope to keep hold of some of her life and choices. Her dress is blue, showing her to be intuitive, so maybe this is the outcome she has feared and ignored and now cannot face, as her red shoes show she has been led by desire to where she currently finds herself.

The man, with his red cloak, would have been driven by more of a balanced outlook, as his cloak shows his passion in building the tower, and with his grey tights in the original pictured image - or shown as white in other decks - and blue tunic being a sign of sincerity, this indicates that he took time in his endeavours. His grey boots show he is already contemplating how he will land, how it will be for him once he meets the ground. Yet the red cloak is on top, a predominant force, and so to him, this is truly a perceived shock as he sees how far he is falling from his powerful position and success.

About the two of them fall what are called Yods; these teardrop-shaped drops of light are about them and like the lightning refer to the Divine. They can be seen as a blessing, God's grace, and so an upheaval which is needed to cleanse the self and to get things back into balance is shown. There are twenty-one Yods, the number of The World, which brings new chapters to our lives. There are ten on the right of the card, showing an emotional completion of a situation, a conclusion. To the left, with the man, are eleven, the number for Justice, bringing logic, truth and harsh facts.

The Tower offered them protection from life's realities and represents the walls that we all build to safeguard our fears and insecurities. We can sleep soundly within our towers as we feel we are safe, but this is an illusion given grace by our egos, as even a house with a smoke alarm can burn down. Nothing is really safe - we just fool ourselves that it is. The Tower acts like a cocoon and would have safely surrounded them with confidence, and The Devil, whom we have met before, is hit by lightning from the heavens. It is this issue that The Tower concerns itself with, as a build-up of avoidance, negativity or ego will always result in destructive forces being unleashed, causing major upheavals. Our inner being and external life will be broken down to make way for a realisation and the new, which will be forced if necessary.

The Tower turns life upside down and brings a sudden harsh view of crystal-clear reality. This state may not be pleasant as we are left with no understandable grounding as to who we now are, as what we have loved, worshipped, valued, or believed in has either gone or been violently and dramatically challenged. With respect to this, The Tower forces us to re-evaluate our lives which may be difficult as it leaves us little to feel secure about. Old securities no longer hold any attraction, stability or comfort as they now bring shattered illusions, tears or distaste. We are no longer shrouded by The Devil's cloak of deceit which the destruction of the tower disintegrates. This is the result of us not being realistic about life when there was the opportunity to do so, or not seeing it coming, and so our world crumbles.

The Tower offers us a lesson to learn the hard way, but when grasped leaves us free to move on and away. A second chance, as it were, offering us the chance to grow and accept our limitations as well as our possibilities. The Tower's function within our lives may appear negative and involve suffering but it shows us a stop sign and forces us to turn around and proceed in another direction. If you can view The Tower's negativity positively, it will lead to a great renewal of life being welcomed in, rather than resisted.

IN A NUTSHELL

Change, crisis, and a sudden drastic upheaval will force you to look at your beliefs, views of the world and your place within it. Lies will crumble, as will anything in your life with weak or rotting foundations.

Flashes of realisation and bolts of inspiration will come to you, shattering what you once held dear or believed in and have never challenged. Or an outside force will make you change your world. Your peace and quiet will be loudly interrupted, forcing changes at the very foundations of your belief structure.

The Tower – 16: Upright

The Tower is a card of ***permanent change, loss, or destruction of what you hold dear***. When laid, there will be major upheavals and ***sweeping changes*** that will turn life upside down; this will be ***unexpected,*** bringing shocking news and events.

The Tower shows a ***failure*** and disruption of events. Ideas and plans will go drastically wrong as the situation changes from what you thought it was to what it actually is. These can be major life events to smaller ones where you thought you had it right and hoped for a positive outcome, yet have deluded yourself or even been misled with presumption or false, ego-driven security.

The Tower brings forced changes on either a mental or physical level that helps to get life back on track, even though it may not feel like it, or even onto a new pathway which is not wanted. ***An existing way of life will be broken down, causing great upset*** in most cases. It is a case of what was once held as a personal fact is snatched away, rocking the very foundation of your views of the world about you and/or of yourself.

Accompanying this card there will be ***flashes of true realisation*** that will force you in a set direction. Strong insights of where you or another has gone wrong will be seen, and which you will not be able to hide from. ***A single thought, look, word or action can change everything in your life,*** and ***everything is seen in a new light***.

The Tower can show ***violence and anger*** and with *other relevant cards,* it may even point to death, a major loss or accident. Whatever the loss, upset or radical change that this card brings, one will be left knowing that the ground has been well and truly cleared to make way for a new pattern of life as ***stark truth and a new reality is brought to light***.

The Tower – 16: Reversed

Reversed, this card can show *a foreseen upheaval and change.* You are a rabbit caught in the headlights of a car as you watch loss and difficulties unfold, feeling **unable to comprehend** or deal with the issue, and so get **transfixed by fear** and freeze. At times like this, we can become numb to the harshness of things and feel very **disassociated** from what is at hand, like Nero fiddling while Rome burned.

A changing situation has been ignored due to **no real ability to deal with the issue**, with the hope that it will go away. Sadly, this will not be the outcome, as it will still happen or is happening.

Dying and dead situations will be clung to, as **delusion, self-importance** or even ignorance will prevail as you simply cannot believe such a thing can happen to you. Issues are disregarded or faced with **grand expectations and lying to yourself** that things can be saved or fixed, yet you are standing in a burning barn with a thimble of water. This can lead to impulsive, **unreasonable** and **irrational behaviour**, including **retaliation and revenge**.

Any actions taken to gain back control will simply deepen the delusion and make events spiral out of control, and yet things will still be at an end. Rebuilding the tower to get things back to how they were is tried for, which brings more pain in the long term.

The flip side to this can be **wanting to run away**; yet either way, the truth is pushed aside or rationalised to fit what you want to happen, bringing fear, delusion and **anxiety in making the changes**.

THE STAR - 17

The Star's number is Seventeen. Its One brings creativity, inventiveness and a desire for movement. While the Seven brings spiritual growth and balance. When reduced (1+7=8), we are given the number Eight, the number of Strength's card, which represents honesty, durability and courage. Seventeen is a harmonious number which brings with it the illumination of problems, leaving the imagination active without illusion. Seventeen lets the imagination be used efficiently and allows faith in one's visions. This number is one of balance and harmony in the process of gaining wisdom and acceptance so that progressive steps can be made forward.

The Star is ruled by Aquarius and linked to the planet Uranus.

After the darkness and the bleak reality shown to us by The Devil and The Tower, we are brought back to the light by the shining energy of The Star which pictures a naked woman kneeling and pouring water from two jugs, one onto the land and the other into a pool of water.

The Star is from The Hermit's lantern, a beacon of hope in the dark, there to show him a way forwards after healing once he had gathered the personal knowledge he sought. A card that shows feelings of relief after a time of withdrawal, loss and searching - peace after war.

The Star shows the woman free from clothes to represent being free from restrictions, unencumbered and liberated with no shame or concerns. She does not have the garland of flowers of the maiden, so has transcended some levels of innocence; yet like a child, she can play again, as her blonde hair is a sign of innocence and youth. She shows us a calm, gentle scene and a tranquil time. Being naked she's vulnerable, yet she has no fear, but faith, filled with hope and inspiration as she is right where she has been guided to be.

She has one foot in the water and the other leg kneels on the grass, showing grounded emotional energy. The green grass, a very earthly symbol, is studded with pink flowers showing fertile ground, which mentally and physically represents healthy energy as well as happiness and blessings. The water is the subconscious self and the grass the conscious. Kneeling is a sign of worship, respect, veneration, which shows your inner faith to the world. Her energy flows with the water showing her respect for life, as she takes an active role in connecting to who she is. This is also shown by her facing the left of the card, the side for movement and active thoughts.

She pours water from two jugs: this represents the continuous flow of life, and our subconscious and emotional energy with the flowing of emotions. Any blocks emotionally, imaginatively and even physically can be set free with The Star, as everything simply flows. The two jugs represent balance, understanding, unity and a bringing together of opposites to create a single focus. Being red, they symbolise desire, passion and direction and her wish for movement and growth. One jug pours into the shallow, clear water pool which was also found in Temperance, showing again emotional clarity and the unconscious mind, whilst the water being poured represents life's interaction as it moves out in ever-increasing circles. The emotional energy created with The Star gently ripples rather than splashing, waves or stillness, but a gentle movement which shows energy and imagination without illusions, bringing a happy, intuitive and positive energy. She is gently gazing at this water pool, enjoying the movement of feelings and being at peace.

The water being poured onto the land is not being wasted; instead, it flows out into five streams representing the five senses, allowing interaction with everyday life, giving us the foundations of our experiences. One rivulet flows back to the pool and the others into the land, showing a fertile time of growth, a time to expand ourselves and look to our potential. Everything is connected, everything is in harmony. This card offers no hindrance to peace or hope and the imagination, as freedom of thought and new feelings emerge, growing to the benefit of those who need them.

Behind the woman is a tree with a bird symbolising life, wisdom and prosperity, with the bird a symbol of freedom, reaching higher levels of consciousness and flexibility as they can walk, swim and fly. The bird, said to be an Ibis, is symbolic of creativity and good luck. This is very much a card which sparks the mind. New ideas creatively bubble up and brush away old, dusty cobwebs, so that potential can rise up and be enjoyed now the restrictions of the past are removed. The Star is like spring, pointing to regeneration and the awakening of dormant hopes and dreams while allowing for the birth of new ones. This emergence of positive thinking promotes self-healing and allows possibilities to present themselves into our lives like a chain reaction: when you feel that you can move forward, then you make it possible to do so.

The card shows eight stars, each with eight points, and an eight-pointed star represents life, death, and regeneration, and of course, Strength. I do not feel they signify the constellation of Orien, as that represents The Hunter, a theme far removed from this card. Perhaps it is the Big Dipper/Plough, which has seven stars and is located within the Ursa Major constellation, that assists us in locating the North Star, a symbol of hope, orientation, and, as such, something to set our moral compasses by; it brings us back home. With the stars shining in the sky, it is night-time, yet here the sky is fully illuminated, and, on the horizon, the white sky shows that this is dawn, the start of a new day. With this new day, there is renewed optimism, the glimmer of hope that gives meaning and direction to our lives when we need it most, and which usually arrives when we are in the process of leaving a difficult situation that has exhausted and tested us. It renews our faith in life and directs us to where we need to be.

The mountains are far away behind the woman, they are in the past yet still visible, so while she is moving away from problems and no longer being destroyed by them, she has not forgotten the lesson they taught. Here the future is focused on without the weight of negative past hindrances as their lessons have been processed.

The Star is an inner card showing inner peace, understanding and a relaxed mind, offering a feeling of wholeness by showing a renewed connection to life, while at the same time allowing for outer growth and progression due to an upsurge of positive energy. The Star is gentle and positive, a healing card that brings joy - its energy is like a light being turned on, illuminating the darkness and allowing the way out to be seen.

Stars are traditionally associated with hope and expectation. The most famous example was the Star of Bethlehem which signalled the arrival of a new era of spiritual development and encompassed all the compassionate qualities of the Piscean Age. Whether you are a believer or not, whether it is fact or fiction is irrelevant: that star was and is important to our current civilisation's present state of development. Humanity has been moulded by the fallout of the Babylonian astrologers' findings when they followed a star in the night sky and found what they were seeking.

On a more mundane note, even Walt Disney tells us to 'wish upon a star'. Stars are always above us and out of reach, they symbolise what *could be* and they offer a beautiful optimistic glow to the unknown dark night sky which lifts our imagination.

IN A NUTSHELL

Healing physically, mentally and emotionally is now possible; there is a return to hope as life fills with a sense of purpose and direction. You can dare to dream and wish as you leave a bad time behind you. Problems will not be permanent as long-awaited solutions will be found.

A time to have faith as spring comes to your life offering fresh new energy to guide you forwards, leaving you feeling extremely optimistic, and you will have a spring in your step!

The Star - 17: Upright

The Star brings **hope and optimism** to even the darkest of situations; it makes us feel like we have come back to life.

If placed in the future, it allows us to see that **difficulties will not persist,** and happiness and **balance will be restored.** If in the present, it shows that a period of suffering has ended or been accepted and worked through, and now you should be **ready for growth.**

Positivity will be in the air and new events, chances and gains may be present to look forward to; if not, they will not be far behind or can be created. **Life is filled with a sense of purpose and direction** and **opportunities** will arrive, so be ready to grab them when they come your way.

The Star indicates *good health*, feeling energised and *full of enthusiasm*, and *luck* will be on your side. You will feel connected not only to your mind, body and emotions but also to your spiritual self, so this is a time to *trust yourself, your intuition, your decisions and your desires. Have faith* in all that you are and all that you are trying to achieve.

We use stars for navigation, so *perspective* is given from within, and we see the direction we are going in a new positive light, yet the past is also seen afresh and in a new light, however bad the journey has been.

Life will be running smoothly once again after upheavals and changes. The Star usually appears after difficulties that have stripped away your lust for life, and you can only really appreciate The Star's energy once you have been denied it.

We can feel playful with this card, *young at heart* and ready to get going now that we are free from the past.

The Star - 17: Reversed

Reversed, The Star still shines but it is not seen or connected to, showing that emotions and energies are not flowing which causes **depression, doubt and physical illness to start or continue.**

Faith can be lost or tested, be that spiritual and religious or emotional and practical, leaving you **questioning, doubting and trying to find the reasons behind disappointments.** At times, this card can show a blip, a bad negative phase which limits us from being happy, leaving us *feeling lost.*

A timid mind or frail body and illness can be shown due to the stress and strains caused by **anxiety**; it asks us to take care of ourselves and our well-being as we deal with hurdles or hiccups on our pathway.

Reversed, we have **pessimism**, even when it is shown to the inquirer that a situation can improve, there is *a reluctance to accept that events can be more positive or different and still beneficial*. It indicates someone who is surrounded by joy or solutions but *can only see the negatives and problems.* This shows there is either *mistrust, fear or a lack of physical energy* due to being *worn down by a situation*, when if the situation were looked at, you would see that positivity and solutions are still present in abundance.

New opportunities will be missed or not created as we view the world with some doom and gloom as we let a lack of movement in our lives blind us to possible change. There will be *doubts as to any future happiness* because of the past or present - at worst, this could leave *wishes unfulfilled* and pathways untravelled.

Life will have lost its meaning and its shine, as *a period of bad luck* runs its course.

THE MOON - 18

The Moon is number Eighteen and connected to deception and misunderstanding. The Eighteen's One shows drive, creative energy and power, while the input from the Eight is challenge and confinement, the Eight contains two Fours, bringing restriction. When Eighteen is reduced (1+8=9), we are given Nine, the number of The Hermit, which brings inspiration and progress but also withdrawal. Inner battles are brought about by the Eighteen. Eighteen presents change resulting from dilemmas and misunderstandings. Deception is a key factor with this number, and the conscious mind is urged into action without just cause, leading to fantasy and error. Our mind's aspirations can prove to be the biggest distraction and barrier to our success, and this number warns us of that.

The Moon is ruled by Pisces and Neptune, with some favouring Cancer.

The Moon's card pictures a large full moon, with a crayfish emerging from the water below, and howling up at the moon are a dog and a wolf.

A full moon can make us feel challenged and reflective. It can shake up our minds, causing stress, uncertainty and worry. The moon is linked to lunacy, as it is said that the pull of the moon on the earth's tides could also create movement within the fluid of the brain, creating disordered, bizarre and altered behaviour. In short, it is said to make us crazy. A full moon shifts our perspective, leaving us with a distorted view of reality and little clarity. Instead, it rattles our cage, making us feel ungrounded and confused. It leaves us with no simplicity or sincerity, and generally gives a time of mistrust with ourselves and others. Without the light of the sun, we have no clear sight. We see only shadows and we lose touch with our realities, wandering dazed and confused within our own minds.

The Moon's face has its eyes closed in contemplation; Waite writes in *The Pictorial Key to the Tarot* that the face's expression is asking for stillness and peace to be with those below. To calm the animal nature so that the mental abyss which is forming can lose its shape and disappear. The face leans to the left of the card, so it will be logic that is affected by the confusion of the moon, and so those seemingly intuitive messages and flashes of awareness may not be understandable, correct, or even devoid of psychic content. The face is shown in profile, so we will not see the complete picture, which with this card can bring self-deception, yet does not mean there is no truth in matters, even if what your mind sees is distorted. The Moon asks us not to put our trust in anything at face value, as we should wait for the influence of this card to pass. Be patient; if not, we will surely be deceived by our emotional and mental clutter, which clouds our intuition, which is present yet pushed aside, mistrusted or ignored. The Moon brings our imagination into play but not reality, leaving the obvious unseen, as moonlight may be bright, romantic, and mysterious, but it still conceals the truth, leading us to fantasies and illusions. As such, we can perceive a mental lie as intuition, and go 'loony' with the mental cycle it can create.

There are thirty-two spikey beams of moonlight, sixteen inner and sixteen outer rays. Sixteen is the number of The Tower, and ideas followed here may leave us building a tower of our own ego, which will fall when we find reality once again after the moon has shifted its position. With two lots of rays, we risk double jeopardy, not only suffering being pushed into an illusive choice, but also the fallout from that if we follow our confused ramblings.

Fifteen Yods fall from the moon, drops of light symbolic of grace and blessing. They show an opportunity to learn within this card, as while we should not follow our rambling mind, we should at least acknowledge our intuition, darker side and fears. The Devil is number fifteen, so this card brings up fears and desires that entrap us, take away our power, and blind us with misunderstanding. With both The Tower and The Devil being aspects of this card, we should heed any issues it brings.

A dog and a wolf howl up at the moon, representing two aspects of our egos. The loyal and trusting dog is a link to our domesticated selves, our social, day-to-day tamed minds. The part of us that wants to fit in, feel safe and loved, howls to seek out familiarity and to be called back home. The wolf is our wild, untamed primal urges, our gut instincts, the werewolf within, which transforms our sensible minds when the full moon appears in the sky. It wishes us to take what we want and has no politeness as it bares its teeth, showing our aggressive primal natures and reactions, and so howls to obey an inner urge. They show a stand-off between our intellect or intuition and our instincts, a time when both are roused and yet neither has the higher ground. They both respond to the full moon, howling, drawn by its energy with no idea why. Yet still, they try to obtain unobtainable knowledge, all stirred up, making it impossible to back down, leading them to be equally confused. Facts are not available, especially the main fact that nothing is actually occurring, other than being denied daylight and overreacting to the situation they find themselves in. The Moon overstimulates the minds and emotions with nothing real or tangible, just a raw powerful, elusive energy that is hard to overcome and contain. It gives drive and energy but no conclusions nor any sense of direction. This results in restlessness, and confusion reigns.

Crawling from the water pool is the crayfish or lobster. The darkness takes away the clarity of the clear water and emotions are now uncertain, with the ripples stirred causing doubt and inner conflict. The water is the subconscious mind, with the crayfish representing the monsters of the mind coming to the surface. The lobster used to be linked to the sign of Cancer which is ruled by the moon and brings emotional awareness and sensitivity. A hard, outer shell can protect soft squishy inner feelings, so this card can show us being outwardly angry, demanding answers and agitated, yet protective of ourselves and going inwards. These animals shed their shells, moulting so they can grow, yet once their shell is set, they can grow no more. This is symbolic of feelings coming to the surface which prod us to look at what no longer fits us, and which we need to be free from. The crayfish is blue/purple: another link to the inner, intuitive self. He comes up from the dark depths of our emotions, representing our deepest fears, our most disturbing thoughts and our nightmares.

The crayfish stands at the start of an uneven mud pathway, showing he sees pitfalls and small stones to trip over rather than a smooth road to travel. As the path is highlighted by the shadows, he does not see it as it is, so his perception is warped. Leading up into the mountains leaves a focus on stress, challenges and a troubling way forward.

The two towers, as in Death's card, are a gateway, a passage from one place or state of being to another. Within Death's card, we pass through these gates with certainty in our minds, a knowing of our reality. Here it would be with illusion and confusion, which could lead to an unwished-for destination. They, like the dog and wolf, also show opposites, but here in the dark, they look similar. The distance between the two can represent a need to bring aspects of yourself closer to make sense of things, representing the divide between fact and fiction. In this original version of The Moon, the distance, like Death, is a watery, emotional blue with a mix of rock and water. In other editions, we can see that the tower to the right stands on a grassy hill with a small stream flowing from it, indicating that emotions will flow, yet in the darkness, they will not be of much use to a mind which is calling for common sense. If this stream turns into a river within the mind, the grassy bank could collapse, destroying the tower and creating bigger problems.

The Moon is a feminine, fertile and mysterious symbol of the subconscious mind which is full of potential. It represents our psychic natures, the dark and light and a phase of change. It shows intuition or deep thoughts bubbling up to the surface. So, we can approach such information in two ways under this card's influence:

1: Leave what we 'feel' until the mind is clearer and don't act, as

2: messages given during this time can get obscured by our minds twisting our intuition or old hidden feelings, leading us to react out of fear rather than love.

The fluctuations of the moon have the tendency to lead us into the unknown, on both an emotional and mental level, as both respond to the other. The Moon can take us to places which we fear and dread as it pulls at the depths of our human nature and acts on our mental and emotional being. It brings irrationality, as nothing can be entirely grasped because nothing remains static for long enough. It acts on our subconscious, telling us to listen to our inner voice but doesn't allow us the pleasure of being able to properly hear it, as it is drowned out by confusion. Deep instincts may emerge from the darkness of our minds, and we are warned about following them, but they should at least be given the chance to be heard so we can understand ourselves better. The Moon drags up old or hidden fears that you would rather choose to forget as well as create new ones. You may not know if a thought or presumption is your intuition, or an old limiting fear, and so this is not a positive time to make decisions.

As The Moon is laid when there is total confusion in the air, it can lead to an equally confusing reading for the beginner. This may occur when The Moon appears in a present position: if the reading makes no sense or the questioner cannot take on board any of the information that you are given, and The Moon is present, then maybe the reading should be abandoned for another day. If so, maybe a cup of tea and a heart-to-heart talk is needed instead. The questioner may not be able to see the reality that is right in front of them, and this is a time to muddle through and be patient. Those new to Tarot may find such a response from a client - or their own confusion if the spread is for the self - frustrating as ears are closed.

If The Moon is laid in a resulting position in a Tarot spread, such as the outcome, then the answer or direction of the question raised may not yet be decided. The answer simply is not available as others in the ever-increasing circles about the person may yet to make decisions of their own, which will impact on situations. Or the questioner is not ready to accept an answer for whatever reason at this time, yet the answers will come to them once their mind is clear.

IN A NUTSHELL

Fears are blinding you and now is not the time to take any action on your inner voice. Confusion is plentiful and you will have no idea of what's what. Nothing will be what it seems at face value, and if you dig for answers, you will not get any clarity; try not to make changes or decisions unless you must.

Old patterns and being stuck in a cycle of thinking or reacting can bring a need to take a break. A reminder not to let the past ruin the present, and to treat new situations on their own merits. Overall, wait for this phase to end.

The Moon - 18: Upright

This card brings a phase of **change met with confusion**, and that is what we must remember with The Moon - ***it is a phase, and so it will pass***.

Events will be changing, and nothing will feel that it has any consistency, leading to the irrational mind ruling with unclear thoughts. Yet you may also be caught up in ***a repeating cycle***, so see if any pattern of behaviour is present.

Emotions will be stirred, bringing ***innermost fears*** into the forefront of your mind which not only leads to ***instability*** from a minor to a major degree but also to ***irrational thoughts and actions***. We can feel that others are wrong and that only we can see the truth as ourselves or situations are ***misunderstood***.

The mind will make monsters from even the smallest of issues and blind us to what is the truth. We will be **confused about our actions, let alone the actions or reactions of others**.

The Moon makes us *irrational, isolated, vulnerable and frustrated*. Our *imaginations work overtime* and due to this, when you are being influenced by The Moon, *you are not in a position to make a wise decision*. Such matters should be left until the mind is clear, as when the moon shifts, we will see the facts, and *acting on your feelings could be disastrous*.

Dreams and instinct should not be followed as your instincts and *fantasies will deceive you*. Pick your battles wisely with this card, as *you will not know who or what to trust*.

The Moon asks that we acknowledge our thoughts and intuition, yet do not take any action or make any choices or decisions, unless totally unavoidable, but wait until we feel more settled. *Take time to care for yourself, do not force anything*.

With matters of *fertility*, the moon is a very fertile card, so everything is okay and possible with those things we wish to create, but it does ask us to look at our feelings and expectations due to the influence of the card.

The Moon - 18: Reversed

With the reversed Moon, we can *make mistakes*, as we do not wait, *we act on our clouded judgements, creating new problems for ourselves* which can make the confusion even worse. This can lead us to *lose trust and faith in our intuition or thought process and therefore in ourselves*.

Reversed, the Moon can give *disturbed emotions and extremely negative thinking* which may be a long-standing problem. Instead of standing back and looking at the confusion we feel arising from our minds, we see things as fact and will not question them as they arise, so we are left with *a distorted view of the world* or the matter at hand. Thoughts will be *obsessive,* and you will be allowing *delusions* to control your life and decisions, leaving you stuck in *an ever-decreasing circle*: a cycle which you may find hard to break free from.

True *feelings can be repressed* out of fear, leading to *nightmares* or *intrusive unpleasant thoughts* as our dreams mirror our worries and suspicions of the world. We may doubt our own mental state: a sign that we need to find someone to talk to, a friend or therapist to help us gather our mind back to itself.

With The Moon reversed, we get *stuck* in phases, so waiting things out can prove fruitless. Until then, there will be a lack of reality in views and opinions, leading to errors and *misjudging others*.

The Moon reversed can show *gynaecological or conception problems* if placed with other fertility cards and the question asked was of that nature.

THE SUN - 19

The Sun's number is Nineteen, representing the creative, cheerful and powerful nature of the sun. The One represents power, creativity, optimism and drive, with the Nine bringing inspiration and progress, compassion and understanding. When combined (1+9=10), we are given Ten, the number of completion and The Wheel of Fortune. Ten shows a great abundance of energy, rewards and together we have a card of energy and purpose that brings happiness. Nineteen brings regeneration and renewal: we are at the top of the wheel. It is a potent, powerful and physical number that brings action and creativity that manifests itself on all levels.

The Sun is astrologically linked to Leo and to the Sun.

The Sun card shows a child surrounded by a walled garden, riding a white horse under a bright, calm sun.

The Sun is our source of light and energy; without it, we would not exist as it gives us life. This card represents a totally optimistic and encompassing energy which is rejuvenating and energising to all aspects of our lives. It shows a release from old setbacks and stresses, allowing for new and productive growth. It brings us solid foundations for the future, allowing freedom to be felt, making the child in us all feel joyous and happy.

The face of the sun is serene, and a bit playful, as it watches us or the small child play; we are faced head-on so everything is in focus, and nothing is hidden. The sun's rays radiate outwards filling the child's garden with warmth, light and the potential for growth. There are twenty-one rays, one for each other major card. Between the right-hand side of the numbers and a ray, presumably a drawing blip, is what has become affectionately known as the *'oh shit'* line, a squiggle maybe meant to be another ray? (Coined by Holly Voley, an RWS enthusiast and expert.) The Sun's energy brings simplicity back to life while at the same time contradicting itself by allowing fast energising changes. It is as if by allowing simplicity to take over, The Sun lets a naturalness and ease take over life's events. By encompassing the other Major Arcana, The Sun tells us that everything is going to be OK: all roads can lead us to happiness.

Behind the child, the garden wall brings shelter and safety. The stone blocks of the wall show commitment and dedication as they take time to build, each stone skilfully placed against the one it best suits, so a sign of time and effort has been taken to create this safe haven. The wall represents security, permanence and often something real and tangible. Walls are built to protect, and while this can be seen as a barrier and restriction, it here creates a safe place for the child to play without fear or worries as all past hurdles are now gone, allowing freedom that has been longed for to be available to enjoy. It allows us to be able to let our hair down and act freely without judgement.

On top of the wall are four sunflowers – four showing safety and, like the wall, the number four brings things that are solid and substantial, and so a real sign of optimism found within physical life. With three on one side of the child and one on the other, they show creation, purpose and potential. Sunflowers are bright, optimistic flowers, symbolising love, honesty, and loyalty, which are said to bring good luck. They get their name from their bright-yellow faces, which turn to face the sun, and here they face the child, as he holds all the hope, potential, and energy of the sun. The sunflowers here are rooted, representing grounded energies, allowing ideas to establish solid and favourable foundations for the future. They are flowers of sunshine, showering us with vitality and liveliness; they tell us that now is the best time, the most favourable time and that this time is yours to enjoy. Blooming in summer through to early autumn, they show the freedom of youth into young adult life when we are still unburdened by responsibilities, making us feel young again. In bloom, they show established growth and the promise of more to come.

The happy and content child smiles with his arms open wide showing us trust, openness, youthfulness and sincerity. The Sun's energy here is to be enjoyed, celebrated with vigour and enthusiasm as we are fully awake and full of light, and we will not want to waste one single drop of daylight. The child can be any age, someone with young-at-heart energy or someone simply fully enjoying what life has to offer, as he shows an absolute enjoyment of life, a time or a situation. He is naked to show liberation, freedom from those things which hold us back and a time to not have to worry; he is pleasing himself, innocently playing and relishing life.

His gaze is off to the one side, so he is not looking ahead as much as enjoying the moment, and looking left, he may be pondering how to enjoy this more, and as a child, such logical thoughts may not be that relevant. Yet, he wears The Fool's red feather in his floral headdress, so growth is still wanted. We have not finished our journey here as we are still inspired. The yellow flowers show happiness and that everything is in your favour. Now is truly a time to kick back and relish all the good things in life. The garland has seven yellow flowers, with red centres, showing the child's thoughts to be lively, vibrant, full of life and with a passion for fun.

In all, there are eleven flowers within the card. Justice is governed by eleven which is also a master number. This brings in a compassionate, spiritual element to the card which shows intelligence, balance and fairness, bringing fortunate conclusions to situations. The Karmic energy of Justice shows us happiness, which is due and deserved, bringing trust, openness and honesty.

We meet Death's white horse, no longer pawing at the ground or dressed in a macabre attire but being ridden bareback by a naked child. With no saddle or harness, we see trust, balance, flexibility and flow from the child's perspective. It shows belief, a faith in the security we have; challenges are not a problem as they have already been mastered. The child rides the horse being uninhibited and breaking free from boundaries, full of both innocence and uncomplicated childlike happiness. From the horse's perspective, he is not being controlled or waiting for directions, nor waiting for the next disaster to observe, but is free to allow life to direct him. His mind is set free now he is unharnessed. The horse gazes forwards with a stern eye, so there is still knowledge and acceptance of responsibilities, and a wish to keep what has been gained. The horse's stare can also serve as a reminder that while we are basking in the sun, others may be carrying the weight of issues; others may not be as free as we are in that moment. Those who have supported us and cared for us may still be doing so, having been the foundation of your happiness, as all things stem from a source. However, while the sun shines, it is time to play, as no one else's efforts in creating your happiness will be seen as a burden to them.

The banner carried by the child shows victory in accomplishments and the presence, again, of desire, yet here is a time to be free from the building and efforts of the past, a time to enjoy what has been achieved. In most versions of this card, it is an orange/red colour, sometimes red, which shows this victory is based on the enjoyments of life. The banner is large and heavy, yet this child holds it with ease, symbolising a lack of effort and problems. Nothing is a problem with the arrival of The Sun, as problems are banished or no longer seen as difficulties; everything has either an answer or acceptance, or has simply faded away.

When The Sun shines on you, its energy is felt through your entire life and extends also to those who are around you and brings with it compassion and feelings of completion and success to your life. The Sun's potency is direct in its effect on our lives, and you will find joy and happiness in everything as life takes on an optimistic glow. Happiness is a state of mind we all possess, and with The Sun, we will not have to seek it out as it will be present, giving hope, achievement, good luck and the chance to be at peace. It is a fresh start and a time to enjoy what life has to offer as all stresses are dissolved.

IN A NUTSHELL

This card's energy brings positivity to even the darkest of situations. It is a card full of healing energy and growth which shines and lifts life, offering a time to feel blessed.

Optimism is high, and all the good is seen within a situation, as things are going well for you. This is not a case of rose-tinted glasses but real solid happiness and opportunities for celebration in any area of your life.

The Sun – 19: Upright

The Sun brings complete **happiness, good luck and good health**.

Life is to be enjoyed and celebrated as it is tension-free and fun; you know that you are free to let your hair down, to **relax and have fun without consequences**. There are feelings of freedom as you are **liberated from past difficulties** which have held you back.

Goals are now in your grasp and your aims are fulfilled. The Sun allows for the future to be planned and gives us a clear path to move along as well as the *ease* to move along it. What we wish for suddenly becomes quite easy to obtain and work towards, with progress even just falling into your lap.

Success and achievement in any area of life are ensured and now enjoyed. **Events will be going your way, a chance to start again, to grow and celebrate**.

The Sun's energy favours families and intimate relationships by offering **commitments** and family celebrations, even pregnancies and births. Where domestic life is concerned, there is **an abundance of happiness and emotional security** as relationships are trouble-free and expressive.

All areas of life are shined upon, and The Sun in one area of your life can spread out to infect others with its positive shine and glow of optimism and luck.

A definite and positive Yes card.

The Sun – 19: Reversed

Even when reversed, the Sun still shines with optimism; its energy and effects are *temporarily hidden* as it is covered by a small passing cloud, so you may find *a small fly in the ointment.*

Happiness is still possible, but **problems will have to be overcome**. Lovers may have to wait for commitment, there may be difficulties for children, or an outsider may try to upset a situation, and there will be **small delays reaching goals**.

If you have fallen off the horse, get back on. If you've sunburn, take more notice of the small things. If you've sunflower pollen affecting you, take a few precautions.

Situations and relationships can be taken for granted, success can be expected but issues need to be worked at, or **issues ironed out**. This is not time to take a break, give up, celebrate early or expect good things to come to you, but rather a time to make sure mutual respect or effort has not slipped. **You are nearly there, keep going**.

When reversed, The Sun shows that **obstacles will blight a situation**. Whatever problem presents itself, it will only be temporary, as The Sun has no room for any long-term bad luck to take hold.

Another aspect of The Sun reversed is **overconfidence, excess pride and being blinded by expectations,** which can place that fly in the ointment also.

JUDGEMENT - 20

The number governing Judgement is Twenty, which represents effort and the stabilising of life's events, a point of transition and renewal. When Twenty is reduced (2+0=2), the Two brings anticipation as well as balance, understanding and resolutions. The Zero shows that anything is possible from this point onwards. Twenty brings transformation to the self. Events are turned about, and confident expectation is felt. It highlights the importance of analysis in aiding shifts in consciousness and the anticipation of realising change.

Judgement is ruled by Pluto, which rules Scorpio.

The card depicts the scene of an archangel coming from the heavens trumpeting God's imminent arrival, while in the graveyard below people rise from coffins with hands raised to greet the Divine Messenger, open-hearted as to what may come as they feel truth and changes on all levels of their being.

Judgement is a card of evolution. It is Judgement's essence that goes before the creation of the true self. It brings us back to our spiritual self, our deep inner being and allows freedom of the spirit, as we are measured by who we now are and not who we once were. Judgement submits us to a clearing of the soul, as the past or one's views and actions are called into account so we can evolve.

An archangel is a high-ranking angel, who appears to warn and tell of God's presence within our lives, bringing a divine moment of truth and revelation. As such, this archangel can also represent moments of clarity rising from the subconscious, or from facts about us coming together like the pieces of a jigsaw, if you wish to see the angel aspect from a more down-to-earth perspective. Archangels are tasked with working with humanity and are bringers of inspirational messages from within or from above. They are not said to come down to earth for mundane reasons, and only intervene when they feel that they are needed or sent. They come during both inner and outer spiritual revolutions, when our eyes get sight of what lies beyond the material more readily than before, allowing us to become more than we have been, letting us put some of our pieces together to see who we really are.

Archangels are God's soldiers, weighing up the soul after death and overseeing the greater path of the spirit during life and in death. These are not to be mistaken for our Spirit Guides, as archangels deal only with the major shifts of the individual, countries, the globe and beyond. They are cosmic signposts bringing with them spiritual controlling energy that directs life, yet not on a whim of our own asking, as we cannot demand judgement. Judgement is not like The High Priestess, where we seek hidden answers, or The Hierophant, where we wish to be shown the way, as we cannot call on Judgement; nor is it like Justice, where we seek truth and balance restored. Judgement is a deep calling from the soul, and it cannot be planned for; and at times, we do not even know we need it. When something higher than us - karma, God, the universe - knows that it's the right time to move onwards, up and away from an issue, then Judgement comes into play.

The angel is in pastel blue, light turquoise in other versions: soft colours of healing, patience, serenity and understanding. The wings are pink and lilac showing us tranquillity and spirituality, so we have a calm, accepting, compassionate archangel seeking to awaken the people below and letting them know it's time to rise up and accept the changes needed to be reborn.

Who the archangel represents is hard to say. He may be Michael, who weighed and balanced the souls of the dead; Metatron, who blew a trumpet; Uriel, with his flaming hair; or Gabriel, who was connected to resurrection, and who acted as the voice of God, bringing good news.

The angel's golden trumpet heralds our resurrection, like a spiritual alarm call. It brings a time to wake up and let go of old baggage as we have no need of it anymore, and we cannot move forwards with it. Once we have learnt all that we can from a situation or a belief, it can be discarded to make way for the new, and this card is about absolutes and reaching defined states, or places within your journey, not just within life as a whole, but also within specific issues. A time to sum up and welcome in the new you, yet it will shift all areas as it radiates outwards in your life. Trumpets are linked to war, so a battle cry from our spiritual, or even subconscious, self is sounded; something is shifting, stirring. The trumpet being gold links to the physical world as well as the inner self, as one often reflects onto the other, with the gold also signifying a higher-conscious awareness.

On the trumpet is a flag that pictures a red cross upon a white background. A flag is a visual sign of passing a message often about intent, status, power and authority, and here is linked to the message of the trumpet. The cross could signify the resurrection of Christ, rising from the dead as would fit the card, yet this is also a square cross, representing balance and a symbol of peace. The cross and its colours show that a marriage of opposites is required to complete a task. Red on a flag implies bravery and life, with the white representing innocence and purity, leaving all spiritual changes reflected on the physical, and all physical changes equally reflected on the spiritual.

The angel, trumpet and flag show unconditional love being shone onto life. We are propelled to fulfil and satisfy an inner urge to create balance between our physical lives and self and our true inner selves, as, when this card appears, it is our spiritual, our authentic self that wishes to be heard. The trumpet calls, stating that time has come to rise up and be true to ourselves and find our identity. There is a realisation that we are more than flesh and bones, routine and obligations. Mundane thoughts must be put aside so we can contemplate our true place within our life, as well as our true identity and purpose within situations.

In the distance are the icy problematic mountains, showing the angel's message can help us face those challenges, but they will not be taken away. A new day is dawning, and this new day will allow things to be seen in a new light. This is not a card that shows energy shifting in our lives, making everything easy and smooth as we gain some inspired wisdom; rather, we will need to face the journey with the inspired wisdom given to us.

The coffins are floating or sitting in water, representing the subconscious mind and the inner self. The sky is blue, often a sign of no trouble in sight, yet those in the coffins may not feel that way as the depths of the waters surrounding them may only offer darker thoughts, bringing fears and worries about what is coming, what the changes will mean if taken, as being called back to life means swimming, or wading to shore through any emotions present.

The coffins show endings, and open, they show there is still hope, situations can be repaired and a time to put things right can be shown. Physical death is not associated with this card, although spiritual change and deep personal realisations are. Judgement's new beginnings are undeniable and definite, as once a lesson has been learnt on a spiritual or profound level, it is never forgotten. Coffins are for burying the dead. In doing that, a new life starts and so while our futures are built on the past, here we do not need to take it with us. Old dead aspects of who we are can be buried with honour as they have gotten us to where we need to be.

The six people within Judgement are dead, with their grey skin showing a life ended. They are naked to show a need for innocence and with nothing hidden, because when we are brought to account, we are like children: we have to give ourselves to a force much higher than ourselves and no amount of clothing would hide who we are. The clothes were also a link to their past life, and this is not about taking the past forwards with you but leaving it behind, as the weight of it is not needed. Six is the number of harmony and beauty, bringing healing energy to the card, seeing the best in life, with six also the day God created mankind, showing life starting. They are divided into threes, which is symbolic of creation and the union of mind, body and spirit, as well as life divided - out with the old, in with the new.

The men, women and children indicate that we are all, regardless of sex, age, race, gender or social standing, on our own life path and that true judgement is only given divinely, however you picture that to be. They combine all that we are to become all that we can be, showing the physical, mental and spiritual combining to create a new era: a time to rise above what has gone before, offering us a whole new evolved human being. They all stand, arms and heads raised upwards, relieved that they can be reborn, carried onwards and given another chance at life and to be true to themselves. There are no well-groomed paths to take them away, just the dark waters to swim or wade through and mountains to climb; but this is a new chance which is welcomed, as staying put is not. There is a relief with this card as all is not lost, yet for one thing to live, we need to let go of the dead wood within ourselves or our lives. With their gazes only being on the angel, they do not seek guidance from each other, as all they focus on is their own enlightenment as everyone is on their own journey.

An inner urge will lead us towards Judgement, or more accurately, we will feel pulled towards it. We will be driven to come to terms with the truth of our own personal individuality. Events, be they good or bad, will come to their conclusion and will be judged on their true merits. What is left remaining is the undeniable truth that we are given to take forward onto our next phase of life or task; when this happens, we are left with no indecisions, doubts or fears as once we grasp them, they are seen as a welcomed challenge, and a needed path to take.

Judgement is not a card felt with pain; instead, it is welcomed with recognition and understanding. An epiphany will awaken the soul from its sleep and then into action. We see the connecting links, the roads which have brought us to where we are. We see who we are to others, to ourselves, and we see the puzzle of our life in a clear light, allowing for sudden understanding to be felt, making the jigsaw and threads come together. It offers a sense of imminent renewal, with sweeping new changes or beginnings which we feel on a very deep level. Its energy is karmic and pulls you as your spiritual self seeks to be heard. To try and escape is to stay still, but follow its prompting and you will grow in your sense of self and understanding of life. Liberation does not just affect the individual; it follows like a ripple in a pool to those whom we connect with, in whatever form they can feel it, which is also reflected by the group rising to meet the angel.

IN A NUTSHELL

A crossroads has been reached, a time to allow inner changes to become a part of your day-to-day life. You will need to express a new you to the world, as events which have been emotionally, mentally, and even spiritually processed will leave you feeling reborn.

Issues that have dragged on will conclude; forgiveness and truth will rule, allowing for life to carry on afresh without hurdles. A deep sense of direction will be with you, one which you cannot ignore.

Judgement – 20: Upright

Both upright and reversed, Judgement brings us to *a crossroads*.

Judgement is karmic and brings *changes on a deeply personal level*. It brings a strong urge to come to terms with life and *a time to move on* and not deny your spiritual or genuine self, a chance to be heard, and to have the chance to *act when it's needed most*.

It asks us to *be authentic*: to really be able to *believe in who we are*, with no feelings of guilt or burdens linked to what we are not, or a time to align ourselves to a better version of ourselves, as with Judgement, *we mature mentally and emotionally*.

This can often bring *a situation that has dragged on for some time, drawing to an end* as lessons are learnt. Judgement brings *an accumulation of past events,* which allows the ground to be cleared, leaving you feeling reborn. Sometimes you will be left feeling that you have another chance, which can leave you feeling tense with the prospect of change.

With Judgement, you can *move on at last* and sum up what has gone before and *let go of the past*, as it offers the chance to make new choices to heal situations. You can judge your own choices, and you will be able to see if you have done the right thing or not.

Our *efforts will be rewarded,* and we will feel compassion for ourselves in the truth that we find or have been given. There will be *anticipation* and excitement as you will be aware that life is about to take on new meaning and that a corner is about to be turned. Judgement has a feeling of arrival attached to it.

Judgement – 20: Reversed

Reversed, Judgement places you *at a crossroads where decisions must be made.* There is still an inner need for change and growth, although it is met with *misunderstanding, fear or confusion.*

Something is not being admitted or owned up to or is being ignored, which stops a new life or a chance for change from arriving. It is a calling for self-judgement and self-evaluation.

This card shows us having difficulties due to fighting or finding the direction that we wish our life to take and as a result feeling *uncertain and irritable.* The heart of this may be *negative self-judgement*, being a harsh critic and stopping yourself from moving on and letting go.

We hide from our true selves and cannot find a balance between who we are and who we want to be, however much that is desired. *Judgement reversed warns us to be honest with ourselves* and allow our spirit or calling to be heard, or a pathway may be missed.

There is the notion that nothing is going right, yet there is no reasoning as to why this is so; there is *a feeling of unease* present. Now is the time to look at why you are making the decisions you are and not jump to conclusions. *Signs have been present, chances have been given or seen which would have helped you*, but you have not felt able to take them, and so *ignored the openings presented.*

When Judgement is reversed, we can also find ourselves *at the mercy of the judgement of others, and it will not be favourable.* Your past actions may not be directing you where you wish to go, as *you have not done the right things or taken the right actions at the right time.* The judgement you receive can be very sobering, forcing you to re-evaluate who you are unwillingly.

THE WORLD - 21

The World is the final card of the Major Arcana and is numbered Twenty-one. The Fool can be placed after The World, as after the world goes through a revolution around the sun, we can get the urge to start the cycle again. The World's Twenty-one gives us freedom, movement and rewards, bringing us significant and important changes to our lives. When reduced (2+1=3), we arrive at Three, The Empress's number of creation and expansion. The Two represents interaction and balance with wisdom, while the One offers purpose, direction and wholeness. Twenty-one gives us independent action and freedom. Rewards are available for those who are presented with this card.

The World is linked to Saturn, and, like The Wheel of Fortune, links to all twelve of the zodiac signs.

The World's card shows a naked young woman dancing, presumably above the earth in the blue sky in the centre of a laurel crown. In each of the corners are the symbolic creatures that represent the Guardians of the Heavens which we have already met in The Wheel of Fortune.

The dancer's nakedness shows simplicity, joy and innocence. Her heart is sincere and unhindered as being naked shows her to be unencumbered by life and burden-free. She has quite a bohemian feel to her, dancing again showing her liberated energy; she does not have a care in the world. She is an independent, free-thinking soul who dances to express her happiness, free from constraints. Her right leg is leading, showing she is moving with her creative self; her dance is carefree and liberated, made up as it progresses with no rules, which can of course show a touch of hedonism.

Her long, flowing hair represents youth, virginity and innocence as in days gone by; only when a young girl was married did their hair get tied up or cut. Here it flows free, showing a time in life where we are getting ready for the next phase, where we can still be in the flow of what we are enjoying, truly living in the moment with no commitments. In the image, her hair is strawberry blonde, symbolic of warmth and commitment to changes and dreams. In other versions, she is blonde with her hair studded with small blue flowers, showing an intellectual calm, a mind which is settled and connected to the higher self or in agreement with thoughts and wishes, with trust, peace and commitment.

Her blue sash with a dash of red at the base of it flows with her as she moves, showing spiritual or higher wisdom. In some cards, this sash has both colours combined, turning it violet. Her hair and sash show movement, grace and energy, the air flows through the card, brushing away cobwebs as she dances carefree and relaxed.

She holds two double-ended wands like The Magician's, yet unlike him, she holds both to the side like batons as she dances, as she is not trying to create; she has already created and is enjoying what she has achieved. The two wands show balance within creativity, a balance of opposites; indecisions are not an issue as duality is no longer in question as all her possibilities are recognised. One wand may represent what she has achieved, the other can show us what she plans on next, as her emotions and thoughts are in agreement.

The victory wreath surrounding the dancer represents optimism and success. To obtain a victory wreath, you must have battled against the odds, and The World states that winning is assured. Whether the prize offered is emotional, spiritual or practical is a personal matter, yet it can reflect on physical attainments. What will affect all who receive it is the sense of achievement that it brings. The wreath has neither a beginning nor an end and so indicates a continual movement of energies, allowing no setbacks or restrictions to take hold, creating a feeling of unity with life itself. The wreath is also shaped like a zero, or an egg. We found with The Fool that zero is a number full of potential to build something new with, and an egg or a womb where new life is formed. This makes her victory wreath also a place to gestate, so again this is a card of being between states, a state between lives. The red ties that bind the wreath show vitality and drive in the physical world. They are placed above and below, so the desire within the mind matches the desire within the physical: all is balanced. Tied in the infinity pattern, like the wreath itself, shows a continuation, no division, one thing leading to another, a continuous cycle.

She is dancing in the blue sky, surrounded by white clouds which symbolise the inner mind, the blue sky simply telling us that everything is just fine. She is above the world, resurrected after Judgement, rising above any issues, being infinite and limitless; the world is truly her oyster.

In each corner are the Guardians of the Heavens from The Wheel of Fortune. They are not holding books and studying here, but relaxed, bringing a touch of heaven down to earth. They bring all the elements together - fire, water, earth and air - and the four corners of the world, showing this is a card of unlimited potential. The Wheel of Fortune is a card of change, movement and fate, whereas The World is more about new stages in our lives where we realise that we can have a say in how life is directed. There is acceptance concerning responsibility for our own will, and this is needed to create balance and true direction within life so that accomplishment can be enjoyed. With The World comes the knowledge that potential has been realised and our talents are exercised and not wasted. This allows for further development to be a future by-product of the original growth; wealth attracts wealth and success creates more success.

The World offers a time to pause, take a breather to enjoy life, so we can dance and feel liberated between stages of our life, as life is about to not just turn a page, but start a whole new chapter. Life is appreciated, accepted and valued; its energy brings us full circle and brings change as well as balance. We can now go into our future with an even load and the security that knowledge brings. Like The Wheel of Fortune, The World shows that life is made of cycles of learning, and rotation is needed in whatever direction it takes. With The World, you are placed on top of the Wheel and from this point, while The World's energy lasts, you are given the freedom of direction, so take advantage of its offerings and enjoy being on top of the world.

IN A NUTSHELL

A time to dance and celebrate, as things have come full circle, be that in big or small events or situations. This allows you to start a brand new chapter in your life built upon the past. You are filled with confidence and aspiration, which leaves you feeling liberated and passionate about everything.

A card of being in the right place at the right time, meeting the right people or person when their help is needed and everything is synchronising, and you can now travel as you go from one life episode to the next.

The World – 21: Upright

The World brings **completion and success** to any area of life. Events, hard work or the effects of luck will fall into place, leaving you **feeling elevated and completely fulfilled**.

The World leaves you feeling totally connected to your life and situations, leaving you **feeling firmly in control and content**. You will **feel passionate about life** and fuelled to carry on and enjoy what has been gained.

A new chapter is emerging, bringing a new phase into your life in which you can enjoy your efforts or rewards. The World fills these positive changes with excitement and **gratitude**, and you will be left feeling that **luck is definitely on your side**.

Like The Sun, this is a big **Yes to questions, as long-term happiness and progress are shown as possible**.

If you are waiting for success, stay on track with constructively aiming for your dreams! Things will fall into place for you and **outcomes will be successful**. The World tells us to **aim high**, to reach up to what we desire as the potential is all about, and everything is in place to make dreams come true.

You may positively be placed under the spotlight, celebrated and applauded for your skills, talents or actions.

You will feel fulfilled in knowing that **you have achieved something of value** for yourself. What was set out to be done has been achieved. Everything is in the right place at the right time, leaving you very pleased with outcomes and progress.

The World also symbolises **travel**. If you wish to make any big moves such as emigration or even a long stay away, this is a positive card to have.

The World – 21: Reversed

Reversed, The World indicates **an unsatisfactory ending to ambitions and goals**, leading to *frustration* and *stagnation*. Getting what you want may fall short of your expectations, making events feel a bit like a damp squib. Success can even leave you feeling trapped and with nothing else to achieve.

Yet, at times, this card can show that *events may fail to complete* and just hang in the air unfinished, as everything simply falls short.

Success is still possible, but more time will be needed to overcome upheavals and setbacks that will be met along the way. This can all be accompanied by *a feeling of emptiness as the past has not yet been resolved and old problems still linger.* There will be a block in the way of success or closure which will be ignored, yet equally, *you may wish to give up*.

Goals require dedication, so it may be time to look at any **wishful thinking** you have and replace it with solid action and determination. You may also have placed your faith in the wrong people or have taken the wrong approach, even with the best of intentions.

Closure can be an issue also in emotional matters, as well as practical ones. The new start you wish can happen, the door you wish to close is still there, yet you must push it with the correct action and passion for change to happen. Until then, *you're not moving anywhere.*

THE MINOR ARCANA

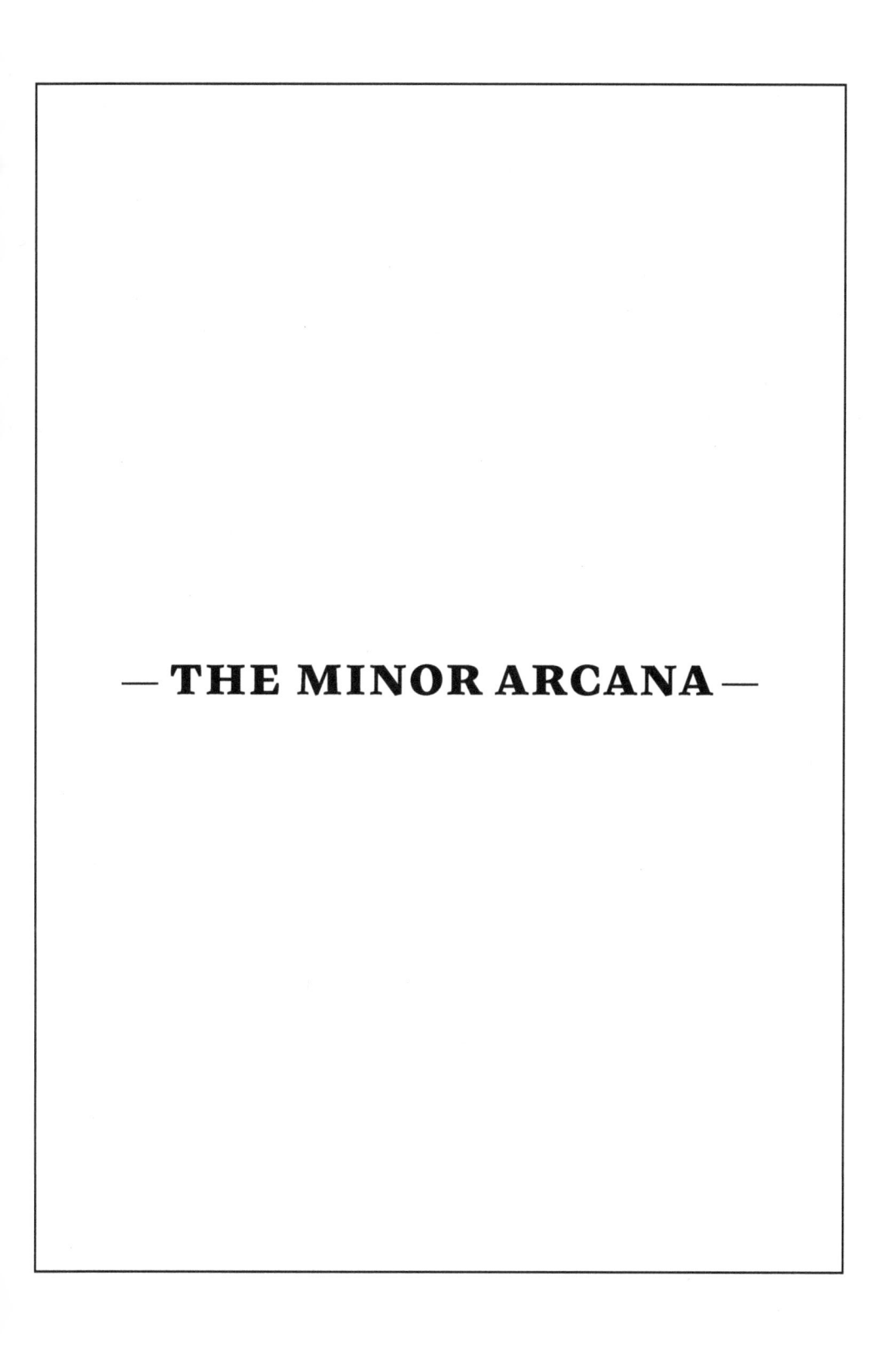

— The Suit of Wands —

The suit of Wands brings us the energy of fire that rules our passions, enthusiasm and drive.

Fire is an element energised simply by use, and while dormant holds the potential to improve and push us forward. Fire is hard to contain, as its force brings a quickened pace for enjoying and establishing life. Wands allow us to challenge our environment and put creative energy to use.

Wands are also known as Staves, Rods, Staffs and Batons. In standard playing cards the equivalent suit is Clubs.

Keywords that define fire/Wands - energy, enthusiasm, drive, gregarious/sensual, friendly, social, warmth, hastiness, speed, ideas and productivity.

ACE OF WANDS

The Ace of Wands shows a hand from heaven offering us a wand.

The first Minor Arcana card is a very energised one, unlike the angels we have met so far who have been flesh-coloured, here we have a bright white angelic hand which you will find in all the Aces, surrounded by a white aura showing a sincere gift or opportunity being presented.

The sky is grey, representing a time of thought and consideration for the acceptance of this gift. In some versions of the RWS it is white, a sign of absolute sincerity, yet also a sign of a beginning as no colour has yet been added. The hand gives us a literal thumbs up, so to start the Minor deck off, we are given a chance to start something new with a *go for it!* The hand is presented from the right of the card - the imaginative, creative, subconscious side of the mind, bringing innovation and inspiration. Like The Magician's wand, this card gives us a boost of energy to manifest and create from those things we can imagine. The hand stirs up the air, creating a grey cloud - again, found in all the Aces - showing that change is in the air and that things will shift if we take what is offered.

Wands represent fire, a connection which comes from wood's flammable nature, with wands creating a burning potential and fierceness in our souls. Here we are given the potential for an opportunity that burns and inflames our desire for achievement, an energy to start our journey off with a spark of something we feel pulled towards. Wands are inventive and driven and have a longing to set the world alight, to make a stamp on life. This Wand gives an exciting chance to do just that.

Our wand is offered to us with a spouting of leaves, bringing new growth, energy, a push, optimism, new potential, and an idea of what could be developed. It represents creative energy and the possibility for a new path to be formed, which, if nurtured and supported, could develop into something substantial. Being an Ace without that nurturing, it could be no more than the potential of an idea, rather than the guaranteed success of one.

The leaves are like the Yods found within the Major deck, falling with grace and as a gift, and eight of the leaves fall from the wand. Its movement through the air allows for these eight leaves to fall, and eight brings us determination, drive and challenge, yet also restriction. Like Strength - 8, courage may be needed to travel to our destination, as without that, an idea, however fantastic, is just an interesting musing. These eight leaves falling away are a sign of those restrictions being lifted, liberation from what may hold you back, leaving a free mind suddenly seeing an opportunity.

The ten leaves growing from the wand could represent the Kabbalah, the tree of life, ten being *'to receive'*, showing at the start of this journey that it is one where we will learn about the universe and ourselves. The Kabbalah is a set of teachings about the understanding of the relationship between God and the mortal universe and the stages of creation. These ten leaves also show this wand to be alive, with, as we have met already, ten being a number of completion, thus giving a real chance to build a new life with this wonderful creative force, like The Fool setting off with his brave new idea.

The phallic nature of this wand is just that, as wands are very sexy energy cards. This shows us fire, but a passion not yet formed into action, but the potential of the male-driven energy to succeed, a passionate spark that ignites the soul and self. It shows readiness for action, a need for movement and an attraction to what is desired which can be all-consuming.

The wood knots show that this idea comes without any dead wood. Knots are formed when branches die and fall away, so here this is a wand that is alive and just needs to be reached for. It comes knocking us on the head, awakening our interest, and we deeply feel a small fire start to burn within us as we can see that this could well become something important.

Below the wand is a castle, which indicates that success is possible. It symbolises the destination or goal which can be visualised with this new idea and opportunity that the Ace of Wands brings. Success is the logical desired outcome of a new idea, as we only ever see the end results with a new flash of an idea and not how to necessarily get there. Yet this wand comes showing us we can really make something of it.

The winding river below shows we will need to cross it to get to the prize. Before that are three trees, symbolic of growth, creativity and potential, all pointing to an opportunity which could allow for long-term growth. We will need to steer our way through the water, and so this could bring an emotional element into play. The hills which protect the castle must be climbed, showing practical energy is needed. Further behind is a mountain range, showing the need to look at facts and potential problems.

This idea this Ace brings may not be possible without drawing on many resources, a fact with all four of the Aces, yet it's a driving urge just the same, bringing a new spark of enthusiasm into our lives. This wand is a gift that promises opportunities, confidence and invention, bringing a love of life and an abundance of physical and imaginative energy. It shows us an exciting creative idea, something new to get our teeth into, which sparks our passion, making us want to roll up our sleeves and get things moving.

Numerological value – **ONE** = Desire for action, new beginnings and movement.

IN A NUTSHELL

A new idea or opportunity will present itself. A good time to put plans into action, as the universe gives you a green light. Grab what comes your way.

Now is the time for a fresh start: allow your ambition and creativity to take you forwards. Seize the moment!

Ace of Wands: Upright

The Ace of Wands brings *fresh, positive and good new ideas*. These will create new opportunities which will make you feel energised and raring to go with an air of *excitement*. These new ideas will bring *potential* and an abundance of *ambition* to drive you forward.

This can also show *a new idea starting to bud* within our minds, so take notice of any new creative and innovative inklings starting to form.

The Ace of Wands shows bursts of positive energy, creative or otherwise, a bit like the universe giving you the *green light or a thumbs up* to move forwards - so grab what comes your way when you have this card. This is an *opportunity* that will be *positive*, *challenging* and may well involve a certain amount of *creativity* and *inventiveness*.

There will be a chance for personal growth, and for *fresh opportunities*, change and *movement*. This card can bring business or creative ideas, and as such a new job, career opportunity or business idea can present itself.

If you want *a new start* or to put plans into action, then this is your card: it tells that the time is right to do so, as this card comes with a burst of energy, and a full tank of enthusiasm to run on - it just needs to be developed. Bringing a time to *act with an idea* or opening we are being given.

This card also represents a phallic symbol, showing *a new sexual attraction* or need for physical intimacy which has not been acted upon. It can also bring *new friendships* which are fun, energised and entertaining.

There is a spark of passion for another person, yet of course, it can also show *a spark of attraction to an idea in any aspect of life where you feel inexplicably drawn to and unable to hold back from*.

Ace of Wands: Reversed

Reversed, the Ace of Wands states that we should *wait before making any decisions: now is not the time to put any new plans into action*. You're too busy, too distracted or failing to direct your energy to make your ideas succeed. The thumbs up is now *a thumbs down* with an amber light in place. This is not an outright no to ideas, but more of a *get your act together* energy.

The ideas you have may not be practical but rather fanciable pie-in-the-sky scenarios, and *bad ideas* will not work in bringing you what you want, leaving you feeling *frustrated* rather than excited.

There will be *no fresh start, and no new or productive ideas* to help you move forwards, so expect *delays*.

A lack of direction will hold you back, often leaving you feeling physically tired and with little ambition and desire, due to *a lack of confidence*.

Sexually, this card indicates that *sexual impulses should be put on hold*, as a relationship is either not suitable with a lack of drive or attraction getting in the way. Problems can manifest themselves sexually, including male fertility issues, or *male/sexual health problems*.

It can also indicate *a lack of creative energy*, such as writer's block, or any time in life when *a new idea is really needed but cannot be created*.

TWO OF WANDS

The Two of Wands pictures a man standing on the castle ramparts, one wand behind him, the other grasped in his hand. In the other, he holds a globe as he gazes out to the horizon.

He stands high on the castle overlooking the village below. Standing on the ramparts, his mind is in a bit of a creative battle, yet he is on high ground, and all is peaceful below, so his needs are based on desire and not necessarily on need. The grey contemplative sky shows us a thinking mind in action.

Below the castle is a village. The field is ploughed and ready to be sown, but he does not wish to wait for the slow approach of the Pentacles, as he wants to get moving and to see the world before he settles. Houses and a church are nestled amongst the woodland along a road, so his environment is secure, even idyllic; everything he needs is at his fingertips, but he has desires which transcend those needs.

The mountains show him to be aware of the problems he may have to face. With the mountains to the right of the card, he may have serious reservations about the emotional implications of his choice, as his picturesque world stems from the wand secured behind him.

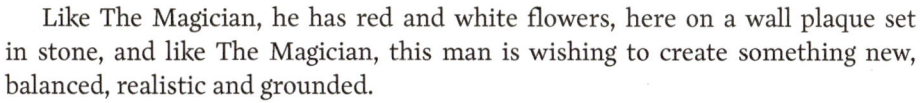

Like The Magician, he has red and white flowers, here on a wall plaque set in stone, and like The Magician, this man is wishing to create something new, balanced, realistic and grounded.

His clothes show this grounded nature, all being shades of brown. He is dressed well, but for owning a castle, he's dressed in a rather relaxed way, with no armour or furs or printed fabric: just a down-to-earth tunic, boots and cloak, as he has dressed for his next adventure. He is far more interested in his potential journey, as, in his eyes, he has not made it yet. He feels driven to reach out for more to complete him. His red hat shows his mind being full of passion for a change, driving him onwards.

One of his wands is bolted to the castle wall: this is the Ace. He has taken it and created something of value with it. Secured to the wall it shows his achievement, indicating that he wishes to keep it safe, and is likely a commitment that he needs to maintain and of which he's proud. Placed behind him, this wand represents the past. Yet the new wand is what he is seeking to explore, not the old one, as that's already his and there to be enjoyed. Being secured to the wall, the fire of this wand is tempered, which is a frustrating arrangement for fire to cope with! This is the old versus the new, often with a desire to keep both.

Yet, he could have outgrown his first wand, having learnt lessons from it which he now wishes to use elsewhere. He may have given as much as he can to the old, so while he cares for it, he is not guaranteed to keep it, which is a consideration he is also taking into account, as he could use it as a springboard to get himself moved along in life.

In his logical-thinking left hand, he holds the new wand, indicating he is giving his situation careful thought. This wand represents his need for more, his need to expand and, held in front of him, his future. This shows him in the process of weighing up his options, and this mental process is also represented by him facing the left of the card. He has managed to maintain his original idea and wishes to continue achieving, as wands cannot stand still. His enterprising nature urges him to continue growing, driven by a need to expand his world. This can bring restlessness and even wanderlust, a simple desire to leave and go and find his destiny elsewhere. The wand rests on top of the wall, so his pondered changes are only possible due to his current achievements. The saying with this card is often *'Should I stay, or should I go?',* or even *'Should I expand or should I not?'*

In his right emotional hand, he holds up the world; he desires movement, a new chapter and he wishes to feel liberated and excited by a new challenge, but he will not rush into anything. He wishes all of the qualities of The World card and is seeking a way forward to claim them. The globe will determine possible directions for his ambition; the world is, as they say, his oyster, but he needs to map it out. He's aware he will have to actively pursue goals if he wants more and is restless within this longing to achieve, as he knows that for his two wands to grow, he needs to change his current position, which will be felt emotionally. His first wand he rushed towards with excitement, unable to contain himself, yet with this second wand, more thought is needed. There is no hurrying, no exuberant anticipation, as this one is not about the thrill but long-term security. He needs to look at his real options, deliberate and make a wise yet also a creative choice.

In front of him is a shoreline, which he is looking over the world in his hands to view. He could be looking at a new distant land to adventure to, or across an inlet, or even just to the shore, but he wishes to experience new things. He values what he has and does not wish to make a mistake but to add to his experiences. He could take it all with him or bring the new idea to his current place once found; or, of course, he could just leave it all behind and move on, taking with him what he has learnt. Either way, he wishes to explore his options and potential, as he knows now that he has the drive to achieve if he aims for it. But first, a decision is needed.

Numerological value - **TWO** = Balance, harmony and interaction.

IN A NUTSHELL

There will be restlessness with an urge for movement and change: you need to decide what path to take.

In order to grow or develop, you need to expand and push out into new areas. Potential needs action to see how far it can be taken; now is about making sure the grass is not greener on the other side, and that you are balanced in your view of a new opportunity or a desire to create one.

Two of Wands: Upright

The Two of Wands brings feelings of **restlessness**, with a need for change and a move from your current situation. What may once have been an idea, is now a realised goal providing the groundwork for **something else to call to you and spark your interest**.

You will wish to improve your situation, as you understand that more is needed to help yourself or for a situation to succeed. This shows a journey of personal freedom, of **wishing a new chapter in life**, or staying and adding more to what you have, or leaving and heading for new shores, new goals or a new aspect to your life.

This card shows control over **future plans**, leaving you deciding which direction to move in while **weighing up the pros and cons**. These plans may still be in the development stage and not yet put into action, yet if they have been, you will still need to think a bit more. Whatever your plans are, this card shows that you have all you need to make a wise move and **a balanced choice**.

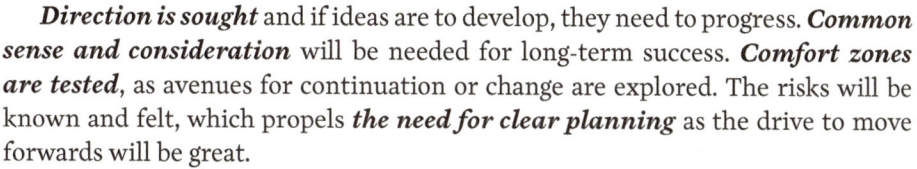

Direction is sought and if ideas are to develop, they need to progress. **Common sense and consideration** will be needed for long-term success. **Comfort zones are tested**, as avenues for continuation or change are explored. The risks will be known and felt, which propels **the need for clear planning** as the drive to move forwards will be great.

The Two of Wands also represents **the building and growth of new partnerships,** business, creative or personal and a sign that they are going well with plenty of room and potential for growth.

The Two of Wands can also represent **house moves** and even **moves to other countries, emigration and travel overseas.**

Two of Wands: Reversed

Reversed, the Two of Wands shows *a worry about branching out* and taking an idea to the next stage. There may be *fears and concerns about not having enough potential and failure*, or even if the energy and knowledge are available to move forwards, generally showing *a lack of confidence*. This can all lead to *obsessively over-planning* and not getting anywhere.

There is *indecisive* energy to this card, and there can be *a lack of options* for the changes needed, yet there is still *the desire to start something new*. In response, there can be *rash decisions*, as ideas are jumped onto simply to soothe *frustration*, which will lead to *mistakes* due to *not thinking before acting*.

There can be an over-enthusiastic attitude that leaves little thought to plans or ability being fuelled by irritation at not succeeding with an ambition: the desire for change or growth that leads us to take *action for action's sake. Acting impatiently* leads to disappointment, as important details are ignored as you rush ahead with such things. *Wanderlust* is in play as the grass is seen as greener on the other side.

This card is a sign *you need to be honest with yourself*, as if you allow disappointment in your life to lead you, it will end in wasting time and feeling more discontent, and you may lose things you wish to change.

Relationships both business and personal will suffer due to *cutting corners*, leaving *others feeling a lack of trust in your abilities.*

Travel and moves will not go well or at all; poor planning or not taking notice of important information could lead you astray.

THREE OF WANDS

The Three of Wands shows a man standing on a large rock, with his three wands looking out over an estuary or port.

He stands on a rocky outcrop overlooking the sea below, showing he has the high ground as before. He can see the bigger picture of his goals and with the distant mountains also any pitfalls and problems. Yet the mountain range is far in the distance and so he isn't perceiving that any problems will arise. From the castle, he could see the ocean from afar, but now, he is out in the world, having left the safety of his ramparts rather than holding one in his hand.

An estuary is a place where rivers come together before leading out to an open sea, representing all the strands of his hard work coming together. A port is a place of commerce, of far-off places meeting, joining and trading, a place from which he can set sail towards his ideas.

He has spread his wings and taken his wands out into the world, but he's still not standing on fertile land, so this is progress based on a well-made decision even if the results are yet to be felt. He does not want to be vulnerable while he puts it all into action; he is full of well-grounded certainty in his plans and his rock makes sure he can stay focused on everything about him as he works from solid foundations, even if roots are not yet formed. He has opened his horizon, expanded his view of his world and here he can watch the progress of his long-term goals. He has made optimistic, positive choices and is now starting to build and wait for the results, full of optimism for his future.

His clothes are bright, and gaudy now, no longer brown, showing him brimming with positive energy, showing others his confident, creative and expansive mind, which is ready for action. His white headband is his link to his intuitive mind and sincerity, and although dressed in brightly coloured clothes, he is no fool, but someone inspired and wise to his own wishes. His sleeve is a silver blue in this original image, bulked about the elbow, looking like armour. As such, it would show him fighting for what he wants, with his right arm showing him reaching for what he wants with direct action and fully emotionally invested. If it were a blue sleeve, it would show his ability to communicate and his faith in his actions, and being on his right creative side, his emotional intent. He has the gift of the gab and will be able to talk to the hearts of others as he talks with passion, and so is an ideal salesperson. His red cloak is his drive and enthusiasm, with the green wrap showing his earthly nature, his need to create in the real world, and also a calm, logical outlook as it's on his left. The black and yellow checked sash show his confidence and potential balance; it makes me think of a racing flag, showing caution is needed, and he is indeed in it to win it, and is watching issues progress with focused attention. In this original image of the Three of Wands, strands of his sash, probably tassels, are seen blowing in the breeze to his right, which are missing in other versions of the deck, symbolising his current achievements and rank and showing us that he is standing where he is due to his own efforts, as well as with the recognition of others, which is also true for the symbolism of his sash. Blowing to the right of the card, they show his emotional connection towards his goals and a desire to not go backwards in life but to stay advancing forwards. He wears purple shoes, so the steps he takes are with wisdom, confidence and purpose.

His three wands form a triangle, a symbol for fire, so he stands within his element, bringing together his mind, body and emotions. He is not lost in his desires but ready for his creations to come to fruition. Behind him are the last two wands, set upright on the strong secure rocks, and together with his past and his decision, he looks forwards.

The wand he holds supports him. It is not held in front but on his right side, so he has an emotional investment in his goals; this is not all about power and prestige but also about feeling good and being happy. This wand may be his selling stick, which he uses to tell others of his wonderful plans.

The sky and sea are yellow, a colour of confidence and assured personal identity, a colour also associated with fire. The card may depict sunrise or sunset, and whichever one it is, it brings peace of mind, as his decision-making comes to an end, yet he may be at the start or the end of his wait depending on it being dawn or dusk. All that is now needed is patience as events manifest themselves and he cannot control them once they have set sail; after all, they could sink. Yet he has absolute faith, as the sea is dead calm.

We see three ships at sea, the ships he has sent to worldly places; for boats to come in, first they need to set sail. Once they come back and are unloaded, he will realise his harvest; until then, he must wait to see how his ideas or invested energy pan out. For now, he knows what he wants and has put his plans into action. The three ships show his active, creative mind and that he is on a creative journey seeking success.

He cannot achieve this without outside help at this stage. Wands are happily communicative and found discussing and seeking outside views, trading in enthusiasm and goals. Together, he and the ship's captains are pursuing an outcome, messages are being sent out, fingers are in the right pies, and he is on top of the situation, out in the world making magic happen. Here he has taken on a leadership role as he takes control of his dreams.

His need for further change is no longer fuelled by restlessness and choice but by established confidence. He has taken the fiery energy that the Suit of Wands creates and is making something concrete which he hopes he will be able to enjoy. The present, as well as the past, are the foundations of the future here, and here we have someone noticeably confident in their ability to achieve their long-term goals.

Numerological value - THREE = Growth, creativity and productivity.

IN A NUTSHELL

A good choice or decision has been made. Be confident in what you wish to do.

You know what you want, so go for it only if you can see the bigger picture. Get ready to take a step forward, as your plans for the future are definitely underway.

Three of Wands: Upright

The Three of Wands shows **confidence over decisions made** and that you know what you want. By moving forwards with your idea and plans, you will not undo any of what you have already built up but add to it generously if all goes well.

If you have made a choice, then this card shows that **a good decision has been made**.

If you have a goal in mind, its rewards will be in sight, as all the groundwork has been laid, and you can move forwards with plans as long as you **stay focused and are patient**.

Everything will have enough momentum to carry you forwards, which allows you the opportunity to think about the bigger picture of where you wish to ultimately end up, leaving you able to set longer-term goals as a result. **You are in the middle of an idea, plan or project which you are passionate about**.

There is plenty of creative energy available, leading to **success in work and creative undertakings**. Although there is still a need for continued hard work, it will be viewed as a welcomed challenge, as an inspired idea has brought you to where you wish to be. **Plans are definitely underway**.

The Three of Wands has a general feeling of **satisfaction based on achievements as you wait for your ships to come in,** as here you are creating your own pathway with **dedication and invention**.

Any partnerships forged will be healthy and rewarding. Leadership will pay off. If you wish to direct a situation or relationship of any kind, it will be received with enthusiasm.

Overseas travel or dealings can also be shown, especially if linked to your choices.

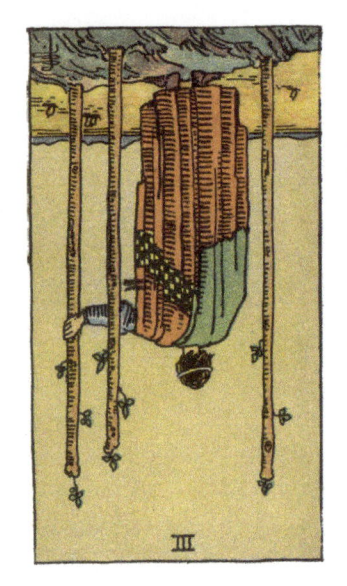

Three of Wands: Reversed

Reversed, the Three of Wands card shows the *failure of dreams and ideas.* This concerns any area of life that energy and time have been invested in.

This card shows *idealism* over projects rather than realism - a bit like *jumping the gun.* So those ships may have sunk or been empty as they came into port, or there is even the chance that they were never sent out at all! This card brings a wish to stay high and dry and not take risks as he may look over that cliff and see the fall rather than the potential.

Ideas will not come to anything, and *plans should be rethought.* By being *unprepared,* you will not succeed, and *bad decisions* have been made.

You may have misrepresented your ideas to others or been misled as to how beneficial something would be, as partnerships or relationships will be based on self-serving natures. However excited you have felt about your plans, *others about you would not have shared your enthusiasm, taking away some of the support and momentum needed.*

There is the energy of being *distracted* with this card. If you need to be putting plans into action, they may be best left for a while, or *opportunities will be missed* as equally as they will be met with *poor judgement.* You may be overstretched and have too much to contend with.

If you wish to achieve a specific aim, then try later and *get goals into perspective.*

FOUR OF WANDS

The Four of Wands shows a scene of celebration, complete with a garland. In the background are two girls waiting to welcome and greet us with bouquets of flowers.

The four wands stand like a doorway, inviting us in. In a line, they act like foundations for a building, representing security and balance, a very stabilising nature, which here can embody the home, and a square, representing the four walls of a house. The wands here show us the footings, the building and the creating of a firm structure, a time for us to concrete our plans. They welcome us in to celebrate what we have achieved, as now we can really start to build. Wands do not like restriction, yet they are shown with plenty of room about them to grow and expand, and they cannot let that go past without the raising of a glass or three, and some applause. These wands are still sprouting, symbolising that more growth is possible, as we can create more as we have a lot to build with.

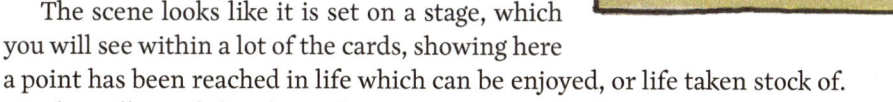

The scene looks like it is set on a stage, which you will see within a lot of the cards, showing here a point has been reached in life which can be enjoyed, or life taken stock of.

The yellow of the sky and, in some versions, also the ground, the stage, is linked to fire, showing a place we are driven to, a place where we feel confidence, a place we care deeply for, as this is home.

Between the four wands, a grapevine hangs studded with flowers and fruits, showing us abundance, plenty and a time not for harvest, but to enjoy what has been achieved, as now is not about harvesting our rewards but having a pit-stop. We are in a way returning home in this card; we have gone in search of our goals and here, we can celebrate all we have created for ourselves. The flowers are in bloom, so this is a time to capture the beauty, and know that everything is growing well. There are two red roses in the centre symbolising love, passion and unity, as everything here is sincere and from the heart. Two of the wands have red ribbons tied to them, showing unity, strength and ties that bind, so we are going to those we love here. Tying ribbons is symbolic of hope and being red, of love and passion, and a prize to be enjoyed and shared.

Here we are now outside of the grey castle wall. We are also on the ground, giving humbling energy. We can stop aiming high for a while and relax, as the castle indicates our current success. This moment is about feeling free as we join with others. A time to feel safe and secure. The castle has five red roofs. One is a house, symbolic of where the heart lies; a home, a place where we can be who we are. The other four are turrets in red that show passion in defending what is loved, and so here is a safe place to rest, a time of feeling protected. Four of them bring back the sense of security we get from our perception of home.

To the right side is a bridge surrounded by pink rose bushes. The bridge takes us back to happiness, home and loved ones, healing rifts. It shows the emotional need for togetherness, unifying everything we have. It welcomes us back to the heart of things. The pink roses bring gratitude and affection, offering thanks as we have not taken any of our luck for granted.

Two women greet us with three bouquets, two with pink flowers and the other with lemons taken straight from the tree. The three bunches show us continued creativity, with the flowers representing new beginnings and warmth. The lemons bring cleansing, a time to touch base and enhance our sense of well-being, heightening our senses. The two women show unity, and an excited welcoming committee, both pure in intent with their white dresses: one faithful, sincere, wanting to communicate and share ideas in blue; the other in a burgundy robe shows ambition. With the flowers in their hair, they are grounded and sincere with an invested energy, so both want this situation to continue to succeed.

The people in the background may still be making the arrangements for this happy time, showing a need for preparation still. Yet with their arms raised, the celebrations may also have begun, as they know it will all go well.

This card shows the time to come home, a time to be at home and a time to enjoy home and the relationship that it offers us. Home can be whatever that means to us, as can family; and here we can celebrate, set down roots and enjoy how far things have come for both ourselves and others. Situations celebrated here will be at a stage of importance, which can bring all manner of traditional celebrations or even improvements to our surroundings.

Numerological value - **FOUR** = Realisation, will-power and logic.

IN A NUTSHELL

You are given time to enjoy your domestic life and be with loved ones and friends. There will be an improvement to your surroundings and a time to celebrate with others. Maybe you will have a holiday, maybe some DIY or even mark an event, but you will feel honoured to belong, so have a good time!

Feelings of happiness and pride in yourself and your home life will boost your confidence.

Four of Wands: Upright

The Four of Wands brings us *a time of comfort, celebration and enjoyment of domestic life*. This can be in any area where you are surrounded by those who care for you, and you for them.

At times, this card can come as a surprise, so **something delightful out of the blue**.

The security of your home life will be important: you will feel settled and content within personal situations. If arising with any relevant Pentacle cards, then maybe the financial security of the home is an issue of importance, such as mortgages.

This may lead to new or improved surroundings, so **DIY projects or house or work moves** are possible, as are **holidays**. Either way, your surroundings will improve, and you will feel settled and happy with those around you.

There is stability within the family, bringing *family gatherings and celebrations*, a time to get together to enjoy achievements and goals being reached. This can include weddings and christenings, as this card has the energy of joining and uniting.

A time to feel safe and relaxed, and while action still calls to you, this card shows **a time to rest**, with the security of knowing that **everything is fine** as you enjoy **a happy and peaceful time**.

In short, **all is well on the home front!**

Four of Wands: Reversed

Reversed, the Four of Wands shows **an unconventional** approach to relationships and domestic arrangements. This may cause difficulties arriving from others as they do not understand your circumstances. Either it does not suit them or what they feel that you are entitled to, and so **other people's views will cause friction**.

There will be a lack of cohesion in domestic settings, you may find that **unhappiness and a lack of security** are causing issues.

You may not fit in with other people's ideals or plans, so you may be the **black sheep** of the situation, as equally as being affected by someone else's independent streak.

Another aspect of this card is that it brings **domestic upheavals** (including accidental loss/breakage of property or general disruption) and possibly even stressful house moves.

Although it may lack the excitement of the upright card, it does show acceptance as you get used to domestic changes and shows *a time of adjustment to changes.*

If you wish to get married or otherwise committed, then wait for the dust to settle if any problems have held you up, as, reversed, this card brings *cancellations, postponements and delays to events and celebrations.*

FIVE OF WANDS

The Five of Wands brings us five children or young adults battling and play-fighting with five wands.

The sky is blue in this card, so while they seem to be battling, there is not a cloud in the sky. What appears to be a tense situation is no more than an exchange of ideas, as no serious issues are afoot here.

They stand on uneven ground, with each believing their point of view to be grounded and valid. At any stage, any of them may trip while trying to express their opinion, causing a bruised knee here and there. The grass is green in newer versions of the deck, but here in the original it is a mix of brown earth and grass, showing that some ideas may be more valid than others; some may grow, others may not.

The wands themselves in this battle do not even touch; they are waved, brandished and held with eagerness as each person thinks that their wand needs to be the focus of attention. The wands here are sprouting, showing these to be the budding views, ideas or ponderings of those taking part. Wands like to communicate and here the wands show an exchange of views, with a touch of a clash here and there. The wands show ideas with merit, so each person has his own Ace in his hands.

The five young people are all brightly dressed. The colours of these five battlers differ in a lot of decks yet the result is the same.

At the back, the one in the blue-checked tunic with yellow sleeves shows someone wanting to talk, filled with optimism. Checks show a balanced outlook, so he may have thought hard about his idea. His red shoes show him taking passionate steps to get what he wants to be noticed.

The one in green, to his right with grey sleeves - in other versions of the deck he has yellow sleeves, for his mental actions, acting with thought - will be a compassionate soul working from the heart, full of contemplation for his idea. His yellow shoes show him taking intellectual steps towards his aim.

To the very left, in shades of brown and yellow, will be someone down to earth and may have a practical or even a spiritual idea with his white headband. His shoes are also yellow, showing thought given to his goal. He has red tights, so he will be driven by strong desires to put things into action. (He is in shades of brown in other versions of the card.)

The boy in the middle is dressed in red and is the only one wearing a hat like the Page of Wands. He may not wish his ideas to be interrupted by other views or logic; his red tunic also shows him to be driven. His shoes are green, which adds some grounding to his passion, so there will be some merit to what he brings to the kerfuffle.

The young man in the bottom right of the card wears a blue spotted tunic. His sleeves are yellow, and his tights are light green. He is wanting to be noticed as different, as an individual, maybe a bit frivolous with a fantastic, yet unrealistic idea; he may also be the one full of innovative, unusual ideas. He has odd shoes seen here in this original image, so may have been unprepared when getting caught up in this discussion and he can show indecision about his idea or standing within the group. In some versions his shoes are brown; here they are red, so he is led by a belief in his views all the same.

So, with their different clothes, they all see the world differently. Their wands have sparked something in each of them individually and they all want to share that with enthusiasm. Each trying to sell or push their idea, but they look relaxed as they thrash out their creative energy.

There is a healthy debate going on, with them all seeking to be heard; the banging or waving of their wands can create more magic as equally as it can cause minor hold-ups. While they all show off their wands, they are not moving forwards and no new decisions are being made. They are sorting out their differences and trying to be heard above the din of each other, a bit like a fiery think-tank. Overall, this can help to decide the direction of ideas and brings in the energy and interaction of a group or another individual, yet can show a flurry of ideas within the self. All of this will aid in the achieving of a goal or aim, even if it is disrupting and initially leads you to no conclusion. Views will differ, arguments could break out and egos may very well get a bit bruised as not everyone's wishes can be accommodated.

While this is a card devoid of pain, it can show that feelings can get hurt as views or ideas are challenged. Many ideas, options or pathways may be open; and here, what direction to move into is open to debate, and with fire, things can get a bit heated.

The energy of the wands is generous and extends to all who seek it, yet when this energy is held by more than one in a situation, then difficulties will arise, everyone's drive is equal, leading to friction and niggling annoyances.

Numerological value - **FIVE** = Truth, analytical and communication.

IN A NUTSHELL

Everything will feel as if it is going wrong. You may be at odds with your ideas, or others will disagree with your wishes, leaving you frustrated as events get held up and setbacks are guaranteed.

All situations can be resolved: it is just a matter of talking with others and not ignoring what is on their minds, and a time for patience. Hold ups are resolved with debate rather than argument.

Five of Wands: Upright

The Five of Wands shows a time when *wires are crossed in communication* resulting in *trivial, petty annoyances* and *silly arguments*. Although these problems can be difficult and troublesome, they will be fleeting and quickly pass.

Decisions are met with the alternate and *differing views of others*, leaving you feeling *frustrated*.

You will have the feeling that nothing is going right when this card appears, *time will be wasted* in what you feel are meaningless pursuits or *disagreements*. Yet it is simply the views of others slowing you down as they wish to debate or add their view to the melting-pot.

There will be little or *no co-operation* within a group, but no permanent damage will be done as *issues are deliberated and debated*, which airs feelings. You will be left wishing a decision could just be made to get things moving, as *a curveball puts ideas off their stride*.

This card is a reminder that we are not lone islands, but what we do or wish for often involves others and they will want their say in how things are done, or how time is spent. Have faith in your position, but it may sometimes be quicker to listen to others and *brainstorm a situation*.

Five of Wands: Reversed

Reversed, this card shows that disputes will not be the minor problems of the upright as they will appear far more serious, showing *a complete breakdown in communication,* and you are flung into a situation where *no conclusions can be made*.

The *ridiculing and belittlement* of views may be present, *ideas are laughed at* and there is no mutual respect for the view or opinions of others, generally showing *a lack of maturity*.

You may be left *feeling intimidated* by the views of others and keep your own to yourself at a time when you will end up following another's idea rather than your own, or even losing out.

There could also be physical fights or avoidable accidents due to carelessness and arguments. Someone will not be playing fair, and *hasty words and actions will cause distress*.

Reversed, we are warned against taking rash actions based on the views of others, to take one small step at a time and to have faith in what is believed in. Now is not the time to steamroller another's views, nor to have yours discarded by others who wish to take advantage or control. *Do not let anger lead you: as with fire, it can explode into rage*.

SIX OF WANDS

The Six of Wand illustrates a triumphant man riding a white horse through a group of people who are cheering him on.

This card is referred to as the Victory Card, as our champion rides here in a parade most likely held in his honour. He wears a purple cloak, with a yellow undershirt with a sleeve and his gloves the same golden yellow, almost orange, of the horse's cape trim. Purple is a colour of success, a colour of status, so he is pleased with himself and his success, and is enjoying being celebrated as he sits proudly on his horse, head held high as he relishes the achievement of a personal goal. The yellow of his top shows his energy, his optimism and happiness. Being a colour of intellect and the mind, it shows that he has worked his way up to this position; it has little to do with chance. In other editions of the deck, our victorious man's cloak is brown, red or ruddy brown, showing a passionate, driven energy or a down-to-earth one, as the success felt is shown by other elements of the card. His brown tights and boots represent the hard work he has done to be here, he has been grounded and thoughtful with each step he has taken.

We see his face in profile, so we are not fully aware of his expression or what he is feeling, but his face is slightly looking down at the crowd below. He could be looking down with a smile, warmth and love, or with inflated pride and disdain; we cannot see, we simply are not shown the whole picture.

This is the only card outside of the Knights, The Sun and Death which has a horse, here representing freedom and rising above problems. To be a winner, he would have had to rise above many issues in most cases. Yet he is also again high in the air being above the people below, so he may be on his high horse, yet maybe just expressing the freedom that success has brought him.

The horse's cape is green trimmed with a golden yellow in the original Rider Waite Smith, yet orange or brown in others. Green is a heartfelt colour of feeling this success deep down, a sign that he is still fresh and vital, as he wants more than a one-off win yet is realistic. The yellow brings enthusiasm and is lively, happy and positive, which is shown equally with the brown or orange, as all are earthy colours showing things down to earth, anchoring them in the real world. He rides in, feeling liberated and connected to all his efforts. The reins are the same green but with eight red flames, the number of Strength and inner control, which the rider holds firmly in his hands, showing control over his passions. The horse looks up to his rider. Some say this to be a look of affection and a willingness to be controlled, others a look of sarcasm or disdain as he is coerced. Yet whichever way it is viewed, his control over his horse is an illusion, as he is only in this position above the crowd as the horse allows it. A reminder that freedom, success and even fame can be fleeting if even one single thing in our line-up changes its mind or goes awry.

The man wears a victory wreath crown made of laurel leaves; his other wreath is tied by a red ribbon to the wand he carries. The wreath of laurel leaves is a traditional symbol of success and winning; as a crown it shows his creativity and ideas have won the day, moving his life forwards as he planned. The wreath on the wand represents the opportunities he has created or taken hold of, and which have brought success because of his drive to achieve. The red ribbon he has taken from the Four of Wands shows he has been wished well by those he shares his life and success with. It's a link to those he loves and whom he's bonded to in his success. The ribbon blows in the wind, flowing forwards, showing his creative mind is already looking to the future.

The crowd's wands are set apart, into a pair and a set of three. This takes us back to the restlessness of choice with the Two of Wands and then putting plans into action with the Three, as here he will not wish to stop his success, so he will be planning his next adventure with the wand he carries, his Ace.

In the cheering crowd, we can see that not everyone is clapping for him, so his success may not impress everyone. The pair to the left of the card have wands with leaves just on the tops, so their enthusiasm may be waning as he has now moved past them and is now their history. Not everyone may be on your side and share your joy; we can see that the woman behind him looks elsewhere, to the future maybe or to the next 'thing' to clap, as his success is of no interest to her any longer. In this image of the card, we can also see that the man next to her is also looking ahead with a stressed facial expression, rather than at the rider, as is the man in blue. They may be looking at our victor's future, waiting for more success or even failure, at what his next move may be. Some may only want you on your way up, some while you are at the top and others on your way down - depending on their needs. Today's newspaper is tomorrow's bin-liner. Again, we cannot see the whole image as we cannot see the face of the person with the red hat nor the person standing behind the horse, yet this is the only one in the crowd looking at our victor. The people who hold the other three creative wands full of leaves will still be applauding him as he approaches them, but we cannot be sure of their motives, yet they applaud, creating momentum and congratulations for our rider.

Our victor has succeeded with the energy presented to him with the Ace of Wands and is confident concerning his future success, as are those around him. Others applaud his success, and he keeps looking forwards, full of optimism. He has driven himself forwards with good planning and grounded ideas; he has followed his passions and dared it all and he has won!

Numerological Value - SIX = Ease, attraction and diplomacy.

IN A NUTSHELL

Congratulations, you have won! Big or small victories, this card brings you success resulting from your efforts. This is a time to celebrate and be celebrated by others, as your success is recognised.

You will feel pride in your achievements and happily show off what you can do or have done as you have succeeded in your goals. A well-earned accomplishment!

Six of Wands: Upright

The Six of Wands is **the Victory Card!** A positive card of **accomplishment**.

This card represents **overcoming your problems, succeeding in your goals,** plus the **achievement and acknowledgement of your hard work**. A sign you have harnessed your strengths and pushed through barriers to get to where you wish to be or to have what you are aiming for.

If your success has been achieved alone, it will be felt by others, as **your efforts will pay off**. Your dedication will be rewarded as **results are positive**; if others share your journey, they too will be sharing in the glory.

As well as indicating **success,** it shows you brimming with self-confidence and brings a time to **congratulate** yourself and receive **recognition and praise** from others as they see how much you have succeeded. You will know that **you have achieved something of value,** and you will feel immensely **proud of yourself and optimistic** for the future.

If you find you doubt yourself and this card is in the layout, maybe it is time to **believe in yourself**, as you have more ability than you may think.

This card shows **you can hold your head up high and feel a sense of personal pride in what you are doing**.

Six of Wands: Reversed

Reversed, the Six of Wands tells that success is possible but there will be delays, and events may be held up and postponed. You have **rested on your laurels**, become **complacent**, not followed up with enough effort or made a move at the right time. That can indicate **negligence**, leading to success slipping through your fingers. There is **overconfidence**, having an inflated ego with **no substance** to back it up.

This card shows ***initial failure or partial success***. You will have to try again in the future if you wish to proceed with plans. ***True victory will just be out of your reach***, bringing ***frustration***.

If you are asking if another could help you succeed, this would be a no. They do not have the experience or means to support their claims and will have their own motives or agenda.

Your actions will lead others to lose faith or trust in you, so the applause you feel you deserve is not forthcoming. Bragging or getting ***over-enthusiastic*** can cause ***disloyalty or jealousy from others*** as you rub them up the wrong way.

Not everyone will be on your side when this card is reversed. If you have not been ego-driven and upset others, you may find that you have gained success, which is met with rudeness, flippancy, dislike or jealousy. Equally, others may just wish to see you fail due to their inadequacies.

SEVEN OF WANDS

The Seven of Wands shows a situation of conflict. The man standing at the top of the hill or cliff is brandishing his single wand against the six wands below.

The sky is blue, so this is a healthy situation, yet for the man standing his ground, it is looking stressful as his face suggests he is serious in his battle.

He wears a yellow shirt and green tunic, with his tights an orange-red. His yellow shirt shows his confidence which is close to his heart, his green tunic shows his sincerity about his position and the passion he is defending it with. His orange tights bring drive and energetic energy to his stance as he feels deeply about what he is defending.

Yet he wears odd footwear, one shoe and one boot, so he may have been surprised and unprepared for the challenge from below. Mismatched shoes can also show our desires and actions not connecting and not being aligned with ourselves. So here, having to struggle against the other wands may not sit easily with him as it wastes time, as equally as it could highlight those things which he needs to challenge about himself in relation to his goals.

He may be in a good position up high, but his footing may not be strong. One of his feet rests in the stream, and the other near the cliff edge, leaving the six wands presenting a real risk to his beliefs and outlook, here he is risking being toppled from his position by the competing wands below.

He stands on a chalk cliff; the grassy ground is uneven, with a stream running through it. The grass shows him grounded, yet the foot in water shows this to be an emotional situation for him. Water and fire can lead to irrational, defensive actions, as fire can be destructive, and water can lead us to feel threatened. The shallow stream will come with shallow emotions attached. If he lets his ego control him, he could lose control and an excess of water could crumble his cliff. He has one foot close to the edge, so he really needs to stay balanced or risk losing his position on the uneven ground and toppling over. Wands like to win with fiery determination: add watery emotions and you have a determined person, but he needs to stay in control and not go steaming in with anger.

On top of his cliff, he is asserting his views and showing that he is willing to fight for his beliefs. He is situated high up, which gives him an elevated view of the surroundings and he may see things unfolding that those at the bottom do not and is urging them to listen, trying to be heard over the din of his opponents. Yet the six below want to have their say, expressing themselves, trying to get to where he is and fighting their way to the top. His position is not secure, and he can easily lose his place, and others would snatch it all from him as six wands bring a victory, and here, he defends with his single Ace. Those below may see things he cannot, so each has their own unique and valid view. They are many, he is one and they want to dominate his viewpoint.

He will not come down without doing all he can to stay on top. So, words, ideas, options and solutions are thrown about, all communicating their value and beliefs. He has enthusiasm for his own creations and passionately defends his position.

We are shown a need to have courage, to be brave and stand up for what we believe in. Others will want to have their say, and they may even want what you have. This card shows a time when we need to stand our ground or risk losing what we have worked for.

Numerological value - **SEVEN** = Spiritual growth, wisdom and endurance.

IN A NUTSHELL

Stand up for what you believe in. It may be a struggle to be heard or get others to take you seriously but make a stand. If something needs to be defended, be prepared for what that means. Don't hesitate to put your foot down.

Others may disagree, others may compete with you, be passionate and determined. Have faith in your abilities and stand your ground.

Seven of Wands: Upright

The Seven of Wands appears when you must *fight for what you believe in*, for what is rightfully yours or for what you understand to be the truth. A time in life when we need to **stand up for ourselves**, our values and our beliefs. This is a card of **determination and of not giving in to others**, as you are called to passionately defend a point, or wish to be heard by others.

You will need to **protect** what you value which can leave you **feeling challenged by a situation** or by others, and which can even **catch you off guard**, yet this is a time to **stay focused**.

The Seven of Wands assures us that a positive outcome is obtainable if we **persevere** and be true to what counts within the situation, but we must listen to others in return. **Events will move quickly**, with others wanting to have their say, so your view will not be the only one being shouted out.

This can be in any area of life where others wish to express themselves, as they are not accepting of the stance you have taken or the route your life is going.

Conversations may be heated as emotions will lead to debates, with ***others questioning situations***.

Competition in the workplace and ***being under pressure*** and tested, in general, are also shown here, but this card shows that you have the determination to win through. Success will be found in the ***faith you have in your abilities***.

Seven of Wands: Reversed

The Seven of Wands reversed shows ***a lack of confidence***, and that you are ***letting others take advantage***. You will be ***indecisive*** and lack personal direction, feeling that your views are not important to those around you, leaving you ***feeling intimidated or undervalued***.

You will be ***overwhelmed*** by demands made on you, and ***you will back down*** to conflicting or opposing views due to ***anxiety and stress***.

Others may gang up on you and play on your weaknesses to get what they want. You will feel worn down by the demands of others as they intervene in your life. You may be surrounded by ***bullies***, or those with more dominant personalities, yet equally ***a lack of personal boundaries*** may be the cause.

You are, however, in a good position to succeed but any ***opposition to your plans will be more successful*** due to you not putting yourself forward in an appropriate manner, if at all. This could show someone who is ***shy*** or has ***low self-esteem*** and with ***a lack of faith in their abilities***.

If your self-esteem is fine, this can show you being ***toppled from power, replaced, or removed from an aspect of your life***. Others will not help you, and ***embarrassment*** is shown. A time when you will lose your standing in a situation, showing that you may have been ***too confident*** and ***misjudged other's*** strengths.

If you are going forwards with any plans which mean competition, such as a new job, or anything where others may also wish to gain, then ***the competition will win***.

UNDERSTANDING TAROT

EIGHT OF WANDS

This card shows eight budding wands flying through the blue sky.

The clear sky shows no obstacles in the way, and nothing to stop what is coming with these eight wands soaring through the air at high speed as they head back down to earth. They are moving so fast that you may not see them coming until the last moment as they land in a flurry of fiery excitement. Arriving out of the blue, they can be a surprise as they land in your lap, especially if things have been going a bit slow of late. They represent the arrival of action, communication and movement.

In the sky, they are full of movement and speed, showing unstoppable energy in action. They will either crash and burn or land well and can indicate that events and changes are still 'up in the air'. They bring a wave of activity, where we need to think on our feet and be ready, and it can feel that everything is happening at once. Being wands, their sight in the sky will bring optimism as progress is finally coming our way. The action of them flying gives a push of momentum to situations, with new solutions, opportunities and news souring above us and landing into our lives.

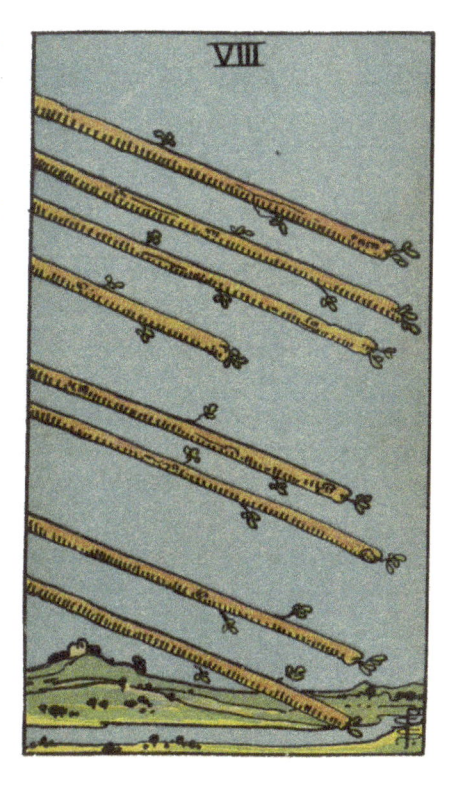

Events represented by the wands come to their creative conclusion here, as energy flows towards a goal and nothing will get in the way. The energy contained by the wands is released, bringing speediness into play, as life gathers force with excitement and rush. When these wands land, they will give us substance, something more than ideas or enthusiasm to work with and enjoy, as the wands are budding, showing a ripeness to a situation. Now is the time to have what you have worked hard for and created, a time to get ready for some fast movement, results and action.

The wands are in three sets, four and two twos. Eight is a number which brings determination, yet one which can bind us. Here it is watered down with the separation of the wands. Four wands bring happiness, as it gives us The Four of Wands and a time of celebration, here flying through the air, some positive news which will make us feel wanted, loved and excited. The other four are divided into twos. This may give you ideas that will excite you, yet will need to be evaluated and even chosen between, as new ideas could challenge ones that you may already have made. Ones which get you motivated and are hard to resist as they arrive twofold, or even two separate issues to choose from, the latter is not really in line with this card, as it is not about duality; but with two twos, who can say? We can also look at this as the four wands being separated as bringing news of others creating their way in the world. News which promotes togetherness, or people from far-flung places separated from those they love simply by distance.

The river below the wands shows emotions travelling and flowing, so a balance of excitement with passion. Traditionally, this card can also indicate travel over water, or air travel, as the wands travel from one side of the water to the other. Yet they can bring the arrival of many things, as they love to communicate, laugh, have fun, build and create, showing all your endeavours coming together with busy, happy energy.

The house nestled in the hills represents security, but the house has no roof, which shows that things may not always bode well. If the wands crash-land, the problems of the past can revisit. Yet on the positive side, it shows the past being left behind with a new flurry of action, and it may be past worries which make these wands so welcomed, as those worries are risen above and left behind.

Far away in the distance is a hint of the mountains, so far away that their problems are not an issue either.

This card brings success, communication, change and movement, a whirl of activity. Energy is in abundance and spare time will be short, as this card shows one, at last, not thinking, planning, or imagining but doing.

Numerological Value – **EIGHT** = Change, challenge, honesty and determination.

IN A NUTSHELL

Expect communications, things to speed up as events come to a quick conclusion. Delays will end and things may get busy, so stay focused.

Little will stand in your way, but remember that communication is key to success!

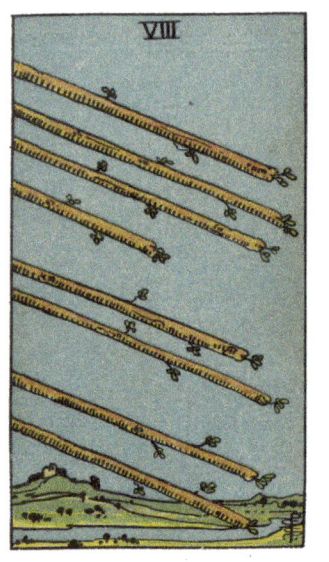

Eight of Wands: Upright

The Eight of Wands brings **an end to any delays**; life will be on the move with a **busy** and productive time promised.

This card brings **a time of excitement, with a lot of rush**, action and occupied time. **A time to strike while the proverbial iron is hot!**

Events and issues within your life will be sped up, which means that **conclusions or solutions will be reached sooner rather than later** with the arrival of this card. This card brings an increase in all manner of **communication**. Your life will revolve around the phone, letters, emails, conversations and messages being passed.

Events are set in motion; there is no trying to change outcomes with this card as it will cause chaos, so enjoy the ride and prepare for a positive outcome. Everything is going smoothly. *If new opportunities come your way to move things along, grab them!*

When it comes to love, act, don't wait - jump in. The same goes with anything you want: now is a time to not wait for it to come to you, but a time to reach for it with confidence.

The Eight of Wands *may also represent air or land travel*, so do not be surprised if you get the chance to see different places.

Eight of Wands: Reversed

Reversed, this card indicates that you will be *too busy and too rushed*. You will find you have too little time and too much to do, leaving you feeling *overworked*.

Events will feel that they are *up in the air* and *obstacles* will be presented. What you hoped would be easy proves difficult, so this is a time to *slow down* and *rethink plans*, look for new ways to move forwards.

Where love or any area of life is concerned, this is not a positive card as it brings the green-eyed monster, *jealousy*, into existence.

This card will leave you *frustrated, annoyed and impatient*. Complications could lead you into *making mistakes* as you try to speed things up, resulting in *chaos as the wands crash*. All you can do is be patient and wait for a situation to resolve naturally.

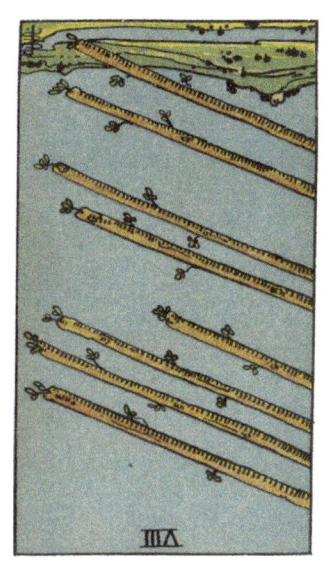

Expected news will either not arrive, or arrive and be misunderstood or be damaging. *Communications will go awry*, so this is not a good time to have serious conversations or deal with anything official.

Reversed, it also shows *news going out*, showing that you will need to deliver some bad, awkward or disappointing news to another person.

NINE OF WANDS

The Nine of Wands shows us a man with a bandaged head, his sleeves rolled up, holding and leaning on a wand. Behind him are the other eight wands neatly lined up, and temporarily planted in the ground, bringing a pause in the action. These wands show his problems, commitments and obligations, as fire can be attracted to too many things, giving us too much to contend with. Fire can burn us out, leaving many things to finish or deal with at a time when we simply cannot cope, so everything just fizzles out for a while.

The eight wands are planted to grow alone for a short time, yet they will need to be faced and finished at some stage, as nine seeks completion. He could well have put too much effort into situations and ideas which have not gone as planned, leaving him feeling a failure, but he's not willing to give up. He is either standing his ground due to stubbornness or due to determination and willpower.

The planted wands form a barrier or fence, yet he does not stand behind them, so he is not seeking to hide, as with the wand he holds, he wishes to stay in the game but stop for a while to get himself together. He has no desire to stay where he is, but as a matter of well-being is protecting himself and his wands for a short duration, as he has battled and needs time out.

His green boots show him to be sincere and feel an emotional response to his situation, he is tired emotionally as well as creatively and physically. His grey shirt shows his contemplative nature or situation, which in some versions of the decks is shown as white. He is standing sincere in the defence of his energy and time, with his rolled-up sleeves showing him ready to fight and to defend his wands however worn down he may feel. His brown tunic shows him being quite practical, and so knows a break is needed yet stands guard all the same.

His bandage shows he has been knocked down, maybe more than once; his self-esteem and ego may have taken a bit of beating leaving his mind in need of a recharge and time to re-evaluate events. Being askew, right now he may not be seeing things straight. The white of the bandage about his head is like a crown, and so he may be feeling spiritually and mentally defeated. He will be trying to clarify his position, needs and wishes as he hopes he can fulfil all his duties and responsibilities when his energy returns. Feeling battle-weary, he is still in a good position, but for a while, he must stop, heal and then he can move on, and above all else, he will need patience.

His facial expression also invites others to take him seriously with a serious-minded stare aimed at keeping away those he wants at bay. He stands tense, one shoulder up, defensive and looking to the left of the card, so his thoughts will be questioning his situation and anyone he feels may attack his position. In this image of the card shown, the whites of his eyes are yellow, which can show envy or jealousy. Feelings of insecurity over what he is fighting for, or the general distribution of those things he wishes for. As with the clear blue sky and green hills, there may be no enemies at the gate at all. Yet looking to his own right, he will feel the emotional impact of his situation.

From his appearance, he has suffered but learnt a lesson and does not wish to repeat past mistakes. He has inner strength represented by the wand which supports him; he may be down and out of the game at the moment, but he has not given up as he will fight back and defend his position if he must. He is not retreating or walking away, as he still has passion and new solutions or ideas he wishes to look into, but the issues he has behind him need to be worked on before he starts anything new.

The calm sky and hills tell us that while he is stressed, feeling under attack and defeated, all his problems can be worked out. This card shows a time to step back and protect your energy, as issues may be unresolved, and perseverance is needed. This is a time for strength and stamina, the energy to see things through, yet for now, energy should be conserved, as you just need to trust your instincts and be confident.

Numerological Value - **NINE** = Inspiration, honesty and understanding.

IN A NUTSHELL

Patience is needed. You may have won the battle, but not the war. You're not through yet, now is the time to re-evaluate matters. Times may be hard, but you cannot give in.

Take a breather and catch your breath but stay focused as things can still complete or go your way.

Nine of Wands: Upright

The Nine of Wands tells you to **be patient, wait** and **stay alert** to changes happening around you, rather than get involved and wear yourself out or down.

Times have been hard, but you should be prepared to continue fighting and pushing your way forward by simply **standing firm and being true to yourself**. Past failure will be in your mind and **caution** will be shown. If you need advice, then find some. Use this time to **think and re-evaluate plans**.

Events will not be moving while problems are sorted out. The planted wands represent problems which need to be resolved, situations have come a long way, yet **the finish**

line is slow to reach. You are in an excellent position to improve your future as *you have learnt from the past* and you're willing to *stay on track* however hard it has been. Focusing on what others have can add to a problem, as *you worry about losing more ground within an issue*.

This card can show loyalty to a cause, person or actions taken and you will not leave *a difficult or tiresome situation* just because you have run out of steam for a while. Others may be counting on your help, but now is a time to *put yourself first*.

Try not to involve yourself in anything that will sap your energy levels during this time, as *tiredness* is a companion to this card. You will be aware of your power and determination, but wise enough to know *you need to sit out some battles*.

Nine of Wands: Reversed

Reversed, the Nine of Wands indicates that you are *surrounded by problems* and see no way of dealing with them, leaving you feeling *overwhelmed*. Any new problems which come your way may be *the straw that breaks the camel's back*.

Issues that require commitment, time and energy to complete will bring *apprehension*, as you will not know how to find the resources, momentum or knowledge to benefit the situation.

This card leaves you *feeling defeated, exhausted and like it's all a lost cause*. You will be *tackling problems from the wrong direction* with no real desire to see it through, as the energy cannot be found.

Creatively and physically, life will be at a lull, causing anxiety.

Often there can be *unfounded mistrust and suspicion* in the air, which results in *being defensive* and confronting those who care as you feel under attack. The fire of the wands can break out here into anger, being touchy and irritable. There are *feelings of unfairness*, as you feel that others have more than you do, which can lead to feelings of insecurity and envy, and even full-blown jealousy.

Past mistakes are repeated and *the past needs to be put into perspective*. Until this is done, there will be doubt, indecision and obstacles ahead as *you blame yourself* for getting things wrong.

TEN OF WANDS

The Ten of Wands shows a man struggling with his ten wands, as he heads towards a town.

The man advances forwards, showing the strain of his load, with his back strained under the pressure as if he has the weight of the world upon his shoulders. His feet are steadily making big routine strides as he shoulders his responsibilities, yet his face is hidden within the wands so he cannot see where he is going, nor can we see his face. Those he walks toward will see his creations, the things he feels deeply responsible for, before they see him. He cradles them in his arms, holds them close, yet they blind him to his actual direction of travel as they obscure his view. He cannot see his goal ahead, but he knows it is there, and the prospect of a successful arrival pushes him forwards, regardless of being blind to his pathway.

Completion with the wands' energy will mean a lot of responsibility to carry along with the success. His ideas, loves and creations need to be maintained and often it's shouldered alone due to fire's independent streak. Each wand has turned into a heavy commitment or problem as he has taken on too much. He may not have foreseen how heavy some of his creations could become, but he carries on regardless due to a sense of responsibility. The wands cross near his left hand, so they are linked as one; he cannot leave any behind singularly, as his commitments are to each as they all matter to him equally. Being held by his left hand, his sense of responsibility is not emotional but practical, which to him is logical. In this original image, we can see only nine of the ten wand bases. In newer decks, the tenth wand's end is shown. The nine show that, primarily, he seeks completion. Near his feet, we see him pursuing an outcome, even if he can no longer see it clearly.

His dull green tights show he feels a lot for his wands, his prized collection as he has fought hard for them. They show he is trying to move towards more growth, but he has lost touch with his environment and his original sense of direction. He will know that he is walking in roughly the right direction, and so aims himself with hope. In some decks, he is also shown with a red belt aimed at showing his determination and passion at the centre of his being. His tunic is a dull red in this image, shades of brown or red/brown in other versions, as he genuinely strives to move forwards and reach his destination, showing his determination to succeed. He has a driven nature which may contain some greed, ego, martyrdom and selfishness. Being a dull red, it also shows tiredness, loss of focus, and his struggle for balance, and so he may regret his determined striving nature. His brown shoes bring in his need for growth, to proceed, to do his best and put down roots; they are his grounding element. So, at one point all these wands would have been easily juggled, as his intent with each was pure, and hard work was not an issue. Under all this is a grey shirt, a sign that he is deeply thinking about his load, even if he does not feel able to stop and put it down.

His hair is blond, sometimes shown as a strawberry blond, rather than the dark hair so far in this suit. Blond hair generally signifies someone young, or inexperienced, maybe with some frivolity thrown in. This shows him leading himself forwards without wisdom but hope at this stage. He may have collected all these wonderful wands and is very near to his completed goal, yet he cannot reach it. He may fear losing face as well as faith as he keeps going, and his lack of experience may well be telling him that he is successful, wise and doing the only thing possible to get to his finish line. Yet, to have these wands, he will not be devoid of wisdom, so that which he does have may come from humbly realising how much his enterprising nature weighs on him, or, simply from how he views his ability to have obtained his abundant set of wands. If the former, he will have a deeper understanding of himself, if not, he may well never reach the town and be overwhelmed by the stress and learn an even harder way.

The wands are heavy, yet he does not put them down and go find help. While this may show a strong-willed person, it can also show stubbornness and insecurity. If he puts them down to find assistance, they may get taken while his back is turned, one may bud and flower more in another's hands or he may miss an opportunity; and so he wishes to hold on, even if it breaks his back. If he asks for help, he is showing he cannot cope with his own creations, the issues of his own making. If he had planned ahead, he could have delegated his responsibilities and arranged help. He may also want to put on a show about how much he is suffering for his ideas and creations, or for those other people his dreams will serve. So, he simply seeks his goal and is a bit blinkered as he cannot see the woods for the proverbial trees.

He heads towards the town: the field has been ploughed so he can set his wands down to grow and form roots which will last him a long time. The house will give security, a feeling of coming home and success in the eyes of others, which is what he has journeyed for. The church is his faith in his abilities as he knew he would be able to make it, and offers a time to rest. But, if he does not look up, he could miss it or even hurt himself or damage the wands if he drops them. Just a few steps in the wrong direction and it could all pass him by.

He is so preoccupied with finalising his success and goals that his task has become tiresome and his load somewhat heavy. He fails to realise that his situation is only made heavier by himself. The weight of the wands makes his journey harder than it needs to be, and rather than asking for help, he struggles unnecessarily.

Numerological Value - **TEN** = Purpose, uniting and bringing together of energies to create a new whole.

IN A NUTSHELL

There will be no time for fun as life is filled with routine. You are taking on too much and you're losing sight of your goal. You feel pressured by your responsibilities yet deal with them adequately even if you are no longer smiling about obtaining them.

There is a need to review what you are doing, and sort through to see what can be left behind, dealt with later, delegated to others, or help asked for, before you make a mistake.

Ten of Wands: Upright

The Ten of Wands is a card that represents **unwanted worries and ordeals and doing things the hard way**. A time where you are **feeling burdened** down, showing **a change of routine is needed. Life will be tiresome** and there will be a complete lack of joy within your daily tasks. Your mood will be low, and **you will wonder why life or certain circumstances must be so hard to deal with**.

You will be working too hard, or adamant about achieving something, maybe even be a **workaholic**. Life will lose its shine due to being too focused on what needs doing.

Problems are usually self-imposed as you have **taken on too much** or have too many worries to contend with, leaving you **tired and under stress**. You will feel unable to see your way out of your problems as they will seem to be never-ending.

This card brings feelings of **isolation** within situations; you isolate yourself by presuming your worries are permanent and untreatable which they are not, so you are left **feeling alone with the weight of all your problems**.

Delegating responsibilities can help to ease the pressure, but doing so is ignored, with the view that no one can do it as well as you can. You fear how badly someone else will do things and it means relinquishing control, a sign **you need more faith in others**.

You will feel lumbered and **under pressure** from an unwelcome person or a set of circumstances. You try to 'do it all' and take on every responsibility offered your way, as you do not realise that you have a choice, which may leave you a martyr to your own limitations.

Ten of Wands: Reversed

Reversed, we often find that the stress is too much. **We drop responsibilities to take a good look at them**, sometimes by force, due to not being able to cope anymore, and a light bulb moment occurs.

Regardless of how you feel, you decide to **delegate responsibilities and ask for or organise help**, as you realise you've bitten off more than you can chew.

There will be **a wake-up call** and burdens will be seen for what they are, as it's a time for being honest about what you can and cannot achieve with the time or tools you have at hand. You will feel **burnt out, worn out** and in need of change, and know that you need to get off the hamster wheel.

A more mindful approach will take your help with any burdens, as issues or **worries are prioritised**. The wheat is sorted from the proverbial chaff as you get a better grip on issues, leaving you with **a more positive outlook** due to the sorting through of responsibilities.

Upsets, worries, stresses and strains on you will be eased, firstly by realisation, and then by action. There will **be a welcomed release of pressure** and a change of routine as you find a fresh way of working with the issues you decide to keep.

— The Wand Family —

Wands are full of creative energy; they are lively souls, full of passion and drive.

They are concerned with energy and how to enjoy and implement life to their best advantage; they like to explore life's possibilities.

They like to play with energetic gusto and excitement, being friendly, sociable and good fun. Wands are the most talkative and innovative of the suits.

Astrologically, Wands are fire signs: Sagittarius, Leo and Aries.

PAGE OF WANDS

The Page of Wands shows a young person standing in the blistering desert, holding a budding wand with both hands.

Astrological Sign: any fire sign, Sagittarius, Leo and Aries.

The whole card is filled with yellow and orange, as everything here is about heat, the heat of ideas and potential.

The Page's golden yellow cloak, with its gold cord trim over the shoulder adding a touch of flair, and the orange lining – red in other versions of the card – bring the sun's power with this card. Showing this Page is fuelled by courage and passion, with a knack for being noticed. The orange tights and yellow boots with flame cuffs add to this, as here is a Page filled with optimism and confidence, who sincerely has faith in his findings. The Page's hair is golden strawberry blond, showing a youthful, fiery, headstrong personality.

His tunic is a bright yellow and decorated with salamanders, a theme with three of the Wand family. A salamander is a small lizard said to withstand fire and heat – they produce a white milky substance that keeps them safe – and which has linked them to the element of fire. They represent immortality, endurance, good luck, change and opportunities. The salamanders' tails are not in their mouths as they are meant to be, showing a lack of maturity, so his ideas may not create a fire, but more of a spark. Some may fizzle out quite fast, yet there is much enthusiasm and creativity, and salamanders ask that we seize the moment! Once the salamander's tail is in his mouth, the energy can go round in a continuous eternal loop. Not meeting shows the energy can go awry as it does not connect; it gives us flashes of fire rather than a loop of intense energy. Yet the fiery determination is still present even if it has not been directed; it is ignited and ready to go. He is like a sun child, full of enthusiasm, shining bright and wanting to reach out to others to share his infectious excitement of what his mind has delivered to him. The bright yellow, which can be a muted gold in some versions of the card, shows his drive, friendliness, ambition and energy, as well as a wish to be noticed.

His hat resembles an early-style pith helmet with an orange, sometimes red feather, so here we have an explorer, someone who needs to explore his ideas as they excite him. His red, or orange, feather will push him to follow any thoughts he has, as his ideas will drive him, making him feel passionate about what is on his mind. In this original image, his feather looks like a flame, with a small red dot at the base which looks like a lit match head. Yet is a red jewel placed over his brow chakra, his third eye, showing his creativity is akin to intuition, coming from elsewhere, forcing him to take notice of his imagination, which he views as facts and certainties. The flamed feather and jewel represent a spark of interest, a sudden burst within his mind which takes his focus entirely. It shows us his visionary and inventive ideas: he sees opportunities where others may just see a pile of sand or a stick. His ideas are strong and motivate him, yet he sees the grand finale, rather than the small details on how to get there and will want to shout about his idea from the rooftops so he can set others alight with his dream. His hat often reminds me of a tin helmet, a Brodie helmet from WW1, something to stop the interruptions of others as he gazes at his new idea. The feather can also be viewed as a 'feather in his cap' showing advantage and achievement, which as a Page is just an idea, yet in the 17th century the phrase meant someone unwise and foolish, and from either perspective shows his ego can run ahead. The feather could even be a pen, so he can jot down ideas as they come to him.

The Page holds the wand firmly with both hands, gazing at it with a smile, realising his new idea. The leaves budding from the wand show he is discovering his potential, and as his gaze goes to the top of the wand, he seeks, as before, the outcome and experience, the grandeur of his new discovery, and a need to enjoy it.

He faces the right of the card, representing his creative goals, his mind lost in the feelings attached to his budding ideas urging him with excitement. His wand can also be phallic, and with the sexual energy present within this suit, it can represent a sexual awakening: a time where sex is mentally, emotionally or physically discovered for the first time, puberty or even within a personal situation for someone more experienced.

The desert he stands in is lifeless, dry and hot, and so none of his ideas have formed roots, but his fertile mind is captivated by the wand as ideas start to grow. Beside him are three sand piles forming triangles; sand pyramids, a sign of creativity; with the triangles, upright, a sign of fire. Shifting sands show a continuous movement of ideas each time a hot wind blows, and sand pyramids tend to collapse after time. His ideas may not be stable, as with each new idea he will want to express himself with a burning desire to let you know what wondrous invention he has conjured up. The sand pyramids are to his left, which leaves his ideas feeling very logical to him, very solid, so he can be very adamant about how things should or could be.

This Page brings excitement, and he will wish to share his discovery of new-found knowledge. He brings the energy of shouting and sharing out what you know, what you have found or discovered, as excitement bubbles out into the expression of new ideas.

All of the Pages are like children with new toys. They have grown enough to be aware of their suit, their element and energy and want to explore and play with it. They have no idea of how to control it or use it to any effect, but they feel its draw on them and react to that instinctually.

IN A NUTSHELL

A time for some good news! Messages or incoming information will inspire you to grab the bull by the horns (or the salamander by the tail). You will feel passionate about something which you will want to explore.

Enthusiasm is abundant as an idea takes your attention. You will be fired up and ready to go; even if your idea has no foundation other than a flicker in your mind, you will wish to tell others about it.

Page of Wands: Upright

Personality - The Page of Wands represents a young person who is **talkative**, very **enthusiastic** and brimming full of creative energy. It brings us **excitement for an idea or opportunity.** This Page is full of **new ideas** and energy like The Fool, except nowhere near as powerful, but still prepared to dive in out of excitement. **The urge to explore ideas** is guaranteed as he cannot hold back; he needs to look into and research potential results. Like all the Pages, he is a student in one form or another; he takes on **new information** with **confidence**.

If an idea fails or he bores, then another one will come along as he will always move on to the next idea as it will be more exciting and novel than the last. So, **if you're wishing for a new idea, then this card will bring you one** and break any creative blocks.

This individual will try to direct their future by **seeking out new openings for change and success.** This Page is **a free spirit**, who is optimistic and encourages hope and happiness as they pass through the lives of others. Their energy may even be a bit contagious and can motivate change, as you feel it possible to move forwards with ideas. Yet be careful as **ideas may not be mature and wise, but exciting and unreliable**.

This Page usually appears as **a good friend who has some news to impart** about an area of personal interest to yourself, as once this Page learns something new, he cannot contain it: there will be **inspired thoughts** spread to all who will listen in a flurry of excitement.

This card tells us to be confident in what we know and to communicate that information or news with those who matter. **You may wish to try everything you can imagine,** yet to **give ideas time to develop** before acting.

Message/event - The Page of Wands is **the bearer of good or constructive news**. Often this energy is brought by a friend but also by post, text, email, phone or messages being otherwise relayed. If you're **thinking of doing something new**, research it first; don't be led astray by being headstrong and impulsive.

Page of Wands: Reversed

Personality - When reversed, the Page of Wands shows an individual **lacking confidence** with a **nervous disposition concerning new ideas or sharing insights.**

The Page of Wands reversed shows a usually talkative and cheerful soul being quiet and withdrawn - especially if they are made to feel **self-conscious**, inadequate or a fool by another for what they believe in, wish to do in life, or worse - have tried and failed at. Unlike The Fool, making **a mistake is a hit to the ego** with this Page. Ideas may have been built up publicly and burned out, leaving the Page **embarrassed** as they were valuable to him, so some quietness, sulking and **disappointment** may be present.

Ideas may have been tried and failed or not gone as dreamed or planned, and everything is seen as a potential failure. The view that **not all ideas are meant to be followed** is not understood, as some are superficial, fanciful and fleeting. Knowing when to let go of an idea needs to be learnt, as is knowing when to work hard rather than to dream, and why you pursue the particular ideas that you do.

This Page reversed tells us that feelings of inadequacy should be erased and that we should talk problems through with anyone relevant to our situation, or another who may be able to act as a go-between to smooth out events. A time to **step back to see why our ideas are not working, and now may be the time to take a fresh look at goals**.

Message/event - Still a messenger but now the bearer of **disappointing, disruptive or even misleading news**. You may be left to feel that others are judging you, or that you're missing out.

KNIGHT OF WANDS

The Knight of Wands shows a fiery knight on a horse, rearing up, ready to go.

Astrological Sign: Sagittarius.

This Knight is dressed in fiery colours with his yellow tabard and orange feathers. His suit of armour shows him ready to battle and charge in, and with this suit, it will often be to where angels fear to tread as he boldly goes towards his goal. He is driven by passion and enthusiasm, with his armour protecting him in case he gets thrown by the horse or everything goes up in flames. His leather gloves are also for protection: as a Knight, he is not fully prepared to handle the fire he wields so they offer some protection, or else he may get his fingers burnt.

He is literally on fire, with flames at the back of his knees coming from his armour, flames around the edges of his yellow tabard and at his back. Orange flames lick out behind him, and his large orange feather is like a flame filling his head with passionate thoughts, driven ideas, enthusiasm and intense, full-on focus on the object of his desire. The yellow of his tabard shows his sense of self, his total confidence, intellect and the energy of the sun. His flames and feather are a deep burning orange, representing optimism and creativity, which is also shown by his orange hair. His whole view of the world will be seen as an avenue to explore. Beauty is seen in things with an overriding passion to connect and create from the physical world; everything is seen through a veil of fire, inviting and alluring, burning in his soul. His flames push him forward, igniting his enthusiasm for exploration.

Again, we have salamanders and here the tails are closer to the mouths, but still not quite meeting. This energy he encapsulates is not mature; he will not have a full handle on it, showing us incomplete action. His adventure has just begun and rests on unformed and impulsive plans.

He holds his wand in his right hand, connecting his creativity to his pending charge forwards, feeling the energy in his whole body as it rests against the horse.

His left hand holds green reins, symbolic of being grounded, sensible, and directing issues. So, he understands the power of the horse and the need to hold tight, yet this is a small amount of earth with so much burning fire that it may not be enough. Three sets of leaves decorate the reins, a sign that he will try to control his creativity as best he can, but with nine leaves in total, he will feel he is nearly at the finish line, when he has only just begun. There are eight small dots between the leaves, a sign of his confidence and certainty that he is up for the challenge.

His horse, a flaming chestnut colour, rears up; both are restless spirits yearning for movement and challenge. That time has now come, as the Knight looks towards the distant horizon with concentration and eagerness, and facing left, action is imminent. His spurs show that he knows he may need to control this energy: with so much fire, if he was to dig them in, the horse, being more powerful, may just throw him. His lack of experience could mean he cannot control its force when at full speed, yet his horse rears up in anticipation of the chase ahead, as both of them are ready to burn a path through the desert.

We have the three sand triangles, as with the Page. With each sandstorm, they will change shape and with each hot wind they will move and shift, and so his shifting passions may not stand the test of time. His desert is arid, with no life - just heat and ideas of what could be, making this Knight as much an explorer as the Page but with added action, pushing forwards in a flaming rush of headstrong intensity. Unlike the Page, these triangles are to the right of the Knight, so he feels emotions with his passion, rather than just the idea alone; he can feel the anticipation of pleasure in addition to success. He will see a bigger picture than the Page, even if it is not the whole thing, as with all of the Knights.

His fiery energy has not yet been controlled by maturity, yet this Knight is still drawn and employed by its force. The mere possibility of challenge deeply excites this individual to such an extent that if one were to try to halt his progress, there would be fierce opposition. His attraction to all that calls to him is consuming; his dislike of being confined within a set view or staying put to him seems bizarre, as he enjoys the learning process attached to discovery, the buzz and excitement.

He may be a bit inconsistent at times, and not be looking at the outcome but at the enjoyment of doing what is at hand. For more long-term stability, where hard work is needed to maintain successes, he may fail, and this card is just a burst of energy to get momentum going, not commitment. Yet, as a Wand, he has a very sexy, desirable energy to him which makes things seem just too tempting to ignore.

IN A NUTSHELL

This Knight brings movement in all situations, including house moves or travel. A sign that positive, fast-moving changes are afoot! He is so energetic that he brings action to whatever he touches. He is full of confidence and rushes in bravely and boldly to most situations.

His friendly and passionate energy is contagious and brings success in getting new ventures started, but commitment may be needed to see things through, and more time may be needed to reach goals.

Knight of Wands: Upright

Personality - The Knight of Wands makes **a generous and honest friend** but does tend towards being unreliable as he is quite **impulsive**.

He can also represent someone who is **physically and sexually attractive**, but not a person ready to commit, as they have too much energy and are not ready to settle down. Even if they feel they want to devote themselves to anything, they simply will not be able to as they are too **restless for change**.

This Knight doesn't channel his energy efficiently, due to **inexperience and impatience** as well as **a desire to please**. He sees no limits to his energy and often cannot do all he has committed himself to. This person is a happy-go-lucky individual who **approaches life with passion and curiosity**.

The Knight of Wands is always busy, energetic and rushed with life. He is always seeing what there is to do, resulting in impatience as the energy he carries cannot be restricted, as he **thrives on challenge and activity**.

He can tell us to **be bold, not reckless, but optimistic and go for what we want**.

This Knight is often found doing favours for people, working hard, or playing sport, and like all the wands he is social and enjoys being with others as it gives a chance for **fun and laughter**. The life and soul of the party!

This card tells us that if we need change or to make a decision, to just do it! Jump in at the deep end. Rise to any challenge, as life is full of gambles. Accept any openings presented but do think about if you can commit to it first, or at least ask if others are happy flying by the seat of their pants till the ride stops.

Event - The event that the Knight of Wands brings is restlessness and the desire to make changes. He will bring **optimistic news** of work, career, moves with home or workplace. But in general, he heralds a time of rush, **travel** and commotion as **exciting changes within a situation are certain**. If you wish to start something new, this card shows you the way.

Sexual energy is shown, and so may also indicate an intimate encounter or **a physical attraction**.

Knight of Wands: Reversed

Personality - The Knight of Wands reversed is still warm and generous but his tendency to be **unreliable** is more pronounced. Due to his **hectic lifestyle,** he will be **someone who will make sincere promises but let you down.** This person's energy is scattered as he tries to achieve too many things at once, resulting in him being too busy and **disorganised.**

Whether this Knight is upright or reversed, he does nothing out of malice. He simply disappoints due to his creative energy combined with his imagination; he presumes that he can achieve more than is humanly possible.

Reversed, nothing is as important as his present idea or notion, and everything else loses its importance. He suffers from **tunnel vision** as soon as a new idea or opportunity appears. He has **no self-control** and just throws himself at everything he is drawn to.

The Knight of Wands reversed **acts impatiently** and needs freedom, but he is also **prone to making mistakes** as he gives little practical thought to his endeavours. He can be left scarred by his actions; as he does not think as he charges at the things or people he's attracted to, his actions burn and upset rather than create.

This Knight can warn us to **stop and think before rushing into anything** which conflicts with our usual mundane life. Magnetic opportunities can lead us astray, hurting others as well as ourselves. He also warns that we would be disappointed with the outcome, as reality would not match the magic of the mind.

Event - The Knight of Wands reversed brings **disruptions** and frustrations to events. There is a lot of impatience about. If you are the cause, make sure it's not because you're **obsessing over what you want**. If it's from another, just get out of their way until they burn themselves out. ***You will be let down and disappointed***.

News waited for or arriving will offer **no solutions**, just dissatisfaction or **empty promises.**

QUEEN OF WANDS

The Queen of this suit shows a woman dressed in gold, holding a wand in one hand, a sunflower in the other, and a black cat at her feet.

Astrological Sign: Leo.

Leaves grow from her gold crown with three small gold circles, each placed on top of a raised gold disc symbolising the sun. Her crown represents her creative mind, budding with positive energy, fully awake and aware, as with this Queen, we have a creative energised fast-moving intellect.

Her dress is a vibrant yellow, the colour of sunshine, embodying all the sunny aspects of the sun, showing her to be warm, passionate, happy, chatty, sociable, full of optimism, someone who people notice. The checked squares on her neckline show her to be emotionally balanced as they come down over her heart, of her conscious and unconscious, her inner and outer selves being in tune. The original image shown here, shows these checkers as yellow and black, on others brown and orange, either showing a blending of her inner and outer self. Someone who understands their potential, and can be the sunny vibrant, loud soul her dress shows her to be, yet still have a wonderful sense of commitment and a desire to be the best she can be, with a grounded, passionate heart. A single brown left shoe pokes out from her dress, showing she may be Queen of Fire but is practical enough to know what moves to make and what to avoid. There is no rushing in with this Queen, yet she is ready for action if it's needed. Under her dress is a small sight of her white under-dress, showing us her sincerity, kept close, so only those who know her may see that aspect in its true light. The rest see a happy soul who likes to be noticed.

Her cloak is rather dull for her element, and here we start to see a different aspect to the Queen of Wands. Being grey, it is the colour of contemplation, it can be used to cover her dress, so she can turn her fire on and off; a bit of a chameleon, a social butterfly, she can choose what others see, hot or cold.

Her cloak's clasp is a red fox, the red linking it to the sun, and holding her cloak together, a sign she is in control of her passions. Near her Throat Chakra, her words will be honest, fiery and full of energy. Wands do not like to waste time, so when she speaks, it will be energetic and often motivational or humorous. Yet a fox is clever, full of self-awareness, quick at decisions. Foxes are playful, they seize opportunities, are quick to adjust to their environments, yet can be seen as cunning and sly. For all her sunny bright energy, she has a darker side if crossed, which is echoed by her lions and black cat. It is wise to not be in a position where she is hunting you.

She sits, legs parted showing her sexual energy and her drive to compete in life; she is no wallflower and can be one of the lads if she needs to be, showing absolute confidence in who she is. Her seated position represents sexuality, she shines a light on sexual freedom, owns her body and feels proud of it, and embraces the intimate nature of the self. She understands the power of her sexuality and physical attraction. She invites life in: her energy attracts people, objects and situations as they naturally gravitate towards her energy as it is bright, welcoming and fresh. Wherever this Queen goes, she is noticed. Her warmth, laughter, openness and vivaciousness draw people in; she is one of those people everyone wants to be friends with, or even be like.

Like The Sun card, she has sunflowers: one she holds, the others are on the tapestry at the back of her throne. This flower tells of her vitality, lust for life and positivity, she is ready to greet life full on. The sunflower she holds is in her left hand, is her positivity and optimism, her logic. While in her right, she holds her creative wand which allows her to achieve with her inventive mind, yet she is a good judge of knowing when to let go.

To the sides of her throne are two lions representing her strength and her sign of Leo, and The Sun. They show her strength comes from her element as it gives her a liberated fierceness. They look left and right, so she is centred in their energy, making her passionate and determined about the things she does. She has fierce energy brought about by being a lioness between the two lions. She will protect and fight for those she loves, and to those she loves she will go out of her way to make sure they are safe and provided for. A great friend, but a fierce enemy. Lionesses also represent sexual feminine energy: they serve the family with a strong maternal instinct, they hunt, so once she sets her eyes on what she wants, she will stay focused and be very aware of any pitfalls.

Her throne's tapestry is decorated with two lions, representing ambition. In this original image, they look like foxes with lion's tails, lacking the majesty with which Smith paints her other lions within the deck: maybe they are meant to be ambiguous? Yet in later decks they are defined as lions. Either way, they bring power, hunt with stealth, pounce on their victims, are territorial and predators. They are on either side of her head and show she thinks about what she is wishing to attain with precision. There are three sunflowers on the tapestry which tells that she wants to create happiness and success in life; in fact, she wants it all. Two are by both sides of her head, showing her optimism and ability to be aware of the positives in situations. We cannot see the top of her throne, so she may be aiming for the sun itself, filled with potential. The king's tapestry is the same; they both want to be seen. They love the focus of others. Having a high-backed throne makes you able to be seen by those at the back of the room, as well as those coming from a distance as they share their sunshine and fire with all about them. Both are hard-to-miss people who command an audience.

At her feet sits a black cat, a symbol of protection from negative spirits, protecting the home, bringing good luck to some. The cat sits at her feet staring at us, a sign the Queen has tamed herself yet will do as she pleases as she is a very independent soul. The cat's stare is waiting to see what we do, ears up, tail slightly flicked, so ready to react with sharp instincts with either affection or claws. Some link the black cat, and thus this Queen, to witchcraft; but the black cat can also show the Queen's more mysterious side, a creative element that can feel like magic as she often lands on her feet and learns from mistakes rather than dwelling on them, and like the cat, she can scratch if provoked. She may or may not be into the supernatural or even interested in the spiritual side of life, but she knows how to manipulate the energy around her to get what she wants. The cat is a sign of her ability to perceive the reality of situations, her strong territorial energy, and her unpredictability and impulsiveness, which she can control if she wants.

To the left side of her throne are the three sand pyramids of the Page and Knight, bringing their shifting energies and passions. Yet to her right is grey rock, an earthy energy, secure, solid and unmoving; the two are opposites. With her grey cloak, this Queen has a determined side which does not shift with the hot winds. Between the two she has a balance on desires, she does not go with each new idea, but rather with the ones she knows will work. Once this Queen commits, she is loyal as those rocks will anchor her for as long as she is happy.

She sits with her body facing front, ready for action, yet her gaze, her grey cloak, the sunflower and even the black cat are going slightly towards the right of the card, showing us that while she is Queen of the Sun, she values the stability of the grey, solid rock.

Her dress, cape and wand are also set upon or flowing onto the solid stone plinth of her throne, as she knows for success to be found it needs to be weighed down with hard facts and reality, or else it will just shift and be burnt to nothing. Her view to the right of the card also shows her emotional need to create and secure success.

This Queen's energy is shown as a desire and lust for life. For fire to survive it must feel life, as it cannot just sit back and watch or simply endure it. Her mind is adventurous, quick and enterprising. She is resourceful and can leave you inspired by the effort she puts into things, as well as the way she sees the world. The practicalities of her home life are an important ruling factor for this individual, and this is where she rules and plays the hardest.

This Queen is traditionally called Queen of Hearth and Home. Leave her to her own devices and she will be content; upset her and she will fight tooth and nail to achieve at least some satisfaction out of even the most dismal situation.

IN A NUTSHELL

Be bold! Self-reliance and confidence in your abilities are important, a time to be protective of what is yours. Show the world you are a force to be reckoned with. Smile in the face of problems, welcome them in, deal with them and do not shy away from anything.

Fun and laughter are good medicine; there is no rush to get to where you are going, and time spent being productive whilst having fun can often be good for you and help you work through issues to get ideas moving.

Queen of Wands: Upright

Personality - The Queen of Wands is an individual who finds security and pleasure within her home life, yet she would feel trapped if she were kept there. She has to be able to *spread her wings* and *assert individuality* which she usually does via working and socialising. *With work, she excels*; and with partying, she is often the one organising.

She is *proud of her home and family* but is *self-reliant* in her approach to life and so needs her *independence* outside of them and often found to be *busy and productive, and happily so*. Her philosophy is that today is our only certainty and opportunities are for taking.

This Queen is *energetic, extrovert, sensual and flirtatious*. She is a *faithful* partner but due to her outgoing nature, she may not instil confidence in an insecure partner - but challenge her faithfulness at your own risk!

This Queen also makes an excellent friend and when she appears, can often refer to *a valued friend, who can offer you help* or support, as well as laughter. *Someone you can trust* to keep secrets and respect you.

This individual is *strong-willed, resilient and fun to be around. Problems are viewed as challenges* to be conquered. She is unpredictable, temperamental, quick to anger and can be fierce when the need arises, especially if her pride is challenged, a loved one has been insulted or hurt, or someone not able to fight for themselves or a cause needs her help.

She tells us to enjoy life, be confident and take pride in ourselves - *be fearless!*

Queen of Wands: Reversed

Personality - Everything that this person does is born out of *dissatisfaction* with their personal life, as well as *jealousy and spite; her claws come out* making her more catty than chatty. She represents *a fair-weather friend and is not to be trusted* in any way with anything. She will give *bad advice* on purpose, and happily *gossip* and share your secrets with others to do damage and boost her *low self-esteem*.

She is *unfaithful and deceitful* and goes out of her way to gain attention and admiration. She dislikes happiness and commitment in others, often fuelled by *jealousy*, so if she represents a friend or partner, then be warned. Her *unhappy* nature will make her reject and burn anything which makes her feel challenged.

Reversed, the satisfaction she seeks makes it irrelevant who or what gets in her way, and in this pursuit, she is *someone who will happily*

lie and manipulate, often for dramatic effect, so she can enjoy the show. In short, she is the proverbial 'bitch', and can show infidelity, be the 'other woman', or someone who is out to gain at your expense for their satisfaction.

She relishes personal glory and only shows emotions for effect and usually at the expense of another. You will rarely see temper outbursts unless it's to promote *manipulation,* as she would rather plot *revenge* than risk losing a confrontation. Unfortunately, you may not know this person has you in their sights until you feel the effect of any actions hitting you.

This Queen can remind us to deal with disappointments, as taking them out on others who have things in life which we feel we have more of a right to, making enemies or *alienating people* isn't beneficial in the long-term.

KING OF WANDS

The King of Wands shows us the King seated on his throne holding a wand in one hand whilst the other is clenched, ready for action.

Astrological Sign: Aries.

As King of Fire, his crown is a golden crown of flames placed over a fiery orange cap. The cap shows his drive and passions and protects his mind from the energy of the flames yet does not diminish their power, more a sign he has learned how to control the flames licking at his mind. The King of Wands is a leader, one of life's doers, and his creative mind needs to be under control. He knows when to unleash his productive energy but has no desire to be controlled by it.

His clothes are the colours of fire with his orange gown and, like the Queen, he is no shrinking violet! His gown has yellow flame-shaped cuffs, pointing to his optimism, success, power, confidence, determination and happiness. His yellow cloak with its golden lining shows a touch of luxury, along with his self-confidence. The salamanders here have their tails in their mouths forming a circle, which, at last, gives us infinite energy. They tell of completed tasks, endurance, loyalty and an ability to create, to make concrete an idea from start to finish as the King reaches his goals. His shoes and a mantle with flame edging, in newer versions of the deck, are green, connecting him to the earthy values of honesty and generosity. In this original image, they are nearly blue, showing a loyal, calm person, and both are correct. The mantle covering his Heart and Throat Chakra shows him wanting commitment, honesty, sincerity, and growth from his endeavours, and that his word and actions can be trusted. He rarely follows flights of fancy, yet is still very driven to win, and his shoes show he walks towards goals with seriousness, as he wants more than experience alone.

The gold lion pendant around his neck represents his courage, power and control over his life. A fierce, positive soul, driven to succeed with absolute confidence in his abilities. He is the leader of the pack. In some Tarot decks astrologically, he is assigned the sign of Leo and the head of the pride.

Unlike the Queen with her black cat, the King has a salamander. In the Middle Ages, people thought salamanders created fire as their skin could resist it, with their skin used to protect precious articles as they symbolised flames and fire leading to rebirth. Fire is created from a single spark, creating a flame capable of jumping to burn and transforming what it touches, leaving this King a powerful force. He is driven to succeed and rivals all when it comes to passionate driven ideas. In ancient times, the salamander was said to lay dormant in volcanoes, which when erupting would anger the animal and so their lava tongues would lick up everything in their path. If this King sees an opportunity, he will grab it with both hands as he is fast to grasp new concepts and will see possibilities others may miss, which is echoed by his body language and his wand on the wooden floor.

Like the Queen, he has a tapestry, this time with lions and salamanders, showing his power and ability to build, create and govern all he does. They are going upwards, again a sign that he wishes to be noticed from afar. Three salamanders show us his creative element; one of them is right behind his head showing his completed ideas, his set goals, ambitions and victories he has already enjoyed. The two lions show his balanced view of his power; one looks as if it is climbing his back so he may deeply feel this energy as a rawness inside of him, pushing him forwards.

The throne's seat looks to be made from wood, as is the floor his wand rests upon. It may sit on a stone plinth showing his prestige, but made from wood it could burn, he could corrupt his power if it all goes awry, but here he uses it to ground himself, a sign he has his element firmly under control.

The King's desert sands are behind him; he does not look at them as he has no use for what will shift, change and move directions with even a hint of a hot breeze. Now he wants to focus on more concrete goals, he has his crown to protect his thoughts, he would not wish to let it all get lost in a blaze of a poorly organised attempt at glory.

The King of Wands holds his wand in his right hand, his creative side, and like the salamander looks out to take in the world about him, looking for opportunities. They both face the left of the card showing action is imminent and desired. He leans slightly forwards, resting on one arm, with the other hand in a loose fist. His posture also tells that he is ready to move to act when he next decides his energy and drive are required or he finds an idea that he knows is worth pursuing.

This King, like The Emperor, also Aries, is an instigator of ideas and change, inventive and daring. He possesses an abundance of enthusiasm and desire to see his endeavours through to the end, leaving him fully committed to his goals. He will wait patiently for opportunities that please him, and if they cannot be found, then he will create ones that do. His ideas tend to be innovative and original as he is one of life's inventors.

IN A NUTSHELL

A time to put your full force behind your ideas or plans to light your passion for what's ahead. Enthusiasm should be tempered as it will not serve you well, so plan well. Commitment is called for; however big or small, rise to the challenge with focus and take control of your own outcome.

Move forwards with ideas and take time to resolve problems and find solutions to what needs solving and do it with a positive outlook. Be inventive!

King of Wands: Upright

Personality - The King of Wands' personality is ***charming and fun-loving***. This King, as with all the Wand family, ***enjoys a challenge to rise to*** and often represents an individual who possesses ***an active and productive lifestyle***, who can be passionate about the work they do or the pastimes they have.

This man is ***deeply committed*** and if this is not with reference to ***a business plan***, then he will either be in a stable relationship or ideally suited to one, as often they show people who are ***married, or in a committed relationship. This can cause issues for others if they are insecure, as, like the Queen, they*** are often quite ***magnetic, sexually attractive*** people.

The King of Wands is often found in positions of authority when it comes to business as his nature is ***enterprising and dedicated*** and can often refer to your ***manager or 'boss'***. This makes him an ideal and ***natural leader*** and an even better salesperson, as all the Wands like to talk and could sell ice to Eskimos. He will love to be with people, and like the Queen, he enjoys being noticed, here for his achievements and skills.

If you need something designing, he will fulfil the role as his ***visionary nature*** finds solutions to answers of a practical nature, and he will see things through to the end - unlike the Knight, who will probably leave it half-finished.

He tends to be very individual and singular in his way of thinking and knows how to direct his ideas and convince others of their benefits as he feels enthusiastic about his creative convictions. He is dedicated to what he works on and feels excitement as he engages with goals and plans.

The King of Wands is ***an incredibly positive and sometimes a very persuasive man*** while being ***an excellent and reliable friend***.

The King of Wands tells us to ***be determined*** and disciplined with ourselves, and in our approach to matters, and go for what we really desire with focused passion.

King of Wands: Reversed

Personality - The King of Wands reversed has *a superiority complex* and has an inflated view of himself and his achievements or aims, but it's all just *over-inflated ego* and little substance.

This King assumes that power and respect are his to enjoy even though *he fails at most ventures* due to this aspect of his nature. His mood will often be *angry*. This can present *temper outbursts* due to others not seeing things from his perspective, and what he is working on not going as he has envisioned it. He acts in a *rash and impatient* way, just wanting to get to the finishing line, and is often *unrealistic* about his goals.

When events concerning others do not go his way, he can be *corrupt and crooked* and *bend the rules* to suit himself. His persuasive nature can lead him into *con artist* territory, and his drive can push him towards fulfilling his dreams at the expense of others.

He is an *untrustworthy* individual, as he is full of empty promises. If one is involved in a relationship of any nature with this person, then he is *unfaithful* and unable to commit as the grass may be greener on the other side, and he will aim to have it all.

The King of Wands is also *one who would pass on bad advice* due to his presumption that he knows it all or because he wants to lead you away from what he wishes for himself.

He warns that *we cannot progress with an egotistical, self-righteous outlook. Others will rebel* if tactics are not reviewed. This King can cut corners, fail, and find himself embarrassed, which often seeks to make his attitude worse.

— The Suit of Cups —

The Suit of Cups is governed by the element of water, which rules our emotions.

Cups represent the feelings and emotions we display, feel, create and direct out to the world or towards ourselves. They show us how our heart responds to events, our sentimental ideals and our emotional judgements.

Cups can also be referred to as the Suit of Chalices, Cauldrons, Vessels and Goblets. In a standard playing deck of cards they are like the Hearts.

Keywords that define water/cups - Emotions and feelings, love, relationships, ideals, hope, expectancy and dreaming.

ACE OF CUPS

The Ace of Cups is being offered from the heavens as a gift of optimism and love, to be enjoyed and cherished by all who receive it. It is a card full of religious symbolism.

From the grey cloud, a hand emerges holding a golden chalice in its palm. The bright white angelic hand is the sign of a gift, one of absolute sincerity. The lack of colour is also a sign of a beginning, as no colour has yet been added. The grey sky and clouds show a time to think about the gift's arrival and to embrace it with equal sincerity. Emerging from the right-hand side of the card, it shows an emotional, creative, spiritual and imaginative gift being offered, something from the heart.

The gold of the cup shows that the gifts this chalice brings can be fully felt in our outer lives, in the physical, and yet deeply felt within the emotional, and sometimes spiritual.

The chalice is a communion cup used to offer the blood of Christ and linked to the Holy Grail, which was said to be the cup that Christ drank from at the Last Supper. The Grail also represents the start of a quest, a time to be passionate about searching for an ideal, something which calls to our hearts. It has three small pendant bells, which symbolise creation. Under the bell at the front are a pair of wings, adding to the divine aspect of this opportunity: this is something which can raise you. Bells are rung during services to bring people to prayer and so the small pendant bells may be symbolic of focus, especially emotional focus, and the spark of life this card brings calling us to attention. To drink from the chalice is to purge sins, release the past, letting us know we can be whole again.

On the chalice is the letter W, which some say is an upside-down M to represent Waite. Yet it could also signify the Hebrew word *mayim*, which means water. Water represents life, motherhood, and creation, as well as cleansing, faith, and salvation. It may be upside down, as when this cup is drunk deeply out of, it is then the right way up.

The dove, a sign of peace, flies down into the chalice with a communion wafer which symbolises the body of Christ, so a blessing from above brought into the physical world as Jesus resurrected, so a new life. With the two we have both the body and blood of Christ, which when taken are meant to give God's grace, purifying us as God then lies within. The cross within the wafer is even-sided, symbolising peace and balance. All these symbols represent harmony and forgiveness, which are needed for new emotional beginnings.

The cup flows with water, symbolic of emotions flowing. There are five streams of water representing our five senses, leaving us in tune with ourselves.

There is an abundance of overflowing emotions with this Ace, and the water flows into the pool below without a ripple; no negativity is stirred up as emotions are calm. The cup literally overflows with life, with the water also representing the subconscious mind with the inner self flowing into the physical side of life.

Falling from the cup are twenty-six Yods, resembling droplets. They fall into the relaxed emotions of the water below adding little divine drops of creation, the ingredients of a new life and a real chance for growth. Twenty-six links to the numerical value of God's name, linked again to the communion aspect bringing salvation, as here a new clean start is being offered.

The lotus flowers are in bloom symbolising many things. In ancient Egypt, they represented the sun rising each day from the darkness, as the lotus plant rises from the murk of dark pond water, representing rebirth and a renewal of life. In Buddhism, the lotus is associated with spiritual awakening, purity and faithfulness. Breaking the surface of the pond water, they show the surfacing of desires, leading to growth, with the pink lotus being representative of the Buddha. In Hinduism, the lotus is associated with beauty, fertility, prosperity, spirituality and eternity. As a lotus grows from the bottom of muddy lakes unspoilt and pure, it represents wise and spiritually enlightened qualities. There are six unopened buds, which show an attraction to this opportunity, as it awakens something within us. The buds themselves represent a folded soul that could unfold and open itself up to divine truth. Three are opened, which show a new future can be envisioned as we can create one within our minds, and here the opportunity is presented. The nine bring the Nine of Cups into focus, the wish card, as this is an opportunity which could lead us to a lot of happiness. The mix of opened and closed brings a time to grow emotionally, to get ready for emotional change.

Aces bring opportunities, not absolutes, and here we are given the chance for a new emotional start. The Ace of Cups brings happiness, smiles and new emotional beginnings which can often feel like a blessing. A fresh flow of emotions is brought to you: a time to heal, remove old pains and feel cleansed of the past. This is the chance for a new life, or even new life itself. Here we have a gift of love, hope, optimism, luck, sincerity and new emotional beginnings.

Numerological value - **ONE** = Desire for action, new beginnings and movement.

IN A NUTSHELL

Love holds the key to everything. There will be a new emotional beginning, which can stem from feelings of well-being to deep love. A time to feel upbeat, happy and joyful as life brings you a deep sense of fulfilment.

Even though this can show pregnancy or the birth of a child, it also brings the birth of a new emotional phase. Smiles are guaranteed and it is a great time to reach out to others. In Yes or No questions, this is a Yes!

Ace of Cups: Upright

The Ace of Cups brings the **opportunity** for **happiness**, spirits will be uplifted and there will be feelings of fulfilment. A time of giving from the heart with **compassion** and complete **confidence**; old anger is released, and laughter will be in the air. When the card appears, **peace** reigns, giving you the chance to let go of arguments, relax and heal situations with love and compassion. This card also tells us to *follow our hearts* and follow emotional impulses.

Optimism and hope will be brought to a situation that will brighten perceptions, and **luck will be on your side**. There will be a new burst of positive, **loving energy** into events or life and the card can be used as *a yes to questions*.

Affection will be in the air, bringing new emotional beginnings which may present themselves in the form of **new friendships, loving relationships** and **emotional attractions**. It brings an opportunity from which something more can grow.

For the onset of new relationships, it shows that actions are pure and from the heart, and for existing relationships it shows respect, faithfulness and growth. Often it will represent **love** itself, a pull on the heartstrings, feelings of sincerity towards another, and **trust** can be given and taken with this card.

This Ace is creative, so can show *a creative burst of energy* so new projects get off to an energised and creative start.

The Ace of Cups can also show **issues relating to conception, pregnancy, birth and wishing to be pregnant**, all issues about bringing a new life into being, and is a positive card in this area. It can also be an indicator of a return to better **health**.

There will be generous **optimism in the air**, and feelings will spark a need for a deeper connection to the object of desire.

Ace of Cups: Reversed

Reversed, the Ace of Cups shows us **unhappiness and sadness**; it brings tears and feelings of **loneliness** and isolation.

There is the need to be in a close relationship, either platonic or sexual, but unfortunately now is not the time. Or there is **a distancing of emotions within an existing relationship or situation**, and feelings are repressed and need an outlet. A **good cry can help heal**, so allow feelings to come out. Long-standing relationships with this card will be unhappy and non-productive and **lack the love or support needed**.

New situations, in which you are emotionally invested, have not materialised or come to anything substantial, as **feelings or sentiments have not been returned or mutual**. Nothing seems to get started with this Ace reversed; feelings are not reciprocated or expressed.

The Ace of Cups reversed brings **a lack of emotional security**, leading to feelings of emptiness which if left, will cloud judgements.

The cup is empty, and time is needed to heal rather than focus on movement and draining more energy. It shows **hope, love and optimism being lost from a situation**. Being an Ace, reconnection can at times be possible, but time to replenish the self is needed.

Reversed, this card shows **creative blocks and issues with fertility or being broody**. Now is not the right time to create and conceive something new. With pregnancies, it shows issues and difficulties as well as general apprehension, including female fertility issues. For general health, it shows you may not feel your best and feel down in the dumps. Your creative self will be flagging, so blocks to your energy need to be worked through as all in all **you are a little bit stuck**. Some time out is needed.

TWO OF CUPS

The Two of Cups shows a man and woman standing before each other, each offering their cup to the other.

In the centre of the card is a Caduceus, a Greek symbol carried by Hermes, a messenger of the Gods, which consists of two entwined snakes with a pair of wings; a magical symbol, said to bring the dead back to life. It bestowed wealth and prosperity via trade and negotiations, turning all it touched into gold, adding strength and balance.

The lion's head represents both physical and sexual energy. Placed between the wings of the Caduceus, the lion seems angelic, which indicates that sexual energy has been transcended by the spiritual, showing us genuine affection and love. Lions also represent danger, and maybe there is an element of risk here as the lion gazes sternly at us. Lions are also found within The Wheel of Fortune and The World as one of the Four Guardians of the Heavens, linked to the fire signs, and within Strength and the King and Queen of Wands. This brings passion to the card, an injection of fire into the watery sentiments, bringing a physical need to find balanced co-operation and connection with another. The lion above the heads of the two people shows that lust or desire has risen above its base level to transcend into something deeper, showing us a spiritual or emotional connection.

Behind the couple is a house nestled on a gentle hill surrounded by trees, symbolising security and safety. The home is where the heart resides, where we feel safe and loved, a house also represents the subconscious mind, both places where we can be ourselves. The hill and trees form a barrier from the world, giving protection. The sky is clear, so no clouds are present to spoil the meeting.

The two figures also stand on firm, even ground, showing a balance in their relationship. There is nothing to trip them up, giving them a mutual standing with each other, as they have reached a stage where a deeper understanding of each other is called for.

Facing each other, the man and woman are shown as both in agreement. They offer their feelings, trust, and understanding of each other with their gold cups. Each of their cups has five decorative balls shown, and so, individually, their cups are communicating a need for truth. By mutual agreement, joining these together will create their goal, which is the Ten of Cups and complete emotional fulfilment. Like The Lovers and The Devil, the woman does not gaze at the man, but to her cup, while the man looks at her. She has a focus on feelings, while he, on action and interaction. The man holds his cup with one hand, so he is aware of its importance, yet action spurs him to care and reach out, encouraging the declaration of their feelings and intentions towards each other. He is touching her fingers, seeking a physical connection, offering a hand of friendship, inclusion and support. The woman holds her cup with both hands, showing she cares deeply for its contents, seeking emotional recognition and showing her deep conviction for what she feels.

The woman wears a laurel wreath indicating emotional victory, acceptance of the connection presented by this card and a sign that all is well. She wears blue, a sign of femininity and intuition, over her white dress, symbolising pure, sincere feelings and her need to communicate them. Her red shoes show she wishes more from the relationship or situation and so desires continued growth, yet not without reassurances, which will be given, as there is an energy of understanding here with an emotional negotiation. Her black belt brings together the success of her victory crown and the desire represented by her red shoes. She will feel desire and a connection to the man, as well as to the world about her. She will have self-confidence and a positive sense of self, showing that she knows what she wants. There is a seriousness at the heart of her desires to connect to another as she understands the potential of the relationship.

The man's crown of red roses is symbolic of mental desire, masculinity and power. The roses are also symbolic of love, which allows for emotions and feelings to grow and develop.

His tunic is yellow, as are his tights; in some versions of the deck this yellow is more muted. The tunic is printed with red and black flowers. The red shows his passion and the black a sign of his potential, the flowers a sign of growth, beauty and attraction. The bright yellow shows him intellectualising his feelings and role within the situation, and also his drive and optimism. The yellow fabric matches the yellow of the two cups, showing us that he is fully invested. The bright nature of his tunic, shows, like his hand reaching out, a need to be noticed by her and truly be seen, like a male peacock displaying his feelings. His boots are light shades of green and brown, so he is being quite practical in his aims, gentle and calm. His tunic is tied by a loose red belt, showing that he brings all of his potential together with a relaxed energy. So his passion lies in a real connection, not just sexual.

They both have darker hair, and with the black flowers and belt, they are not naïve to the world as both already have life experience.

There is equality and fairness within this card, which helps to create a balanced situation between the man and woman. There is understanding and solidarity in their closeness and the sharing of experience, showing friendship and unity first and foremost between two people.

We may not always have a new intimate relationship being shown here, as this can be any relationship that has affection and fairness at its heart, two people or even two sides coming together to create a new level of understanding.

Numerological Value - TWO = Balance, harmony and interaction.

IN A NUTSHELL

A time for friendships, platonic as well as romantic, to grow and gain strength. This can often be a new relationship being built or an old one being enjoyed. There is mutual respect and co-operation between two people, a group or two sides. You will feel cared for, loved and appreciated.

Where romantic connections are concerned, relationships will deepen.

Two of Cups: Upright

The Two of Cups symbolises **friendship** first and foremost: a close bond between two individuals, or even groups of people coming together. New relationships can be shown - **platonic as well as romantic**. Either way, it shows **genuine friendship** and sincerity at a relationship's core. This card shows that strength, **trust** and reliability are present within a relationship. While, regarding established relationships, **commitment and sincerity are guaranteed**.

Within loving relationships, this card often shows **a time to commit to each other and secure emotions**. This can be **declarations of love**, deciding to live together, proposals and even marriage.

Differences can be reconciled, and compromises reached in troubled friendships or relationships, as understanding and **co-operation** will help resolve differences. The energy this card brings to relationships is creative and inspiring, so you will feel uplifted by your connection to another soul.

Help and support are there to be taken from someone who cares about you, and with life in general, there is balance present or restored to issues.

Partnerships may also be important to situations, and this card is a positive sign that you are in a good partnership. If you are in need of advice, you will find **a trusted advisor** to help you.

Two of Cups: Reversed

Reversed, the Two of Cups shows **breakups** in relationships, friendships and all manner of situations resulting from **personality clashes**. This results in **arguments, sulking and pettiness,** as people are **not seeing eye to eye**.

Situations may be more **ego-driven** than with a need for unity and co-operation. **Power struggles** will be present in situations, as within partnerships and relationships one person will wish to have more, or total control or even be able to do as they please. This will lead to frustrations as events do not go their way, or for the others involved as their views or feelings are being ignored, or maybe, even being bullied. There is **a lack of mutual respect**, and there will be **incompatibility** within relationships.

Friendships and loving **relationships will be taken for granted**. Relationships will feel like they are on **an emotional roller coaster**, constantly up and down but never truly settled. **Sexual or physical issues**, including unfaithfulness or physical distance and separation, can be present as the lion's energy is brought to earth, and a sign that such things need to be resolved.

Grudges are held here, making relationships hard to enjoy due to the mistrust the past, hurt and misunderstandings brings with it.

There can be an avoidance of connecting to others and the refusal of much-needed help due to feeling **a lack of trust in others**.

THREE OF CUPS

The Three of Cups shows three girls dancing and raising their cups high in celebration during the late summer or autumn harvest.

On the ground, the three girls dance amongst the harvested fruits and vegetables. Harvests are a time to celebrate being able to sustain yourself through the winter months, a time to also celebrate your wealth, abundance and life itself. A harvest brings ripeness, richness and vibrancy to life, which can be shared easily with others. While a harvest happens once each year, we have lots of mini harvests in our lives: our monthly or weekly wages, a promotion, an engagement, a marriage, a christening, a hen do, a new job, a day off, a night out - anything which has been worked towards and results in a happy gain.

The pumpkin lying in the bottom right of the card symbolises growth and abundance and is a sign of prosperity and good luck. By its side is a bunch of grapes, an abundant symbol of rebirth. They bring happiness, especially when turned into wine! The apples behind the girls, which have fallen to the ground, show temptation, a time to give into fun. This is surplus fruit, as they have more than enough to go around. It has been a good harvest, and everything is ready to enjoy. Ripe fruits and vegetables come with the joyful energy of celebration, the rewards we gain in life, and those things in life that make us want to sing, dance, and gather with friends and loved ones to share our joy. Scattered on the ground, they show an excess of happiness, a time when there is more than enough joy to be shared with everyone.

The women show us differing stages of life; the maid, mother, and crone. The woman dressed in white will be innocent, naïve and the least experienced. She will be enjoying the party for the party's sake, drawn by the socialness of it all. Her long hair, decorated with grapes and vine leaves, shows her youth. She holds her cup up the highest, fully enjoying the freedom the situation offers.

The woman in an orange-yellow dress is filled with enthusiasm and playfulness. Her white undergarment shows her to be sincere, with her blue shoe representing her inspiration. She also wears vine leaves and grapes in her hair, although just at the back, showing a less frivolous energy. She holds a bunch of grapes in her left hand, symbolic of abundance. This and her blue shoe show her thinking ahead to next year's harvest and how to maintain this happiness. Some versions of the deck picture her with blonde hair, like The Empress, symbolic of beauty, fertility and love. Here in the original, she has fiery orange hair, showing passion and drive, someone invested in the success of this happy celebration. Both show her emotionally invested in the growth and continuation of her situation, and her rosy, flushed cheeks show her physical contribution to the situation and to the happiness at hand.

The third woman, with dark, strawberry blonde hair, whose face we cannot see, wears a purple dress with a red robe and yellow shoes. Her clothes show a lot of enthusiasm, ambition and determination. Her purple dress shows that she is someone in a position of power and could be the person in charge of the success being enjoyed. The red cloak adds to this, as it brings drive and determination. Her yellow shoes are a sign of confidence; in other versions of the deck, they are brown, showing her to be also grounded and realistic. She too has her hair down, showing liberation from normal constraints - literally, a time to let your hair down.

These last two women's cups, being at the same height, show a mutual celebration, joint efforts, and a happy understanding of what has brought them together. Now the time has come to enjoy the fruits of their labour, and their dance forms a triangle, a symbol of fire, bringing balance and cycles of growth and manifestation. Being three, we also have the number of creation, so this harvest can offer more for the future, but right now we can just let our hair down and enjoy our rewards with others.

Enjoyment is shown as life is shared with others and problems are resolved. Experience is a great teacher, and this card shows a release of pressure via joint effort and fun. It's a card that brings a time to enjoy life and efforts, the company of those whom you enjoy being with and those who are a part of your success or life.

Faith is being rewarded by physical enjoyment here and smiles are assured. Now is a time for harmony and feelings of connection with others. While the future is considered here, it is the here and now which is the focus.

Numerological value - **THREE** = Growth, creativity and productivity.

IN A NUTSHELL

Time is spent with friends or loved ones, it's party time! Be it a one-to-one with a friend or a gathering to celebrate, there will be smiles to be enjoyed with others. Enjoy the company of others and rejoice as you share an experience. There will be something to celebrate.

Sometimes you just have to let your hair down and play, even if you're only celebrating the sun shining!

Three of Cups: Upright

The Three of Cups gives us *celebrations* and *social events, happiness in the air* as time is spent in *relaxed enjoyment* with those we care for. A time to *savour the moment* as with others, you celebrate what has been gained or given, or even just for the sake of it.

The Three of Cups shows that you will be *enjoying yourself* with close friends and/or family, even colleagues. This may even include engagements, the office Christmas party, passing exams, a lunchtime glass of wine with a friend, the birth of a child, etc. A *time to eat, drink and be merry!*

It reminds us that we need to let our hair down occasionally, meet with loved ones, take time out and off, *reconnect* and *help others,* plus share time with those we care for.

This card gives us a time in life to feel *confident and happy,* leaving you feeling generous and warm towards others as well as to yourself. This card can level out people's status, so old and young, rich and poor can all meet in celebration without such issues being a barrier as at this celebration: everyone can have fun.

Personal relationships are intense and exciting with this card and show that a relationship is going well and in its honeymoon stage, full of intimacy and fun, yet still new.

Personal appearance and image such as buying new clothes, diet, exercise or changing hairstyles can also be represented by the Three of Cups, especially if it is done with friends. Yet this can also show the simple act of putting on your best clothes and doing your hair to go out and have some fun!

Three of Cups: Reversed

Reversed, *after the party, comes the hangover!*

This card can bring **self-dislike and even hatred**, even **shame,** as your life or actions may not gel with your beliefs, emotional life or expectations of your physical appearance, leading to feelings of **no self-worth and personal self-disappointment**. This can lead to **extremes in behaviour**, an **overindulgence** of pleasures such as eating, spending, drinking, promiscuity and drugs, anything which makes you feel bad about yourself, as it is contrary to how you wish to be, or how you wish others to see you.

It can also show **a focus on vanity** and placing a high value on the body beautiful, and labels. To the other end of the spectrum: totally denying a right to any kind of enjoyment at all, with a denial of pleasure and controlling the body in some manner. This also includes overworking and not taking a break, all of which is aimed to punish the self. This is often accompanied by **shallow feelings** based on how things look to others and what others think.

So, either excessing too much and hating yourself for it or refusing to give yourself some of what you need, and you may swing between the two, yet both can be a sign of **depression and a lack of self-esteem**.

This card brings a deep need for emotional fulfilment that will present as *a need for physical and sensual attention, which may be regretted*.

Friendships may make you feel confrontational and in competition, stemming from *feeling insecure* with those whom you should feel at peace with. This can suggest *friendships and relationships are superficial*.

Romantic relationships can be extremely short-lived, even one-night stand short, which has stemmed from a need for contact and naïvety in seeing the others' true intent when something deeper was hoped for.

There is **no sense of fulfilment** reversed; there are no rewards given for hard work, leaving you *feeling short-changed and used*.

FOUR OF CUPS

The Four of Cups shows a man sitting under a tree, with his arms and legs crossed. He looks gloomily at the three cups in front of him whilst a fourth cup is being offered from the heavens.

The four combined with the cups shows a restriction to emotions; it can hem them in, causing a dull time which leaves us feeling emotionally disconnected, and here we are also shown disgruntlement and boredom.

The blue sky is clear, showing a lack of any real issue at hand but still, the young man sits alone, away from everyone, isolating himself and daydreaming. Yet his body language shows it's an unpleasant daydream, focused on what there is, or what there was, rather than what could be.

He sits under a tree, which can be symbolic of protest, not budging to make a point, yet traditionally, it shows protection. So here with his three cups, he feels safe and in a miserable comfort zone, dwelling and feeling that he has no one who can help or even who cares. His Base Chakra, his energy centre which connects him to his physical life and gives a positive mindset, is in direct contact with the earth, so he should be grounded. Yet with his body language, he is stuck, wrapped up in negative thoughts, refusing to see beyond his restrictive view of his world. In this original image, we can see rings on the trunk where a branch once hung. In newer editions of the deck, this part of the trunk looks like a hole, yet it is where a dead branch has fallen. It was dead wood, something that could no longer be supported if growth were desired.

The grass is green on his hill, as he looks down on things, passing judgement on how he wishes things to be, or how they should have been. Yet with his blue sky, his green grass and his healthy tree he is in a good place; he just cannot connect to that right now. In the distance, there are mountains that represent upset and pain, yet they too are not affecting his situation as they are far from where he sits. They sit on his emotional right side, so he will feel the tension they and the past represent, without his logical mind having a say.

His focus on the three cups before him is intense; he gazes at them with a miserable expression. His mind is not in the present but lost in thought, lost in a world of woe, his arms being crossed, a universal sign of sulking. He is unresponsive to the suggestions of others and closes himself off to interactions as he wants to be left alone. His Solar Plexus Chakra is covered by his arms which will also bring him feelings of insecurity as he cannot link to his inner confidence, nor balance his feelings.

He wears blue trousers, showing inspired and even spiritual thoughts and faith, showing his expectations. His shoes are brown in some versions of the RWS, but here they are purple, showing wisdom. In brown, his connection to the earth, or the practical solutions in life. With his feet not standing on the ground and with crossed legs, he is disconnected from both. So, here we have someone who is normally in tune with their life in a bit of a funk. His red shirt, which is closest to his body, shows him full of hope, passion, and drive, covered by a long dull green tunic. Under different circumstances, a healthy green tunic would ground him emotionally, make him calm, and smooth out burning desires, but here it smothers his wants and needs, leaving him greedy, needy, or wanting. Especially with it being a washed out green, it adds a depressive weight to his being. An inner search is afoot, and so he has lost touch with the world around him, lost somewhere between his head and his heart, his wishes and failures, feeling thoroughly disillusioned.

The hand from the cloud offers him the Ace of Cups, trying to gift him optimism and new hope. Yet it's not seen, as he is stuck in thought, lost and feeling sorry for himself as apathy has set in. The goodness of the situation cannot be seen, yet this is a chance for him to move on, should he take the cup being offered to him. It could be a new opportunity to move away from things or to make the situation he is studying a lot better, but he ignores any solutions.

Instead, he stares at the three cups, and at a time which brought him happiness and had promise. As the cups are upright, they are not things lost to him, but things he has lost faith or interest in, or which have simply run out of energy. The Three of Cups is not a party which can last forever; all good things come to an end. He knows that he wants more from them but is unsure of what he really desires or where to even look for it. He is too busy looking within to see the answer that may lie outside of him in the real world.

This card can show a need for a kick in the butt, but it can leave us feeling very unhappy, as we simply cannot find joy in things we once loved or wish to recapture.

Numerological value - **FOUR** = Realisation, willpower and logic.

IN A NUTSHELL

There is stagnation, and discontentment as well as boredom with a situation. A malaise has stepped in: you cannot see the beauty in life as you're looking within feeling despondent.

A lack of ability to see what is under your own nose can appear to others as a lack of respect or even a lack of gratitude. While you are looking inwards, life carries on, yet a way forward is about you if looked for.

Four of Cups: Upright

This card represents *boredom* and appears when there is *dissatisfaction* with life or within a specific situation as *disappointment* is felt. You may have a right to feel unhappy, but this is *a time to shake it off rather than dwell on 'what ifs' or 'maybes'*.

There may even be feelings of *defensiveness* with the arms crossed, letting others see that you would rather be left alone as *you're trying to work through things* on your own. This leads to offers of help being turned away or ignored, making you *isolated by your state of mind or mood, which could well be rude and abrupt*.

Life loses its shine for a while, leaving you full of *self-pity and sorry for yourself*, making it impossible for the good things already within your life to be seen and felt. As a result, events that are developing about you go unnoticed as you get lost in an inner world of wishing, leading you to *miss opportunities* while you *daydream* your life away.

Life may feel empty, but there are openings about you to take advantage of. They are just not being looked for in the right places - that is, if they are being looked for at all, as motivation will be at a low! Remember, action flows where attention goes and if your mood is in a bit of a funk: try to help it pass.

The Four of Cups advises us to *take a fresh look* at a situation or a state of mind, if only to realise that life still holds many possibilities. There is more to life than the problem in which you are absorbed.

Four of Cups: Reversed

Reversed, this card's energy has a positive effect, as it brings *exciting changes due to opportunities being realised*, as you come out of a time of self-absorption and wake up from your daydream state. These opportunities will probably have been under your nose for some time and are obvious to everyone else, so you may have to jump at chances before they fade.

There will be *enthusiasm* once again about what you already have in life, and your *passions will be revived*. It will be a time to want to take action and get back out into the world again, leaving you open to the people, solutions and suggestions about you.

Your existing life will not seem so bad after all, and you will want to make the best of your current set of circumstances. Their virtues are seen in a new light as *you start to climb out of a self-induced rut*.

As you move away from this down mood, you will **be able to see the world from a new perspective** which will give you momentum and **brighten your mood** even more than before.

Now is the time to move on from the past, to forgive or forget and to let go, so that you can get some fresh energy flowing through your life, or else you may find that you've missed out on too many good things. If you are stuck within old frustrations, with tears or anger being triggered by old events, then this card shows that now is a time to leave it all behind. Others about you will be able to help, yet you may need to ask if offers of help have since been taken away.

FIVE OF CUPS

The Five of Cups is a card of disappointment and regret and shows a man grieving over the three overturned cups as their contents have been spilt and lost.

The man stands, facing away from us with his shoulders hunched over and his head down, looking defeated as he has submitted to his loss. His hair is dark grey, showing a deep contemplation is consuming him, with all his thoughts linked to his situation, and also echoed by the grey sky. His long black cloak is a sign of death and mourning as he stands here bereft of hope. What he has lost has profoundly affected him and has led him to retreat inside of himself to heal. While he may not see it, the black of his cloak symbolises the potential which can come from his sorrow, and his brown boots show he is seeing things honestly, through a grounded lens of reality, seeing situations, events, others and himself as they are.

Three cups lie turned over with their emotional potential spilt onto the ground. Blood flows from two of the cups and from the other, there is a green liquid. The blood shows the pain of the heart, a real emotional attack that has left him feeling injured. The green can link to the Heart Chakra, showing a deep emotional and spiritual pain. So, a loss which cuts deep on many levels. Green also shows jealousy and envy, with red also representing spilt passions, guilt and shame, so these may also form a part of the loss here. The man may be a victim, as equally as he could be the wrongdoer, as there are no signs of which.

All is not lost here: two of the five cups remain upright behind him showing hope, which is also shown by a few things within this card.

The river to the front of him is fast-moving, with the water symbolising the upset, turbulent emotions he is facing. He may be looking down, yet each glance up means he sees his emotions streaming by as he has not turned his back on his loss. Being fast-moving, he will not be able to swim through the river back to his castle, which will force him to take the bridge and deal with his issue or stay put.

The bridge gives a way to move on from problems, offering hope in the form of reconciliation and a time to 'mend bridges'. A bridge connects two locations and represents separated people, groups, or locations; and with this being a five, communication is both possible and required. It's to his right, so to get there, he will have to use his emotional self, but some healing and emotional realisation are called for first.

In this original picture, beyond the barren area he stands within, the grass is green, symbolising a move to the greener ground is possible in time and that this is a temporary situation, not a permanent place to stay. In some newer versions, the land is completely brown and dead on both sides of the river where he stands, with the green grass just being about the castle, suggesting a longer route to healing, as opposed to this original, which shows that healing can start the moment you take a few steps. Regardless, the ground is hilly, indicating a path that requires some focus and care to travel.

Over the bridge is the castle, so safety awaits him once his situation is realised. The castle symbolises his home, his well-being and his security, which the river separates him from. He may feel a long way from home and disengaged from life, yet like the river, he can still see it if he looks up and has not abandoned it. Getting back to this place of happiness will be a goal and what he misses, yet also what he feels is lost.

The two upright cups indicate that although there has been a loss, the future is waiting, which is mirrored in the moving water, telling us that life does not stop regardless of upset and hurt. This is not a stagnant card; things are changing already. These two cups, which represent balance, connection and unity just as in the Two of Cups, are not seen; either he ignores them, or in his grief does not see them as he focused on the loss of the Three of Cups, which here represents a happy situation being overturned.

The two upright cups show hope in repairing a situation. They show that there is something to salvage, yet it may not have the wild passion of the three lost cups; but with a lesson learned, situations can be more mature and secure.

At times, we need to take time to ourselves to mourn our losses, to gather our thoughts and pain so that we can heal. The emotional loss shown in the Five of Cups may leave us hurt, upset and lost but it will also give us the chance to challenge our situation when we are ready, a chance to retrieve something from our loss. We are simply frozen for a while and need to do some soul-searching.

When he realises that life holds another chance for him to enjoy, he will be able to move away from his regrets. He will then carry the two remaining cups over the bridge to a new future, but resolution with the three spilt cups will have to be sought first, and so he has to feel the sting they bring and that cannot be avoided.

Numerological value - **FIVE** = Truth, analysis and communication.

IN A NUTSHELL

The focus will be on upset rather than solutions. Regret will not change things, yet all upsets need time to heal; find acceptance and move on. There is no point beating yourself up over what has gone before, as you cannot change the past.

Look to the future and salvage what is left, this is not the end but a bump in the road.

Five of Cups: Upright

The Five of Cups shows *the effect of an emotional loss.*

Circumstances will change within relationships or a specific situation. These changes will bring feelings of *loss, regret, anxiety and panic* over what has been lost, as well as *obsessing* over every word said and action made. We can be left feeling betrayed by our own actions or another's, and alone.

This will lead to worry over past actions and *a reluctance to accept the changes presented.* There is a tendency to think about *what went wrong* instead of what could be, and the present could be lost because you're being too concerned with the past, yet *healing cannot be rushed.*

The dust needs to settle, as what has been lost cannot be regained in its old format. Things have now changed and can be seen as they truly are.

The emotional breaks that the Five of Cups bring are not permanent, as often referred to as *'crying over spilt milk'*. This card shows *situations can be repaired* if you come to terms with what has occurred, be that a simple argument, a lovers' tiff, to a major separation. When it comes to separations, it can show them to be *a temporary relationship break-up.* Yet can also show *someone fixated on an old relationship or situation,* who is trapped in a cycle of negative spiralling thoughts rather than taking action.

Feelings must be felt and dealt with to make or break a situation. If they are worked with, a deeper relationship may follow, teaching one or both partners a bit more about the other. If not, then there will, after time, be a friendship to enjoy. Yet of course this does not just refer to romantic relationships, but all relationships where *acceptance* is needed before you can move on.

Five of Cups: Reversed

Reversed, the Five of Cups shows the two remaining cups being picked up and used as their value is realised as *life goes on*.

It shows a difficult time has been gone through, and that now you are passing out of it, freed from the pain it once caused you. *Hope is felt* and actions are taken to get back to normal, or a new normal, being left a bit *wiser;* and we can feel elated by all of this.

Negatives are turned into positives, here is a time to realise life has potholes which we fall into at times, mistakes happen, and we do not have to be frozen in place by them. We *heal* and move forwards with a deeper understanding, feeling stronger and seeing situations, people and ourselves in a new light.

There is *acceptance of a situation,* a realisation that allows life to go on without regret and remorse, as the past or an event is put into perspective. An emotionally distressing time is moving away as *apologies are made, offered and accepted*.

Friends may help in your break from the past by acting as mediators or councillors, so *reach out to others if you feel the need,* as communication is welcomed with this card.

SIX OF CUPS

The Six of Cups pictures two children in a garden with the older child offering a younger child a cup of flowers.

The children represent warm childhood memories or recalling the past, the safety of earlier years and of perceived simpler times in our lives. They also show the inner child and that home is where the heart is, and they take us back to a time when life felt easy.

The little girl is a young child as shown by her mitten, as well as her blonde hair which represents youth. It is an image showing a moment in time, where she is offered the gift but has not yet had the time to take it, as her face looks up in pleasant wonder. Her clothes are mixed, showing her youth and playfulness; the orange cowl shows her enthusiasm, which is echoed by her spotted dress. In the original pictured, it is pale green with black polka dots, in others yellow with orange dots. One shows her as trusting, loyal and loving, and the others full of energy and lively, both fitting for a child, with the polka dots showing her to be young and full of energy. Her blue under-dress shows us her calm, trusting nature. Her shoes are red, showing optimism, a desire to receive, curiosity, positivity and excitement. The white of her mitten is a sign that she trusts the gift giver, innocent to it being anything other than pure.

The older child is wearing an orange hat called a chaperon with the tail called a liripipes - a hat which is also a shawl. In some versions, their hats are alternate colours, with the younger child in orange and this older child in red. Whilst for keeping warm and dry, it is also a bit of frivolity, a fashion statement; the name liripipes can also be interchanged with liripoop, meaning a person who is silly. This being orange shows this child to be wanting fun, gifting the other child some silliness to enjoy, with a desire to please as he hands the cup and flower to the child in a loving gesture. With the blue coat, he is an equally trusting soul, and his brown boots show him to be sincere.

In this version of Rider Waite Smith, both children's clothes are a bit ragged. The girl's clothes are frayed at the ends, and the boy's tunic is patched at the sleeve, representing that this is not about money, wealth or status, but genuine affection for affection's sake, and seeing the past, minus its hardships.

The children's two ages indicate differences in time, and how both the 'time or era', or our age when events occur, can allow us to perceive memories frozen in time. Memories don't mature with us: they come imbued with the feelings we felt at the age we experienced them, leaving us travelling back in time to revisit them.

The cup handed to the small child emulates the act of passing down gifts and belongings, traditions, heritage, ideals, beliefs, yet also support, affection, generosity, gifts for celebration or love. And all of this is done with warmth and sincerity. He is gifting something which will one day be a memory.

The four cups in the foreground represent the memory of this scene, as four's action on emotions is to restrict them. This gives a narrow view of things gone by as when we find a memory, it's seen from a set viewpoint, and with this tunnel vision. As in the Four of Cups, we can get lost in how things were, yet here all four cups are together rather than separated. The Ace is being gifted, and so there may be rose-tinted glasses being worn, with us only seeing the good from the past.

The last cup is placed on the concrete plinth bearing a coat of arms. The shield represents protection, the cross deep belief in the past, with the coat of arms itself a sign of history and memories honouring past events. Placing the cup high on top shows respect and reverence for the past. About the base of this plinth is ivy; it spreads onto the grass near the eldest child. It brings with it an energy of holding on to the past, of immortality and affection, all those things which fond memories are.

The white flowers are placed in the cups as if they were vases, so a playful use of symbolism. It shows we can take the past and use it imaginatively as equally as we can stick to the old ways. The flowers are either Astra Whites, symbolic of friendship, welcome and warm remembrance, or the White Cypress flower, symbolic of eternal love, and also remembrance. With five petals these small white flowers are a sign of hope and protection.

The house represents home, a place to go back to, a time of safety, family, childhood, youth, happiness, being carefree and being surrounded by friendship. Back to a time when we were free from responsibilities.

The garden brings safety, echoed by the guard patrolling the grounds with a spear. He walks on the pathway which is secure and strong, a sign of protection and safe boundaries. His presence allows the children freedom to explore, have fun and enjoy moments of innocent joy in the safety of familiarity. Sometimes we just need to go back home and be with those who love you.

Beside the house is a tower built on firm ground, showing it was built with sincere ideals. Yet it is still a tower, so these may not be your ideals, but those gifted to you in years gone by, and memories may give you a need to review the past.

The Six of Cups brings the past back into your life with feelings of warmth and comfort, to a time when our needs were met, and to a time when we could play. We feel genuine affection and friendship flowing from the past, bringing us gentle moments of thoughtfulness and reflection.

This card concerns itself with the past and the security found in nostalgia. Stirred-up memories will prompt you to look at people and events from the past. The gift representing the past is offered to the child, who represents the future. She reaches out with her right mitten, as white as the flowers, showing the emotions of the past meeting the present. A time to reach into the past to help with the here and now, a time to greet memories and open our hearts to who we once were, a time for innocent sincerity.

Numerological Value – SIX = Ease, attraction and diplomacy.

IN A NUTSHELL

The past will bring answers to your problems. Memories will help move you forwards; it is a time to connect to what you have lost or experienced so that you can move forwards with a spring in your step.

Old names and faces can pop up, giving you things to consider, reviving old dreams, and talk will be of the past.

Six of Cups: Upright

The Six of Cups shows the **returning of the past that will affect your present.** This may be in the form of thoughts and memories. This can be prompted by events or more usually people, yet also a song or a smell taking you back to earlier times in your life.

Your past will be presented to you in one form or another, and feelings connected to this are **nostalgic, heart-warming and welcoming**, bringing up past issues for you to review and reminisce.

Your mind will be in the past as **happy memories** take centre stage. You can look back on events to get inspiration for the present and future, even if that actively means connecting to the people involved and connected to those memories.

The past will be a topic of conversation. We may even feel a bit **homesick and whimsical** about our past and enjoy some time reliving the past alone or with friends.

The Six of Cups often means that an old relationship will resurrect itself or an old friend will be unexpectedly heard from. **Places and faces from your past** including family, old friends and ex-lovers can appear and influence you, a time for **reunions and celebrating the past**.

Yet this card can also show **random acts of kindness** which fill you with hope, happiness, leaving you feeling connected to both yourself and the giver.

Six of Cups: Reversed

Reversed, the Six of Cups shows **we will have to deal with the past and it will be unpleasant**. Remembrances may not be warm and happy but filled with feelings of insecurity and upset as **unhappy memories** surface.

The past will be unceremoniously dug up and **you will have to face events that you thought or hoped had been left behind you**. You will find yourself stuck in old memories, wallowing, or haunted by events, **trapped in the past** and unable to move forward.

The past is not ready to be forgotten as it holds too much importance when it should be let go of by either yourself or another; instead, it is romanticised or agonised over.

There's an air of bitterness to this card; there are no small acts of kindness, as the past brings up unwelcome gifts of **nasty comments and rash statements** born from past disappointments, grudges and losses.

As the past is not forgotten, **anything embarrassing, illegal or immoral will be found out**.

This can also show that someone who wishes to **live in the past, does not wish to grow up, or those who do not wish to cut the apron strings from childhood or youth**. So here you may meet a 'Peter Pan' or someone always going back to when 'they were young' and negatively judging the present in relation to their past.

SEVEN OF CUPS

The Seven of Cups depicts seven cups sitting in the clouds, while below, a man contemplates which one to choose.

The man is hidden half in the shadows and half in the light, which shows him to be in a state of indecision and confusion, and yet in the process of trying to make a wise choice. His silhouetted appearance is a sign he is overshadowed by choice, and that the choices themselves may just be in his head. He ponders options, yet he is a figure, an outline, so he may not see the whole picture. His back is to the dark with the light in front of him, which may blind him, indicating that he is not illuminated as to what he wants, and so he gazes at the cups in the clouds, poised to reach out, if only he could choose one. Fragments of ideas lead him forward, with his imagination embellishing his visions. He has an active mind, which is moving from one idea to another, focused on dreams and adventure, each one full of *what ifs and maybes*.

The cups and their contents sit in grey clouds and so are not concrete or realistic but mere daydreams, hopes and wishes. Until action is taken, and choices are made, these are just figments of his imagination. He literally has his head in the clouds, completely bewildered by the choices and outcomes his mind gives him. And being grey, this may well cause tension and anxiety while he contemplates.

Each cup holds something different to tempt and confuse the man.

The first cup has a woman's head or a mask, and this represents the outer self. It displays the mask we put on for others and our public image. So, his curiosity here could be on how others see him, how he is perceived, his insecurities and how he wishes to portray himself. He may wish to change who he is, and it will be to please how others see him, so here is his fragile ego.

The shrouded figure represents the inner journey towards our true inner self. He may wish to develop his spiritual self, work on his inner being and look within his subconscious. He may wish counselling, guidance or to spend time evaluating who he really is. A red aura surrounds the figure, so he may see an inner journey as a means to, again, create a different version of himself based on ego and sees only the outcome and not the hard work it would take.

The snake is for temptation and learning through desire and knowing what to say 'No' to. He may wish to lean towards intimacy, yet snakes also bring fertility via rebirth and growth as they shed skins. So, he may wish to stay on a path but be wiser? The snake slithers out of the cup, so does he wish to be free from desires, or be free with his desires? Deep down, this can be an inner trust issue.

The castle is for adventure, yet this also looks like a tower, so does he wish to hide inside of his ego and build castles in the sky? In doing so he is impractical and deluded by his wishes, not willing to work at anything he wants. Or he may prefer the safety of the castle walls to retreat and not risk conflict or insecurity, to feel safe.

The jewels represent material treasure: they are piled high, hanging over the edges of the cup, showing an abundance of wealth. This cup shows riches, so he may be looking at his greed, what else he can take, or find to enhance his own prosperity. He may be focusing on thoughts such as 'when I'm rich ', 'when I win the lottery'...

The laurel wreath is for victory, yet it also has a skull etched on the cup, so really victory or death! He may be focused here on success and power, looking at personal achievements with a fear of losing what he has gained, or even losing what he may gain, which stands in the way of him trying.

The last cup has a devilish imp, or a Wyvern, showing his inner courage being challenged, a need for him to confront his deep-seated confusions and fears about who he is. It leans over the cup, looking to pounce at him, tongue licking the air as it senses the man's fear and insecurity. Wyverns breathe frost, so this may be an aspect of himself that sends chills down his spine, yet once greeted, he would see it as a strength instead.

So here the difficult challenge is laid down - all that you must do is choose one! This may seem easy, but you only have one chance to make the right decision, and you are being led by your imagination.

Numerological Value - **SEVEN** = Spiritual growth, wisdom and endurance.

IN A NUTSHELL

Choice, decisions and questions about choice and decisions! A card which can lead us to opportunities or pathways to choose from. Yet due to there being more than one choice or one with many aspects to it, we are unsure of what to do for the best. We may not wish to lose one thing to gain another or make a choice only to realise we have made a mistake.

We may need to prioritise, or even stop dreaming - either way, once we have chosen, there may be no going back, so choose wisely what you pick, ignore or throw away.

Seven of Cups: Upright

The Seven of Cups tells of *a time for decision-making and usually an important one*, where the weight of confusion may make it hard to do. If the importance of the outcome is not realised, then it should be, as any decision made under this card will direct your future. Once a decision is made, it may well be final and hard to cancel. When opportunities present themselves under this card, put sincere effort into what you desire for your future. You may need to ask another for their view or **be honest with what you really want** and try not to become the victim of illusion.

You can be spoilt for choice also, with too many options, too many ways to move forward when only one can be chosen. ***Being faced with more than one alternative to choose from*** can indicate a need to be more focused and less distracted by what shines and glitters, in order for you to see what are shallow opportunities, false promises, or wisps of fantasy and what are not.

Time may be a factor here, so make sure that imagination is kept in check.

If you have been waiting for a time to be able to make some fresh choices, then this card shows that ***you will be free to make a new choice or a decision concerning much-needed changes***. This will be with you in the present or coming to you, depending on where it's placed in the spread, which can be a welcome relief if choice has been denied.

Seven of Cups: Reversed

Reversed, the Seven of Cups points to a need for change when there are **no options available**, or the ones that are presented are undesirable or unsuitable. This will leave you in a situation where **no changes or happy adjustments can be made at present**.

Your head will be in the clouds, and you will be focusing not on choices but on wishes which have no foundation other than to distract you from what is real. The risk of **delusion** is present as you have become **blinded by dreams. Daydreams and fantasies may be propelling you towards a mistake.**

Now is a time to be realistic and get to grips with what needs to be worked with, as you are hiding in wishes, hopes and make-believe.

The cups can come crashing down, falling from the sky, breaking your dreams into pieces and leaving you feeling **overwhelmed by your imagination**. You will be unable to see what you really want and get **lost in micro-nitpicking of your visions**. Leaving you stuck and prone to feeling boxed in by your own irrational or impractical wishes and even **procrastinating**.

EIGHT OF CUPS

The Eight of Cups shows eight neatly stacked cups in the foreground, and in the darkness, a man is shown turning his back on the cups and walking away.

The cups show an emotional connection to a situation which has, in the past, brought emotional rewards, but now lacks 'something'. His cups have been cared for, tended to, and neatly stacked, showing us that they are not being thrown away, but they miss an ingredient shown by the gap between the cups on the top row. He walks away from the security of the situation, so he can find the missing piece, as they do not hold his attention as they are. Here, he sets out on a journey, focusing now on his search for the missing cup.

Whichever way you look, the eight cups fall into a set of five cups with a set of three. Either a set of five next to a set of three, or five at the bottom and three at the top. This can be seen as his pain, with his celebrations and joys, and a need to bring them together. Or that he has built his life upon his past disappointments, built connections and affections but still needs something to bridge that gap and fill the empty space. It shows the Eight of Cups is all about the pursuit of the ninth cup, as something is missing from his life.

Although the card shows darkness, it is daytime, and we are shown a solar eclipse. The new covering moon brings a time where change can be felt on a deep emotional level, with a need to leave old cycles of life, or self, behind. It brings a time of inner awareness, yet not the total illumination to see things with clarity. The energy of The Sun's card would be mostly hidden, with the watery cards' number eight causing restrictions, here constraining emotions and confining them. The eclipsing moon would prompt the man's need for change, an instinctual calling, with the slither of the sun giving momentum to get moving and make changes before the light fades completely, or the sun returns and blinds him with optimism, and he stays put.

With little light to show him a way forward, the man will feel the confusion of The Moon card. He will have a subconscious prompt that change is possible and deeply needed. He feels a deep emotional pull to leave old cycles of life, or the self, behind. A time of inner awareness, without the total illumination to see things with clarity. The moon presents a window of opportunity that allows possibilities to be felt. In the darkness, man may not see a clear path, yet there is the understanding that change is needed.

Secure situations have limitations, and sometimes they need to be left or challenged to allow for growth and so he is setting off because that missing gap simply needs to be filled. He is seeking satisfaction and completion even if he is equally pensive and puzzled by his unknown destination. The moon watches him with a sad, tight-lipped expression – maybe wondering why he would leave such a lovely collection of cups and a great situation in search of something new, which may equally be a thought to those around him.

The man is not full of illusion or deluded but more driven to seek more to fill his life with, as his red boots and cloak show him to be pushing forwards, full of desire to find what is missing. His steps will be filled with purpose, even if not with a real sense of direction.

The man walks uphill to reach higher ground; there is no pathway, just grass and rocks to trip him up. In the dark, this means his journey could be up and down on uneven terrain, prone to mistakes and slip-ups, yet he has a wooden walking stick, so with grounded emotions supporting him, he's determined to keep moving forwards. His walking stick can be seen as a wand, a fiery energy taking him forwards with a desire and passion to create and find a missing jigsaw puzzle piece. He feels the potential ahead of him, so he forges his own path, determined to move forward.

There is a desire to escape stagnation, which is shown by the rock pool's shallow water, where nothing can escape till the tide dictates. He has walked through this water, these non-flowing emotions, these stale feelings, so he has deeply felt his discontent; this is not a whim. He knows he needs to move onward to avoid damage or loss to his neat stack of cups, so he starts his journey in hope of new perspectives, answers, opportunities or a new road to travel.

This card brings an inner urge to make more of ourselves or a situation: we may not know what or why, but we seek to add to what we are or what we have achieved for deeper fulfilment.

Numerological Value – EIGHT = Change, challenge, honesty and determination.

IN A NUTSHELL

Trust your intuition; yes, you can improve what you have, so be willing to reach out of your comfort zone to find it. You may feel that you are in a deep rut, and all ruts can be climbed out of, allowing you to see things from a new perspective.

Have faith that you can find a new outlook: it is out there, even if you are confused as to what you may find; it's a journey you have to take to stop stagnation.

Eight of Cups: Upright

The Eight of Cups shows **a desire to leave or change a secure relationship or situation that has been outgrown**. As we grow or evolve, so do our needs and goals, leaving us knowing we need more than we have and willing to risk our current security to find change or growth.

We feel **disappointment or dissatisfaction** and it's felt on a deep emotional level that now is the time to **cut ties and break free, so we can find what's missing from our lives**.

A current situation does not have enough stimuli to satisfy any longer, yet the situation is still cared for, but the winds of change need to blow life back into it by stepping outside of it.

This card shows the questioner having **courage** with a **realisation that feelings and personal requirements change over time**. Admitting to themselves that they need to create more for themselves or feel more satisfied in an area of their lives. To be able to keep a situation alive we need to leave our apparent security to grow, even when the outcome may not be clear.

Security does not always prove to be beneficial, and this card shows this being realised, it can cause frustration, stagnation and place barriers to growth. A magic ingredient is called for and the search is on to find it, leaving us **restless for change** and to improve what we have.

You may find yourself **stuck in a rut** and have an idea as to a solution or be completely in the dark yet willing to gently seek change to be able to **see things from a fresh perspective**.

Independence and space are needed as you are tiring of old routines, and **a challenge outside of an established situation is needed**.

Eight of Cups: Reversed

Reversed, this card still shows disillusionment with events and situations but warns that the *impulse to make changes should be made carefully*, as feelings can often be temporary and not founded. So, a case of *'look before you leap'* as mostly this card is one of *staying put and making the best of things, and not being deceived by The Moon.*

Be positive before making any decision out of *boredom*, as *your current situation or relationship still has plenty of life and energy left to give*. So instead of walking away, stop and *try to make changes within the situation itself.*

You will feel that life is stagnating or passing you by, which may be due to having built up something without thought for the future and you are now finding yourself trapped within it. You may also feel too scared of the hurt it will cause to others, as well as the insecurity it will bring to yourself if you make changes.

You may find yourself *making excuses* to avoid looking at the changes you need to make within yourself and correcting your own behaviour. If you wish to *escape a situation,* honesty is needed with yourself, as it will be yourself you wish to escape from; and if you leave, you will take yourself wherever you go.

Confusion will cloud judgements and you may feel the *grass may be greener on the other side,* but with this card, it rarely is. Once you have decided to leave your current security and situation, it may not be waiting for you when or if you try to return.

We can also be shown here someone struggling to improve a situation, who keeps failing as they are not working with the right intent. They may be *trying to force change out of insecurity or because they think it will please another.*

NINE OF CUPS

The Nine of Cups shows a contented, happy man sitting in front of his neatly displayed nine cups.

Often this man can be seen as a merchant. Yet I feel him to be a relaxed, prosperous man, as he's not selling us anything here. He wants to keep what he has and presents to us his possessions as you would a new car or an engagement ring; he is simply asking us to look at what he has achieved. He has a plump face, a sign of good living and being free from worry as his basic needs are met, with plenty left over.

His striped white and grey outfit - which is blue and white striped to represent a merchant in some decks - while slimming (there may be a touch of vanity here), along with the white and grey under-shirt, shows he has deep thoughts about what he has achieved, as he does not take it all for granted. His hat is orange in the image, yet red in others and shows him still fuelled by ideas, enthusiastic and wanting to play with the ideas he still has. Extra bits of fabric decorate his hat, showing that he can afford an excess, a bit of swagger as he shows off. His hat symbolises his actions, his daring, which have allowed him to step out of his comfort zone to gain his cups; as they haven't just fallen into his lap by magic. His red tights show the same passion: each move has been made with purpose. They show a bold, daring personality with a strong sense of self-worth, someone pleased with what he's gained. He has a small black belt, the black showing his potential, and here the ability to see bring all his mental desires to fruition. It is thin and under his belly, so it represents a bit of indulgence in the world about him as he enjoys what shines to him on what could be seen as a superficial level to others.

His clothes are not clothing to labour in, but for relaxation, showing a time to be able to sit back, relax, and enjoy his rewards. It is as if he has just spurted out for new tights and a bright hat to show the world of his gains, but not worried so much about the rest of his outfit, opting for comfort. (A bit like showing a new Rolex off while in your PJs, Hugh Hefner style.)

With his green shoes - brown in some versions of the RWS - and wooden bench he is grounded, with both connecting him to the practical side of life and his earthly gains. Here is not someone egotistical and superior, as he chooses to sit on a basic wooden seat, showing he is down to earth and not lost in his accomplishments, simply happy with them and enjoying the good life. At heart, he is keeping it real. Both his feet face in different directions, showing he may not have any firm decisions about his future, as now is about just enjoying what he has gained.

His legs are open, showing passion, desire and that he is ready to act if he wanted to, and so with his hat and feather, he has not finished accumulating the things which make him happy. He knows his cups need to be maintained and worked at. This is echoed by his folded arms forming a lemniscate, bringing balance and simplicity, showing that he wants to maintain all he has. His arms go across his Solar Plexus Chakra so he may be quite protective about what has come his way; and some may see smugness, as getting what we want can bolster our ego. It may also show that the opinions of others are not needed, as he feels confident and safe. Either way, he will not be giving any of this away. He smiles a genuine smile, showing contentment: in this moment he is truly happy.

His nine cups, representing his accomplished desires, are placed in a semi-circle around him like a horseshoe, a symbol for luck and protection. A sign he wishes to keep what he has close to him, everything in easy reach so he can cherish them all equally.

The narrow table holds his cups, with room for nothing else as he is only focused on his gains. It's draped in blue fabric, which shows his spirituality side, or rather, his current inner self reflected in plush fabric and his need to communicate to us what he has in his life. Notice the abundance of material isn't neatly pleated. He has not taken the time to make the display as neat as he could have. So, he may not be focusing too much on his spiritual side as he's too busy being down to earth, enjoying pleasures and comforts. As such, right now, his spiritual values are placed in the physical and it brings him happiness, as material or emotional gains are a higher attainment, which still creates joy for him on a spiritual level, as his display voices his happiness, confidence, and excitement to all who can see it. He's found peace here, even if it may be superficial to some. This can lead to a relaxed phase of life in which deep contentment is brought to the soul as wishes are granted.

What is beneath the curtain? Who can say? Maybe it's all the imperfect things he wishes to hide from the world, or maybe nothing at all, as he only wants us to focus on what he wishes to display, his newfound smile and pride.

The cups are raised above him, placing them out of reach of others and showing them off for all to see, like prize-winning cups. You can look but not touch, which shows he places a lot of stock in them. His faith, his hope and his future are placed on the shelf behind and above his head; he may well even find them more important than life itself.

Traditionally, the Nine of Cups is known as The Wish Card, pointing to the fulfilment of a wish and all the happiness that brings. It brings personal achievements as aspirations, as his dreams are fulfilled with his success displayed so that he can fully enjoy the emotional satisfaction that he has obtained. He has his heart's desire!

This card brings happiness and a feel-good factor into one's life which will make you feel enormously proud of yourself.

Numerological Value - NINE = Inspiration, honesty and understanding.

IN A NUTSHELL

Wishes will come true, so make a wish...

What you want, you will get. Happiness, contentment and feeling blessed will find you feeling proud as punch. Everything is going your way, but do not sit down too long, as work is still needed to take you forwards. Yet it is a wonderful time to fully enjoy yourself.

Nine of Cups: Upright

The Nine of Cups is traditionally known as the **wish card**, and also *a yes* to positive questions. Desires, hopes, ambitions and dreams will be fulfilled, and **success** will be assured.

The Nine of Cups is not a card of finalisation, it simply states that **you will get what you want**. It is not a sign of long-term happiness but a time to grasp what you want - after that, as with all things, it is down to you to make things more long-term.

This card brings physical and emotional security, **a time to reap rewards**.

The Nine of Cups shows **accomplishment** in any area of paramount importance in your life; you will naturally be left **feeling pleased with yourself**, a bit like the cat that's got the cream, so a bit of happy **self-indulgence** is enjoyed. **Satisfaction is guaranteed**: you will feel proud as you realise that your **dreams can come true** as you get what you want or are given the chance to go for it. Feelings will be **positive, happy and contented**.

This can also show someone happy and **feeling blessed** with what they have; someone already in awe of how much they have achieved, yet happy to aim for more.

Definitely, a card which will make you smile.

Nine of Cups: Reversed

Reversed, the Nine of Cups leaves **wishes and dreams unfulfilled**; what you hope for does not come your way. This can be from **bad timing to being unrealistic** with what is desired, making your goal impossible to obtain.

Wishing, hoping, and dreaming are not going to get you anywhere; **now is a time for direct action and to rethink dreams**.

This card brings **sadness** and **disappointments**, leaving feelings of **disillusionment** as you are let down by your own desires or wishes. You may not have put enough effort in, or it can simply be that **now is not the time for progress** or the time for you to have what you fancy or are working towards.

At times, this card can also show that you have been gifted what you've asked for, and the old saying *'be careful what you wish for as you may just get it'* comes to mind. You have what you wish for, but it has proved to be **unfulfilling and unsatisfying**.

Longer time limits or a different route should be set regarding specific goals; success goes to those who **keep dreams in perspective**. Idealised wishing will not yield results.

TEN OF CUPS

The Ten of Cups shows a family; two adults are joined under a cup-filled rainbow whilst two children dance beside them.

The main element shown here is the family setting: mother, father and two children showing happiness and unity. Together they all stand on firm ground representing stability, giving a secure and solid foundation to their lives and unit.

In front of the adults is a stream, a reflection on them more than the children, as it shows their flowing, fluid emotions. The children are joyful as they have not experienced the harshness of life, whereas the adults will not be naïve to such things. Yet here everything is flowing, so it is a time to be at ease and be problem-free.

The house in the hills represents home, the secure, safe environment of a protected family setting. Everything here is idyllic.

The children represent a carefree and happy situation full of enthusiasm and innocence with their colourful clothing. One wears the colours of the woman, the other the man, showing that they are in tune with each other, linked and together. Some editions of the deck dress the older child in the same golden yellow as the cups, showing that good things can be directly brought to the family, the home, and to who and what we love. As they play their game, they do not notice the rainbow; absorbed in their dance, they express their enjoyment of life, as for them, this is just how things are meant to be: safe, joyful and liberating.

The two adults bring security and love, to their own, as well as the children's lives, a union that extends beyond their relationship. They wear clothes which are quite humbling; they may not have riches, but they have each other. Her underskirt is purple, showing us her spirituality, wisdom and devotion. Her blue dress covers this with loyalty, serenity and matches the man's blue trousers, showing their spiritual and deeper connection to the family situation as well as each other. In other versions her underskirt is brown, showing a grounded, down-to-earth and practical energy, a physical connection to her life as it draped onto the earth. In purple, it shows a spiritual connection to her physical life, so both are apt.

The man wears yellow boots with red cuffs, which show his desire to maintain this scene and security. His coat is orange/red, which shows his optimism and mental commitment, a zest for living and for enjoyment within this situation, along with the steps taken to create this situation. Yet this is not an intellectual moment, but one of wonder, happiness and joy, as a richness of love is at the top of their agenda.

They stand facing away from us as this is their time, their scene to enjoy and they want to absorb all they can from what they see. The man has his arm about the woman's waist, showing familiarity and a realness between the two of them. They both stand with arms outstretched towards the sky filled with their cups, praising their luck, their connection to each other and their emotional abundance. They are opening their arms to the opportunities about them and welcome all the goodness here with open, trusting hearts. This scene has a 'happy ever after' feeling to it: everything is perfect, representing domestic life combined with expressions of love and harmony.

The ten cups, an expression of their commitment and love, hang in a clear blue sky within a rainbow, symbolising that our dreams can come true. Blessings can be bestowed upon us all through those whom we love, literally here, blessings from heaven. A rainbow is formed after rain, something we can only appreciate when we have gone through a few emotional downpours, and here they are in awe, standing, arms raised, welcoming this gift from the heavens into their lives. Traditionally, rainbows are symbols of good luck, hope, faith, peace and serenity. They bring encouragement and miracles showing new beginnings on the horizon.

The Ten of Cups is a time of happiness within home and family lives, showing us that domestic happiness will be at its best. Emotionally, things will be very harmonious, with lots of love and laughter to go around, feelings will be sincere, and emotions will be committed. Life will be going very well and will feel blessed, allowing not only for the enjoyment of the present but also the planning of the future.

Numerological Value - **TEN** = Purpose, uniting and bringing together of energies to create a new whole.

IN A NUTSHELL

Happiness is guaranteed! You can wallow in your good fortune and share that happiness with others. Everything is positive. Love is in the air, along with commitment. Healing of life, love and self is now possible.

Forgiveness, unconditional love, respect and harmony are brought into play and there will be smiles all around.

Ten of Cups: Upright

The Ten of Cups gives an **abundance of unconditional love and emotional security,** by offering us the sanctuary of family; be they related or friends, we find our emotional home and relish the joys and peace found there. A time is given to feel totally safe and welcomed for who you are. This card shows **a happy family,** or situation where everyone is **satisfied** with the part which they play within the group, showing unity and sincerity. Everybody will be pulling in the same direction. *Everybody is on the same page and smiling*.

It's not just family situations that bode well with this card; so do new or growing relationships and friendships. If you are wishing to start something new, you will find *others to be very welcoming to your ideas*. Do reach out to those you wish to know better or to ask help from, as all will be well with whatever you are trying to achieve.

If you wish to *heal a rift and difficulties with another,* this card can help, as the rainbow forms a bridge to help you both find a new peace and understanding between each other. Now is a time for *happiness*, and this card makes that possible.

This ten can bring us sudden joy and happiness, like *a miracle out of the blue* - all that is positive is now brought together for everyone to enjoy and to *celebrate*.

The Ten of Cups brings *commitment* in relationships such as weddings or engagements. This can also cover any union between people or groups, the bringing together of those things which would make you feel totally emotionally content.

Whatever this card brings, it will enrich your sense of self as well as your overall well-being and make you happy, as this card brings us all *the happy endings which we all hope for*.

Ten of Cups: Reversed

Reversed, this card brings *family and domestic upsets*. Although it can show stress and upset in other reliable situations, especially where other people are involved, such as work.

Rifts can appear in families, relationships and connections of all kinds where there has been long-standing security or a previous harmonious unity.

Happiness, what is positive in your life, can be *taken for granted*, leading to potential loss, so this card shows *a time to review matters* especially if you feel you would be better off leaving. If you feel the need to walk away from a situation, it may not be for the right motives, and you may be *self-sabotaging* something good.

Close relationships and friendships are *close to failure*, as the security a situation of this nature produces is causing friction for at least one member of the group, making them feel trapped, *bored and hemmed in*. They may feel they are losing their identity and need to be reassured or allowed to pursue their goals to develop their own sense of personal identity. This stems from being too settled and secure, which has allowed a dull routine to start to break things down, leading to *complacency*.

A lot can still be gained here, as reversed this is a warning that serious loss can be encountered if actions and feelings are not challenged.

— The Cup Family —

Those belonging to the Cup family are caring and concerned with their own, as well as with the feelings and emotions of others. They love to love.

Cups are also the most intuitive of the Tarot suits and often found with psychic/spiritual/religious as well as psychological and other ministering interests.

Astrologically, Cups are water signs: Scorpio, Cancer and Pisces.

PAGE OF CUPS

The Page of Cups pictures a young boy holding a cup containing a fish that looks up, seemingly talking to him.

Astrological sign: Any Water sign, Scorpio, Cancer and Pisces.

Standing by the sea, we are shown this young man's emotional personality, but he is not touching the ocean, as the emotions within are too much for this Page to deal with. As a Page, it would be difficult to deal with that level of emotional complexity as the sea represents deeper feelings, yet it does also represent the unconscious mind. The water is a bit choppy, so the emotions here are not static but changing and moving. The Page stands on a stage, as with other cards, showing an important phase of life. With the waves rising to his side, it offers firm ground, which is good as he is not looking at anything other than the fish within his cup, and with his grey, contemplative sky, his thoughts will be deep. Other versions of this deck show the sky as a pale blue, showing that all is well, yet takes from the element of reflection, and of course, can also show a need for caution, especially when following such absorbing new ideas.

The pale pinks and blues of the Page's clothing show gentleness and reflection in this young soul. The pink shirt with billowing sleeves and tights shows a playful, fantasy-driven imagination that views the world through a soft lens. Pink is a very innocent colour, full of affection and harmony, so he is at ease walking through life from an emotional perspective. The tunic is trimmed with gold cord and a deeper pink trim: the gold shows an extravagance, here of imagination and the darker pink trim amplifies emotions and feelings. Around the throat, this can reflect talking with excited imagination, so tall tales of magical journeys; around his legs, it indicates someone walking in a world of their own and imaginative play. This shows someone with heightened emotions, yet being a Page, not mature ones.

The tunic is blue with the white lilies found in the Ace of Cups, on long golden stems. Being golden they show his feelings grow from his conscious world, the things he sees about him. The lilies bring growth from enlightenment, which grows here on stems of consciousness. His blue hat shows subconscious communication and faith, the blue scarf a sign that imagination flows easily into reality, making a division between the two hard at times, as it drapes down from his mind to over his right shoulder. So, his thoughts flow out, passing logic, and resting within his emotional view of the world. While it looks like a blue feather to the side of his hat, it is fabric, showing an excess of imagination; if seen as a feather it is also a symbol of communication with the self, so someone here lost adventuring within their mind and imagination.

At the centre of his hat is a very small blue circle representing his psychic nature, the third eye. In some images of the Page of Cups this circle is golden, also showing a higher spiritual connection. With creativity, this Page also has intuition, even if it is outweighed by the imagination. It is small, yet still full of potential.

In the original image shown, his belt is black with a gold buckle. The black represents his potential and depth, while the gold emphasises how his potential is secured by conscious desire; a touch of magic to hold it all together as his dreams become real to him. Other editions of the RWS show his belt as dark indigo, a spiritual colour that adds devotion, fairness, humility and creativity. Being loose, the belt shows that he cannot yet bring ideas, precognitions, and dreams together as they are all in his head. Nothing is tangible, even if they lean down his left side of logic, it all just gets caught up in wonder.

From the cup, a fish looks at the Page, perhaps talking to him, as the fish represents imagination, creativity and psychic ability. The fish coming from the depths of the ocean and the Page's smile shows this is the birth of something new, the fish connecting the Page to deeper thoughts, emotions and imaginings which tantalise him. The young Page gets pleasure from just looking at the fish, but this does not mean that he is yet ready to act on this creativity. His artistic, dreamy, or spiritual nature will be in a fanciful, inquisitive and imaginative phase but sparked. With the Page of Cups, this indicates that abilities and potential are being realised via imagination, allowing the mind to come alive as he starts a journey that will tell him a lot about his own, and others', psychology and emotional responses. Yet right now none of that is relevant or understood. Once this Page has done with the fish, it will be set free, as it would upset the Page to cause harm, and when he is ready, he will catch another.

He stands turned towards the left of the card, the logical thinking side, yet he does not look in that direction, as he looks solely at the fish, as right now that is his absorbing reality.

The Page of Cups is ruled by an imaginative and creative outlook on life; he thinks about feelings and dreams. This young individual is seeking the solace of their creative mind and so tends to be a quiet, intuitive and sensitive person. This is someone who loves themselves and who loves their world, with everything based on its emotional or imaginative content, and what journeys or messages can be gained from them.

IN A NUTSHELL

Be playful, dare to imagine what could be. Listen to your intuition, see what messages lay within your dreams or daydreams.

News may come relating to children, births or pregnancies, but if this is not for you, then have some fun and follow your imagination to see where it takes you.

Page of Cups: Upright

Personality - The Page of Cups is *a gentle dreamer* who is *sensitive, quiet, trusting*, very *imaginative* and creative. They may represent someone who enjoys art, writing, stories or any activity that involves the use of a quiet but active creative mind.

Out of all the Pages, this one can refer more to a child, so can represent *a child or baby.* An innocent card that can be a reminder to us all to play, dream and have fun once in a while.

These individuals are understanding of the feelings and needs of others and are always good to have around in times of trouble due to their *caring* and soft nature. They are often empathic, taking on the miseries of others as they feel responsible for other people's unhappiness and wish to resolve it.

The Page of Cups is also *a daydreamer* and could show *wishful thinking*.

This card can indicate the beginning of *psychic growth*. Intuition can be stirred up and although it excites, it will be thought about a lot rather than acted upon. Yet if you have had some psychic insights or a dream, this Page reminds you to look at it rather than dismiss it, as it may have stemmed from your subconscious mind or spiritual self.

Now is a time to *trust yourself*, have faith in your world-view, however passive it may seem to others.

This Page tells us to also use our imagination to help with any spiritual or practical problems we may have, as our imagination is a valuable tool.

Message/event - The Page of Cups brings *news or situations that concern children*: a birth or pregnancy, even good news relating to a child, someone young and imaginative or even a pet.

Page of Cups: Reversed

Personality - When the Page of Cups is found reversed, we have an individual who *lives in a daydream world*, and wishes to avoid reality, suffering from *an over-active imagination.*

This person will get over-excited about *unrealistic* concerns and be *over-sensitive to criticism.*

The Page of Cups reversed will often feel confused because circumstances or surroundings will not match the majesty of his mind and feelings. No dedication should be expected from this person, as they will be *wrapped up in a dream world.*

This is someone *unaware of the consequences* of their actions, which can show *naïvety and being overly immature*. There will be *the view that things are unfair*, as life will seem harsh to them.

In psychic and spiritual terms, imagination runs riot and fears are stirred up, leaving the psychic side of life experienced from a *superstitious* perspective.

The Page of Cups reversed warns that we should try to analyse irrational thoughts and fantasies and try to pacify an over-active imagination and fears with facts.

Message/event - The Page of Cups reversed brings *emotional upsets* and hurt feelings due to over-sensitivity, so *trust issues* can surface or be created. The troubled feelings of someone young or emotionally sensitive will surface, bringing *tears and wounded emotions*.

You may also show *concern for a child or even a pet's well-being or health*. For those wishing for pregnancy, this would not be a positive card.

KNIGHT OF CUPS

The Knight of Cups shows us a young man with a winged helmet and winged shoes astride his grey horse.

Astrological Sign: Scorpio.

Here is a young man in armour, who is at battle with his emotions; an emotional warrior trying to coax them to go where he wishes them, but like water, his emotions will just flow where they are taken. He may wish to look in control in his shiny new suit of armour and be emotionally mature, but he is at their mercy. His decorative tabard or surcoat bears his coat of arms: red fish and blue waves. The red fish show his emotional passion which jumps from his mind and calls to him through every fibre of his being. The waves show the flow of those emotions. Whatever he falls for, or whatever cause he wishes to champion, he is on an emotional crusade - and if you listen closely, you might even hear him dreamily sigh!

The winged helmet and footwear show spiritual aspirations. Both show him to be a messenger of emotions and earnest feelings, rushing to tell you how he feels, so at times this horse will go at great speeds with this young person. His winged helmet symbolises the rush at which his emotional thoughts can travel and change direction, with his emotions in flight. Missing in some versions of this card is the ring of red at the base of the wings, which shows them stemming from a passionate mind. However unrealistic he may be, it is born out of a heartfelt, intense search for a place to show his true self in the outside world. He cares and he wants his feelings known and accepted by those, or what he is aiming them towards.

His blue belt shows his single-minded nature; all that soft blue shows him to be earnest, and the image shows him focused on offering his sincerity via the cup he holds. In some RWS decks, his belt is white, showing us that his emotions and desires feel like a deep spiritual connection to him as it joins all aspects of his body and mind, laying central to his body. He looks over the cup, looking ahead, raising his cup up for another soul to see, extending his emotions outwards to display them and offer them up with seriousness.

He has arrived where he is in a flurry of feelings and now stands declaring his love, affection, and principles while his steed comes to a halt. Some say that he rides Death's horse, as Scorpio links the two cards, and this Knight can have a sting in his tail if passions are not rewarded, as they can feel like a grave wound to this young heart and soul. Death's horse, however, is white, and this Knight's horse is grey. In newer editions, he is often on a white horse to show his innocence and becomes the traditional knight in shining armour riding in on his trusty white steed. But the original is grey, showing his sincere, contemplative nature as he gently ventures in with his heart held out to that which he longs for. The horse is moving at a slow pace as he approaches the stream, and the Knight tentatively offers up his emotions, waiting for reciprocation, acceptance, or understanding. The horse's straps are decorated with waves and a soft blue, a coy romantic energy in which the Knight rides forward on waves of feelings and devotion.

His held-out cup represents his feelings of romanticism, desire, expectancy, sexual attraction and a need to be acknowledged. He is in love with a glamorised idea of what love and physical attraction represent. The Knight is lost in his imagination, giving him a dreamy nature, full of hope and anticipation that his affections will be returned. He is wearing his heart on his sleeve here and can show idealism and naïvety towards anything in life. He comes to us in a wave of simplicity, full of ideas and hope. He faces the right of the card, the side of emotion, so there is no logic in his seeking of love – but is there ever?

His surroundings are fairly barren; the water from his suit has not been used to fertilise the ground, and too much water with the muddy cliffs could bring them down. He is not dedicated to growth in his world as he's not worked out yet how to make the emotions he has, the water he is connected to, make the seeds of his desires root, grow, and blossom.

The stream is shallow, showing unsubstantial emotions with no real grounding in reality. It meanders slowly, adding a kind of half-hearted but gentle effort to this card. He is not getting off the horse to touch the water or even dip a toe in. He has not crossed it but stands raised above and away from it, showing us that while he is lost in his emotional wishes, he is not ready to get to grips with real emotions, nor truly ready to uncover what his suit really holds. He instead invites you to walk through the stream to meet with him, to meet his ideal of what love, passion, attraction should be, to see things from his side.

The Knight's dreams are full of possibility, but without the maturity that such matters need to have longevity, he may find it difficult to commit himself to the Cup's full energy. He is unprepared for commitment, and to confront the issue would shatter his idealistic view of the world and dent his armour.

The Knight of Cups is an idealistic dreamer who will often go to what shines and falls in love with new things at the drop of a hat. He brings a time when we act out of love and passion for what we are doing and sincerely feel we are doing the right things for the right reason.

IN A NUTSHELL

The Knight of Cups brings an emotional situation where the focus is on an emotional outcome. It shows the heart has a goal in mind. This can often be a romantic attraction, yet it can be any situation where daydreaming about action is present, rather than the action itself. We can fall in love with someone or something even if feelings have no firm roots.

This Knight's energy can leave you disappointed due to a lack of action or reality, a matter of enjoying the dream as it may not lead to anything substantial, but it could also make you feel pretty wonderful and excited.

Knight of Cups: Upright

Personality - The Knight of Cups is **a romantic and intensely devoted individual** susceptible to romantic **daydreaming** and is given to **high aspirations and idealistic desires.**

High principles feature with this Knight, with a firm belief in what is right or wrong. **A sympathetic soul** who brings inspiration and chances for change. He has persistent energy when he is chasing a dream and the word "No!" is often not an answer that deters this Knight, as he feels he must win you over to his way of seeing or feeling.

This may cause this knight to be a tiny bit **unrealistic.** He can often be found gently sighing over what might one day be and is easily hurt by rejection, as he is a lover, not a fighter. He brings **an earnest, serious approach to matters,** yet how to turn a wish into reality may not be present.

A bit of an 'emotional peacock' would also describe this Knight. He enjoys how things make him feel and so can be shallow, even if he appears to be deep. This Knight is flirtatious and **seeks intimacy** but can tend to wear his **heart on his sleeve**.

He is **Prince Charming**, riding in to save the princess with a bunch of flowers, someone who sees life through a veil of romanticism, **someone in love with love** and who will want to rush headlong into commitment. It may not always be a princess he seeks to save, but also anything which he feels he can help in a humanitarian or caring way.

He tells us that **hearts should be followed**, but be sensible and take our brains with us. He can lose out simply as he dreams and wishes more than the action he takes. Reminding us that a faint heart does not win the maiden, nor keep her.

Event - As an event, our romantic knight brings **a new opportunity for a romantic encounter and a sexual or, more, an emotional attraction,** a time for your heart to skip a beat! It could show someone sincere in their feelings for you, albeit a bit starry-eyed!

It can also show that if you're *in love with an idea,* you're still in the dreaming stage. However, no solid work has yet been done to secure any outcome, a case of being idealistic rather than realistic.

Knight of Cups: Reversed

Personality - When the Knight of Cups is reversed, we are confronted with *jealousy or anger* over an emotional and deeply personal disappointment. He realises that life does not always follow an idealistic pathway and is hurt. This Knight's armour has been dented!

To deal with hurt emotions, *this Knight lashes out by twisting facts* to even the odds in his favour and has a sting in his tail. To gain control, he may use *emotional blackmail* and *pass the blame* onto others; play with people's emotions trying to get what he wants; act in a *passive-aggressive* manner; and use others for his own emotional needs. He can act in a *misleading and seducing* manner in any area of life in which he feels slighted or hurt to empower himself. He will not confront situations personally, as he prefers emotional chess and manoeuvring others to his view.

He has *a fragile ego*, so *rejection* can turn this Knight into an unreasonable and bitter soul who will be unrealistic to the core.

All that matters to this Knight are his bruised emotions. Our once intrepid romantic turns into *a possessive individual* who refuses to accept the failure of a situation due to a broken, immature heart and a dented ego. He can cling to ideas or people, refusing to let them go.

All he does is influenced by his feelings of loss and disappointment; he reminds us to keep our motivations in check when we are hurt and feel stung by life or love.

This Knight will also, in an instant, leave a situation if something shinier comes along, be that an attraction, a cause or an ideal.

Event - Feelings within attractions or relationships are not mutual, showing *unrequited love*. This could also show a situation where you wish to have an old partner back even though you know it's not healthy.

Ideas here will be totally unrealistic: you will be in love with the outcome but unable or unwilling to do the work needed, and you may also feel very envious of those who have obtained what you are desiring.

QUEEN OF CUPS

The Queen of Cups shows a woman seated on the shore with her throne adorned with baby water nymphs.

Astrological Sign: Cancer.

The Queen of Cups sits on land whilst her feet and dress are gently lapped by the sea. Within the water, a small piece of her dress's hem in the water resembles the ripples of the sea itself; these ripples are missing in some newer decks, revealing the hem simply to be wet; yet the ripples show her a part of the ocean, understanding of its emotional depths, and her element. The ocean depicts her deep, calm emotions, yet she sits on the shore, as if she went in, she would risk being overwhelmed by her ocean, as it is boundless and deep. On the shore she has a balanced secure emotional outlook, facing emotions rather than swimming in them. The combination of land and water supports her dreams and visions, yet her foot touches them, so she can feel their ebb and flow. It allows her to be able to detach from the emotional element if she needs to ground her fantastically imaginative and loving mind.

She sits at the opening of a cove, an inlet or on a small, sand-banked island, and any would suit her. An ocean inlet is where emotions flow via a channelled route; in a cove, emotions collect and get caught up until the tide changes; a small island can show her need to be alone to recharge and connect to her feelings. She embodies all those things, yet in all, she is surrounded by the calm movement and flowing feelings of the sea. The ocean tides link to the moon, showing her intuitive nature, including clairvoyance and psychic insights as her caring nature will naturally make her empathic and sensitive to the energies about her. The tides also represent her emotional state which can fluctuate, and each ripple will change the way she acts, reacts and is within herself. Like the Page of Cups, she sits slightly facing the left of the card; the emotions she feels will be her reality and will be how she rationalises all she is and all she does.

The chalk cliffs are symbolic of emotional peace, protection and of home. The chalk will easily erode with a storm or high tide, just as she is easily affected by even a slight change in the currents about her, and a sudden flood of feeling could too easily eat away at her emotional calm.

At her feet are pebbles and a shell. The small pebbles all in different colours, worn smooth by the tides, indicate her emotions have helped her build who she is, her throne stands amongst them, aspects of herself which have been smoothed and moulded by her feelings and emotional experiences. In the very bottom right of the card is an indistinct image which is a conch shell; within it is the Seed of Life. The shell is linked to the vulva; the conch itself is an aphrodisiac, a link to Aphrodite, the Goddess of Love. We find an Egg of Life with the Knight of Swords as well, and within this Queen's card, this conch shell represents fertility, conception and pregnancy. The physical desire to procreate, bringing us her maternal side. Yet it is not in her focus or even a clear drawing, but out of sight as she gazes at her cup, as without love, it is all meaningless.

Her throne is made of stone and carved with Undines, also called water spirits, elementals or nymphs. They are small and cherubic, symbolising her emotional goodness and a simpler, purer love. Water nymphs embody the element of water, making her Queen of Water or Queen of Emotions. The one at the base of her throne holds a fish, representing intuitive messages from the subconscious mind, or from her spiritual self, as with the Page of Cups, yet here, set in stone, they are the seat of her character. Above her head and under her seat, they show that their energies form both the foundation of her true self as well as the way she thinks, as emotion is everything. The giant clam shell at the top of the throne shows her fragile emotional nature. When prodded, they clam shut, like her Cancerian aspect, which can hide inside a hard shell when things go wrong. Yet, by reverse, you can also be 'as happy as a clam'. She also wears a clam clasp, placed between her heart and throat, and so she will not always be able to hide her feelings in her words or actions. She will express all her positivity, love and sentiment; when unhappy, she will shut down and be silent. She sits on a deep red cushion, which is a brighter red in other versions of the deck. It shows her controlling, sitting on her feelings of passion, as if they ran free, they could cause loss and pain, anger and aggression. She does not wish passion to take precedence over emotions; she knows she would not be able to control her feelings as readily as the Queen of Wands. It shows her sexual energy is very present, but her emotional comfort and happiness have more say; she wishes for a guaranteed emotional commitment

She wears a long white dress with hints of blue, showing her sincerity and simplicity, the puff sleeve showing us her romantic side. Her cloak is printed with waves, her connection to the flow of the tides and feelings. At her throat is the clam clasp like the colour of her cushion, showing her to understand the weight of the emotions she speaks of and how they heal and help others. The cloak's deep pink lining displays her sweet nature, her approachability and her need for things to be rosy: a very playful, innocent and tender colour. She wears no shoes, but stockinged feet, not quite barefoot but still showing her need to be free to touch and feel her element. She sits relaxed, with her knees apart. She is aware of herself and her sexual energy but shows herself to be demure, with the ankles clasped.

Her gold crown is tall, placing a value on her thoughts as they impact her emotions, as this is where her intuition lies. Her crown acts as a channel for higher emotional wisdom. This Queen is linked to the emotional values of The Empress, which is the third card. There are three Undines within her card, and on the crown are three small loops, empty spaces which hold potential as with a Zero, with three being the number of creation. The crown has two sets of nine circles; gestation is nine months, so a link here to creativity, maternity and motherhood.

To add all four sides of her crown by adding the two unseen sides, we come to eighteen, the number of The Moon, which rules her sign of Cancer. This brings in her ebbing and flowing emotional, intuitive nature which rules her. Emotions are at the centre of her world. However large or small an issue, however much space it fills in the lives of others, it will be her feelings, her own inner being, which govern her actions, or reactions.

Her chalice itself is very ornate and she gazes at it lovingly. On either side are winged angels showing the higher aspirations of love. Each angel sits on four beads, bringing security and safety. The two angels and four beads tell that unity between another soul is needed for her to be happy. She may need a grounding force to focus her feelings, the four of The Emperor for safety and commitment, the joining of two minds both focused on sincere love. Her cup is protected by a lid, which symbolises controlled and understood emotions, and ensures they cannot be lost, taken or fall out. She understands that consequences arise when emotions are not controlled and she cherishes her own emotional world above all else, so they need to be cherished and kept safe. The cup represents all her affection, love, compassion, her soft gentle approach to others as well as herself. The small cross on the top, symbolising flowing emotional happiness, is where her faith lies. Beneath are, presumably, fish eggs, representing creation, birth and new beginnings. The ruby set within the cup is symbolic of protection, peace, and wealth, here of emotional prosperity. The cup protects her heart and mind from pain, with the hope it will increase and safeguard her emotional well-being.

Around the cup are three small images, one an eagle and another a lion. The eagle will soar above the world, and give her a panoramic view of her feelings, while this can be confusing it can also give her a better picture than just a single viewpoint. The lion protects, linking to family and those she cares for deeply kept close and safe from emotional harm. The first image is indistinct: I feel it may either be the astrological symbol for Cancer, which is her sign or an open clam with a pearl. Pearls are linked to the moon, as is Cancer, and they symbolise fertility, femininity. They can also represent virginity, or more relevant with this Queen is purity, of emotion. The Queen of Cups' chalice is similar to an altar to worship at; to her, it is everything, as her gaze is firmly and lovingly fixed on it.

She lives in a watery world where all is defined by emotions, feelings, empathy and creativity. Her dreamy gaze cultivates intuition and creativity with her soft, loving and nurturing nature. This queen is a sensitive individual who openly responds to emotions and who seeks emotional fulfilment above all else. She is only totally content when her cup is full to overflowing and is bereft when it is empty and overly concerned when its level dips below the cup's lip.

IN A NUTSHELL

A loving woman who offers comfort and emotional support, and an intuitive soul who seeks to evaluate a situation by how it feels. She understands how emotions work, is trustworthy and can offer great counsel and advice when problems hold you back.

Compassion and kindness are needed, and you are told to follow your heart. A time to listen to others and be passive so that you can feel what is needed.

Queen of Cups: Upright

Personality - The Queen of Cups appears to be emotional and deep, and indeed she is, as **her greatest need is for emotional security,** not only for herself but also for those that she cares for. She is **compassionate and forgiving** towards others and willingly shares her cup with those she loves and dotes on, and even with strangers whom she feels need her help.

Love is easy to give for this person; it is a natural aspect of their personality and is often found to be highly creative and artistic and will **work from the heart** rather than the mind.

To those she loves, **she is gentle, caring, protective and maternal.** She is a sensitive nurturer with a strong urge to make sure that everyone has all they need and that everyone is happy as **happiness is important** to this Queen. She would rather be poor and happy than rich and miserable. To her, true wealth is measured by love, trust and sincerity.

Any advice she gives may also be of an ***intuitive and empathic*** nature; she is attuned to feelings and emotions and will grasp your problems, however confused you are or however hard you try to hide them. Her need to help others can drive her, so **listen when she talks**, as she has the emotional wisdom you need.

The Queen of Cups has a protective shield she uses to keep distant those that she is not sure of away from those that she cares for, as well as from her own delicate and easily hurt emotions. She may offer you **a shoulder to cry on** and help you, but you may be left feeling that you do not know her, as she will only open herself to those that she feels secure with. However, once she gets to know you, she is quite playful and relaxed.

The Queen of Cups can be a clingy worrier, but it is born out of love. She represents **a woman who cares for your well-being**. With this Queen, we should **listen to our intuition and listen to our hearts**. We should give love and emotional wisdom to those who need it, and **trust emotions,** but not be governed by them.

Queen of Cups: Reversed

Personality - When this Queen is reversed, she shows us *a hard, as well as difficult exterior shell* which she presents to the outside world. This is to prevent her from being found *vulnerable* and being hurt, as this is what has occurred in the past and she is *scarred deeply and wounded*.

Her *trust has been betrayed* leaving her *moody, suspicious and unsympathetic towards others*. If you wish her forgiveness, you will not receive it. *Emotions will be bottled up*, exploding when they become full or are triggered by events.

Her nature is *smothering*, and her lack of emotional satisfaction will be too much for her to bear, and she will *fear* anything that could bring further changes to her emotional state.

Reversed, the Queen of Cups is *overly emotional* and *depressed* about events. She is prone to be *materialistic*, as when her yearning for emotional happiness fails, she seeks comfort in her material well-being, which can also include *physical comforts such as food and alcohol*.

She will be *dramatic* about emotional conflicts and although not a liar she may be *prone to exaggeration* and be the proverbial 'Drama Queen', building even the smallest molehill up to be a mountain. This Queen shows us a need to understand that *there is no such thing as a half-empty cup but only a half-full one*. With a need to not be *gullible*, but selective in those whom you trust.

KING OF CUPS

The King of Cups shows us a mature man seated on a throne, resting on a stone plinth, placed like an island in the middle of the turbulent ocean.

Astrological Sign: Pisces.

Unlike his Queen, he does not touch the water, which is choppy, yet offers one of his feet forwards, holding it back and resting it over the plinth of his throne's base. This lack of contact with the water can indicate a lack of commitment, a dislike and discomfort of deep emotions, someone not in touch with feelings. Due to the intellect of a king, he may feel uncomfortable within the realms of emotions and not truly connected to his element, so he can, at times, be like an island, struggling with emotions versus intellect. Yet he is shown to be a master of emotion, the King of Water, as he holds a sceptre, a symbol of worldly power, showing him to be truly in control of his feelings. The choppy waters could overwhelm him, yet he remains still in the face of emotional adversity; calm, patient and totally in control of his element. He is here far out at sea, at the mercy of deep, turbulent feelings, yet he does not panic or flinch. Being out within the ocean, he will not be dictated to by tides or the moon like the Queen of Cups, but he will be affected by strong currents and storms. For him to be pulled about by his feelings would leave him at the mercy of them and risk drowning in a literal sea of emotion. Maybe both representations are correct, as, like us all, he will have differing sides to his nature.

The King has a grey sky about him, as with the Page, white in some editions. The grey shows a contemplative element to this King, someone deep in thought and cautious. Those cards with a white sky may well indicate his pure emotional nature, someone sincere.

In the sea, we see either a fish or a dolphin to the left of the card. In some versions of the deck, this creature is only seen in part. If a dolphin, it represents harmony, as it jumps and plays in the rough waves with ease. Dolphins are seen as guides, showing that land is near, and the King to be a signpost to salvation in troubled times. They bring a healing, kind, and affectionate energy, so while he may look all out at sea, he knows where land is. If a fish, then it is his subconscious mind jumping up out of the rough waters, content and happy, showing us his depth. This King is not lost or in danger, but simply in his element and choosing to stay dry.

In the background, a red sailing ship rides the waves. The red represents his desire to navigate emotions, to stay on top of them and to move as he wishes within them. He does not wish to swim within the water; like his foot hovering over the plinth, he wishes to control his interaction with his own emotions. Yet is fully engaged in how they work. The ship shows the passage of life and his emotional journey, as well as that of others he meets, making him an excellent person to guide others.

Under his ornate red and green decorated golden crown, he wears a blue cap, which shows his faith in his feelings, in emotions and in reading them in others. He may wear this here to slow down his imaginative, intuitive and psychic connections, as his crown will act as a channel and his cap represents a need to focus his insights. Being a Cup, he is sensitive and empathic, yet as a King, he will wish control. His crown has waves about it, showing his emotional mind. We can see three large red stones, which show his desire and ambition for dominance over his element, with a need to be able to use it to create and be channelled to where he needs it. Below is a green wavy line, which can show a healing mind, a loving energy, yet one which fluctuates. Overall, this shows him at ease and to be a safe, benevolent man who cares. His emotions, which stem from his thoughts, will be governed by a more organised set of rules than the Queen who scatters hugs to anyone in need.

His fish pendant shows that his imagination and creativity are controlled, and an integral part of his nature has been caught and is no longer swimming free in the depths of the ocean. He has harnessed it, allowing his imagination to be used in a more concrete fashion, giving form to those things he dreams up. He knows what ideas to abandon and what ones to build, as he knows illusion, dreams and high hopes when he sees them. He does not wear his heart on his sleeve, but here, over his heart, his fish is his subconscious messages or emotional wisdom, delivered from his heart with sincerity and well thought out delivery.

His green shoes show he approaches life with harmony. Being the colour of the earth, there is fertile energy here, showing his fatherly nature. They are made from fish skin, representing that he walks with emotional purpose; everything is done with respect to how it feels to him or how it feels for others; and that his imagination is of great benefit to him in his daily life. His cloak is green and yellow in this original image, gold in other editions of the card, trimmed with red. Along with his blue tunic, we are given the primary colours, so he could paint a rainbow if he wished, offering hope, healing and optimism. He is shown as a quiet, unassuming soul, calm and sincere. When shown as golden yellow, we see his emotional confidence. As a spiritual and mental colour, it shows him thinking in emotional terms, metaphors, imagery, cause and effect, as he is a strong visualiser. The red shows his power, authority and drive. The blue tunic shows his ability to communicate, his intelligence, and his loyalty.

His gold ring is worn on his right hand, the side of emotions and sentiment. A king should wear a ring on the index finger to represent power, but on the middle finger, it shows balance and responsibility, said to balance the personality. So, his character is balanced by the intellectual energy of a King and love.

His sceptre is a symbol of his power as a King. It is not adorned with jewels but plain, so he is keeping it simple and understated. His clothes may be colourful, but he wishes to wield his power simply, quietly and in an understated fashion.

He does not look at his cup or at his sceptre. Instead, in this original image, he stares to the right of the card at what is beyond our view. In other versions, he looks to the left of the card with an untrusting, suspicious gaze. Here, we see his eyes facing in line with his head position. He looks to his own left, the side of logic, which is to the right of the card representing emotions. He watches his feelings, and his expression shows a directness as he looks over the horizon. His position of being seated to his left and to the card's right can also show that deep down, there may be conflict as he does not face us head-on but angles his body slightly towards the emotional side of the card, as if he does not wish to be open to our gaze or have eye contact. Emotionally, this King will value his privacy; he would not wish to be the centre of attention. Both eye positions are linked to this King, depending on the fluctuation of his mood.

This is a King in charge of his feelings, actions and reactions. He is calm, personable, gentle and often quiet. He shows a very loyal character, someone who can be relied upon to be honest, wise and dependable. His emotional wisdom can make him seem distant at times, but under that, he is very warm and tender, although he may reserve those feelings for those he is most comfortable with. A creative, inspired, intuitive, healing soul who can help us navigate our way through situations. He is someone who cares deeply for all he has and has the knack of having the right words to help you see your own solutions.

IN A NUTSHELL

This King is a man who cares about you. He is attracted to the good in others and often shares his time willingly, helping others work through their emotional issues. He is firm, with no desire to deal with emotional outbursts yet enjoys emotional communication and can help guide you.

He can be reserved and prefer dealing with the feelings of others than with his own. He can be highly creative, and often fatherly.

King of Cups: Upright

Personality - The King of Cups is **warm-hearted, a relaxed and caring person** who is happy and cheerful. He is often **someone who loves or cares deeply for you and your emotional well-being, someone who cares** about your happiness.

He has *a lively sense of humour and intelligence, mixed with inspired, intuitive imagination.* He has initiative and enjoys using his perceptive and resourceful nature to help others. He has a **compassionate** nature and like all the Cup family, he does not like to see suffering in others; he likes to know that he can, if he chooses, make a difference.

If you need guidance, then this King can help, as he is a giver of **good advice**, someone who will help you see the best in who you are. **He is quite a passive, quiet and philosophical soul, with firm morals**, yet he does not impose them on anyone. He is very **tolerant and accepting** of others, so you can talk to him about most things without judgement. He has a loving, supportive energy about him.

Emotional commitment is a serious issue with this King, so he may appear to shy away from it. Unlike the Queen, he is more likely to hold back from delivering declarations of love. Yet, **when he loves and cares, he does so deeply and with all his heart,** but he will double-check with himself to make sure his emotions are not flimsy, or that yours are not insincere. Once he openly declares his feelings, that bond will be hard to break.

He makes a good husband, partner and father, and does his best to be *a positive role model.*

This King may be the King of Emotions, but he can leave you wondering at times what he is feeling. As a result, he can come across as being so deep that he could drown himself or appear to be emotionless. This is not the case: he just has his emotions firmly in control and gently simmering under the surface. He is a **kind-hearted** soul, who thinks about his messages or words of love, support, or wisdom before he delivers them, as he feels how they will be taken by others. He may be *a man of few words.*

He shows someone who is an emotionally stabilising force.

King of Cups: Reversed

Personality - When the King of Cups is reversed, he is *an emotionally unstable and self-pitying individual, intolerant and prejudiced* against others. He will be uncaring and impatient. He will be selfish and avoid dealing with issues.

Reversed, he is drowned by the ocean waves with no control, bringing *panic and confusion.* Showing us someone *emotionally unstable* and who will see danger in everything while he floats like an *angry, anchorless individual out at sea.*

This King is *his own worst enemy* and is emotionally harsh and bitter. Everything is the fault of another, and he could make you his *scapegoat, as everyone else will be to blame.* Rather than accepting responsibility for his feelings, he would rather choose *denial* of emotive issues rather than the pain or the choice of reality.

If you wish advice from this man, it will be *biased bad advice,* and he may even gloat at your misfortune or what he sees as your stupidity. He enjoys seeing others lose what he cannot have himself.

This card tells of *a man who is uncaring towards you.* If you are involved in a personal relationship or any situation with this man, *he will be losing interest in any commitments you may have. He will create barriers* between you and himself if he is not able to express his feelings to your face. He would rather cause disagreement leaving you to press the issue or to walk away, making it your fault and not his. This can leave *relationships or situations going in circles,* as he does not wish to take responsibility for a situation which he has changed his feelings about, and which he wants to leave or not be involved in any longer.

He reminds us that we should not blame others in order to avoid taking personal responsibility.

— The Suit of Swords —

The Suit of Swords is governed by the element of air, which rules our thoughts.

Air deals with our mental and intellectual natures - how we process thoughts and what our thoughts lead us towards, how we respond to the intellectual and emotional actions of others. Swords show harshness, bring pain and difficulties as the mind is followed instead of emotions, and any emotions felt are uncomfortable due to the starkness of the truth they bring.

Swords are known by many names, including Knives and Daggers, and in playing cards they are equivalent to Spades.

Keywords that define air/swords - reality, thoughts, fighting, arguing, truth, worry, defensive, striving, mental clarity, fairness, lack of emotion, reality and loss.

ACE OF SWORDS

The Ace of Swords shows a hand from heaven holding a double-edged sword adorned with a golden crown.

As with the other two Aces, a pure white hand offers a gift from the clouds which are a slightly darker grey than in the other three, heralding something a bit more challenging. The hand enters from the left of the card and so here we have the intellectual, cutting action of the Swords.

The sword represents the mind, our intellectual selves, the part of us which needs to look at life and events with crystal-clear reality. The double edge of the sword shows its truth can cut either way as we do not have control over whether it will fall in our favour or not. The Ace of Swords offers us a moment of clarity and sometimes a need to see or balance two sides of a situation, although only one can win. The steel of the sword is a cold blue, showing no warmth, just facts that are cold and unyielding.

The sword rises through the crown looking like a backbone, a spine, with the golden crown representing the conscious mind, our ego, our true sense of self, how we act within the real world based on our beliefs. This Ace makes us sit up and listen. It calls directly to the way we think, which decides what we feel, and this can be quite uncomfortable as it rises and pierces the psyche. The crown is a sign of our power, our ability to direct our lives with clarity if we are honest with ourselves and others are honest with us. It can also represent our connection to our subconscious minds as well as our spiritual selves, our link to our divine nature, so the truths we get can be blasts of inspiration from spirit, our own subconscious as well as from outside forces. Like The Tower, the crown can be dislodged and often this Ace's arrival can make us feel uneasy.

The crown is decorated with red gemstones, showing that strong, fervent, and powerful thoughts are linked to this card. Thoughts of protection, realisation, anger, power, ambition and determination, thoughts, yours or another's, that drive what is not serving you to be cut away. There are nine gems, showing the intensity and passion of the mind and ego and their need for finalization and security. This can show the worry and concern of the Nine of Swords as we look at what the future will bring, or the ninth card of the Major Arcana, The Hermit, a card of focused thoughts and, with the grey sky, contemplation. This Ace can shake us up. It may be a gift, but it can be hard to accept at times as it brings clarity, killing the ego and awakening us to who we are. Nine wishes completion, and this Ace wishes to start us on a journey which will remove us from the deluded or uneducated place it finds us in, to a place where we can fully utilise it. So, a card of personal truths, like the lightning in The Tower, a flash of consciousness gifted to us even if it hurts as it cuts its way through to the facts of who we are.

Hanging from the crown are an olive branch on the left and a palm branch on the right; both are symbols of peace and victory. The olive branch is a symbol of life, harmony, hope and victory, the palm branch again showing victory and peace. Hanging from the crown, they show a time to rise above the conflicts of the mind, to allow truth to set us free so we can be at peace with ourselves and feel liberated. This is a sword that gifts us the removal of illusion so we can make clear choices, as the scales are cut away from our eyes. Whether we like it or not, this is a gift of freedom.

The six droplets of light are Yods, showing the sword to be a divine gift, giving us truth and clarity which we can use to get ourselves back on track, showing us the way forward and allowing us to own ourselves. They fall from the sword evenly, with three on each side of the blade, so for positive or negative, the changes they bring to us are needed. This is a transformation you can create via a new way of acting, being or thinking. Six links to diplomacy and harmony, and to balance and peace being brought into your life, so as with all the Aces, this can be used for growth. The two sets of three Yods on both sides of the blade show balance being restored to situations as we are liberated from what no longer serves us. Three being a creative number shows that whichever way this Ace affects us, we can grow.

Below are the mountains showing harshness, problems and cold facts, as this card may not make our pathway easy. Those jagged mountain tops look painful, cold and unwelcoming and the place where you would find The Hermit. Yet with this card, they are the only way forwards shown, and we are left with no illusions, as the Ace of Swords' energy is forceful and demands change, especially the removal of deadwood. Something will be cut away from within our lives, leaving us facing our minds, beliefs, views or opinions.

With the arrival of this card, confusions are cut away: we are left with the truth, however ugly it may first seem. This card also has the title of 'The Old Order Changeth', as all new beginnings with this card come with an ending, or separation from something we have held dear.

This is a Sword of justice, as equally as it can be the surgeon's knife cutting away what is diseased, or the pen which writes down that which needs to be expressed. This card clears mental chatter and clutter, allowing for a fresh, open and honest beginning, even if it has an 'ouch!' moment attached to it.

Numerological value – ONE = Desire for action, new beginnings and movement.

IN A NUTSHELL

Nothing will be the same again, even if you do not want the gift of truth, this card will bring it to you. Deep within, this card calls you to recognise truth, as illusions and ties to things or people are cut away.

You will know what must be done or let go of.

Ace of Swords: Upright

The Ace of Swords represents *strong emotions* but allows *no delusions* as we come face to face with *something in our lives which needs to be let go of,* be that a thought, view, opinion, person or situation.

This card can show the anxiety we feel when faced with changes. We are told to *stick to facts*, be level-headed and leave emotions by the wayside to be able to just get on with it, as *things will not go back to how they were*. Where we need to come to a decision, we will be able to judge things with *a clear mind, and even optimism and confidence, as the facts are laid bare*.

This Ace brings the gift of *clear, precise thought and mental direction*, as illusions are stripped away, leaving clarity and *inspired thought*. It brings us *truth and honesty*. Success can be reached via a clear mind as reality is seen once the clouds have been sliced away.

It is often interpreted as a card of *triumph, a victory over adversity*, with the sword high above the mountains. However, it is often a harsh victory that can bite and be felt as a *no to questions or a roadblock* as we are directed back to the path which we should be on with, sometimes, brutal honesty. It can show that truth may not make us feel victorious in the short term but will leave us with no doubt as to the solution being imposed or sought as what we wish for can be denied to us as it is not suitable for us or available at that time or be granted and feel difficult.

The arrival of this card shows *permanent changes*, an opportunity to discard or have taken away that which is no longer needed. As the Ace of Swords is dual-edged; the rubbish cut from our lives may not always be something that we initially feel is bad which is when sadness can arise. *New thoughts and beliefs can replace old, outdated views*, and *answers are* found for problems, as this can show *a new way of thinking*.

With problems, this card calls for *rational thought and direct action* based on truths. Changes made under this card will be felt on a mental level as they will *challenge the way that we think about an event or person,* and they will be wise choices to make.

The sword can also represent the pen, the written word, which can include *truths arriving by any written means.*

On a health level, the Ace of Swords can point to medical treatment, i.e. operations and injections.

Ace of Swords: Reversed

When the Ace of Swords is laid reversed, it shows *confusion caused by speculation and assumption.* New ways of seeing things will not be possible, leading to feeling victimised, fearful and wanting to fight back against *a battle which cannot be won.*

This card makes us hold back from accepting change, as we *give in to fears* or refuse to let go of something. *We may not believe the truth*, leaving us unable to move forwards.

There can be much *negativity* accompanying this card's arrival. *Illusions will cloud reality,* leaving us seeing something which is not productive within our life as still holding value, leading us to *bad decisions and not letting go*.

The mountains will be on top of you. The hardness of reality will be too uncomfortable, with a refusal to find a way forward. *Failure* will lead to a lack of truthful communication or *not listening*. This can be due to someone *lying*, or only seeing what you wish from another's truths and lying to yourself.

Negativity risks spilling into your outside world, in the form of *accusations, temper outbursts or even violence.*

New problems will be caused, and old ones will not be overcome. What has occurred or been realised will not fade out of avoidance of an issue, but instead will become a thorn in your side.

TWO OF SWORDS

The Two of Swords pictures a woman alone at night, blindfolded and holding two swords.

The woman wears a grey nightdress which shows her unprepared to make a decision and wanting rest from her situation. She is outside, alone in the cold night air. With the grey of her outfit, she will be in contemplation, isolated and frozen in place as there is no warmth shown here. Her nightgown covers her whole body, showing that her mental state is controlling and keeping her in this place. In other versions, it is shown as icy blue. All aimed at showing her isolation with her cold thoughts. Her slippers are the same yellow as the moon, representing her indecision as to what direction to take. They can be beige in some versions of the RWS, showing a non-committal and neutral position being taken. Both of her feet face outwards in opposite directions, showing her to be in two minds about her situation: to go one way or the other, to choose this or that. Each foot is backing one side of the debate or problem. She sits with her legs slightly apart, wishing movement with an awareness that action is needed, but she cannot move two ways at once and feels stuck with an unresolvable set of options.

Her blindfold is the same grey as her nightdress, so she cannot see what she needs to see to make a clear, unprejudiced judgement. The blindfold is placed on her by her own indecision. She could remove it but has chosen avoidance and denial, as she is consciously avoiding acting on an issue and holds onto inner conflict as a result. The blindfold does not cover her third eye, so she still has intuition on her side, yet with the waxing moon, she may not feel she can trust it.

Her seat is cold stone, leaving her situation stressful, uncomfortable, unwelcoming and even intimidating. She sits upright, which helps her to maintain her balance with the two large swords, but also shows her rigid and unable to move without incident, as even a slight shift in her position could cause further problems if those swords fall.

The two swords represent decisions, options, avenues, sides, solutions, choices and ways forward. Yet to confront and deal with the swords could mean difficulties, as whichever one she chooses will cause tension and upset, especially for her if she chooses the wrong one. The swords are at angles, showing a lot of effort is needed to keep them balanced. They are heavy and could fall at any moment, causing pain and disruption, yet at least the decision would be made for her. To put them down means she would have to change position, remove her blindfold and deal with things via deciding which side to pick. This is a decision which she is not ready or able to make. Resting on her shoulders shows her shouldering a mental burden. If she tries to remove her blindfold without putting the swords down, it could cause personal injury and a loss of control, so she sits hoping it will just resolve itself as she is blind to a solution. Her arms cross her Heart Chakra, leaving her emotional energy blocked and ignored as she tries to avoid conflict. Her crossed arms also show her conflicted, with crossed interests which she cannot resolve. She could even be at a crossroads within her life that she cannot face.

It is the night, showing us that she cannot see things clearly, leaving her situation not seen in truth or clarity but in confusing shadows and moonlight. The waxing moon shows ideas and solutions which are not fully formed, and the moon, in a state of change, is leaving her confused. A waxing moon makes the low and high tides be of similar depths, so she may not be able to see the subtle differences about her and there may be no definition to her choices. She waits for a sign which is not present and tries to keep the status quo. In some versions of this card, fog surrounds her head, representing her insecurity, confusion and doubts as she simply cannot think clearly.

The water, like her emotions, are trapped, showing that her emotions are stuck, ignored, and literally not faced. This trapped water, left behind by the receding tide, shows the shallow trapped emotions and thoughts she has been left with, which she cannot remove. The water is gently moving, so her emotions are in motion, showing her difficult emotions and problems, which are ignored and literally not faced, but they are not moving enough to force action, as she avoids making waves. In the water just behind her, algae grows, forming on water that has little movement, showing stagnation and inaction, and that her problems may be long-term. She seems stuck, yet she turns her back on the problems; she does not wish to face her confusion or slip up on the algae or rocks. The water is too shallow, so no boat would have a clear passage, and to escape from this place would mean risking being taken by the currents once into deeper emotion-filled waters.

Behind her lies a sandy beach or landmass. The dark stops us from seeing the definitions, so what is there is unknown and confusing. It is pictured here coloured in pastel colours as if the sun is setting, telling us that something has to end here, something must be dealt with to be able to move on. Other versions of this card show it to be a sandy brown colour, showing the indistinct nature of her solutions.

She is allowing her indecision, an inability to face a situation, to cause unhappiness in her life. She fears the conflict of the swords if their balance is tipped, which brings her and her situation to a stalemate. She may be in a no-win situation or stuck between choices where no outcome or pathway can be seen or is favourable. Yet she is not seeking a solution. She is allowing fate to have its say and hoping her problems will just resolve themselves and go away.

Numerological value - TWO = Balance, harmony and interaction.

IN A NUTSHELL

A time to wake up and smell the coffee! You may wish to avoid a confrontation or deal with an issue, yet it is not going away.

It is better to face issues head-on and in control, rather than when things fall apart, and a decision is forced on you.

Two of Swords: Upright

The Two of Swords brings us **a stalemate situation, an uneasy truce and personal conflict** between yourself and one situation or another. **Thoughts and feelings will be torn** concerning what to do for the best and **the problem will be ignored or avoided**.

Indecision will rule, leaving you not knowing which way to turn. You may opt for ignorance being bliss, but that will only work for a while. The effort and pressure of keeping a situation static will come crashing down at some stage, leaving you to face **a situation which you are wishing to avoid**, the proverbial 'elephant in the room'.

There will be tension combined with **a temporary peace** that will not last. Eventually, arguments will occur, however hard you try to ignore a situation. **Decisions are waiting to be made**, problems need to be accepted and the need for **change is pressing in**. If the situation is ignored, **the answer will be forced onto you**, taking away your control as hiding away from issues just gives **a false sense of security**. **Turning a blind eye** will not work long-term, as denial will backfire.

With this card, you will be **feeling ill-prepared to make a decision or accept a situation**, leaving a defensive, hopeless attitude. **Ignoring a problem** will not make it magically disappear, although there is hope it will.

The proverbial 'brushing things under the carpet' is summed up by this card, yet that just ends with lumpy carpets which trip us up. Everything will be based on what you wish it to be, rather than what it is. Changes will be ignored, and **an old status quo will be clung to for dear life**.

The only solution with this card is to **try a bit of give and take** and be prepared for heated discussions as you deal with what you are trying to avoid. The uncomfortable feelings or truth you are wishing to escape cannot be hidden forever. Now is a time to **call a truce, agree to disagree**, accept and **be open about your inability to make a choice**, but do something before someone else does.

Two of Swords: Reversed

Reversed, the Two of Swords promises that *compromise can be reached*. We can succeed with this card if we *challenge a difficult problem,* as *arguments can and will be resolved.* So, you may as well be active within the resolution so that you can have an influence on any outcome. Either way, *situations will be forced to a conclusion.*

At times, waiting to see which way the swords fall can be the only solution. We *sit on the fence openly and honestly*, and with that, the outcome is accepted, as you have already agreed to fate taking a hand.

Yet if the swords have slipped and balance is lost, it creates more pain, awkwardness or heartache. *What you have been avoiding comes crashing down, forcing you to deal with matters*. Blindfolds will be removed, leaving you seeing your reality and forced to listen to what needs to be heard. This could lead to an unsettling and unhappy experience, but it will be *a conflict bringing change as the plaster is ripped off*.

The Two of Swords reversed point to the letting go of past emotional ties that have caused distress. There will be feelings of *relief* as this card's energy passes and the weight of the swords is released. You realise that life does not have to be a complete struggle.

THREE OF SWORDS

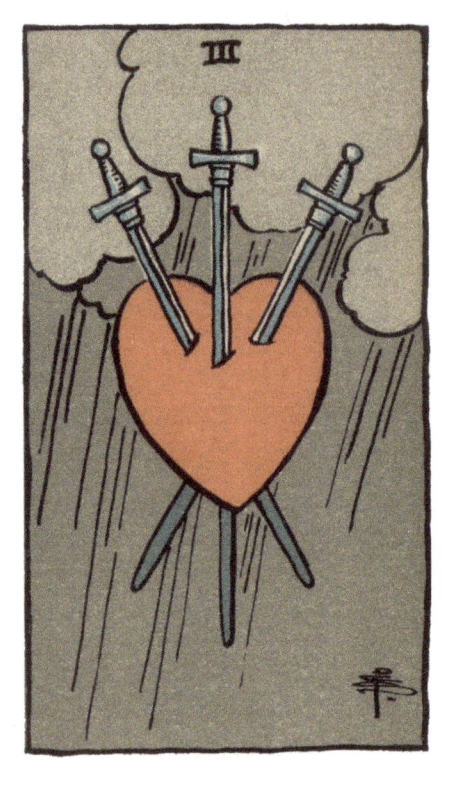

The Three of Swords brings us an easy card to interpret as a heart is pierced by the three swords, while behind are grey storm clouds and rain.

This is a card of sadness, loss and anger. The storm clouds gather above the heart, showing us the emotional storm brought to us by the card, and at times also the sudden nature of this pain's arrival. Storm clouds symbolise isolation, sadness, grief, loneliness and even depression, and they come filled with watery emotions, building in the sky till they burst.

It is expected that into each life, a little rain must fall and here rain falls in sheets. We can imagine that the air is cold and sharp as our upset comes down on us in a storm of emotion. The rain represents tears which can wash away and release pain in order to find peace with situations. This is a card that can bring freedom and a greater understanding of our own emotional selves, but not before we feel its overwhelming message. The blue sky and sun are lost, taking away optimism, hope and happiness, leaving us with sadness and loss. The grey of the sky leaves us looking inwards at our hurt.

A lone red heart is shown, indicating that the pain, truth and facts which these sharp swords bring will cut right through feelings, sentiments and emotions, hurting as they go. They go straight through the heart, so no slight nick, but an incision directly through feelings, bringing pain and rejection, which is isolating, even if shared by others. The heart is the seat of our emotions and holds the feelings we cherish the most. It's where our hope, love and trust lay, where we dream about optimistic futures and where we link to those we love. To have this ripped open causes unhappiness and can leave us feeling completely lost.

The swords themselves show the disruption of a situation in which you have faith and trust. They are swift, so even if you see them coming, you will not be prepared for their cuts. This truly represents anything which, like a knife in the heart, cuts deep, leaving you distraught.

Sudden pain is shown by the image of the heart being pierced by the swords. Truth is felt on a deep emotional level, and loss is faced. The three swords and three dark clouds show the creation of a new understanding of life arising from the storm. This growth may be hard to see when suddenly your world is filled with pain, yet it is from such moments of harsh reality that we grow and can often raise other difficult problems or realisations to be dealt with.

The Three of Swords shows an emotional storm is blowing, leaving hearts broken, tears falling, and nerves jagged.

Numerological value - **THREE** = Growth, creativity and productivity.

IN A NUTSHELL

You will feel hurt, upset and disappointed. Words, actions, or events will cause you pain and heartbreak, and even if they are not wanted, they will force truth and, at times, liberation. You may feel angry and hateful, and you must vent these emotions healthily to move on. It is a time to learn from pain, so you can understand yourself better and not hold a grudge.

Take each tear as it comes and allow yourself to move forwards one step at a time.

Three of Swords: Upright

The Three of Swords brings **heartbreak and tears**; a situation will arise causing emotional pain and feelings of **loss**. You will feel emotionally wounded as life throws you **painful knowledge and truths**, leaving your mind filled with upset, clouding your judgement as everything will be tinged with **heartache**.

The Three of Swords can bring **anger towards others or situations**. There will be frustration with the disappointments you have suffered, leaving you feeling **unable to let go of emotions**, often due to their sudden and unforeseen nature.

The **separations and disruptions** with this card will cut you deeply emotionally, causing **sadness**. **Distress** will be caused by the words or actions of another, leaving you with feelings of deep **heartfelt loss**.

It could be any area of life that will be affected, but the damage this card brings will be followed by **sadness and tears**. You will be left feeling hurt and distraught with what remains and often left *feeling rejected and alone*.

The only way forward is to feel the pain and not reject it, or else you will stay stuck. In a lot of cases, what has hurt you was dead or dying even if you were not aware of it, so this is a time to cleanse yourself with tears rather than wasting time trying to regain what has been lost.

Yet do remember to give time to **grieve**, as often pain cannot be rushed.

Three of Swords: Reversed

Reversed, the Three of Swords shows you have suffered a loss that although painful and disappointing is moving away, with the ***pain easing***.

This card shows a time of ***healing*** where you start to see the beauty in life once again as every cloud finds its silver lining. ***Life goes on***. The ***wounds may still ache*** as the swords fall away and you may still feel anger, upset, frustration and not wish to fully accept events. An unwillingness to totally let go and face the future may linger still, yet there is ***an understanding that it is time to accept issues***.

You decide that the past should be left behind as you start to move on and grow from what you have been through rather than letting it destroy you. Forgiveness or forgetting aids healing, as now is about ***moving forwards and starting afresh*** as ***you start to think clearly*** and are not weighed down by loss.

You are no longer focused on how things could have been, as a ***time to let go*** is reached.

FOUR OF SWORDS

The Four of Swords shows the carving of a golden knight resting on a tomb inside of a church.

The church shows us a place of faith and also represents a place of protection from the outside world, so the knight has sought a safe place to rest and heal. It offers him solitude, peace and a place and time to retreat from and reflect on life.

Above him, a stained-glass window shows a priest blessing someone kneeling before him. This indicates a scene of healing, and the faith that things can get better. Above the priest's head is the word Pax. A Pax is a flat object passed about the congregation during mass, kissed by each person as they entered the church. It symbolised a healing kiss, a kiss of peace to the person as well as their spirit. When the light shines through this window its image will cover the knight with its colour, yet it is also what the knight would see if he looked up towards the light. It is the healing he seeks for his mind, his spirit and maybe even his body. There is a thick black line between the priest and the kneeling man, so our golden knight may need to rest to be able to drop some of his barriers in order to regain his strength.

The knight's armour indicates a fight has drained his energy, showing him taken over by the necessity to rest or retreat as the swords have won the battle, but not the war. Here he is needing recovery and to catch his breath. The man is golden, representing a time to give in to the higher self, to see things from a higher perspective as now his outer daily life may need to be on hold for a while. Looking like a statue we see his need to be still, to not interact and, with his eyes closed, to go within. He wears no helmet which leaves his head bare and without protection and unable to protect himself from his thoughts. Right now, his mind needs to be free, not encased by a helmet which would leave him seeing the world through a narrow opening designed for battle, as now the battle is over and he needs to come to terms with his lot. There is a need for a higher meditative connection to restore the mind and find enlightenment and a time to find some peace forced into this knight's life. His head laying on a pillow represents a time to rest the mind, even literal sleep if the body is tired. He may even be physically unwell and his whole self needs to take a break from the stresses of life.

His hands held in prayer symbolise asking for help, guidance, healing and safety. He wishes to seek a higher source for the solution to his issues as he needs this withdrawal from life to be productive.

The tomb is a sign of burial, death and an ending. Within this card, it symbolises a quiet time out, a renewal being sought and of putting the mind to rest. To heal, we need to work through the disruptive things in our life, we need to sleep on our problems and allow our higher and subconscious selves to sort through the jumble of feelings for us. The tomb brings life to a full stop, taking us away from others, which can lead some to see this as a prison card. At times, this can be a decision made by the self, yet more often than not, this card shows enforced incarceration and withdrawal, a time where we have no choice but to be away from the world to get ourselves back together. In other editions of this card, the knight lies on a white surface, as opposed to a golden one. The white adds purity and sincerity to his needs and can often represent a new beginning from a blank slate. So, his desire here is for a fresh start, a time for old issues to be resolved or removed.

Above the tomb hang three of the swords whilst the fourth lies under him. The three swords above the knight, just like the Three of Swords itself, are a reminder of the pain he has endured and yet which still hang over him, needing to be resolved. One hangs over his head, showing his thoughts are affected and lines up over his eyes leaving him having witnessed a painful truth. The middle sword hangs over his heart bringing painful emotions and the last over his Solar Plexus Chakra, showing him to be feeling insecure and off-balance.

Next to these three swords is a line running down the side of the window, and at the end is the carving of an animal's head. This may be the jackal-headed Anubis, which we found in The Wheel of Fortune, or just a jackal or a fox. The latter two devour the dead, and Anubis takes the dead to weigh their hearts: the bad are eaten and the good ascend to heaven. Within a church setting, maybe it is here to take away his pains, those small or large things which have died and brought this knight to this place of refuge, to allow him to be reborn when he leaves. The weighing up of his issues may remove mental burdens once he is strong enough to carry on, as this carving may be symbolic of those things eating away at you. It hangs over the groin area of the knight, which can symbolise passions, ambitions, drives and those things which have been lusted over which need to be put into perspective while he hides away and heals.

This single sword on the tomb is golden, linking him to his outer life, leading to life events having forced this break, something from his day-to-day physical existence. If this is not a willing break, then it will be by force, as a situation which has affected the mind or body simply could not go on any longer, leading to illness, intervention, stress and upset. His ability to fight has been taken away and so he seeks the refuge of his mind, away from everyone, as he needs to deal with his issues alone. Like the Ace of Swords, this golden sword shows the potential for clarity, healing and truth to be gained from his situation and that he can fight again; but for now, he needs to escape it all for a while.

While the three swords show pain, suffering and a need to resolve problems, the sword on the tomb shows that this is not an ending, but more a time to heal after an ending or a situation which has stopped play.

This card can refer to illness and a time to recuperate, but mainly represents a retreat from the harshness that the swords bring, a time to be away from the world and heal, which can take time. This is a temporary shelter from life, not a permanent one, as in time, that single golden sword will clear the mind, so emotions, thoughts and body can get back up again.

Numerological value - **FOUR** = Realisation, will power and logic.

IN A NUTSHELL

Healing is needed. A break from life, a situation or stress will be required or enforced: you should take more care of yourself, and this is time to do just that. There is a need to unwind, relax and even meditate, a time to listen to your body and mind, especially if you have been dealing with a difficult issue.

Anything from hospital stays to a pyjama day is called for, as time alone to heal is needed. A time of retreat from life to recharge your batteries and find some inner peace and a new direction.

Four of Swords: Upright

The Four of Swords shows a time to **retreat from other people, a problem or from life in general.** Some time spent alone is needed to find some space to mend and resolve feelings. Any situations which are taking your energy should be left, as literal retreat can also be shown.

This card often comes when we have been **ignoring a need to rest or resolving a problem.** When we keep battling with our issues and working too hard and we simply cannot go on anymore due to **exhaustion**. Yet it can also arise from **a sudden conflict or dispute** which knocks us down, leaving us **praying for things to get better.**

This card gives a break from routine and allows us to **get the past into perspective** and let any changes be felt and understood before moving on. It is a time given to us to meditate on what is no longer good for us, to **heal the past or the body.**

Time to be still and quiet will often come as a relief with this card as **you will be tired of fighting or worrying.** A calm time with oneself is guaranteed and needed, even if your focus is on a singular issue for the duration, as you will be seeking **peace**. It can at times bring a need **to lick our wounds after setbacks** damage our pride.

If the retreat brought to you by this card is not enforced, it may well lead to feelings of **isolation, anxiety and loneliness.**

This card shows a lack of physical as well as mental energy and can also represent **stress and illness,** so life may also be postponed due to health factors. Either way, **a break is needed and given,** as life goes quiet and unproductive for the duration as you get the body and mind rested and thoughts back in order. It can show **a literal break from life,** as life's traumas have taken their toll and

reflection is needed. If situations have made you want to hide away, now is ***a time to focus on recovery***.

Four of Swords: Reversed

Reversed, this card shows us ***a renewal of mental energy and a return to good health.*** Mentally, emotionally and physically, this card brings ***recovery and hope.***

After a period of illness, stress or withdrawal, there will be new-found energy that will fill you with ***optimism***. There will be ***an acceptance of a situation*** and you will be in a positive frame of mind. Life will be enjoyable again as you ***no longer feel restricted by health, life or circumstances.***

Problems may well still exist but now is the time to ***get back out into the world,*** as you will have a new perspective and feel regenerated, leaving you ***feeling productive and ready to resolve any issues remaining***. So, go out and be with others as a time of being isolated ends for you.

The Four of Swords reversed shows ***a time to act***, a time for progress after delay as now the three swords are no longer hanging over you and your mind is clear once again.

Life has been stagnant and now you seek to take direct action to get life moving again, as ***you feel free from the past and able to start focusing on your future once again.***

FIVE OF SWORDS

The Five of Swords pictures three men. Two of them are walking away from the one who is left holding three of the five swords.

The clouds are grey yet the sky's still blue, showing this to be a scene where the fight is over, the storm is clearing and we are shown the aftermath, showing that events here were not successful. Ego has won the day, ultimately bringing failure. More trouble is yet to come.

In the background, the mountains show problems on the horizon, and everyone in the card faces in their direction. They are all aware of the tension this situation will cause in the future as well as right now in the present, even if one of them does not seem to care. The sea ripples, yet there are no waves, just undercurrents pushing the deep ocean emotions about, showing the discontent present.

The three men all take different roles in the argumentative situation they find themselves in, as they have battled with verbal and mental sparring and are now feeling the results.

With five swords in the image, a couple of people have already left the scene, and either abandoned their swords or had them taken by the victor, as their opinions were fought against. They have accepted defeat, refusing to play or unable to compete, so to have the men in the background whose swords are lying on the ground, with the conqueror at the front now collecting up his prizes.

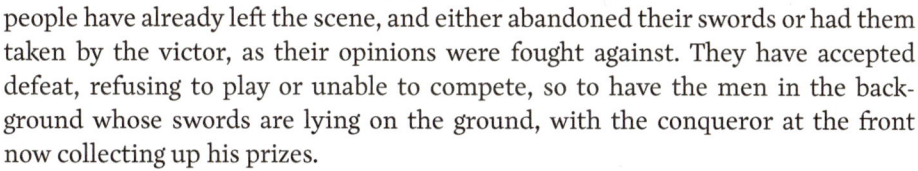

The man furthest away stands with his head in his hands, showing signs of despair. In the original image of the card shown here, he is dressed all in yellow, an intellectual colour, so his view may have been single-minded and unbendable. The Universal RWS shows this man in a brown tunic with the left side a darker brown and wearing yellow boots. Here he has walked into his situation with confidence, down-to-earth, but with two shades of brown, one suggesting shadow, he has not been clear in his approach, a person who may not have had the ability to mentally spar with such an opponent and feels the loss on a very personal level. His sword, representing his honest or opinionated view, may have been all he had to negotiate with.

The other man with his back to us stands as if pondering his next move, thinking about the predicament he is in and may even be considering turning round to stand his ground. His green, yellow and orange clothes show him to have been optimistic, practical, friendly, logical and open in his approach. We see one green sleeve on his left arm, so his part in the argument was, again, like the other man, down-to-earth, even gentle and caring, yet practical. On his right shoulder he has an orange cloak, showing he would have been enthusiastic about what he felt, yet he may not have been as confident as he needed to be with it just over one shoulder. He has dark hair, showing a mature, experienced person, in other versions he is shown as blond: a more immature, yet sincere energy. His clothes can also differ, with a brown cloak with orange tights and belt, with grey boots to contemplate his next step. Yet this still shows him down-to-earth and open with his view and opinions.

These two do not seek to band together or comfort each other, so they too could be fuelled by ego, or not in a position to offer support out of their own shock.

The man in the foreground has passion with his brown boots, orange in some versions, red shirt and tights. He is someone who will talk with drive and enthusiasm for what he wants; each step he takes is out of determination, firmly grounded in his beliefs. Having the green tunic over the top of his red garments shows that he sees merit in his aims; he feels his potential, he wishes growth, yet all that red will make him take actions out of desire rather than consideration. He is more driven, determined and able to shout louder with a more dominant, brash personality. The wind blows his red hair out of his face, so the others in this situation will be seeing this person as they truly are. This may be a shock, as the winds of change blow in his favour, harshly affecting the others. Right now, he is the bringer of the storm and owns the stage this scene is set upon; his mind is full of fiery ambition for his own dominance. In some versions, his hair is strawberry blond, symbolising him as young and therefore immature.

Holding three of the swords, he holds onto the pain and loss of the others within the image, like the Three of Swords we met earlier, yet also to his own, even if he does not see it.

Holding two of the swords over his left shoulder he shows that he feels his opinion is the correct one; they, the others, are wrong. The other sword he holds to the ground in his right hand, so an emotional element, so, right, or wrong, he deeply feels his sense of conviction. He smiles, feeling confident that he has won whatever the battle was, as he defends his opinions and pride, yet his attempts at communicating were just ego and bullying. His smile is at the expense of the other's upset, showing a smug and self-righteous expression. His shoulder is slightly raised in a shrug as if to minimise their shock and disappointment, as if it's his right; he may even be feigning sympathy. He is detached from his actions, believing the best man has won. He does not mind that he has hurt others to get what he has wanted as being right and victorious are all that matter. He is often referred to as being unsportsmanlike, as, like a spoiled child, he takes what he wants and will fight if others try to beat him to it, or shout until others back down.

However, the others have turned away from him, abandoning their swords which represent their wisdom, beliefs, thoughts and expressions, and are facing the ocean and the mountains in the background. By turning their backs on him, they show they no longer wish to do things his way. He has won. They are tired of fighting and the only outcome that can be made is one of failure in defeat.

The lone man holding the swords has the victory, but at what price, as his victory is hollow? He has pushed the others away due to his presumption that as he holds the most swords, he is by far better equipped to hold a position of authority, regardless of the expertise that the others may or may not possess. This man, although appearing victorious, has lost the fight, as he has achieved his position by going against the views of others and using force. His ego has ruled the situation. He has intimidated the others into submission, yet he has not gained any respect. The remaining two swords, if used, could create a temporary truce but they have been given up on and reconciliation is walked away from, as the others realise there is no hope. Being on the floor can also show the uneasy balance within the Two of Swords being lost as a situation has been faced.

You can be the holder of the swords in this card, as equally as you can be one of the defeated, yet whichever role you play, no one will really win, and this situation is more of a 'lose-lose', as no one is listening to each other as an inflated ego rules the show.

Numerological value - **FIVE** = Truth, analytical and communication.

IN A NUTSHELL

Pick your battles and consider the consequences of actions and words. Mutual respect is needed, you do not know everything, your opinion is not the only one – nor should others presume theirs are either. Arguments could get out of control; words best left unspoken can cause situations to fail as people reveal their true colours.

Resentment, disagreement, and a war of words will leave you feeling a bit hollow. Try to see the bigger picture and move stubborn pride out of the way, even if you feel justified to air your views and have your say.

Five of Swords: Upright

The Five of Swords indicates that *others will be upset* as words, beliefs and actions will leave *feelings of hurt, intimidation and humiliation. People will be turned against each other* due to opinions and presumption that one person has the right to steam-roll others. *Here, enemies can be created*.

Due to the lack of unity between you, a situation, individual or even a group, a *war of power* will erupt, bringing *arguments, resentment* and *disagreements*. This card shows all sides will disagree, no one is prepared to put their views aside and listen to the others. *One person or side will dominate* and will not relinquish control or power, and they will succeed with *a lack of honour or principles,* at the expense of others.

The Five of Swords informs us that *stubborn pride* will achieve nothing. *Defeat and failure* are the only outcomes of this card: *compromise will not be found* as beliefs are hard to change.

The phrase 'cutting off the nose to spite the face' can be used here, as it's an act of hurting a situation and causing yourself harm in the process, while soothing your own fears, resentments, beliefs, or ego.

Circumstances will go round in circles, and you will achieve nothing of benefit, as too much will be expected from a situation and limitations should be understood. Accept that you will not be able to have what you want at the present moment, or within the present set of circumstances.

Here you may well find those people in life who cannot accept others for their beliefs, skin colour, sexuality, gender or anything which is different than they are. This includes the work, school, family or relationship **bully**.

If you hold the swords, it may be prudent to realise you do not know everything and the views of others are as valid as yours. If you are the one walking away from a fight, understand you could never have won against such **arrogance**, and a new way to resolve issues is needed.

Five of Swords: Reversed

Reversed, the Five of Swords states that you should **watch your back** and **be on your guard** against the actions of others as **you could well be made a scapegoat**. Trouble will be laid at your door due to others not being able to get their own way.

This card shows you really wish a testing time would be over. You are **in a war** which you do not wish to be in with an opponent who is stronger-willed than you, and who will not let the fight stop as they carry on the argument.

The Five of Swords reversed shows force within relationships or situations due to **selfishness or dominance**. Control is sought from an insecure individual wishing to stay in charge and not lose power. This can spill out into **physical violence** or aggression as one person wishes to take control. They cannot let another's view or opinion drop and feel they must impose their own views in **fear of opposition** arising.

Out of anger and frustration, an **unfair decision or accusation will be made**, leading to being discredited by others in one way or another. This could be **embarrassing and humiliating** and be done out of **spite** by others trying to dominate a situation.

At its worst, there will be **dishonourable, unfair acts** which will lead to feelings of **shame** being felt. Yet there is bound to be another who can help, as **you will not be the only one affected**.

SIX OF SWORDS

The Six of Swords shows a woman and a small child being ferried across the water by a man, while the six swords stand upright in the boat.

The boat represents our journey through life and our ability to navigate through difficult emotions. It shows a voyage to somewhere new, as here, life needs to move onwards as we often need to change our outlook to heal, understand or learn.

The boat sails into calmer waters, as to the right of the boat, the choppy sea symbolises churned-up, disturbed and troubled emotions. On the right, negative thoughts will stir negative emotions, and negative emotions will stir negative thoughts. A cycle of unhelpful thoughts is being broken as they sail into the calmer, smoother water to the other side of the boat. On their left, it shows us their minds are starting to settle; they will be starting to see the truth and logic of their situation without so much emotional chatter. Their emotions and mental states calm as they travel away from problems.

The boat and journey show a time to leave problems behind with an acceptance of the past, or with a need to move on, with a grateful release of pressure. The boat provides a break between the waves and the smooth sea, signalling that distance is being put between them and their problems, which is also shown by sailing from one shore to another.

Like the last card, the three people are playing different roles. The woman, or mother, is huddled in a cloak, the dull brown/yellow shows a lack of energy and avoidance of taking part in her rescue. She has wrapped herself in her cloak, her head down, even avoiding comforting the child, absorbed in her thoughts. If she looks up, all she can see are the swords and the stressful danger they pose, leaving her feeling frozen by her situation, vulnerable and despairing. Her legs sit amongst the swords, reflecting on the loss and pain she is entangled in, and which has prompted this change in her life.

The child sits close to the woman, dressed in blue, showing spiritual trust, as this child knows it can do little to change things. Cuddling up to the woman, he wishes to feel secure, yet all he can do is have faith in the others to provide a safe journey as there is no comfort being offered. In other versions of the RWS, this child's clothing is an indigo blue, which shows devotion and a spiritual higher element of trust placed in the situation.

The man punting the boat is putting effort into sailing them to a better place by taking charge of the situation. You can imagine the silence here, as everyone does what they need to do to move forwards. He can represent real help or even life itself slowly moving us onward as we make decisions to leave things behind us. The man's blue sleeves and green trousers show him to be moving forwards with sincerity and communicating confidence to everyone. The rest of his clothes are very down-to-earth and practical, so he is doing what needs to be done as the others here cannot. He holds a lot of potential with his black belt, showing that he fully understands his ability to help change the situation. The remaining problems will benefit from that wisdom and be more readily resolved once dry land has been reached. His black pole being used to punt the boat, like The Fool's stick, also represents potential. The only way is forward if that potential for a fresh start can be felt. Emotions will be stirred up as he punts through the choppy waters, so this journey may be one full of tears, anger, impatience and frustration as well as hope.

The three of them have nothing apart from their clothes, boat, punt and swords, leaving them with just the clothes on their backs and the problems which have prompted this journey. While their journey will not be a *sailing off into the sunset* situation, it is one which escapes and rescues.

The six swords are bolt upright in the boat, indicating that problems are still present and visible. They cannot be thrown overboard or left behind as they keep the boat watertight, so they will need to be dealt with once the boat finds land. The thoughts, troubles and problems they represent still need to be voiced and dealt with but for now, they just stay lodged in the boat. To tackle them now would be inadvisable, yet thankfully, a turning-point has been reached. The swords are placed into a set of three, one and two. We find the Three of Swords on the right side of the woman, showing the emotional pain she carries with her on this journey. In front of her is a single sword; the Ace, being directly in front of her, shows us she is in no doubt as to her reality, as the truth will sting and be very present within her mind. On the mental left of the boat and the child are the remaining two swords, bringing us the energy of the Two of Swords and its indecisions, and can show that balance was tipped by themselves or by others, which forced this escape and brought such welcome relief. The sword in the centre of the boat and the three to the right bring the Four of Swords, bringing a need to heal emotions and recuperate from those choppy waters of the mind.

The grey sky shows this to be a situation of thought and contemplation as they head for dry land, which is filled with gentle hills and trees. A calm-looking place to start again, find some firm ground and deal with issues. The land is the same colour as the water, so they know it will not be emotion-free, yet it is the only place to go. So, a place they can have faith in even if they have no idea what it will really be like. The destination can sometimes be depicted as shades of white and blue, yet the message is the same.

The journey represents the process of travelling away from past troubles and showing we must willingly participate in the act of letting go and moving on, even if it is just to allow it to happen. You can play any role within this card: you can be the one who seeks faith in the process, the one lost to the situation or the one helping it all change: helping, trusting, or relinquishing control. This card brings relief that situations are moving, even though problems still need to be resolved.

IN A NUTSHELL

Things may not be at their best, but they are improving and better than they have been and an end to troubles will be in sight.

You will feel a sense of relief as the tide changes, you will know situations are not completely fixed and are aware there is some distance to travel. You will feel more confident or less stressed about finishing what you must do, giving you time to re-evaluate what you want or wish for.

Numerological Value - SIX = Ease, attraction and diplomacy.

Six of Swords: Upright

The Six of Swords tells of the calm after the storm. **Stress and tension will be reduced,** as it is now **possible to move away from a problem** or situation which has caused you conflict and friction. You may feel battered and bruised by the situation, and unsure of what to really do, or how you're going to resolve issues long-term, but things are changing for the better.

Acceptance of difficulties will be gradual but assured and *the worst of a situation has passed* and can show *a literal escape from a situation.* You are now able to look once again to the future and make plans. Even if you cannot enforce them just yet, *you can dare to dream once again.*

Even with an easing of pressure, the past is still present in the questioner's mind. Any problems that this card represents the departure from are probably in the recent past. Due to this, you may, although *relieved*, may not be totally optimistic as *the healing process begins.*

This card shows a positive turning-point in one's life, yet the journey will be slow and determined, and at times, you may feel you are not getting anywhere. Right now, you are still all at sea, yet know that better times are coming. ***Now is not the time to confront issues*** but to let the dust settle and find a new way of dealing with things.

The Six of Swords can also show leaving problems behind rather than working with them, yet wherever you go, those same problems will still be with you.

Physical journeys or moves taken to relieve stress can also represent a rite of passage in someone's life, something they need to go through to grow and which will define their character for evermore.

Six of Swords: Reversed

Reversed, this card can make **an already difficult situation worse.** Leaving a situation will be aggravated by slow progress. There can be the temptation to just turn about and go back and return to a situation which brings stress, leading to **sabotaging your own happiness** out of impatience, *fear and vulnerability*.

Emotions can be overwhelming as escape plans fail, and *panic* can lead you to go in circles between the new and the old. *You will fear going backwards, but not feel able to go forwards.*

Someone may be rocking the boat causing problems at a difficult time, so you may need to ask others to sit down, or even do so yourself. As things will only be made worse, not better, by such actions.

The Six of Swords reversed brings **complications and delays**. If you are trying to solve an issue, then an unsatisfactory result will be reached, leaving you feeling that nothing can improve. Yet this is down to being stuck within an issue mentally, so **thoughts, views and beliefs will be your enemy**. You may find communicating your feelings difficult, or when you do, others will not listen to you for many reasons.

Problems will not be resolved, and new ones may arise. It's time to break a cycle and confront any vulnerabilities you feel you have. If help is needed, seek it.

SEVEN OF SWORDS

The card depicts a scene of a man carrying five of the seven swords, quietly sneaking away from two swords planted in the ground behind him.

The man stealing the swords is brightly dressed in mismatched clothes. His red fez is traditionally a sign of an oppressor or bully and matches his fur-lined boots. Their colour shows he is acting and thinking from a position of passion; he feels his views are important, as are his actions. His belief will be that he knows what is best and acts with that perceived authority. With the touch of luxury with the fur trim, they may be a tad self-serving, as he looks out for his own interests. His blue tights show a need to communicate through his actions, yet his tunic is covered in small dots or squares, showing someone independent, showy and with firm beliefs about how things should be. In the original image shown here, his tunic of green with slightly darker green circles gives him an element of faith in his actions; a friendly, trusting colour which can point to a friend's actions yet could be for show; whichever of the two can, from the wearer's perspective, show him feeling sincere in his actions. Others place this tunic as orange with darker orange dots, a fierier extrovert energy. His white under-shirt lays close to his body representing his pure belief in his actions. His overall appearance shows someone with opinions and who is optimistic and daring. His clothes being bright and not matching show someone who is easy to see, which is not what you would expect from his sneaky body language. This can show him as The Fool, throwing caution to the wind and being an opportunist, or even someone being sneaky and hiding in plain sight.

Taking the swords, he may hold the belief that it is best for everyone, yet it removes a chance for others to have their say or defend their position. He may be a thief taking the swords simply because he can, or seeking power by underhand means. Alternatively, he could be a kind yet reactive, impulsive soul who is removing dangerous ideas from the camp. He is not dressed as a soldier but as a commoner. He could be a common thief, an opportunistic passer-by teaching people a lesson, or someone seeking to even the odds, as he enters the enemy camp, which is a dangerous task. He is not dressed discreetly, so his subterfuge takes place when all is quiet, as in the distance seen between his legs is another camp in front of a hill. He could be from this other encampment, a soldier having put plain gaudy clothes on, or someone employed by them to interrupt and disarm, so the battle can be won more easily. Yet, just as easily, he can be from the camp in the foreground, again in his own clothes, so his entrance goes unchallenged as he is trusted, so his disarming of his comrades goes unnoticed.

He tiptoes, sneaking away from the tents, looking behind to make sure that he has not been seen or heard as he leaves the army camp. His smile and face show he is happy with his haul. He has a look of contentment as he has taken the swords and got away with them, so now he can control the outcome of any real or perceived hostilities or trouble. His eyes are closed, so he may be dreaming about his victory, his haul, the ground he has recovered, as well as the message he has sent out. In this original Seven of Swords, Pamela Colman Smith has given the thief white curls outlined in black. This shows a black and white mind, someone with firm beliefs about what is fair, right, and wrong. It can also, with white hair, be representative of wisdom, age, and experience. This thief's motives may not be all they appear at face value, as they may stem from direct balanced thinking or even sincerity, maturity, and diplomacy, and in this, it still may only serve them, yet rightly or wrongly, it could also be aimed at the benefit of the situation at large.

In the distance, the small group of soldiers discuss, eat and drink, relaxed in their confidence as our thief's actions go unnoticed. They have faith they will win this skirmish, or else they would be guarding their tents and weapons, but their guard is down, and they fail to defend their stance, views, or belongings. Alone, the small army symbolises aggression, forced actions, attitudes and verbal attacks, which are bypassed, undermined, or even misdirected by distraction, tact, and the forcing of negotiations from the taking of the swords. With two camps, this presents a war of opposites: them and us, ours and theirs, you and me, mine and yours, a collision of opposites.

As with the Three of Wands, the yellow sky can show dawn or dusk, most likely sunrise. If at dawn, the man's actions are with thought for what is to come, as are the others in the card, preparing for the day by their campfires. Yet those by the fire could show celebration after a day's battle, with him evening the odds, retaliating, or retrieving what's been taken. In any case, the men in the camp are not on the lookout for the traitors in their mists, and the grey smoke from their fire will obscure what is going on around them, clouding their view of their position; similarly, the man with the swords can only guess what their plans are and may misinterpret bits of conversation drifting on the morning air. The brightly coloured tents, with their doors open, are inviting, tempting loss as the soldiers are overconfident. Their multi-coloured tents are a sign of multiple opinions and views, as well as putting on a good show by displaying colours, expressing their views and beliefs to all who see them. Tents show a temporary situation, so a battle of wits, a war of belief: who has the bigger view and the strongest opinion.

The man takes five of the seven swords, and within the card, we see both the Two, Three, and Five of Swords. He has left the two swords behind to communicate a need for a stalemate situation, a temporary truce to things, an *'agree to disagree'* situation, as two is the number of compromises and balance. One of these two swords is higher than the other, suggesting that one view, his or the one promoted by his actions, is superior to the other. The five he takes show him to believe his views are better and more informed, or that he is not prepared to have his views overpowered by others, with five being the number of communication, intellect, and analysis. He holds these five swords in two lots: the two on his right shoulder represent his need to not face an emotional situation head-on as he turns his head from them; over his left shoulder are the other three, showing the logic of his actions. Here, he could be trying to defuse pain, especially with the two swords left behind, or causing it, as he has the power to upset or control a situation regardless of other people's needs, rights, or feelings. He smiles over these three, showing he feels victorious over the situation. With the number three representing creation, he has brought a new dynamic to the developing battle. The hilt of the middle sword is at an angle, so that new dynamic could be a new perspective, a literal new angle of approach in dealing with his situation, or a new view presented to others.

By taking the swords, he has armed himself with his opponents' weapons and stolen their thunder, their tactics, their ideas. This acts to avoid him being attacked by them, as he has evened the odds that were originally against him. He has left the remaining two swords with the enemy to create a result in his favour. He is defusing any potential danger to himself, or others, through forward planning, shrewd words and actions, mind-games and psychological manoeuvring.

The blame within this card is often placed at the thief's feet, as he is the one sneaking and stealing. Yet he could also be moving or hiding, re-changing the swords of those who would hurt him, or even taking back what is his. Those in the camp may not be the victims, but those who seek to hurt. Again, this is a card where you can be any of the players; at times things are not what they seem.

Numerological Value - **SEVEN** = Spiritual growth, wisdom and endurance.

IN A NUTSHELL

A time to change tactics is being presented. Diffuse others or situations by being diplomatic, bite your tongue if you have to and do not rise to the bait. Stay aware of all that is going on around you to stay focused on keeping things calm.

A time for the intellectual part of you to act, not the emotional. Stay alert to the actions and words of others.

Seven of Swords: Upright

The Seven of Swords tells us to **approach problems intellectually**. This may involve **changing tactics**, doing, and saying things you may not feel comfortable with to **keep the peace** in times of trouble, as **diplomacy** is needed. It can also show a time when it may be wise to **research your enemy or problem**, so you know what or whom you're dealing with.

You may need to **defuse a situation** with a lot of tact or tongue-biting and even avoid issues, even if it makes you feel uncomfortable or uneasy. This can leave you **feeling guilty due to secrecy and underhanded actions** when you would rather be more relaxed and open.

There is a need to go behind people's backs to achieve something or have what you wish. Yet by the same token, others can be doing the same to you. **Playing mind-games** does come with its risks, so stay focused.

Conversations may be overheard or interactions seen, leading to misinterpretation. Conversations may even be started to gather information or reactions rather than out of true friendship. Opinions or truths are being tested to be used against you or to satisfy another person's need for control, information, or power, so watch for **a spy in your camp**.

Be aware of all that is happening within situations. **Be wary** of the subject at hand and any others involved within it. Views and beliefs will not always be apparent, and when expressed, they could disarm you, causing embarrassment, vulnerability or reputation within a situation. You are **in the enemy's territory, in the lion's den,** so tread carefully as you will need to **be mentally agile**. You may even need to stay silent to resolve your issue.

This card warns against impulsive behaviour in any way. **Careful and forward planning** should be implemented to avoid circumstances or another person getting the better of you. If you wish to **act alone** with an issue, this card suggests it would be beneficial.

Seven of Swords: Reversed

Reversed, this card shows ***dishonesty and deceit.*** If you wish to get away with something, ***you will be found out,*** as deception will come to light.

Cheating, lying, withholding of information in any context will be in the air. The cat will be out of the bag, as attempts at keeping something quiet will not go to plan. If you wish to take a short-cut to solve a problem, it is best avoided as others will point it out unfavourably.

The main message with this card is to ***think twice before you act or speak, or give anything away,*** be that a belief, opinion, fact or idea. It may be taken, turned against you, or utilised by them in some way, with them claiming ownership.

Acts by others to diffuse events will just be an act of bullying, so now is a time to hold quiet council with yourself until you know who you can trust and only respond with facts.

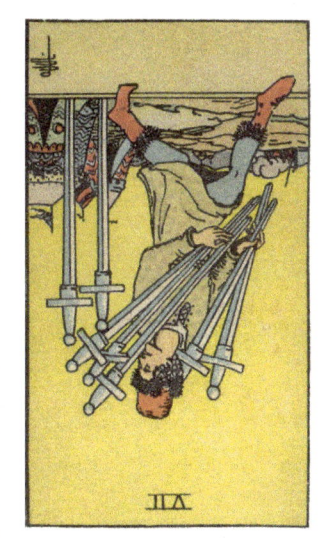

This card shows your life may be made the subject of ***rumours.*** By not protecting yourself or ignoring an issue, you have left yourself open to someone with a ***grudge,*** or to someone who wants to ruin what you have, or even simply for the joy of ***gossip.*** And it will happen right under your nose. ***A time to be careful about who you trust*** as someone has their own motives to go against you. ***Their words and intent may trick you***, yet they are setting you up and revealing true or false information about your life. If verbal banter is risen to or paid back in kind, it will not help, as it will backfire and cause distress.

On a material level, this card can show ***theft and material losses,*** as another will desire what you have.

EIGHT OF SWORDS

The Eight of Swords shows a woman standing bound and blindfolded, with the eight swords surrounding her.

The woman is dressed in an orange/red dress and pale brown shoes. The colour of her dress is one of enthusiasm, power, action and optimism, yet she looks far from empowered and optimistic and is showing little action, as her bindings stop her from enjoying those qualities by restricting her. Her shoes show her fully aware of her predicament, with the brown earthy element stuck within watery emotions. In some versions of this card, her shoes and undergarment are both a light orange, symbolising a lack of physical as well as mental energy. Her clothes reflect what she hopes for herself yet feels unable to attain, as here she is psychologically trapped by her own restricting beliefs.

The fabric used to bind her is loose, so she can remove it if she wishes. It matches the dark grey of her undergarment yet like the couple in The Devil's card, she stays fixed in place rather than freeing herself. She is bound by a deep fear of moving out of her situation. The blindfold creates a fear of the unknown and issues are exaggerated within her mind. It covers her third eye, leaving her blind and without her intuition. Her fears will be heightened, yet like the ties about her body, they could easily be removed. She could also walk away from her situation as her legs are not bound, but without sight, she fears falling and making things worse, leaving her mind tying herself up in knots. Her blindfold may stop the truth from being seen and a way out through the swords, but it feeds into her limiting self-belief about being powerless. They are grey, bringing deep thought, as she ties herself up in her problems. Someone or something has bound this lady up on a mental level, allowing a problem to take authority in her mind, tying her to a situation, and she feels perplexed, helpless and inadequate in making any changes.

The tide has gone out, leaving her standing in rivulets of the remaining, still seawater, mud and sand, bogged down with static emotions. When the tide returns, she could drown in her feelings as her thoughts trap her here. The muddy sand represents her lack of footing and stirs up shallow emotions. This prompts fear and creates a cycle of negative emotions followed by disempowering thoughts. The ebbing current of the tide shows the bulk of her emotions are not present, but a more niggling fear of what ifs and maybes as she avoids her problems and creates a panicked hurdle within her life. Algae has started to form, leaving her shallow waters prone to stagnation as she waits for someone to save her.

Behind her stands a castle representing safety, comfort and success, but it is not seen or faced. The castle is high up on the rocks, so she may perceive the journey back as too hard and hopeless. Her inner doubt can be telling her that it's just not possible as she won't be able to make it. She is separated from her place of safety, isolated and not able to see further than her current situation and beliefs.

The swords form a prison for her, thoughts hemming her in and trapping her or rather, stopping her from looking to where she would rather be. They represent her limiting beliefs leaving her psychologically confined, feeling powerless, stuck and unable to challenge her beliefs. The swords are planted in a set of one, two and five, so she stands caught between the failure of the Five of Swords and the avoidance of the Two, with the reality and truth of the Ace in front of her, all being ignored. She is a victim grounded in her fears which prevent change and movement, as fears are the greatest jailers, keeping us confined in prisons of our own making.

The woman within this card is trapped by her own mental processes or actions. Intellectually, she is stuck, as she could move if she chose to. She is not fenced in by the swords and so could leave via the opening in front of her, or simply pull them up.

It shows a time when you believe your own negativity and when you have allowed others, or your own beliefs and narrow opinions, to control your world. This may leave you feeling frozen in place, powerless and too scared to make any moves as your mind tells you it will all fail. The magic within this card often comes in the form of outside help and being helped by others, so all is not lost.

Numerological Value - EIGHT = Change, challenge, honesty and determination.

IN A NUTSHELL

You will feel trapped, powerless, unable to make changes and victimised, which may disempower you even more. No way out of a situation is seen, as you listen to fears allowing them to imprison you.

Ask for help, or take it if it is offered, as the insights of another can help you to move away from your own self-imposed limitations. Let go of old restraining fears if you wish to be happy and move forwards.

Eight of Swords: Upright

The Eight of Swords brings a time when *you will feel trapped and unable to move out of a difficult situation*, which will restrict any incoming opportunities. This situation exists because you tell yourself it does, leaving a situation of your own making. Regardless of how big any monsters and outside forces are, it's your fears, expectations and worries which keep you stuck.

There will be an *inability and fear in making decisions*, as all you can see are problems, situations and others holding you back, yet *there is a pathway out of your current situation* if you look.

With this card, you should not pass blame, as you have either originally caused your problem or have embedded yourself in it by *negative thinking*, usually while trying to avoid an emotional situation and not tackling outdated beliefs. This card shows *a need for personal honesty* and a realisation that *you are the roadblock you are seeking to remove*. This is a card which represents *being your own worst enemy*.

You are trapped in a situation which is taking your confidence, self-esteem and happiness. Quite often with this card, *you will need help from another,* to help you see that things can be changed or are not as bad as you think they are.

There is a need to take a break from your situation so you can focus on what is holding you back. *Self-imposed boundaries* can be broken free from, which means letting go of *limiting beliefs*. Often you can be seen by others as playing the role of a victim, or apathetic and defeatist, as you will be *feeling persecuted and imprisoned by your issues*.

Another aspect of this card, if it were to turn up with cards such as Justice upright/reversed and The Tower, could refer to actual imprisonment.

Eight of Swords: Reversed

Reversed, the Eight of Swords shows *you have realised that you can break away from a restricting situation or person,* and indicates *you are now able to think rationally and clearly*.

The truth or the reality of your situation has been seen, allowing a new beginning to emerge as you realise your own connection to your limitations and that *old ways of thinking are now let go of.*

You will be aware of a shift in your views which gives you the key to freedom, and the road ahead will not seem so full of pitfalls as *you start to feel empowered* by being able to see solutions.

You see how addictive your old way of thinking was and how it left you blindfolded in a comfort zone with no real consolation, and *you start to take steps to make things better.*

You see that you can change your conditions and there is hope.

You grab hold of the reins and take personal responsibility for your situation and throw away 'victim mode'. This allows you to *feel personally empowered* and free from old negativities, as you step away from fears, often with *the help or kind words of another.*

NINE OF SWORDS

The Nine of Swords pictures a woman troubled and in distress, whilst hanging beside her are the nine swords.

In the darkened room, the nine swords hang on the wall over the left side of the bed, showing that they are impacting her mental state, leading to her thoughts, fears, expectations, and sorrows not being tempered by understanding emotions or wise thoughts. The hilts of the swords form an interlocking pattern, a neat pattern behind her, her past, firmly set in order within her mind and feeling unescapable, and which when lying down hangs over her, blocking clearer thoughts.

Three of the swords are in line with her body. One passes behind her heart, triggering emotional pain, causing her to reflect with worry over losses. One lines up her with her throat, showing worry over words and communication with all those things said or unsaid. One passing above her head, her mind, represents concern over certain thoughts, opinions and beliefs, all bringing mental anguish. Her mind is being tortured by what might be, when or if the swords come crashing down or ever need to be used, as well as how they were used in the past.

Her grey nightgown shows her vulnerability, as well as her sincerity to find peace and her deep desire to rest. Yet, she is plagued by her mind, which stops her from recharging, leaving her full of anxiety as she contemplates her fate.

In the original image of the Nine of Swords shown here in this book, her hair is blonde; in others it is grey. When blonde, it can show a need to be rescued and a naïvety, and feelings she cannot cope with as she does not have the experience. It brings a vulnerable element to the scene, leaving her feeling unable to face her fears. When grey, it is the opposite, as grey hair is a sign of maturity and wisdom, yet here that wisdom is not felt. The grey hair shows that worry here is intense, leaving her disconnected from her wisdom, as the weight of the swords hanging over her is full of words, actions, beliefs and attitudes. She is fearful of their perceived threat. She may believe that due to her experiences she should and must know the answers, yet struggles to find the ones she needs. She may also feel that old wounds should be healed, yet they still haunt her. This places an extra burden on her already over-stretched mind, leaving her facing a new day with the confusions of the last still wearing her down as she sits in scrutiny of herself and her insecurities.

She sits in bed, a place where you are meant to rest, a place where the subconscious mind can work through the day's issues. Instead, she is bolt upright, head in her hands, full of despair. Her mind is racing, churning, busy and unable to shut off as she worries about worry, either projecting her fears onto the future or going over what has already happened. Her pillow is beige, a neutral colour, so a safe place to rest her mind, sleep and find a new order to her thoughts via shutting off from them for a while. But in her current state, that is not available. This all leaves her tired, stressed and not seeing things clearly as her mind turns the shadows of the swords in the dark room into mental, tormenting monsters. Her mattress is thin, showing a lack of comfort: nothing to soothe and comfort her mind or body, as laying down she may feel the hardness of the bed beneath her.

Carved into the woman's bed, two people are fighting, showing she is concerned about both intellectual and emotional confrontations, and maybe even physical ones. Below where her head would lie, she is trying to sleep on her issues to see them clearly and to gain understanding. Yet the scene is of one person being defeated by another with a sword, bringing the total of swords in the card to ten. Nine as a number wishes completion, wanting to resolve any leftover issues; the Ten of Swords shows a situation at its worst, while the $10 = 1 + 0 = 1$, the Ace of Swords bringing a need of a bolt of mental clarity to release her from her nightmare state, and from the fears she cannot rationalise. The carving shows two trees, a number of balance, with the trees symbolic of history, growth and her foundations. This can show that her mind is focused or being triggered by things long since passed, which is echoed by the bed itself which resembles a wooden chest, a place where keepsakes and memories are stored. Within this can be memories and events going back years. Sleeping on her past will cause the future to be blighted by fears created by events gone by.

The design on the bedspread is of red roses and the signs of the zodiac. The red roses have a yellow background and show a desire for growth, change and movement, as they do within The Magician. She wishes to be grounded and creative enough to find her own way forwards and to intellectualise her feelings with the yellow. If only she could lie down and cover herself over with this energy, she may find some calm. Yet this bedspread is mixed with the zodiac symbols against a blue background, representing a sense of fatalism covering her. To lay down and cover herself with it may make her feel pinned down by her worries even more, as she has already thrown it off and now sits overwhelmed with concern over what dreams have visited her. But even sitting up, it weighs on her legs, stopping her from walking away from her concerns. In her worry, she relinquishes her control to let destiny do its bidding, with a faith that time or fate will resolve her problems, even though it is something only built up in her mind. The passage of time can be linked to her problem, as the twelve signs can be linked to times gone, or even that projection of fears on times yet to arrive. The zodiac represents all the personalities, so here her worry could be on the welfare, actions or beliefs of others; how she can help, avoid or heal from her connection to other people, leaving her to worry not just about herself, but of the bigger picture of her life.

When the morning light comes, it will illuminate the room and she may well see that the shadows are gone, and her fears are not founded. Yet that alone will not be enough, as she will just see harsh swords, truths and fears hanging over her still.

Often, this can be called the Worry Card. Sleep can be affected with the arrival of this card, yet it shows you feeling isolated and consumed by thoughts that make life a living nightmare. Fears are often not founded but exaggerated by a lack of clarity, leaving you full of anxiety and hopelessness, with no escape from an issue psychologically.

Numerological Value - **NINE** = Inspiration, honesty and understanding.

IN A NUTSHELL

Worry, worry and a bit more worry! There will be anxiety and concern over a situation. Yet the fear and anxiety will not be the result, just what you are feeling. Sleep may be lost as you focus on the many things which can go wrong.

While you project your fears onto a situation, time is lost in an unnecessary world of angst. Let worries go: the results will not be as bad as you think.

Nine of Swords: Upright

The Nine of Swords brings upset caused by worry, doubt and more *endless worrying*. When this card is laid, there are feelings of *concern, hopelessness and anxiousness over a situation past, present or future.*

The mind is awash with doubts. *Past events go round and round in the mind*, replaying small details, analysing events, sometimes filled with guilt or regret over actions taken or not taken.

Yet *the future or a forthcoming event can be shown,* which is being approached with a *pessimistic* frame of mind, as you worry about the things which can go wrong. *Nerves* rattle you as you face something with crossed fingers, *hoping for luck to be on your side*.

There is real *fear* concerning what a situation may bring and *confusion* as to how one will cope when it arrives. This leaves you feeling helpless in the face of an incoming disaster, real or imaginary, which sometimes implies making a *mountain out of a molehill.* This card can bring *sleepless nights* and show sleep issues, as *apprehension* sets in, and the once logical Swords are now found seated in emotions.

However, the Nine of Swords indicates that while thoughts and *fears intrude into your life*, affecting you on many levels, the *worry is uncalled for.* So, whatever the irrational fear that you are being subjected to is far worse than the actual reality of the outcome ahead. *The bad things you think will happen will not occur, or they will be a lot easier than you think.*

Old trauma can be represented here: issues buried deep down which are trying to come up from the past, showing *abuse* of any kind, which affects you on a mental level, leaving you haunted by the past.

Traditionally, this card can also, sadly, refer to female problems with hormones, such as PMT, which sidetracks the mind, including grief over miscarriages and other unhappy pregnancy issues.

Nine of Swords: Reversed

Reversed, the Nine of Swords tells that the *aversion* felt concerning events is severe and can often present itself in the form of *anxiety and panic attacks.* Sleep problems can turn into long-term *insomnia and nightmares.*

Thoughts run wild, leading to *despair*, leaving one with feelings of hopelessness: *panicked*, like a rabbit caught in a car's headlights and *powerless* to move out of the way of problems, and the pain you feel they will bring. Thoughts can be all-consuming and *obsessive*.

Superstition can take hold, as *irrational and illogical beliefs and fears* drive you forwards or hold you back. You will feed into the suspicions of others rather than seeking facts and you will lack the knowledge to see things as they really are. Fear will lead you to avoid issues out of dread of what will happen, leaving you overwrought. There can be fright over actions that are needed, resulting in *fearing shadows*, as *fact cannot be told from fiction.*

Past traumas, hurt and abuse can be hysteria and anxiety as the past cripples the present, showing that it is time to start working on resolving the past as it has taken enough of your time.

Depression can be caused by the confusion of a problem either ongoing or expected and the absolute fear of its outcome, leading to *hiding away to avoid any further problems*. Yet, as with the upright card, a lot, if not all, of what is focused on, will not happen.

Unfortunately, this card can also show *paranoia, repetitive actions, suicidal thoughts* and actions, as the mind cannot free itself.

TEN OF SWORDS

The Ten of Swords shows a man pierced by all ten swords, showing the end of something of value as misfortune takes hold. As with the King in Death's card, he lies in the mud, destroyed, his ego and sense of self beaten, except unlike the King, he is alive.

The night sky shows a time of ending, a time of transition. During the dark of night, when he would not have seen it coming, the man was overcome by the ten swords being put in his back. They represent a situation that has happened and is raw and crushing, as it is at its worst. He was not expecting this situation, even if he saw it as a possibility, as the swords in his back show the attacker came up behind him.

His tunic is a light brown, which covers his heart, showing he will be fully grounded by his situation and very aware of the reality of his situation. He may not like it, but he will be open to it as it is forced upon him. The brown of his tunic shows someone practical and sincere, yet bad things happen to people, good or bad, and here he lies.

His red robe, representing his drive, passion, and energy, has been removed, torn from him by the attack, and lies covering his lower body. He will be aware of his lost ambitions and his current lack of ability to manoeuvre his way out of issues, so solutions are hard to see as they lie torn from him. He is skewered by the swords into his body, and his robe leaves him feeling every inch of his destroyed dreams. Placed over his legs, it shows a wish to leave this fateful place, to escape, yet that is not possible as he is lifeless and totally overwhelmed. The robe shows a loss of status, identity and authority. It indicates the end of an aspect of life, something which he loved or desired being snatched away from him.

What the man has believed in, loved or cherished has been challenged and ended with a painful, harsh reality. The swords pierce the length of his spine, leaving him paralysed, and he can do nothing but wait for help or death. Like Death's card, a lesson must be realised before the birth of a new era, and here he has nothing left to give. He lies defeated by events, learning how harsh life can be. The swords are absent from the top of his head and his crown, so he will be fully aware of his situation. His mind will be in no doubt as to what has occurred; here, there are no delusions present. A sword goes into his ear, representing hearing those things which destroy. One pierces the base of his neck, his heart and all the way down his spine. Because the swords in his ear and neck prevent him from moving his head, he is forced to watch the dawn of the new day and the fear it may bring. His pain cannot be avoided; he can see everything clearly, leaving no room to deny his situation. A single sword can kill, but ten are used here, and his red cloak could indicate he was proud, did not listen to warnings, and was ignorant of things he should not have been. Yet, his brown tunic adds a more down-to-earth element, as while he travelled through the day-to-day of life, he may simply not have thought that such a thing as this could happen to him. His life has collapsed on a mental, physical, emotional, and spiritual level. This forced situation has no chance of repair as he finds himself at the rock bottom of The Wheel of Fortune.

For all the swords, the only blood shown flows from under his upper torso from the sword in his heart which goes in the deepest. His heart is bleeding, leaking out his life force, showing his life will be changing and he is powerless to control it, as the emotional pain is too much to bear. He cannot fight the situation as there is no point, which leaves him with no choice but to accept his situation.

He lies motionless as he feels and comprehends his loss, grounded within reality, and in a way, given into his situation. Yet there are three positive aspects to this morbid scene of mental and physical destruction. His sleeve is grey. This will allow for contemplative action to be taken, as, with a little energy or ability, he will be hoping he can bring some changes, to push himself up, even if not right away. This is echoed by his right hand, held in a Hindu/Buddhist gesture called a *Prana Mudra*, which symbolises the energy of life. It is used to activate blocked energy within the body, which the swords will stop the flow of. This shows us his hope that the swords can be removed, which he holds as he lies lost to events, a sign he does not wish to be in the situation he has been forced into. It is a quiet prayer made from desperation and a need to carry on. The third sign of hope is the sky, as with Death's card, here is the sunrise, a new day, however unwelcomed it may be as he knows he must start all over again. Yet it offers a new chance of life, a new chance to live and fight another day, so a new day is dawning as life goes on.

The sunrise highlights the mountains and the difficulties they bring, which the swords force the man to face and the painful reality they bring. In the new light of day, he can very soberly see the details of his situation and knows that this is a dreadful change with further stresses to overcome as he will need to face those mountains head-on.

Between him and the mountains is water, which is extremely calm. He is beaten, his anger has been broken by the swords, he is defeated, and the situation just is what it is, there is nothing to fight. He has no emotional energy left as his mind shines a light on the reality of his predicament.

This card shows an extreme of emotional pain caused by our reactions to events, a harsh time where we realise that we have little control and that life itself is bigger than our wish to be happy, content and productive. The sun does not always shine, and here we are forced onto new, often unwelcome pathways as situations fail, end or suffer too much damage.

Numerological Value - **TEN** = Purpose, uniting and bringing together of energies to create a new whole.

IN A NUTSHELL

Things will be at their worst as events come to a painful ending. This is a card of disaster: things will not go well or as planned. From this point, things can only get better, which may be little consolation, as you will feel defeated and you will wish to give up.

A new day has dawned, showing time to let go of the past, leave disappointments behind, and move on, yet first you need to find your feet.

Ten of Swords: Upright

The Ten of Swords shows us **a final, inevitable ending** that will bring emotional pain, leaving feelings of **unhappiness and loss, leaving us facing a stark reality**.

A **situation will suffer irreparable damage** and be at its lowest point. This is a card which tells that what we are wishing for, working towards or value will not work out well, and things will break down, as **emotionally we will be feeling as hopeless and lost as the situation**.

A **'No' to questions asked**, as things will be **a disaster** and **situations will end badly**, yet at least you will know the truth of how things are. If you wish to know how something will go, this card shows no life is flowing towards it, and no growth is possible.

Misfortune will accompany you **as unwanted changes will be forced onto you**, which will be difficult to deal with. Reacting badly to these changes will be a real possibility, as **a situation will be at its worst**.

There will be feelings of **wanting to give up and feelings of betrayal by life itself**. You may feel **shocked and numb** as you work through the pain, as there will be no hiding from the truth of your situation. **Views and beliefs will be shattered**, leaving you demoralised and **without a sense of purpose** or belonging.

Whatever the loss brought about by this card, it will allow for new beginnings, if the change is not resisted but accepted as it's the only real option you have. A time for the phrase, *'life goes on'*. A time to **trust the universe** and go with the flow rather than holding on to what has left your life. While moving on may seem a million miles away, in time, it will be where you are heading.

Ten of Swords: Reversed

Whatever disaster has befallen you, the Ten of Swords reversed indicates the **acceptance of a forced change** and shows a willingness to move on. Negative events from the past are seen in a new light as you start to move on. You have taken the change to task and dusted yourself off.

Although the pain of the upright is moving away, there are **still difficulties to cope with while one adjusts** to a new situation or way of life. Now is the time to **start putting life back together again**; nothing will be the same, yet the human need for growth kicks in and you are driven to move onwards.

Reversed, this card can indicate the **emotional baggage** which can be carried from past hurts, and which can cloud judgements as you move forwards, dragging the past behind with one foot in the past. Before starting afresh, any loose ends, unresolved feelings and **open wounds need to be put to rest**.

Solutions can be found for old problems, often from first accepting that the old way of doing things is now broken, was not productive or simply cannot be regained as it is permanently lost. You are left with the truth, which is a particularly good place to start from.

Regarding health, this card shows that **recovery** is possible, but it will be slow and require a lot of effort on the patient's part, especially with respect to their state of mind.

— Sword Family —

The Sword family is concerned with the battles of words and intellect, as well as the resulting victories and defeats. They are mentally active, rational, decisive, and direct.

They may often be found in positions of authority. They are the fighters, the soldiers, and warriors of the Tarot deck.

Astrologically, Swords are air signs: Gemini, Libra and Aquarius.

PAGE OF SWORDS

The Page of Swords stands with his sword ready, as the wind blows and the clouds gather.

Astrological Sign: Any Air sign: Gemini, Libra or Aquarius.

This Page stands poised, taking the high ground, looking over those below or further away. Pages are immature energies, with this one being as sharp as a tack and exploring his intellect. While swords can be witty and clever, they also know what words to say to get what they want and can also use them to their worst effect. Like all Pages, their talents are new toys, so each reaction to words spoken is something to play with. Standing here, he can see what is going on, wishing to stay ahead of the gossip or news, hearing interesting tidbits of information drifting on the wind. The high ground shows a tendency with this Page to feel they know it all, yet they only have partial bits of information most of the time, or no understanding of others' emotions even if they know the whole story. It is all just entertainment to them.

The hill shows grounding energy for the Page and with those red boots, it points to confidence. They seek those things which drive that passion, so go out of their way to express their mental energy. One foot is on tiptoe, suggesting quiet observation of the situations below, which links this Page to spying, eavesdropping and being underhand. The foot raised leads to a half-grounded individual who can move forwards with words without all the facts. His left, logical, foot faces the mountains, the sign for harsh truths and trouble. His right tiptoed foot is on the side of feelings, as it is often an emotional reaction that he seeks from cutting words.

To the back are the mountains which he leans towards, showing a need for conflict and reaction from actions and words. His search is for truth, logic and mental clarity, yet he leans two ways, with one foot facing the mountains and the other just dallying nonchalantly to the other direction. Showing this Page's loyalties may not be as good as you may wish them to be for someone so quick-minded.

The blue sky indicates that this Page can come sneaking up from nowhere to ruin the day as the clouds gather, and the wind blows, showing a storm is coming which this Page stands to face. After all, he has probably created it, or made someone else's storm a tad worse, and wants to watch the show, even if from a distance. By turning his head away, it is almost to show he is innocently just minding his own business.

The Page of Sword's head is in the clouds, and above fly ten birds. Ten is the number of completion, yet here is a Page far from complete, as he is too young and impetuous. The air he carries may make him feel he has more of a grasp on the truth than he actually has. The birds also show his soaring intellect, yet it is not very grounded, as he sees things from an intellectual perspective, without any maturity.

The trees bending in the wind are cypress trees, symbolic of misfortune, and so no good will come of this storm. The river below them will have its surface disrupted with this storm's wind brewing, so he brings stirred up emotive reactions from himself and to those he meets.

His sword is also missing the top third, and this represents his mind, actions, logic, and perception of things. He may believe he knows everything as he looks down from the hill and clouds in judgement of others, with his ten birds believing they can see everything, but he may only see a small part of the scene rather than the entire picture. Unlike the other pages, who are focused on their element, this one is not even looking at his sword, assuming mastery when there is little to none.

In some versions of the RWS, this Page's hair is fiery auburn, showing a mind alight with its new ideas. In this original, it is orange, showing the same passion, yet the ponytail is green, showing that with this Page's drive and ambition comes an envious, calm mind.

The Page wears a purple tunic, the colour of wisdom, and is worn over the yellow, showing confidence, a strong sense of self and within this card, childish mind games. You must watch for the element of truth in the hurtful words this Page's sword wields, yet they will only show a version of the truth, with no empathy or depth, just observations rather than reality: very much a half-cocked energy, which will mislead more than enlighten anyone listening to it. The white shirt shows an innocence with this Page, as with all of them, which stems from inexperience, yet with a sincere draw towards its element. So, words can be the result of simply speaking without thinking, out of curiosity, as well as planned and aimed for effect and the instigation of arguments.

The Page wears no armour, so this individual would fail to take any attack in return, as his defences are as ill-prepared as he himself is. He looks over his shoulder to make sure he is not attacked from behind, making him wary of the actions of others, showing us mistrust. This Page would rather lash out than risk hurting himself. He can shout and use his idealistic sword, but he cannot cope with such behaviour when it is returned, and doing so results in tantrums and irrational anger. But all the same, the threat that he poses is real and should not be ignored, as some of the harshest truths come wrapped up in spite.

The Page of Swords is a warrior of words: air represents intellect and thought, but with this Page, it is misdirected and misused. This person is sharp-tongued, direct and totally inconsiderate of the feelings of those whom he approaches. And approach he does with full vigour and often with immaturity. This Page reacts out of jealousy, insecurity, from only hearing half of a story as well as for the sheer hell of it.

IN A NUTSHELL

Words will cause upset. The truth or one person's truth mixed with immaturity, or a lack of personal experience will lead to temper outbursts or upset.

Someone will enjoy causing conflict, and even though what they say may be the truth, it will not be delivered with love. There will be gossip. Tittle-tattle is juicy, as what is private is brought up to be explored by someone who is not respectful of feelings, and rumours are likely.

Page of Swords: Upright

Personality - The Page of Swords represents ***an immature person*** whose main aim is to cause ***deliberate conflict*** and who enjoys causing trouble. This Page may be the child who is going out of their way to cause discord, or an ***insecure and angry adult or teenager*** who wants to upset another. Yet, he could also bring a sincere but unfortunate slip of the tongue, a misplaced word, an accidental spilling of the beans which causes upset and uproar.

The Page of Swords is often ***an individual not to be trusted, even though they speak the truth in most cases***. This Page will tell others your secrets and ***gossip*** about private matters. This person may not outright lie but will seek to ***imply matters*** when telling others. The ***truth can be damaging,*** and this Page will make it their job to tell it to those who would suffer or react the most from it.

Be careful about who you trust in your circle, as this person's mental ***curiosity*** will lead them to want to know as much as they can. They may go out of their way to find information if it sparks their interest. They will simply need to know facts or even tantalising tidbits to ***sensationalise the troubles of others***. If you point out their actions when found out, they will often back down, embarrassed or with ***an insincere apology,*** while cursing you under their breath.

The actions of the Page of Swords represent someone who is not mature enough to sort out problems sensibly, lacks scruples, holds grudges and gains enjoyment out of watching others having to cope with any difficulties caused. This Page does not care for the feelings of others nor to the outcome of any trouble caused and is quick in ***passing verbal judgement***.

Equally, this Page may have a bee in their bonnet and will make sure you know how they feel. Rather than talking in a mature way, expect sulking, snapping at you and going quiet as they build up to their storm.

The positive to this Page is that underhand, quiet actions can be to help move a situation along, and to get an issue noticed, yet with a wish to remain in the background. This can act to inform others of issues which are being suffered by another, with a desire to help and to smooth things out, representing a positive manipulation behind the scenes from someone who expresses their knowledge of a situation to those who can use it.

This Page warns us that words can hurt, and to think before sharing other people's details, secrets or moments of venting. We often do not know the facts, just one side with little of the full history, if any.

Message/event - *Expect gossip and rumours.* Any action from another that results in your washing being aired in public. Someone will go out of their way to cause trouble for you, yet it may be an innocent slip of the tongue, so check before you react. *News will arrive, which will be unwelcome and will cause tension.*

Page of Swords: Reversed

Personality - When the Page of Swords has been reversed, the threat posed is more hostile, bringing us *an extremely irritating and vindictive person,* with a tendency towards **lies** and even paranoia, especially within close friendships and other relationships. This leads to *secretive and underhand actions* to channel temper, frustrations and feelings of injustice.

Imagined relationships and problems can also be made up with this card reversed, as the mind creates facts to support non-existent situations. He is *a fantasist,* so may boast or lie about things, yet they may lay solely in his head.

This person will *go to silly extremes with their anger,* perhaps because of emotional problems or *feeling awkward or inadequate* when dealing with social situations. This may happen especially where they feel that they don't get enough attention. These people react out of frustration to situations where they feel that they are losing ground.

This Page displays *a spiteful nature,* which can be cruel and nasty and often leads to unwarranted aggression, *manipulation and lying to get their way.* They shout loudly, feeling a need to defend their views and beliefs even though others are not attacking them. Reversed, there is *no sincerity, apology or remorse,* as here is a very insecure and frustrated soul who feels *justified in their actions.*

Reversed, the Page of Swords reminds us that *others are entitled to their privacy, and apologies may need to be offered.* It is a good time to *look at anything being obsessed over* as it can lead us to be hurtful, irrational and lash out at others for no real reason.

Message/event - The Page of Swords reversed indicates that ***trouble will be caused for you by another:*** you should try to understand why this individual behaves in the way they do. You are warned that getting involved may fuel the situation and make matters worse. ***Do not react*** to rumours which amount to tale-telling or petty hostility, but do not be surprised at any silent or abusive messages, calls or letters, or even petty vandalism.

KNIGHT OF SWORDS

Within the Knight of Swords card, we see a young man in full armour galloping at speed, his sword held ready for battle. Without fear, the Knight rides into the coming storm.

Astrological Sign: Gemini.

The cypress trees bend in the strong wind, symbolising upset, regret, sorrow and an indication that the storm has arrived as the sky has darkened, filled with grey, rain-filled clouds.

He is the only Knight charging into battle, with his face showing a battle cry as he aims and targets his attack, throwing himself into the heart of the action. His armour shows he can and will protect himself. So, reacting to his presence can often be a waste of time and unpleasant, as while he is not a master of intellect, he knows how to use his words, knowledge and intelligence to aim himself toward what he wants. His visor is up so he can face the storm head-on. He is a force to be reckoned with – explosive, persuasive, and mentally driven to achieve his goal. Like the Page, the top of the Knight's sword is missing again, representing that he may not know all he thinks he does, yet all Knights bring incomplete knowledge along with a lack of commitment, and this one is no different.

The wings on the back of his knees, like all the bird motifs in the card, show his desire to fly, to soar high into his element, to take to the air with each stride full of intellectual purpose. Being ruled by his mind, he wishes to be seen as strong, knowledgeable and well-informed and as a capable warrior, flying high and allowing others to see his perceived qualities. Yet birds fly from one place to another, only seeing glimpses of things as they speed by and above what is below, bringing in an ego which can presume it is better than others and superior.

On his helmet, he has a red feather and a small flower shape made from seven circles called the Egg of Life, a geometric symbol for the potential of life, representing the first stages of a cell's development. The seeds of his thoughts have grown and while they have not hatched, he is following the path they lead. He is sure of his mental creations, sure that his mind, intellect and reasoning will develop into something certain. His red feather shows his passion, his intellectual drive, his rational certainty that his way of thinking is correct, as he is driven by a logical mind. His mind is conceptual, philosophical and his concepts can be very compelling to this Knight as each thought brings a new option into play.

His purple cloak, red in some editions of the deck, symbolises wisdom and covers a red tabard with blue birds. The red of the tabard is closest to his heart, so his need for power will drive him more than wisdom. Blue is the colour of the sky, calm and communicative, so he is relaxed with his high-flying ideas. The birds don't seem to resemble birds of prey, but maybe pigeons or magpies. I don't feel they are bluebirds as those are symbolic of happiness and peace. Pigeons represent memory, recall, homing in, and are used to deliver messages, and this Knight charges in with his own messages of urgency, perfection, facts and figures. In some countries, magpies are a sign of bad luck arriving; in others, they are a sign to look at both sides of an issue to avoid being blindsided. As birds alone, they drive him to soar high into his element of air. His tabard would be covered should he not be galloping into battle, so it represents his true colours, which you may only see when he is in full charge, leaving his purple cloak a self-perceived show of ego and wisdom. When in red, we automatically see his need for authority without the illusion of wisdom.

The five birds above the Knight represent his mentally active mind. Five is a number of communications, showing us his need to speak, act, get things moving and charge in with a touch of conflict, as he seeks to use his intellect to impose or manipulate change. This is also echoed by the five birds on the horse's harness as he rushes forwards with his opinions and beliefs.

He charges into the fight, ready for anything on his grey horse, and moving to the left of the card, he is bound for stress with wars of intellect and words. In newer decks, the horse is a lighter grey. Grey, a colour of contemplation and calm, implies that the horse is a part of the storm. You could say that he is the Knights' grey matter, his intellect and deliberation, as he rushes in like a tornado, yet to the Knight he is the quiet epicentre, as, like the other three Knights, he has complete faith in his abilities, his mind, and the ways he sees things. The horse is going at speed, showing a time for instant action, with no time to waste as they charge into view, so this is a Knight you may not see until the last minute as he arrives full of intensity with his adamant beliefs. He looks confident on the horse, so he is unlikely to fall and injure himself, but he may trample over others if he is not careful, or if you get in his way. Another difference in this original image is that the horse looks back at the Knight, its eyes full of stress and strain, rather than at the path it is taking. This could be problematic, considering the speed at which they are moving. In other versions of the Rider Waite Smith deck, the horse faces forward, focused on the road, representing the Knight's focus on the charge. This original suggests that the horse may not be as confident as the Knight, so mentally there may be some deep insecurity, but as the fight has been started, continuation is the only route open.

The heart on his horse's harness indicates he propels himself forwards with his emotions intellectualised, so he may appear cold, straight to the point and with no room for sentiment. For him, sentiment is not needed as it is too messy or unnecessary. His love is with the battle, the thrill of the chase, winning, succeeding, to be at the top and take down those who do not feel the same with his mind and clever disposition.

The horse is decorated with two birds, again showing this Knight's link to air and his need to swiftly swoop in on his goals. There are also four butterflies which we also find with the Queen. The butterflies bring inspired thought, death, resurrection and changing thoughts as they flutter about the head. Here set on the horse, they show him charging in with ideas; certain others will see things his way and be equally inspired. Both the butterflies and the Egg of Life show that while he is in full-on battle mode, his mind can be changed, yet it would have to appeal to the drive within him and bring instant satisfaction or action. The two birds show balanced thought, as he is not in disagreement with himself, there is no duality to be found within this Knight; to him, his insights are true, seen from high above the opinions and needs of others. These two birds are not in flight, so they are not free, representing the ideas he has already captured. The four butterflies bring a restrictive energy to this Knight's battle charge. Fours can suffocate; they like order, and butterflies flit about with little order. Here he has also captured his inspiration which can crush it. His brainstorm is not tempered with experience, which can lead his fantastic ideas to be lacking in substance. Yet he has placed them on his horse, so this is what he is chasing: an inspired thought.

He rides over dead grassland and mountains. His chase does not bring growth with it, as he brings the stress of the mountains which he has come from with him, along with a need to have it all right now. Growth takes time, and this Knight does not have any; he is not viewing things through a lens of what can be created long-term, but what it can give him Now. Everything needs to be done in this instant, so he may run out of steam before he achieves anything substantial, as grass needs water and sun to grow, and he just brings a storm.

The Knight of Swords is a spontaneous individual, bold and challenging, who seeks new opportunities of an extreme or dramatic nature as he charges in, throwing caution to the wind. He has a fast-acting intelligence that requires constant stimulation to provide him with inspiration; he cannot stay still, as he needs to prove himself right and put his cleverness into action.

To mention that this Knight is not at all concerned with the thoughts of others would not be an understatement. He is an intellectual soul, serious about what he can gain from a given situation and not about how others may perceive, feel, or react to his actions. He uses his sword to take him straight to where the action is and will cut at anything to get there.

Fortunately, this Knight is always rushing from one experience to another, as is represented by the speed shown within the card. Although this Knight's direct charge is often chaotic, it is also mostly short-lived.

IN A NUTSHELL

Batten down the hatches: a storm is coming. Spontaneous upheavals and upset will be caused by single-minded views and beliefs. Another will see something about you as a challenge to confront. Don't take things personally, as another person or a situation moves through your life, leaving tears in the debris they leave behind.

If this is not a person, then expect some chaos to arrive with a need to ride the storm through.

Knight of Swords: Upright

Personality - The Knight of Swords is *a free spirit who thrives on spontaneity* and is very *adaptable*. He is *someone prepared to fight for what they want* and will not back down easily, bringing a lot of chaos to situations.

This Knight actively *seeks out challenge and change*, as he has a restless and inquisitive nature. He is never satisfied, as he wishes to sample everything in life that comes his way which usually has him referred to as *a 'jack of all trades* and master of none'. He does not stop long enough to grasp the entirety of a subject, as he is *easily distracted* by anything new and *bores easily*. He is not likely to remain in one set of circumstances for too long without becoming *disruptive*. His mind literally bursts with solutions, arguments to and for things, and he must bring them to people's attention.

The Knight of Swords is an individual who dislikes emotional commitment and may find it *hard to commit to anything* of any nature at all. He is mentally active and needs to be mentally stimulated, as *he enjoys the thrill of the chase*, change and acquisition, yet not the commitment to anything he pursues be it a person, career, or material goods. Once something no longer sparks his interest or goes slow, he seeks something new to conquer, as he cannot abide tedium or routine and seeks *instant gratification*.

He is a crusader, yet as his actions stem from *ego or immaturity*, he fights his personal battles from the perspective that *his actions and words are paramount*. He tries to influence others with his logic and viewpoint. It is often his way, the highway or a battle!

He has an *attractive and charming personality* which he knows how to use, yet he *can behave cruelly towards others*, being selfish and dismissive of others' concerns. His thoughts, needs and desires are all that matter to this Knight.

If you choose this individual as a lover or friend, then beware. He will use you or otherwise let you down by making you feel unwanted.

This Knight can tell us to *be quick with decision-making*. To move fast with an issue, but not to get ahead of yourself.

Event - As an event, the Knight of Swords is *a person or a situation that brings highly charged and chaotic emotions.* As this knight is always rushing from one experience to another, any trouble brought to you will quickly pass, leaving you upset or angry and wondering what has happened as it passes quickly through your life.

Relationships with this person will be short and may be painful.

Knight of Swords: Reversed

Personality - The Knight of Swords reversed shows someone with *a lack of patience* who is unrealistic and *devoid of any real purpose in their life.*

This card can show *someone getting into trouble* with authority or others in their life through *antisocial or confrontational, angry behaviour.*

This knight can also show someone not to be trusted and can be referred to as the *thief card.* Someone who will steal ideas, information, time, energy, goodwill, views or even goods.

Reversed, he can be *nosy, arrogant, self-righteous,* with an enjoyment of interrogating others. He feels it is his right to know what is going on and will go to lengths to find the information that he seeks. When he realises that he does not like what he finds, or does not see what he wants to see, he reacts negatively with the aim of *discrediting and ruining another's reputation* or hurting them.

He is the proverbial 'bull in a china shop'. *He creates disruption* wherever he goes as has no regard for what he leaves behind. As far as he is concerned, you should not have got in his way. He is *hatred propelled, wanting war, not peace.*

When reversed, the Knight of Swords warns us to stand back from those things we may wish to say or do out of anger and frustration.

Event - The Knight of Swords signals that *your plans will be ruined by the deliberate actions of someone else,* or even by an Act of God. This may also refer to theft and other losses. *Mass disruption to plans* will be caused by someone who doesn't feel that you deserve what you have, or even by getting unknowingly caught up in another's issues by being in the wrong place at the wrong time.

QUEEN OF SWORDS

The Queen of Swords shows us a woman holding a sword, with cut bindings around her wrists, welcoming what is coming towards her.

Astrological Sign: Libra.

She almost sits in the white and grey clouds with her head in the clear blue sky, above the clouds, above the storm. A wind blows at her back in the distance where her past resides, which is not affecting her, yet those clouds hold watery emotions, which she rises above. Facing to the emotional right of the card also echoes this, yet she is not angered, upset, or driven by them. The clouds are to her left, so it is a matter of viewing them mindfully and rationally. In the clear sky, she can see the truth without judgement and with a calm outlook as her mind is sharp and she understands her problems. We see her in profile, as this is a Queen who only shows us what is relevant, and not always the whole picture, as that is private.

Above her head, one solitary bird soars, representing her mind rising above problems. It shows that she seeks answers alone with purpose and focus, leading her to trust her own judgement. She observes the whole of an issue without interference from outside. One is a masculine number and, as a warrior, this lady is strong, forceful and determined.

This is mirrored by her sword which is held straight up, indicating justice and truth, whether it be good or bad. She holds the sword in her right hand, showing that she guides her wisdom and words through her emotional filter. She understands deeply how life works and will not be swayed by emotions. Like Justice, she is also Libra, so her scales weigh up between fact and fiction and need to balance. She is not someone you can lie to and not be found out.

She wears a cloak made from cloud- and sky-printed fabric, trimmed with orange. The clouds here are white, yet even white they show that she is wearing her past and that she knows more rain may fall. This aspect of her cloak shows us not a pessimistic nature, but one accepting of loss as a part of life, even if not wished for. The white clouds also bring free-thinking, blue-sky energy where her mind has no real limits to what it can understand. Wearing the sky shows she no longer feels the need to fly. She has done that; now she is happy to bring the air down into her personality, rather than taking it out into the world at full steam, sending others flying without due cause. The orange trim and lining of this cloak is a sign of something which would not be expected with this Queen - silliness, frivolity, optimism, a touch of individualism, a need to be different, a desire for life and maybe even a bit of eccentricity. It shows her enjoying life, something which may be missed at the first glance with this Queen. In some versions of the RWS deck this lining is red, showing that she still has desires, passion and a need for power. As it is the lining and trims, it's an aspect she will wish to keep private yet will show to those whom she is close to.

Her white dress is symbolic of her pure nature and sincerity. It covers her entire body, as she is not about how things look or feel, but the reality of how things are, so she keeps it simple. On her white gown is an orange V-neck, yet could be a necklace - which in some versions it clearly is - and which stops over her heart. So, like the lining of her cloak, this lady still has passion, drive and enthusiasm. She is not as cold as the card may suggest. In the necklace versions, there are five beads, four clearly seen with one just under her cloak, showing a need for determined, passionate communication. Even if it is harsh, it will be wise and compassionate.

This Queen has a butterfly clasp pinning her cloak. It rests just above her heart, so when she speaks from her heart, she will often be inspirational; she can raise you up with her words, to motivate rather than damage and to help you see different perspectives. Her words may help you grow, as they are words aimed at transformation, an aspect of the butterfly.

She has a red shoe showing, so she is ready for action and to communicate. Her life is not static but ordered, and she still wishes for movement in her life. Her feet are on the yellow ground, as found with the Knights, so she sits amongst loss, a place where things have died, yet it has become her intellectual grounding. She invites movement into her life, with an open left hand, held out to greet what may come with truth and sincerity. It shows her wisdom: she knows how to play the game of life and is ready for anything, be it good or bad. She is open to life and has the wisdom to know it is easier to greet your enemy, emotions, trauma, or problems rather than shut it all out. So, while alone, she is not blocking the world out.

About both her wrists are red ropes which have been cut away, representing situations she has left behind her. Being red, they show situations she was passionate about, things or people whom she cared deeply for yet has been separated from. She has dealt with the pain and is no longer trapped by it, and so she, or life, has cut the ties that bound her by using harsh honesty to set her free. These cut ropes show grief, struggle and conflict in her past, situations leading to a desire to be free of emotional pain. They are left on as a reminder, so as not to make the same mistake twice, nor to forget why a situation is or has occurred.

Her golden butterfly crown shows her thoughts are inspired, calm and gentle. Her words may be direct and powerful, yet she is focused and quiet. To her, everything is logical, everything has potential. She knows that from death, new life can come, as she has been through many transformations herself, leaving her with a stillness that only comes with the acceptance of life's unpleasant events. She understands the phases of life and how we transition through them. Her hair is light auburn, a sign of a fiery, passionate personality. She is willing to feel; she has not lost the ability by any means; she just has a firm understanding of how feelings affect reality. This card could show her grey, aged and a crone with her losses, yet it shows her still youthful, and as such, still waiting to see what life can offer.

The orange fabric under her crown links to her creative drive, her individual way of seeing the world. It provides a buffer from the flight of the butterflies and her mind, which allows her mind to be still and take the inspiration they need rather than all there could be. It mirrors the colour of the land behind her, as if it drapes down and onto the earth far away, showing her past losses once again present within her mind, forming a part of who she is.

Behind her, the stream represents flowing emotions. Divided, it shows a time where emotional bonds have been split between her and another, a time of separation and loss. Her problems are known, realised and rationalised, bringing wisdom and an understanding of life. The cypress trees do not bend as with the Knights, but their leaves blow, showing this storm from the past may be behind her but is not forgotten and has made her who she is today.

Her throne is very ornate: the feet at the bottom show her stability and grounded energy. Once she has put her foot down, she will not budge, as facts are facts which cannot be changed. At the base is a large butterfly with two small birds beside it and with two sickles above, which are small scythes. They may represent both sickles and sickle moons, and above these are two smaller butterflies. This Queen is often called The Widow Card, and these two moons would represent death and rebirth. A sickle moon is either a waxing or waning moon, showing the first or last phase of the moon's cycle, a sign of life and death and the changing seasons, here of life, and in one respect, rites of passage as we experience life's harder moments. A scythe is death's instrument which is used to cut down the living, and being sickles, these are more personal. They are held by an individual to cut down those things which are dead or not wanted on a personal level, causing pain as they are cut from our lives. The butterflies are her inspired mind and her re-birthing nature; all of what she has lost, endured, or suffered has allowed her to be free and able to fly above the pain, using it to her advantage, giving her mental strength. This is all carved in stone, elements which she cannot change, and which support her world-view. The two small birds may be doves, bringing peace and emotional clarity to the carving, so that when her intellect takes flight it is tempered by this calming balance at her foundation. There are three butterflies which show creation, so she can create more in her life, yet it will be built with wisdom and careful thought rather than physical or emotional needs alone.

The widow element with the Queen of Swords can represent someone feeling alone and isolated, single, widowed or divorced. This can also be represented by a type of cherub called a *putto*, which means a boy/child, and is also carved on her throne. They were often placed on gravestones and memorials, pointing again to grief and her sitting on the grave of her losses, accepting and grasping her painful reality. The carving shows she has lost in life and suffered major setbacks yet uses those upsets to guide her intellectual energy and that she is on top of her grief. As a cherub, it shows protection, as they guard and watch over God's interests, praying for and keeping watch over souls who need confidence and restoration. This shows a Queen who still has hope, faith and dreams, yet approaches life with fairness and simplicity, as the logic of the mind is very healing. Here, isolation is not the end.

Her gaze is fixed on the future, with the past behind her, and she is ready to battle with anything which challenges her, but she will always do so in a fair and appropriate manner. Her face is stern, so she will take no lies or nonsense and can rarely be fooled. Yet if you are fair to her, you will not even notice her sword.

The Queen of Swords is a strong individual who has suffered at the hands of emotions and even fate, but importantly, has survived. This person has a definite determination to cope, persist and succeed with life, as she knows that life is not always a bed of roses and is prepared to fight her way through difficulties. Life has taught her there is power in surviving adversity.

IN A NUTSHELL

Now is the time to focus on facts and not be led by feelings. The past needs to be cut away if it causes you pain and a more rational stance taken. Honesty is the best policy as lies will not be tolerated, so listen to your instincts and try to see the situation independently.

A woman with emotional intellect can help you, but expect honesty which may hurt you a bit. This is a time to accept events and not be fooled by your own emotions. It is time to put your foot down, set up firm barriers and be diplomatic rather than aggressive or tearful.

Queen of Swords: Upright

Personality - The Queen of Swords is **an individual who is alone** either through choice or circumstances. Someone who has accepted their situation through mental reasoning. **She has suffered in life but has lived to tell the tale.**

Traditionally, she is called the widow card, and although she may be widowed, divorced or otherwise alone, it certainly does not mean that she will be alone forever.

This card, although showing **an extremely strong and direct personality,** can also show **loneliness** and a certain sadness at being alone. This is coped with, and she is often found with a smile and a quick sense of humour.

This queen is **strong-willed, sharp-witted, patient and intelligent.** She copes well when staring into the face of adversity. Experience has taught her it is far more beneficial in the long run to **face problems** than to run and hide, as they resolve themselves more quickly when dealt with. Although some may view her as one of life's victims, she would strongly disagree, as she is far stronger than you may perceive.

She makes **an excellent diplomat** in times of trouble, as **she remains cool and calm. However, be warned, as she demands truth.** She is someone quick to deal with issues with her **direct thinking and calm, calculated approach to problems.**

This Queen is a very *individual, independent soul* and may not always be single. She can also be a strong woman who is happily in a relationship, or even someone in a relationship who feels isolated or alone for many reasons. It can also cover those who others believe to be strong and durable, yet may still need friendship and company to relax in.

She will willingly give her advice and her *unbiased* opinion when it is needed, although in doing so she may offend, as *she is direct and straight to the point*. If this lady offers you advice, it will be no-nonsense and worth listening to. She will cut through any emotions which blind you to show you the truth of a situation, or even of your own failings - yet it will not be done in judgement.

If you wish to fight this woman, be prepared, as she will not suffer fools, nor will she back down where truth and morality are concerned.

This Queen tells us to *be organised with our thoughts, to clear away mental clutter,* to be rational and to face up to circumstances; to be as direct, unbiased, independent and as forceful as possible and not to let emotions get in the way at all.

Queen of Swords: Reversed

Personality - The Queen of Swords reversed has let disappointing relationships or lost opportunities turn her into *a bitter and sullen person* who is often *unkind*. Grief has blinded her, and she may be *living in the past and scared of the future.* Her troubles have made her view life as a reflection of those hardships, leaving everything a negative, a potential loss or a fight she cannot bear to take on.

She has allowed herself to become *one of life's victims*, who can be *overly critical of others.* She dislikes emotional weakness in others, even though she suffers from the same condition. She can often come across as *demanding and unreasonable,* as *life is seen as unfair* from her perspective.

The Queen of Swords reversed has *a vengeful, insensitive nature.* She will smile at the misfortunes of others, as it makes her realise that she is not alone in her pain. As she has *no trust in others or in life in general,* she tends to lash out verbally by being sharp-tongued towards others, whom she feels are 'less' than her. This leaves her ego-driven and *self-centred.* She will be suspicious of anything which may pose a threat.

She is a gossip and a troublemaker. This queen is not to be trusted, as what you say to her will be talked about and twisted maliciously behind your back. She is very strong-willed, so she can *intimidate* others. As she tells her twisted version of events, others will often agree rather than take her to task over what she says.

Reversed, she warns us to remove ourselves from negative ways of seeing the world. How we treat others reflects on how you in turn will be treated by them. *It's time to let go of the past.*

KING OF SWORDS

The King of Swords cards shows the King resting on his throne, holding his sword at an angle.

Astrological Sign: Aquarius.

Like the Queen, the King's sky is calm and dotted with grey clouds, and unlike the other Sword family members, there is no ill-wind blowing. This may be due to the air elementals, which stand carved on his throne behind his shoulders. They show us that this King is the storm. Air elementals, also called air faeries, sylphs or sylphids, connect to the element of air which is the pure nature of this King. There are three of them, one above his right shoulder, the other two to his left. Elementals can be good or bad as they are neither positive nor negative; they fly on the air currents delivering their gifts of intellect, communication and logic like voices in the wind. Here, there is no wind needed to deliver their messages, as they are set in stone as an aspect of this King's rule. The two on his left shoulder, on the right of the throne, are talking to the King. One reaches its arm out to his ear, so even on the emotional right of the card, there is a breeze of reasoning blowing. The one on his right shoulder is barely discernible, with his eyes facing the sword he will be focused on its actions. Three brings growth, so this King is not all rigid facts and figures, but someone who uses his cutting intellect to create from.

His throne has the same butterflies and sickle moons as the Queen. The pair of butterflies behind his head show his inspired nature, and his ability to see the potential for transformation. Two sickles and two butterflies show that every balance within this King stems from clarity, inspired thought, and an acceptance of change, both gains and losses. This is an element also shown by him leaning more towards the logical left side of the card rather than to the emotional, as he will be the one delivering such changes. Above his head is a third butterfly between the sickles/moons. With the butterfly between the changing, re-birthing nature of the moons, and the destructive nature of sickles, he has rebuilt himself in the past and transformed himself due to loss, battles and his own private wars. The three butterflies, as with the Queen, show this King's creative nature via the use of his mind, as he can make or break situations with his intelligence. Butterflies within a symbolically male card show the spiritual and philosophical side of the King. It points to his spiritual or higher transformation and his belief, plus his faith in pure logic and fact. The back of the throne goes straight into the sky, showing us his mind has no limits. Like the King and Queen of Wands, he wants to be seen from afar. Yet this is not a social invitation, but more to highlight his wise and just nature; he does not mind being noticed, he just wants to be noticed as a warrior of the mind and be taken very seriously.

Two birds fly to the right of the card, showing his soaring intellect and his ability to see things from all angles, his ability to rise above emotions. They also show the duality of the mind as he weighs things up. He is indeed a person who can and does pass judgement on others, which often carries an emotional impact.

Like the Page, he is on an earth mound higher than others so he can look down and see the bigger picture. This is not to attack or to hurt others, nor out of curiosity, but to be able to judge, with respect, for the situation. His mind is clear, driven by rationality, and as the clouds are far behind him, he looks at us with a strong gaze, seeking only facts. He leans away from the clouds to the right of the card, choosing not to let emotions be an issue. He is not in favour of them, as they do not hold clarity. He knows they are there, but instead leans towards action and thinking.

His sword is set to the left of the card, representing facts and reality, and in his right hand is a sign of how he will face feelings, slicing through them to get at the factual heart of things. His magical air symbol, the double-edged sword, is used to cut away at anything which needs to be eliminated, especially if it is to reveal the truth. For that, he will favour using laws, rules, ethics and morals above feelings and sentiments every time. This can leave his judgements feeling ruthless and unfair as he restores balance. Yet without emotions balanced with logic, as with the Queen, and his sword not being straight, at times he may not make the right choice for others, as he needs to satisfy his own belief in fairness above all else. His left hand, like the King of Wands, is in a gentle fist, so while he sits upright and aware, relaxed with his legs crossed at the ankles, he is still ready for action. He wears a ring on the middle finger as a sign of responsibility to all he touches.

In the far distance behind him, we can see a mountain range butting up against the grey-edged clouds. His experience will lie within those troublesome peaks yet show to us the stress which he can bring if unfairness is at hand. To the right of the card, we can also see a lake overshadowed by the mountains, smooth and calm just like this King, showing he has deep emotions even if they are not displayed.

The King's golden cherub crown represents his protective nature and his need to serve. Like his Queen's throne, this is also a *putto*, a grave adornment; placed over his mind, it brings his own losses into direct focus, as he understands loss and pain. It brings from him a direct desire to bring fairness to his life as well as to those who need it. This shows us someone who stands up for justice, truth and conscience. His crown also has four indents, not stones or jewels, but simplistic indents within the gold. Four mentally brings order, it can be a restrictive number, yet this King only focuses on what is right, to him or a situation, not how things feel, so this suits him, as everything is balanced on his mental scales.

His orange cowl – red in some editions of the RWS deck – covers his head and throat, draping onto his shoulders. Like the Queen of Swords, this acts to channel some of that logic into something understandable to others and give him a bit of buffer to the full onslaught of total logic; it allows him to be able to play with his ideas rather than be controlled by them.

KING OF SWORDS

He wears more orange under his cloak and tunic, so he too has a hidden extrovert side to his nature. He has a calm energy, filled with fun and sharp, sarcastic wit. As a person, he can be quite upbeat and extremely focused. He will keep that for those he knows well, as he would like you to deal with the serious person he is, rather than the friend he can be once he knows you better.

His gown is blue, most definitely not the colour of warm emotions, and is similar to that of The High Priestess. It shows his exterior, as he wants you to see he is stern, with little time for emotions, and that he holds the answers which will help you get on the right track. Even in relationships, he will say what he means and mean what he says. He can leave those who wish warm, comforting words feeling that he is cold or uncaring. He is just not wired for sentiment unless it is warranted in his opinion. His logic is there and given to others to show them their own pathway, failings or judgements about the world about them, and with his sword not upright, again it could simply be his opinion, his truth. His cloak is a blue/violet colour of communication, faithfulness, wisdom, independence, power and compassion. This shows his sense of commitment, high ideals, beliefs, faith and respect for those he deals with.

A brown shoe is seen from under his clothing, a down-to-earth colour. This shows him grounded and practical in his approach even if it is an intellectual one. Being his right foot, it shows he leads with care, common sense, doing things seriously and with effort, as he will not rush decisions but overturn every stone to get to the truth.

His gaze in some versions of this card shows his eyes staring off to the left of the card, the side of his preferred logic, finding him seeking facts. In this original version pictured here, he stares at us, so he is someone who demands the truth from those he focuses his attention on.

This King is the King of Air, and as such, it makes him the most direct and forceful soldier of his suit or even of the Minor Arcana. His intellect is solid and secure, as is his ability to reason. When you deal with this man, you are forced to answer to the laws of logic and judgement. He is firm in his beliefs and actions; he does not dream about things which need to be done, as he acts with direct force and inspired thoughts. Out of all the court cards, this person is the most analytical and the strongest when it comes to mental combat.

IN A NUTSHELL

Logic and organisation are needed. Now is not the time for emotion, but for fairness based on facts. Communicate honestly. Be ethical, have high moral standards to be able to do the right thing.

There is no room for mental or emotional clutter. Be forceful in your actions. If you need someone to help you fight your corner or to help you focus, look for someone qualified, who only works with facts.

King of Swords: Upright

Personality - The King of Swords respects *truth and facts*. He will fight his or anyone else's corner if he senses unfairness is occurring. Mentally, he dislikes disorganisation and clutter as he is very ordered and direct. He holds *strong moral views and has high standards,* which he follows above all else. He has a great love and respect for the truth and is *logical* through and through.

The King of Swords can also depict a physically mature person or one that appears older than their years. He is quiet in his approach and will use few words, as he *directs truth to where it is needed.* He is someone who may wish to overturn situations to find honesty. Yet he is not one to shout or be temperamental but *silent, precise and incisive*.

This King is *non-emotional* in his approach and takes issues very seriously. *Rational intellect informs his decisions,* and emotions will never be found clouding his judgement. This person may bring conflict with them, as he is only concerned with *facts and reality*.

He has the ability to see a situation as it is. He will *base decisions on what is good for the situation* and not for lone individuals.

It would be unfortunate if this person does not share your views, and he can, at times, represent *a person who has authority over you*. His advice will be based on *fairness*. This King will listen to your points of view, but if you are being unfair or unfounded, you will not succeed in making your point heard. If you wish someone to be *incorruptible* and a tower of strength, he will provide this.

In his personal life, he is witty and possesses *a sarcastic sense of humour*. Relationships with this man may at times be cold, as he does not display emotions openly, even though he is *committed*.

This King tells us to be strong and forceful in our actions, to get an overview of events and analyse them before acting, and *only deal with facts* as they are all that are relevant, although he may represent another person who is very educated in the matter at hand and will help fight for the truth on your behalf or give you the correct advice.

King of Swords: Reversed

Personality - The King of Swords reversed is *callous*. He lacks all understanding of the feelings of others and *resolves problems to suit himself*. He will *mislead, lie, bury facts* and use mind-games to win and succeed. He is *someone who will not fight fair*.

The King of Swords reversed is *corrupt, unethical* and opinionated to the point of rudeness, with no room for anyone else's view, as he will view them as weak, wrong or deluded.

This King is *a dominant bully*, sometimes in authority over you, by life's circumstance or his decision to impose his views where they are not needed. He is someone who *demands respect* yet deserves none, and will ask for favours, yet not return them.

Manipulation and mind-games come with this card. This is someone who knows what buttons to press to get what they wish, even if that means scaring and instilling insecurities in others. His attitude is *imposing and commanding*. He likes to surround himself with people easy to influence. He is never in the wrong from his perspective, as he feels justified in his actions.

He can be *a control freak, desperate to achieve or to keep power,* and does not mind who or what he destroys to keep his world safe, even when it is not really under threat. He fears independence in others, preferring to dominate other people's actions, thoughts and beliefs. He will often hate anything or anyone who is different or better than him in his view.

There can be *illogical* actions, thoughts or ideas. *Temper outbursts* may lead to *aggressive as well as verbal shows of strength* as he tries to dictate and command others.

This King is *an unhappy perfectionist*, a sign of deep insecurity as he fears failure. His ego could not cope with a loss and will respond by waging *a psychological war* on those he feels threatened by, leading to failure never being his fault.

He warns that *motives are misplaced* and that imposing views on others may mean you do not have to face change, but enemies may be created.

— The Suit of Pentacles —

The Suit of Pentacles is ruled by the element of earth, which rules our practical lives.

Earth energy shows the actions and the results of our labours. Life's practical and sometimes mundane side is represented within this suit, as are our creative natures. Pentacles show harmony, fertility, growth and stability.

Pentacles can also be called Discs, Coins, Stones or Rings. In a standard playing deck of cards, their equivalent are the Diamonds.

Keywords that define earth/pentacles - security, practical, honesty, health, persevering, slow and sure, physical.

ACE OF PENTACLES

Like the other Aces in the Minor Arcana, our last ace also shows a hand appearing from the sky, here offering us a bright golden pentacle.

As with all the aces, we have the pure white hand angelically emerging from a cloud, representing the genuine nature of the gift offered as an opportunity for growth. The hand comes in from the left of the card, showing that pentacles are connected to action, thinking and progress. The hand cups the coin, offering us a sincere chance for change. This pentacle is linked to our material or physical life and, being gently cupped, shows us the fragile nature of the coin. It is something that needs care, consideration and patience to grow.

Engraved on the coin is a pentacle, a five-pointed star (found reversed within The Devil) within a circle, representing the element of earth. The circle symbolises the universe, our lives, our creative space, our own world as well as the world at large. The pentagram represents the four limbs and head of the human body, with the head at the top in its positive position, showing the spiritual and mental aspect of the self in control. It's a symbol for luck, health, fertility, prosperity and security, so it offers us an opportunity of a material, practical, spiritual and physical nature. The pentagram can mean financial opportunities, health, money, or gifts arriving, yet it can also be seen as a positive boost of help or luck being delivered.

Below the hand is a well-tended garden. The flowers are healthy, the lawn mown and the pathway free from weeds, showing that things are going well. You are starting from a secure base and will be able to get off to a good start, with security and solid growth possible. Pentacles need time to grow. They cannot be rushed, whether this is linked to mental health, the body, money, work or home. A slow road forward is presented, as the Ace of Pentacles is like a seed needing time to grow. However, it comes with a gentle push to show us potential and possibility. The garden shows us what we already have, wish for, love or cherish and have worked hard for in our lives. The offered pentacle is a chance to improve on that.

The white lilies are flowers often associated with death and rebirth, representing purity and the restoration of innocence after death. The new beginning offered here takes you back to who you are, as a down-to-earth and sincere energy is presented. They grow strong in the garden, with six stems on the left of the path, the number of beauty and harmony, hope, feeling and emotions. Being on the mentally active left of the card, they show the mind sparked with creative ideas and intention. The single stem on the right side shows hopes and positive emotions forming with the new potential realised. White lilies were also used in weddings during the time this deck was created, symbolising a time to renew life, a new start and, here, to put down roots and make something of life in the real world.

The red rose bush symbolises desire and love, and a link to the number six of the lilies. It is a bit unkempt, but in a happy way, showing growth has started. In some other versions of the Rider Waite Smith, this can be shown as new light green leaves growing along the top of the bush. Everything here is about happiness, potential and growth. The bush forms a rose arch which again is linked to ceremonies and symbolises a gateway to happiness, a phase in life. The neat path leads towards it, showing no pitfalls or rocks to trip you up. The combination of the red and white flowers, with their lovely grounding energy, tells us of passion and purity, and a sincere drive to achieve more from life with their lovely grounding energies.

The archway allows us movement from one world to another, as we find ourselves in a protected garden looking out on the world. It offers a chance to move out of the security of the garden to make more for and of ourselves. The arch is not blocked, so we have a two-way opening. We know we need to take our opportunities out in the world to enable the care of our own gardens, or our own physical comforts and lives. The pentagram is a gift in dealing with our practical lives in one way or another, so you can add to your richness, literally or metaphorically.

Yet through the arch, we can see the mountains representing harsh facts, trouble, stress and the realities of life. We know a risk may be present, yet positive movement is offered to go out into the world to create. The mountains can show the Swords we have just left, with a need to heal and gather ourselves back up before we take this new opportunity, or an awareness of the risk we may have to take. The garden gives us somewhere to come back to, home, a place of security or the opportunity can be to stay put and nurture what we have, as this Ace is very grounding.

The garden is the safety we have created or seek, and what we wish to improve and grow from. We can now think about building, with the pentacle being a foundation stone in the secure grounds of the garden. It offers a time to germinate new seeds and be able to provide for, develop and nurture what we have or are wishing for. A time for peace and for us to connect to our lives with some prosperity, be that emotional, physical or material.

We can step through the rose arch with a proposal of a new life, a chance of a new job and anything which will allow us to feather our nest and feel a sense of contentment and hope, leaving us feeling lucky. Here is an opportunity for happiness where you know that you have secure ground underfoot. We are given the opportunity to make something of the gift in whatever form it takes, even if it is for the sake of enjoyment only. A time for health, money, or luck to be flowing your way.

Numerological Value – ONE = Desire for action, new beginnings and movement.

IN A NUTSHELL

Help, happiness and health are presented. Generosity will be in the air and for you to benefit from as abundance flows in your direction. You will be overflowing with happiness, leaving you feeling grounded and happy. You are on firm, secure ground for any new plans you wish to start building.

Goals all seem possible, and solutions are delivered. The timing is right for you to move forwards with financial and practical goals, with openings being presented to you.

Ace of Pentacles: Upright

The Ace of Pentacles brings a positive new beginning. A card which is filled with the offerings of **good luck** and can bring **gifts, good health and help of a financial or even practical nature**.

Career and financial opportunities will be offered, allowing for the chance of more prosperity. One will be **rewarded** financially or practically, for work done as well as for the sake of it, and **abundance** will be in the air.

This Ace also shows security as being vital to the enquirer, which may not yet be a reality but wished for. If so, then this is a good time to **step out of your comfort zone and aim for a goal**. Creative energy will be high, so use it for pleasure as well as business, as opportunities taken, or goals strived for under this card, will have abundant rewards and benefits. You will often be aware of any risks to your wishes with this card, yet you will also be aware of the hard work you have done to get to where you are. Here you can be assured that you are **off to a good start** with **a secure base to work from**. Now is a time to start putting some roots down and building foundations in life.

The Ace of Pentacles represents the beginning of **success** and shows that practical and money-making ideas will present themselves and have the potential to work out well. Or more simply put - **money is coming your way**, or **money will be found to do what you need to do**.

In relation to health, this is a wonderful card as it brings **healing**; energy returns and a sign that **a return to better health** is available. Feeling better in yourself after a time of illness is very possible. The earthy aspect of this card will leave you **feeling calm, down to earth and at peace** and can even appear when you realise how lucky you are to have the life you have.

Ace of Pentacles: Reversed

Reversed, the Ace of Pentacles shows the **refusal to accept financial responsibility** in general, which may leak out into other areas of life. You will be better at spending than saving when this card appears reversed, as the money falls out of the hand. **Bad financial judgements** will be guaranteed, so **it is not a time to trust opportunities**, however good they look, and **nothing should be rushed to completion**.

Financial opportunities or help of a practical nature will fail or not arrive. **Funds, a new job, or assistance wanted will not be found.** Now is **a time of loss** as opposed to gains, as your financial arrangements and plans will not turn out as expected.

Financial opportunities will be missed, leaving you feeling stifled and trapped by your situation and **desperate for a way out**, leaving strong feelings of **insecurity over finances**.

Materialism may take you away from realism and into a world filled with **fantasy** rather than hard work and dedication. **The path you wish to take or have already chosen goes nowhere,** as nothing takes root or grows.

Generally, this is a card of **bad luck,** as everything comes with an unwanted risk, or **an outright 'No'.**

Health may also be an issue with this card, including **depression and stress**. Physical energy will be low, leaving you vulnerable to infections and **feeling down in the dumps**.

TWO OF PENTACLES

The Two of Pentacles shows a dancing man juggling two pentacles.

The man juggles with the two pentacles held within a green infinity loop, a lemniscate, which we have seen before in the deck. It is a sign, with these pentacles, of the eternal struggle or dance of life to keep things balanced, financially or otherwise. Here it shows a continuing cycle and a time to keep a phase of life moving uninterrupted. Being green, the cycle is earthly and linked to health, mind, body, comfort and wealth, with a need to keep things flowing with harmony and calmness. This shows a scene of focus, attention and slight concern on the face of the juggler, but the sky is blue, so all is well.

He juggles to stay in tune with his situation, keeping flexible with each movement to stay focused on money, energy and happiness. One of the coins is lower than the other and these coins can be seen as two options, the weighing up of a decision, as well as money in and money out, energy in and energy out. Here it's the 'out' he aims his gaze at, his left hand, and as the old saying goes 'money out with the left, in with the right'. So, he dances, juggling his life, finances and responsibilities, making sure that he does not drop the ball, or coin. He is quick-thinking and busy staying balanced, so that life runs smoothly and cheerfully. This is also linked to him looking to the right of the card, as he has an interest in staying happy.

He is dressed in fancy, colourful clothes with his high hat and scalloped buttons and fashioned hemline, and he wishes to keep the standards he has. His high red hat shows he has lots of thoughts, aspirations, potential and high hopes, and he wants to hold onto his power. His hat is filled with his dreams, which he cannot act on right now, yet are on his mind. Letting one of the two coins drop is not wished for, as he desires to stay in control so he can move past this point to those dreams. His brown tunic shows him grounded and down to earth, with his heart committed to his aims. There are six buttons on his tunic, linking his actions to attraction and harmony, which again shows his desire to keep the happy things in his life with no loss of status. The buttons are separated into two lots of three, so there is a creative element, and he may be weighing up desire versus responsibility, wishing to be free from the juggling. Yet he knows, as he gazes at the lower pentacle, that now is for thinking and balancing, and not straying from that, as staying focused is needed for balance. At the neckline you can see a red lining in this original card, so he is still very driven to have more, to enjoy those things he wishes; but for now, they are kept inside, under his hat, stored for later when he has the time, energy or opportunity. At his neckline, there are two more buttons which are undone, allowing us to see a hint of red; as undone buttons, they can show that he is relaxed, that he wishes to communicate by opening his throat area, but also that he understands the cause of his position, or his undoing. He knows what wrong turns he has made or any challenging choices that have brought him to where he is, and so he is taking responsibility. With eight buttons altogether, we find a restrictive energy, showing him, buttoned up, holding it all in and doing the best he can, often with Strength's calmness. The rest of his clothes are orange, a bright vibrant colour: his overall clothes show that he has already spent money, diverted funds to how he looks, so here he may be trying to recapture some balance after an indulgence. The orange shows his confidence and an optimistic, playful element, so here money, financial, practical, or even emotional matters may not have been either needed or felt to have been taken so seriously up until now. His belt end dangles from his waist, so he may have had to tighten it. He could have had to reduce his spending while he juggles, as he is not able to make any changes in the present as that would disrupt the flow of his juggling. The belt links his thinking mind and his desire with a need for enjoyment; orange wants to shout and be seen, to enjoy life, so he may be here due to simply enjoying life and a need to continue to do so. It shows also that he could be finding this dance fun, a challenge, just as exciting as the situation which has gotten him here, as he happily maintains this balance. His green shoes show him grounded, relaxed and not feeling stressed, as this is just routine. The position of them shows us he is thinking on his feet, using common sense, and trying to stay ahead of the coins as they move from hand to hand.

His backdrop is a clear blue sky, with two ships sailing on the rough sea. The ships represent life and the need to steer our lives at times, and not become victims of the currents. Life always keeps moving: it does not stop while we pick up our dropped coins or focus on keeping them in the air. So, life may be passing our juggler by, or so it will seem. With the rising and dropping of the waves, they show in part life's ups and downs, and the deep, turbulent emotions which losing his rhythm could create.

The ship at the front, with its yellow and orange sails, carries his optimism, enthusiasm and ideas. The far ship, with red and white sails, is a sign of his hopes and wishes yet to come, and his passion and sincerity to get it right. (They can both be white sails in other decks.) The ships sail the waves behind him. He is not ignoring them but rather he is so very focused on his juggling that life goes on without him. He may miss new opportunities or potential mistakes as he cannot, with all the will in the world, focus on everything. Behind him they can also represent his past, and what he is now trying to calm and settle within his life. The ships on the rough seas show us shifting fates, as not all our ships will come in: some may sink, storms will blow them off course, and of course they can offer us a rough journey. As a result, a lot of his dreams or new ideas will stay under his hat and he will have to leave them for a later day. He cannot worry about what he does not have within this card, just what he does. He thinks long term, as his boats will eventually come to shore, bringing new changes with them; but for now, all that matters is keeping things moving and balanced.

The two pentacles are at risk of falling, even rolling into the waves, so although he is happy in his task, flexibility, and a readiness to maintain balance will be needed. This is a card that reminds us that life can be quite dull, yet content if we focus on what we have and keep it all running smoothly. It may feel consuming at times and never-ending. We can feel unable to go ahead with new ideas, but here you are asked to just stay in control, be open to changes and see where it takes you. It will be the balancing of issues that moves you onward, not the abandonment of commitments.

Numerological value - **TWO** = Balance, harmony and interaction.

IN A NUTSHELL

Stay flexible to changes. Life will have its ups and down, so enjoy the ride rather than fighting it. Brush off your juggling skills as they will be needed, as you multi-task your way through life or a problem. Stay focused on what is important.

Bring humour and fun into this juggling act; keep stress at bay as much as you can as you work towards a calmer time. This situation is only temporary.

Two of Pentacles: Upright

The Two of Pentacles brings a time when **money and responsibilities need to be juggled** to keep life running smoothly. **A busy time** where you will be coping well and a time to **focus on important responsibilities rather than hopes and wishes,** as you cannot keep everything afloat.

Financial as well as life **changes are on their way, even if it is just something to add to your busy routine.** If the card is laid in a future position within a Tarot spread, it is worth taking note so that you can be prepared, as you will have to **stay on top of a situation**, as some **quick thinking** will be called for.

Yet **changes should not be actively sought** if it means losing focus on other important areas, as they will come when the time is right. **To rush deliberations, ideas or plans without proper examination could be disastrous.** This is more a time to let ideas percolate in the mind while you get on with the **routine** of life, especially when it comes to **weighing up alternatives**, looking at options and trying to work out what life changes you wish for yourself.

The main message of this card is to **be flexible and prudent, as life or finances** will become a bit challenging. You will find that you have to **multi-task** and keep things **balanced,** be this in terms of your finances or your time, or of a situation needing your attention.

We can also be shown the challenge of keeping more than one part of our lives in balance at a time, such as home and work, work and play. It can also signal that **financial partnerships are doing well.**

This card shows *a sensible approach to life* in general and indicates you will cope well with any difficulties, if they are dealt with using *humour and spontaneity* and *going with the flow*.

Upright and reversed, it can show balancing two relationships or areas of life at once, aiming for a happy balance, such as work and home, or two people who do not like each other and working on finding a positive solution.

The Two of Pentacles also represents the *divisions of goods* and property, such as wills and divorces, going well.

Two of Pentacles: Reversed

Reversed, the Two of Pentacles indicates that you are *unable to cope* with financial difficulties; they are leading you into *debt* or putting you at risk of losing something of value. The ball will be dropped as you are *trying to cope with too many issues or problems at once*.

You can find yourself hindered by *unpredictable events* getting in the way of your spending, as things beyond your control overturn a balanced and often financial situation.

There may be *impulsive behaviour* such as excessive spending or gambling, or just *making bad choices* on what is focused on, leaving you *living beyond your means*.

Poor financial planning is at hand, leading to confusion over finances and responsibilities, with issues seeming never-ending. Emotions can be turbulent as you lose focus, leaving you *feeling overwhelmed with financial or practical matters*. Responsibilities can be abandoned due to wishing excitement, which has disastrous financial or practical results.

You will be *too busy* and too focused on a situation, resulting in *other areas of life suffering from neglect*. There is *poor time management*, and things are getting on top of you. It can also point to the work/life balance not working well within a relationship. It can show *financial or work matters causing problems between couples*.

For questions concerning intimate relationships, it can show two partners being entertained at once, indicating *unfaithfulness*, as someone weighs up which relationship is best for them or simply to enjoy both. As with the upright Two of Pentacles, it can also arrive when you struggle with keeping two or more people or separate areas of your life apart, yet it is needed as they do not gel or mix well, having little understanding or respect for each other. Here it shows you are *failing to keep one or both sides,* or people, *happy due to your link to the other*, and you may be asked to take sides.

With any issues connected to wills, inheritance, or any legal or moral division of goods, there will be loss.

THREE OF PENTACLES

Within the Three of Pentacles, we are shown a team of three people discussing the plans for a building being constructed.

Teamwork is represented by the three men talking about the plans and work progress, with each one playing a vital role in the completion of the idea.

The man holding the plans has the blueprint for the building and wears an orange hooded cloak with printed darker orange squares. This shows him wealthy enough to buy such individualistic clothing; he has been successful in life and does not mind who notices. His nature is optimistic, with a touch of flair and lots of drive, yet with controlled ideas, and here, he is the master of the project, the architect. He is the visionary of this building's creation, a professional who knows how to put the fine details down for others to see. He may even have funded the project at hand, showing him to have provided the opportunity for the other two and the larger community - since the building is a church - to enjoy. His brown boots show that his expectations are not as fanciful as his cloak, and he is very aware of the actuality of things at hand. He will not expect projects to be rushed and is aware that real skill takes time to implement. We can see the slight hint of blue trousers, which show a sincere, intelligent and calm energy.

The building plans show a detailed set of directions are being followed, as the men discuss the work being done and yet to be done while they make plans concrete. Mutually, they look at the blueprint and make suggestions of how progress should be made. There will be flexibility to change or tweak plans if needed, as everyone is invested and wishes progress to be made.

The monk's shaved head tells us he has renounced all his worldly possessions. He offers a contemplative, cautious element with his grey habit. He may also be someone responsible for taking care of the project and may well rely on it for his own sustenance in the future, as this building may be where he will live and work. He brings to the team a spiritual element, suggesting deep, personal satisfaction as he is doing what calls to him.

The stonemason stops his work to talk to the others. He is someone qualified, dedicated to his expertise and working hard to perfect the plans given to him. With each stroke of his brick hammer, he carves out the designed plan. As a craftsman, he symbolises a need to master a situation, to be recognised by the onlookers for the skill, knowledge and talent possessed, and equally to be rewarded for that. Here his work stands up to what has been required. Thus, he is encouraged to carry on, knowing he is doing an excellent job. He wears the traditional leather apron of a stonemason, meant to protect them from their tools and sharp stones. He is someone eager to do things well and to their best advantage, not rushing in and cutting corners, doing everything safely, professionally, with the right tools and to detail. He is dressed in blue in this original image, showing his confidence, faith in his work, and intelligent mind, with his white shirt showing us his pure focus on his position and situation.

He stands on a bench over the other two, with neither expecting him to get down, showing mutual respect as everyone's input is valid and warranted, and work needs to progress rather than be interrupted too much. The wooden bench shows him grounded, fluid and adaptable, knowing also that he needs the help of others to make things go to plan, and he is sensible enough to know that he is not working alone, as he is the one tasked with bringing their dreams alive. It can also be a sign of a step-up within a work situation, being elevated due to skills and abilities.

The plans shown are for a church, symbolising a place of refuge and safety, showing that their plans are for a lasting venture or opportunity. Together, they are building something which will support not just these three, but also their families and congregation. They have designed, prayed over, been given the chance, and are working hard to build something solid. It will be a durable investment, which in turn will bring protection and safety for the long term.

They stand in front of a large arch which has two smaller arches within it. The smaller arches represent decisions and the balancing of views. The stonemason stands in one, with the monk and architect in the other as they defer to his wisdom on how things can be done as they reinforce each other's efforts, wisdom and choices. An arch is symbolic of support and structure, and to walk through an arch is a sign of a new life being presented, a time to renew or start a new phase. The blackness behind the archway shows that there is more potential yet to be gained from this situation, more which can be built and enjoyed, yet also that the outcome is not known as it rests on actions taken now between these three men.

Above the two arches, the three pentacles are arranged in an upright triangle, a symbol for fire. In the centre is the symbol for earth, a circle with a cross within, representing the desire and passion that has been put into action. Ideas are being turned into reality. The mason's triangle can be brought in here, which represents the Holy Trinity, the unity of different energies in creating the whole; it brings God down into physical form, so shows a divine, blessed, creation in action, a calling being answered. On a practical level, it shows detail, ideas being squared off, determined ambition and precision if viewed as the triangle of the Masonic square rule and compass.

Below is a carved, inverted triangle, symbolising water and emotion. Within is a five-petalled hibiscus flower, facing upright like the pentacles, shows the five limbs and head of the human body, and inside is another earth symbol. The hibiscus flower symbolises beauty, delicate design, immortality, inspiration and respect. So here everything is honoured: the people, their skills and what they each bring to the project and to the wider repercussions of their work, and how it will impact themselves and others practically and emotionally. The water, flower and earth show that feelings are grounded, sensible, responsive and calm, as the creative energy and unity of those involved are greater than any worries. Their drive and grounded passion aim to set dreams into reality.

While this card is often taken from the stonemason's perspective, you can find yourself being present within any of the three roles shown: doer, contemplator or planner. The Three of Pentacles is a card that brings acknowledgement for efforts and rewards for abilities. Plans are important with this card and show that a framework is needed to be followed, and that situations are progressing with dedication and hard work.

Numerological value - **THREE** = Growth, creativity and productivity.

IN A NUTSHELL

Keep going, you are doing well. Others will be happy with what you are doing and may want to help. If praise or compliments come your way, know that it is for a good reason, as you are worth it.

If you stay focused on plans, stopping to review them when you can, you will happily reach your goal. Enjoy the boost in self-confidence given here. Expect to get the job, pass the exam, be offered a promotion, and generally get a pat on the back.

Three of Pentacles: Upright

Three of Pentacles indicates that *goals are getting closer to being realised*. Plans and ideas have brought you pleasure and enjoyment, leading to firm foundations having been laid within your life, work or financial goals. With hard work and determination, recognition and *rewards are on their way*.

Now is a time to *stick to plans* made. Even if you have made a mistake, you can make things better. If you find yourself unable to move forward with an idea or project, then it is time to *ask other people for help*, as your collective knowledge will be beneficial. *Teamwork and being a team player* are important tools with this card.

Take time to *listen to others*, converse about your plans and vision for the future. Now is a time to *pay attention to rules and facts* - *'measure twice and cut once'*. Going it alone will be hard, as others will be needed to help, assist and even open doors for you. Even if you are independently moving towards a goal, support - practical, financial or emotional - will be vital, as others will provide much-needed elements to success.

Of course, if you have not created any solid goal and wish to make changes, this card tells you to *make a well-thought-out plan of action before taking any action*.

Businesses and careers are going well when this card is laid, and any new projects that you are involved in will be of benefit to you. With slow and thoughtful planning, a solid foundation can be built, which will bring you a lot of happiness in the future.

You will win the ***support and admiration*** of another that may result in anything from ***a pay rise to promotion or even praise***. Either way, this card offers a boost in self-confidence and can often be felt as a well-earned pat on the back.

This is a positive card to have during unemployment, as it shows ***a return to work*** as ***your skills and abilities will be of interest to another***.

You have all the skills you need to create what you wish. ***Have faith in others*** and put your master plan into action.

Issues in any area of life will be ***going to plan*** with this card, as approval is given, tests will be passed, paperwork will be fine, consent will be given, and everything goes through without any hitches.

Three of Pentacles: Reversed

Reversed, the Three of Pentacles brings ***delays to ideas and plans,*** often due to not enough effort being implemented or even from ***not having the correct skills or knowledge.***

You may be ***setting your sights too high*** and are ***being unrealistic*** at the present, a sign that you are trying to run before you can walk.

You may wish to go it alone and be independent, but outside help is a requirement which cannot be ignored. ***You cannot do what you wish without the correct skills, money or support***. Problems and ***frustrations will continue,*** leaving you demoralised and with ***a lack of faith in yourself or a situation***. Getting others' help is vital, yet is being avoided, either due to a lack of funds, availability, skill set or even ego.

Promotions, work advancements and pay rises will not arrive. In any area of life where you seek approval or recognition, it will not be given. Professionally, you can lose status, work or money and even be demoted or passed over.

Plans can also suffer from ***shoddy, careless work, rushing and/or not asking for guidance*** as you believe you can do better than you are capable of doing. This leads to hard work and dedication being avoided or ruined. Skills can be lied about; you are ***not up to the job,*** and it will be obvious to others.

You may find that ***others are not being honest, working as hard or slacking,*** and so those linked to your dream may be damaging your plans. ***Teamwork will be unsuccessful*** due to a lack of respect, egos and disagreements. You or another may feel their work is up to scratch when it is not.

Plans will fail. Tests and exams meet with failure, and requests will be met with a 'No', or just fall through as nothing passes inspection.

FOUR OF PENTACLES

The Four of Pentacles shows an individual with four coins, one on his head, two beneath his feet, and one across his chest.

We are shown a man holding on to his wealth. He sits on a stone seat, showing his position to be secure, solid, and immovable, looking uncomfortable.

He wears a black cloak with a hint of red and an orange lining. In some versions, his cloak is deep-purple and black with a bright-red lining, indicating that he wishes to keep his passion, desires, and need for adventure to himself and not display his inner self to others, or worse, allow others to tempt or take from him. In this original image, his dark cloak makes him look as if he is in mourning; he is not, but instead he is tinged with vulnerability, which has closed him off to the outside world. His facial expression is neither happy nor sad, as he stares with a mixed expression, and while the black within his cloak shows his potential, he has an air of miserliness, control, mistrust, or presumption as to how things are going for him from his appearance. It has some red within it, showing his passion for life, his confidence, yet is overridden by the black, showing he has a lot of potential but holds it close, too scared to spend or risk wasting it. The orange lining has polka dots and brings to light a playful, extrovert soul, someone who wants to enjoy life to the fullest, but again it is hidden and held close. This could be due to living to excess in the past and regretting it, or it could be due to him being too afraid to spend and take a risk due to other circumstances, fearing what losses, or even gains, they may bring into his life.

His clothes here are a dull purple, almost brown. The light-blue hem shows his trust in his situation and reliability, as it is about his legs; he would have sought out his situation, so he could trust that no changes could be made. The tunic, being a dull purple and like his cloak, is also a sign of mourning, a gloomy colour which shows someone stuck in a way of thinking. His red shoes show he still has a driven nature to him, yet that aspect of him seems to be weighed down by his dreary cloak. Oranges and red would show a desire to spend and have fun, but this man curtails that and holds it all tightly to himself.

His golden crown shows his outer success and is fashioned into a battlement design, showing he may be struggling with his mind, maintaining his power, or a situation. He does not wear the clothes of a king, so his crown may be more a representation of his ego and self-expectations, with firm feelings relating to his security, safety and possession. He rules over everything he feels is his, not letting anyone else near to him or giving anything away.

His body is not in a welcoming position. His arms across his chest hold on to a pentacle and cover his heart, disconnecting him from his emotional wisdom. His arms place his hands in the opposite directions, with his left hand facing right and the right facing left. This creates a circle, representing a situation that is ongoing and a manifestation of his limited vision. The right and left hands being interchanged show his protection of his emotional well-being, and that his mind and thoughts agree with his actions. His right arm goes across his Solar Plexus Chakra, stopping him from connecting to his confidence, feelings of security and self-worth, so he may not understand his own value but just that of the coins and what it would mean to lose them.

His left arm pushes his shoulder up, leaving him hunched on one side, looking unapproachable, and his whole demeanour shows a lack of excitement with what he has. His effort is put into keeping the status quo; his body language keeps us at bay, so progressive conversations will be hard to have, as he does not really wish to communicate his situation or reasons to others.

One of the coins rests on his golden crown, showing he sees the world through his financial status; everything comes down to value, cost, loss or gain. The coin allows for no spiritual energy to enter through his Crown Chakra, as it halts any flow and intuition. His mind is blocked by his view of his wealth, in whatever way he perceives it.

His feet rest on the last two coins, leaving him unable to ground himself to his physical world as his feet do not touch the earth. This leaves him disconnected from the flow of life, common sense, and practical solutions. He is rooted in his possessions and those things or people he cherishes, which can come from poverty as well as from greed, with a fear of losing what he has. Both situations can make you cling tightly to what is yours. His feet face opposite directions, so he may be unable to make a decision. This can also be shown by the duality of these two coins. Which is the best way to spend, save, or invest? His heels are also tilted upwards, as the coins are raised at the back, pushing his knees up, which shows he wishes to take no action, yet if he did so without careful thought, his coins could be taken, lost or damaged, and his only foundation lost. The coins don't touch the ground completely as he lacks confidence and maybe even realism, a sign that he fears his own short- and long-term security, which could be limited here as these two coins are on concrete, and without earth they cannot form roots and grow. He is protecting his body, staying safe and not taking any risks, as he simply would not know who or what to trust.

His position shows his earthly, emotional and spiritual possessions and can represent any area of life that you are holding onto for fear of loss. Although this tells of financial security, it also warns of avoidance, being restricted and held away from the grounding, nurturing earth and spiritual healing energies, the practical and the subconscious, movement and new ideas. There is no access route for energy to gain entrance, as all his energy doorways are closed. He sits huddled up over his coins, protecting them with an adamant desire to stay safe.

Four is the number of securities, strength and stubbornness, and this person has fenced himself off with the four pentacles. In the far distance are mountains, so the problems he feels may be a result of issues once experienced in the distant past, giving him a stagnant view of life and leaving him over-cautious.

Behind him lie the security and richness of the city, yet he has his back towards it, guarding what he has, making sure no one else can see or take his wealth, inventions, ideas, goods, loved ones or security. His possessiveness protects him from loss, yet he cannot move so is forced to stay where he is to protect what he values. Everything is held on to very tightly, creating static energy where nothing can be lost, yet nothing can be gained, and he breaks even. He may have reasons to protect his belongings and wealth, as it may not be enough, and he cannot afford to lose any. He seeks to maintain his situation as best he can, which places him in an uncomfortable situation with little comfort and joy. He may feel vulnerable with his wealth, scared of losing or making mistakes, and even, at the other end, greedy and want to keep everything for himself.

While there is a castle in the background, he has turned himself into a fortress. He is the beginning and end of the support he gets or gives, and for whatever reason, he has turned himself into a little island. He is protected by his perceived security, allowing nothing to move which can lead to vulnerability and isolation, at the price of stability and the effort of control. He symbolises those who try to hold on to what they have, to those things in life which make them feel emotionally and physically safe while focusing on finances, wealth and welfare. He is wishing for more security, more income, more growth, yet is not willing or able to risk anything to create it.

Numerological value - **FOUR** = Realisation, will power and logic.

IN A NUTSHELL

Vulnerability may make you hold on tightly to what is yours. You may be secure, but nothing will grow, so expect no changes to any situation, which is a positive if you wish to keep the status quo.

Control may give you confidence, but it is a sign of insecurity. You are allowing your fears to control you or a situation, as you are viewing life through a lens of what you do and don't have and wish to hold onto.

Four of Pentacles: Upright

The Four of Pentacles shows a financial or emotional situation that, although secure, neither gains momentum nor loses. This informs us that *security is static*, allowing for *no growth*, giving you *a comfort zone*.

Financially, this card can be positive, as it shows *security and enough money to go around*, but not prosperity, as money coming in equals money going out. Leaving no room for mistakes, emergency buys or fun, placing you between a rock and a hard place. *Money is viewed with concern* and held onto, either due to past or present poverty or greed. There is the knowledge that what you have may well be needed, so is looked after with caution. This can come from *a poverty mindset*, born from hardships in the past or present.

Yet it does not have to mean limited funds. It can show someone wealthy who is extremely cautious and *protective of their money and investments*, and what to do with them for the best.

Security is opted for and so risk or changes are avoided. What there is, is kept hoarded, *safe and protected*.

This card shows *a situation of no change,* so success is not a given. It shows that *you cannot lose; nor can you win*, or gain. So, a bland, balanced outcome is shown to a situation where no or little change will occur.

Emotionally, this card shows you are conscious of allowing others to get close to you. You worry they might take advantage of any *vulnerability* you have about relationships, or what you have materially. Yet if you hold people back, it stops relationships from deepening or even starting.

This can also show a *defensive, possessive attitude* towards others, with an over-protecting personality which clings to those in their lives. It can represent the *control freak* in any area of life where a lack of control leads to panic and stress.

If you are thinking of making a big purchase or decision, you need to hold onto your money and ideas. Step back and protect your funds. Go slow with any decisions to avoid losses.

Four of Pentacles: Reversed

Reversed, the Four of Pentacles tells that *if a risk is needed, take it,* as it will help to counteract or avoid stagnation. You may feel vulnerable, but now is *a time to make changes.*

It is a time to *open your heart and mind* and let go of fears which have stopped you from moving forwards. *Take a chance with people, work and money* as well as emotions, as here insecurities, attachments and control are let go of. There is an understanding that you've been too strict, stern, controlling or self-contained and *movement is needed,* so open your purse or heartstrings.

Refusing to allow change or not spending money in the past may well be the cause of problems which now force you to act. *What you have neglected and left to stagnate will need attention.* The walls you have built up around yourself need to come down, even if you are reluctant yet willing to take action.

You will see the things you have previously feared in a new light, leading to a release of control over the things in life you have tried to protect, either by force or a sudden new outlook being gained.

This card can even take you as far as wanting to *throw caution to the wind* and *take risks,* which can be beneficial. There could, however, be *problems and disputes from others* about how much caution is to be thrown to the proverbial wind leaving *overspending and disagreements* being an issue.

The message with this card is to try to *be realistic about sudden urges and desires to make changes* concerning any aspect of your life, but do make them.

FIVE OF PENTACLES

The Five of Pentacles shows a cold and dismal scene of two people in rags, at night, walking through the snow.

The cold and darkness of the scene show a situation of discomfort with no solution visible to the couple as they look in the opposite direction of the window shining down on them. The snow has covered the path ahead, and its coldness forces them to focus on their basic needs and survival.

The pair have fallen on hard times, yet as we can see from their clothing their lives have not always been like this. They do not interact, nor help each other: they just try to stay moving, yet they are at least together and going in the same direction. The woman walks ahead, ignoring the man's difficulties. A weariness may have fallen over their relationship as they struggle with issues inflicted upon them or caused by their own actions.

They are both wearing unsuitable clothes, unprepared for this cold spell. The time for such luxuries has passed, and now they think about how to make things work out for the better, how to keep warm and moving forward.

The woman has grey hair in other versions of the Rider deck, as well as a yellow-spotted skirt. When her hair is shown as grey, it shows her contemplation of her situation; it represents stress and weariness, indicating someone accustomed to hardships and expecting nothing more. It can also show age and wisdom in someone who can no longer support themselves and is trying their best. She has red, auburn, fiery hair in this original card, which shows, as with her clothes, someone who has enjoyed life. Here her head is covered by her brown patched shawl, showing she is just focused on the basics, rather than wishes or dreams. She huddles up in her shawl, face down against the cold night air, as she just wishes to get to a better place in her life, away from the coldness of her reality, yet she cannot see where she is going. Her skirt is green with polka dots, a sign of a fun life, good times and a time of energy, optimism and being sociable. In either yellow or green it shows that she has enjoyed better times. She may have overspent and been too optimistic with money in the past, and is now suffering the consequences, or simply a time of bad luck. If she could, she would love to go back to what she once had. Her blue clothing shows her loyalty and sense of commitment, and the skirt shows a more carefree past where she could do as she wished. She has no shoes, with her right foot and leg bandaged. Emotionally, she has been hurt or tripped up and is now walking without a feeling of attachment to either life, others or her dreams. Her skin is also a shade of green in this original image. She may be envious of others now that she has lost her status or cannot gain what she needs to help her move forward and may be sick with envy.

The man behind her wears patched-up or torn dark indigo trousers, showing his situation to be more long-term. The dark colour shows he has potential and is earnest as he tries to keep going, but this potential has been damaged and he can no longer rely on it. His tunic is blue with yellow and green sleeves, showing how he used to feel: trusting, confident and intellectual. The mix of yellow and green could be to denote faded or even dirty fabric, which again links to the long-term aspect of this person's plight. As he walks along, old thoughts and feelings will be a distant memory that he cannot access any longer; he has no desire to go back in time but, instead, simply wants a fresh start. He has a blue band about his red hat, so while he seeks security and refuge, there is still a part of him which is hopeful for more.

His left foot is covered in a thick bandage or a plaster cast, showing that as he walks, he does not think of new directions to take to heal his situation. He may also be doing the same thing repeatedly, with no new ideas, options or opportunities arising for him, being set in a state of mind which is no longer any use to him. Yet he wishes to fix what is broken. His lower right foot and ankle are bandaged, representing someone who is emotionally hurt and wounded. He is dependent on his crutches to move forwards, which can symbolise social assistance, help and benefits, yet not enough to get him out of his situation. He may even need love and kindness, but none has been forthcoming, and so he supports himself as best he can. He sees no solution anymore as he is unwell, out in the cold and in pain. Each step will take effort and be considered, leaving all changes hard to achieve due to his circumstances. He is unshaven and neglects things which seem unimportant. He gazes into the sky in other versions of this RWS card, asking God why He has forsaken him, hoping for a miracle. This original shows his eyes looking downwards, as if he has given in and is despairing of his situation, avoiding eye contact. The bell about his neck tells others of his situation, like a leper warning of his arrival. This shows that other people may be aware of the problems he brings before he arrives. The bell may symbolise that we can become our circumstances if we permit it. It allows our misery to disable our efforts to succeed, as we become despondent and lose our hope and confidence. The woman may also be in front due to this, wishing to disassociate from the man and what he represents, not wishing to be held back by another's bad luck.

The couple walk past a building, presumably a church, yet with the pentacles in the window, it could be a commerce building or charity. The window is lit, but they just walk by without noticing it. This is a building that could give them sanctuary, help and assistance, yet they are so caught up in their difficulties they do not consider it. They may have already been rejected and left to deal with things alone and so do not seek help to risk being rejected again, or maybe they are too proud to ask. They may be homeless, jobless, penniless and in need of help, but they have also lost faith in help or are blind to it due to their circumstances.

The stained-glass window depicts the top half of the Tree of Life, showing they have no foundation of their own, yet this is a place where they can come for practical, emotional and spiritual support. Even if it is not an outright solution, it will give them temporary help or shelter. At the base of the stained-glass window in the middle, formed out of the stem of The Tree of Life, are circles with a line down them. This is the Phi symbol, a Greek letter which represents the Golden Ratio, which represents an ever-increasing spiral. This is telling us that even a small financial or security issue can rapidly bring even the richest of folk to desperate situations, and we need to focus on the pennies rather than the pounds. Yet of course that can work in reverse also. It calls for the minute details to be taken notice of within life. With the top half of the Tree of Life being depicted in the window, it is spiritual connection or growth which they seem to have lost, showing spiritual poverty as well as a financial one. At the top are two castle buildings, each with two windows and four leaves. While they are a symbol of success and goals achieved, something to aspire to, they also show duality, a need for balance and cooperation. The number four features here; four windows, four leaves, and here eight, its duplication. This brings restriction, a need for constraint to maintain success. The trappings of wealth may also be shown by this, a message that money, luck aside, needs dedication to make, keep, and grow. Yet, it is far above them, out of their reach, and a message they can only utilise with money itself, even if some of that help can be found within the walls of the building itself. They walk by, ignoring this shining light in the darkness, as it does not give them what they need right now. Yet it would feed their soul if they let it. Being too wrapped up in their physical situation has disconnected them from the spiritual, as it does not solve their situation or keep them warm.

This card tells us that sometimes loss is caused by the severity of unrelated circumstances, as events beyond our control make an already difficult situation worse. Our attention is drawn elsewhere, and so we leave other areas of life vulnerable to decay. Luck is at a low point with this card, and we suffer losses. We find it hard financially or with security issues, leaving us feeling vulnerable, unwanted and at a loss as to how to fix a problem.

Numerological value - **FIVE** = Truth, analytical and communication.

IN A NUTSHELL

You will not be feeling secure, and you may well feel as if you're on the outside, looking in towards the success and happiness of others, and feeling left out. This can leave you feeling rejected, unwell, stressed and even unloved.

Difficult times can leave you struggling to find balance, and although this card can link to unemployment and financial worries, the hard times can link to any area or issue which makes you feel unable to find a solution or ask for help.

Five of Pentacles: Upright

The Five of Pentacles is a card of *financial hardships, worries and material losses,* including *unemployment.*

You should *safeguard your finances* when this card appears, as it warns that money will not be readily available.

Now is a time to *take a close look at spending,* as even a slight change could leave *a secure situation spiralling out of control,* as *bad financial luck* lands at your door.

Whether unemployed or not, financially this card shows *poverty*. It shows a lack and loss of material comforts or pleasures. It is a time when you will not be able to make ends meet, or struggle to maintain a balance.

You should *pay close attention to the small details* and fine print, especially regarding financial or work matters. If signing contracts or documents, be careful. Financial problems will cause arguments or general difficulties within partnerships and personal relationships. Financially, look after the pennies to save the pounds.

Emotionally, this card tells that you should also *take notice of the details in your personal life* and don't let trivial things slide.

You will feel like you are on the outside looking in, out in the cold, *disconnected from others* or shunned due to work and finances. Maybe you are *trying to 'keep up with the Joneses'* and *live beyond your means.* You may fear judgement if you do not match up or are the *'poor relation'*, unable to keep up with friends or family financially. This can leave you *feeling detached from other people or a situation* due to your life not feeling enriched in a way you would like it to be.

You may not fit in due to circumstance, and you may be listening to feelings of *rejection* rather than ways to move forwards. You will feel as if you do not belong where you may wish to, wondering why *doors have been closed to you* and you have been left out, being given *the cold shoulder*.

Health can suffer; accidents, illness and setbacks may have created a difficult situation for you which you need to work through without further *neglect*. Make sure you do not become the situation you are in, but see yourselves as a traveller, passing through.

Five of Pentacles: Reversed

Reversed, this card indicates that any *financial hardships will begin to improve,* taking a great strain off you both financially and emotionally. This may be from a change of luck, or even due to seeking what was once reluctant advice.

While there may not be an instant resolution to issues, **situations start to heal.** Our minds, bodies and practical situations start to sort out their issues, leaving us feeling grounded and open to finding the help we need. The lack of faith we had is replaced with **a new understanding and renewed trust in life** and respect for what we have.

If this were The Wheel of Fortune, we would just be getting up from under the crush at the bottom. Now is the time to let go of the issues which have been neglected and **seek solutions**, as the initial pride or fear of further rejection of the upright has worn off and **a way forward can now be seen**. Here, help and support can be forced on you, as well as sought, but at last, you can start to **get back on your feet.**

Doors that were once closed to us are now open or in view, and we can start to **make plans** once again. **Options, solutions, and answers come our way,** which enable us to start to resolve our situations and problems.

Life warms up and old cold shoulders melt. Life may not be perfect, but you are welcomed with open arms rather than with a refusal to help, as **a time of problems and isolation from others' ends**.

SIX OF PENTACLES

The Six of Pentacles shows a wealthy man offering financial help or charity to a beggar.

The man distributing the money has come from the city behind signalling his success, wealth and influence. He wears the blue and white striped clothes of a merchant, which is sometimes shown on the man in the Nine of Cups, with a red belt. His belt is low about his waist, which shows a need for comfort; there is a slight bend in the stripes so he will be eating well. As belts bring together physical desires and mental thoughts, this is someone driven by his needs, and he has obviously done well. A long tail or lilipipe goes from his hat, round his neck and below his belt with a tassel for a bit of extra flair, showing wealth with its excess of fabric, as he is wealthy enough to dress for fashion. It also symbolises, being purple, that he makes wise choices, his mind is focused and he will see the bigger picture. His dark red coat and tights show leadership, drive, power, and again his status, which in some versions of the RWS is echoed by the luxury of a fur trim. In this original drawing, the fur is seen under his arms and coat as a lining. He will not act out of impulse, or emotion but with calculated thought to do what is best with his power. His green boots show him to be grounded and down to earth, so, for all his luxuries and his elevated social position, he can see things from a practical perspective and connect to other people's needs.

As a merchant, he is not trading, as there are no goods to be seen. He is not paying wages for work done as the other figures are begging. So here he is passing on his wealth to those in need. This may be a gift, yet, as it is weighed on his scales, it may be a loan and he may be a money-lender.

His golden scales show that balance in the outer physical world is being granted, which can show a Karmic situation in action. Within his left hand, he shows fairness and logical understanding. His evenly balanced scales mirror his own financial and moral state but also show that this is not a gift for the sake of it, as everything must be balanced. Cause and effect equal karma. What you give out you will get back, and what you get you will need to return in one form or another.

Using The Hierophant's hand position for a blessing, the merchant drops some coins into the beggar's hands, and if you look carefully, you can see three remaining coins in his hand. He has seven coins to share here, and like the Seven of Pentacles, he may be mindful as to how he invests his money, as the harvest will be important to him. He will be seeking a reward here for his own efforts. This card has thirteen coins, which brings us to Death, a time of transition and change, often forced; a defining moment. As nothing is accidental within Pixies' work in this deck, this may be intentional as the aspect of asking for or getting help can be life changing and humbling. The three coins left in his hand show that he is not losing funds as he is planning and creating. This is constructive and collaborative.

The beggar he blesses with coins wears a straw-coloured blanket with a simple cap, showing his needs to be basic and sincere, and in need of an injection of generosity and kindness to help him find his feet. The dull yellow of his clothing could show that he has lost his energy and momentum, which has affected his security, and he now needs to find a way forward. He probably just wants to eat, provide for others in his care, or seek investment in an idea; he looks up with gratitude. To this man, the money giver grants four coins, a number, as with the Four of Pentacles, which gives balance, and which could give him some security, but not enough for growth. So, maybe the wealthy man is wishing to keep the beggar subjugated, or he may be trying to help him see beyond the blocks he has created for himself. As this beggar shows no injuries which could stop him from working, the wealthy man may be giving him enough to allow him to want to seek and to invest in his own security rather than settle for 'just enough'. The four coins also fall in twos, which shows a beneficial situation between the two men based on understanding and fairness. This indicates that this may be an agreement, a loan or even an exchange of time and energy.

The man in blue holds out his hand, also gazing up at the merchant. His cloak is either patched, so he may have been in need for some time, suffering from long-term bad luck, or it can be seen as having an empty pocket with the lining hanging out. The red of the lining is a warning that he may not be wise at spending or otherwise negligent in his approach to his security. His cloak shows him to be a loyal soul; he may be suffering due to staying faithful to a job or situation yet has not been rewarded. Yet he could also be loyal to bad habits which he cannot break, and the merchant would be wasting his funds, time and energy if he helped him.

The merchant is not asking them to stand and take the money but leaves them kneeling on the floor. He does not place the money into the man's hands but lets the coins fall. He looks down on the beggar, not wishing to have him stand to face him directly but to grovel. This can leave the merchant looking less benevolent and more interested in increasing his own need for power, showing off and boosting his ego in a condescending manner. Equally, he could sincerely be helping and wishing them well, and it is the beggars who feel awkward or embarrassed having to ask for help.

The six pentacles are not evenly arranged, which shows the main imbalance of three positions occupied within the card. At times, we need to ask for help, and at others, we need to give it. One of the coins hangs over the merchant. Like the Ace of Pentacles, he is the opportunity, the gift, the chance for change within others' lives. The man in blue sits under the scales and above two of the coins. He sits under the energy of truth and balance as with the Two of Pentacles, so may need to learn how to control his finances or life. He may need to learn how to balance and juggle things to stay on top of his situations and be honest with why he is where he is. He may be begging as he cannot control his own issues and has created his own problems. The other man who is gaining funds sits under the last three coins. Like the Three of Pentacles and as a creative number, he may be asking for a loan to fulfil plans, being elevated due to his abilities, aiming for solid growth and foundations, focusing on a skill or solution. Deep down, he may want to create his own success and needs help with that.

We can play any role within this card, as it represents the distribution of help, guidance or funds which may not be welcomed. The beggars have had to go and seek this money giver, and so the receipt of any money, work, advice, or help given may be hard to receive, in whatever form it takes. The individual giving the assistance is financially or morally in a position of some importance, as he is able to give help to the others yet may need to weigh up what he can give and if he will get it back, as well as if it will be squandered.

There is an air of charity, yet having wealth distributed creates balance, giving what is no longer needed or being used to help another. It is a time to be grateful for what has been given to you, as it will help you move forward. This is not a time for 'looking a gift horse in the mouth' or withholding your ability to help if it is needed.

This card also shows that financial situations will be put right by the means of justice being brought into action. You may well receive what is yours, even if it puts you in a position of having to rely on another person or a situation.

Numerological Value - **SIX** = Ease, attraction and diplomacy.

IN A NUTSHELL

If help is asked for, give it; or if needed, ask for it and take it. If you need funds or help it will come your way. Don't be shy and take what you need but know it will have to be repaid. Improvements in finances or situations will be down to the charitable natures of others.

Yet if you have what another person needs, be that help, money, advice, or care, then be generous. What goes around comes around.

Six of Pentacles: Upright

The Six of Pentacles indicates that if you are owed money or are in need, then *financial or practical help and advice will be offered.* You will find *temporary solutions* to your problems which will tide you over.

With work or financial issues, it shows you will be able to survive financially but not be able to do much more. Your job will be *a means to an end* and financially unsatisfying. Yet finances will improve even if it's just pay-day! The Six of Pentacles can show anything from a regular income (which includes Social Security) to a loan, credit, *the distribution of another's wealth or charity* in whatever form it may take to help you work your way through a dry financial spell.

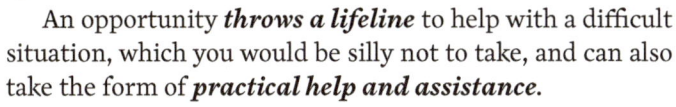

An opportunity *throws a lifeline* to help with a difficult situation, which you would be silly not to take, and can also take the form of *practical help and assistance.*

Another aspect of this card is that of *balance and control being restored to a situation.* Demoralising actions sometimes need to be taken to end problems: this is not a time to be proud but to *do what you need to do* to help yourself or your situation.

In all events, *debts will be repaid,* sometimes in kind or literally.

Wills and settlements can also come under this card, bringing the balancing of goods, money, and shares between people.

If this is not relevant, as you are financially secure, then it's maybe yourself who is able to be *a benefactor* helping with your time, money, mentoring or practical help. You may act out of generosity, yet you may still need to think carefully about what you are giving and why the other person needs it. It can even be as simple as doing a simple favour for someone, yet to them this may be a great help.

You may wish to invest in someone's future and help them grow, as you see their potential and you know that you hold the key to them getting started.

Unless mutually agreed and enjoyed by both parties, the Six of Pentacles can also show *inequality in relationships* where one partner, friend or loved one earns more than the other and the imbalance is felt by one or both, yet is a situation filled with love and respect.

Six of Pentacles: Reversed

Reversed, the Six of Pentacles indicates that *a reliable situation (usually financial) will be disrupted,* and *opportunities will be missed,* leading to disappointment.

If there is a need for financial assistance, none will be forthcoming. If money is owed, it will not be received. In short, *debts will not be repaid,* and no charity or assistance will be given, be that financial, practical or emotional, as *you will not find the help you need.*

Financially, things will be or seem unfair. You will feel that a fair deal has not been done. You will be *short-changed literally or metaphorically,* as you will not have generosity, honesty or respect extended to you.

You may *regret getting into debt.* In the past, you have not considered the consequences for the future, and now may be struggling to make ends meet or remove the damage debt has caused.

This card can bring *mean, condescending, snobby and patronising attitudes* which you may be getting or giving, as someone is seen as lower or less than another. You may also refuse to give help to another when it is needed and when you are able to do so, showing *a miserly, uncharitable attitude.* Yet if asked to lend money, be careful, as it may not be paid back.

Within relationships, affection and money may be held back, leaving you trapped in a situation you cannot leave. This can be due to *financial, physical, or emotional dependency,* as another person controls what you can or cannot have. You may have to ask or nag for money, help, or support within a relationship or family setting, as someone holds back to suit themselves, gain power or out of selfishness.

SEVEN OF PENTACLES

The Seven of Pentacles shows us a bush full of coins, which are being tended to by a man.

The man stands resting on his hoe looking calm, tired and thoughtful. While there is no tension in his face, the sky is grey, showing his gaze to be contemplative. He may have concerns over his pentacle vines, yet he stands relaxed.

Behind we see mountains, so he is aware of the consequences of no harvest, which may add to his contemplation. He is at a crucial point of the season. His coins are ripening, and for that, the sun is needed. A grey sky could be harmful, so deep down, he ponders the outcome of his efforts. In some versions of the deck, this is highlighted by some of the leaves being brown, and this too will be a concern, as he needs to stay on top of blights and other issues which may destroy his pending harvest and rewards.

He is dressed in down-to-earth colours, showing he is interested in the practical side of his venture. His white undergarment shows his sincerity in his project, and the blue shirt and leggings show his faith and trust in his situation and hard work. In some Rider Waite Smith decks, he is shown wearing odd-coloured shoes, both brown but different shades. This can represent a *make-do and mend* attitude, as he saves his time, energy and money to dedicate himself to what he is successfully growing here in his field. His brown shoes, resting on the mud and grass, show him totally engaged in his endeavours; he has little time to think about much else.

He rests on his hoe, showing he is taking a break from the work which he has put his all into. Hoes keep soil turned and remove weeds, showing his care to the finer details of his work and commitment to his goals. The soil is well cared for, allowing for roots to grow healthily. He knows his pentacle vine has merit and value and hopes it will bring rewards, as he has done all he can to make it so.

He gazes at the six pentacles on his vine: this shows his past actions, his efforts and his dedication. They represent beauty, attraction and what he loves, a creation born from a desire to grow and expand. The pentacle vine is healthy but not ready to be harvested, showing a time for patience, as picking the crop too early could kill the coins and destroy all his efforts. The man gazes at his potential harvest, gains and achievements, yet for now, he can only stay on top of the weeds and wait with a mindful approach. So the here and now, although relaxed, is of importance. He looks towards the growing coins respectful of their growth, understanding what their loss would mean. His investments are of great importance, as he has spent time helping them grow. He knows he can have a good harvest if all goes well, and that his efforts can be rewarded.

This coin at his feet can be viewed as an extra, unexpected piece of growth stemming from the main plant, yet it will need to still be allowed to grow to be of value, or even planted somewhere else to give a second investment. Or it can be seen as a coin consciously taken from the original plant, the original invested idea to start something new with. Yet with either serendipity or design, both still need care to keep producing the luck you want. This coin is like the Ace of Pentacles, representing future potential made possible due to his past efforts. He stands amongst his growing pentacles, happily exhausted, aware that he cannot stop for too long, as his garden needs constant care.

As he is resting, it shows that a return to hard work is the next step to be taken. Yet for now, he stands between the past and the future, and he can only focus on the present as it is his only reality. He cannot worry about the grey sky but keeps it in mind, as he stays aware of each weed as it pops up.

Traditionally, the Seven of Pentacles states that projects and plans already set in motion can to a certain extent be left to grow on their own as their foundations are strong and durable, yet your focus must not slip. Now is a time for waiting, caring until the time is right to claim your rewards. What you are developing should be able to support you in the long term if you are careful and keep nurturing the situation.

Numerological Value - **SEVEN** = Spiritual growth, wisdom and endurance.

IN A NUTSHELL

Now is a time to get ready to reap what you have sown, as what you have invested in will be paying out soon. Your efforts will be paying off and what you set out to do will be in view. Use this time to sit back and see how far you have travelled and how well your decisions have paid off.

Long-term goals are set for the future, yet the hard work is not over. You need the patience to see things through, which makes you very mindful of your present situation.

Seven of Pentacles: Upright

The Seven of Pentacles represents **an important time of evaluation**, a moment to relax and look at what has been achieved by your time, hard work and effort, or even money invested.

There will be a **reflection on the past whilst considering the future.** If plans are to work out, then **effort and commitment are still needed,** but this will not cause difficulties, as matters concerning **work and money will be going well,** as is any area of life asked about.

This card can bring **work changes,** which are more than likely within a current job or area of expertise. If existing work is unchallenging, then now is the time to make the relevant changes. If you feel you are toiling for no good reason, then reflect on how you can better use your time or money. This can be anything from a temporary change in working hours to areas of larger importance within a career. **Now is the time to make changes, as you have already laid the groundwork.**

Emotionally, this card shows us that **emotional investments are going well.** You are on track, even though there is a road left to be travelled. All is going in the right direction, as you have invested your emotions wisely.

In all things, there are no guarantees, and you cannot expect hard work alone to get to where you wish to go. **Stay focused on the bigger picture** and long-term success, as well as the daily running of situations. This card asks for **a mindful approach**, and to be aware of each moment you are in, while things continue to develop.

This card shows that the harvest, **finishing line, results and celebrations are not far away, and however tired you may feel, do not give up.**

Seven of Pentacles: Reversed

Reversed, the Seven of Pentacles brings *lost opportunities and a lack of personal achievement*. You have gone blindly into a situation without considering your circumstances, nor the effect these decisions will have on your finances, practical or emotional life.

Your energies have not been focused, so your *efforts have been wasted*; you have looked for a quick road to success rather than the hard work needed for the long haul. *There will be no rewards and you will feel tired of trying*.

Investments, financial or otherwise have not been productive and you are left feeling disappointed, and that all you have done has been for nothing. *Bad career or financial moves* can leave you *trapped in a static career or difficult circumstances*, where there is *no room for improvement* or growth.

Now is the time to stop what you are giving your time, money, or energy to, or not to enter into such agreements with yourself or another. If you want things quickly, you will not be able to benefit, as impatience will not serve you well. The Seven of Pentacles reversed also points to *inconvenience and trouble within the workplace,* due to working towards unspecific goals, or the impatient natures of other people, and rewards are not forthcoming.

Life can even have disrupted your efforts, as that grey sky may have brought problems out of your control to ruin your hard work. Even with the best will in the world, investments and dedication can be overturned by fate, bad luck and other people. If you wish to know if an idea or offer will bring rewards, then this is a 'No', as the harvest will be lost in one way or another.

EIGHT OF PENTACLES

The Eight of Pentacles shows an apprentice hard at work, fully engrossed in perfecting the coin he is working on. This card is often called The Talent Card, as it brings a dedication to knowledge or to a skill or ability. Here the young man is engrossed in the perfection of carving a pentacle onto one of his eight coins.

He sits astride his bench, so he can allow it to double up as his workstation, showing him to be an innovative soul. The bench, being wooden, is also a grounding energy, allowing him to be patient and focus on his physical endeavours, as he slowly dedicates his time and attention to the carving of each disc. He is working without gadgets using just the basic tools of his trade, so his interest is in the work for the work's sake, wanting to feel connected with each move he makes towards perfecting his skill.

The sleeves of his blue tunic are rolled up, symbolising hard work. The shirt's blue shows us his faith and dedication to his work. Being in such a focused state may well also show a spiritual link or that he has found his calling. This is echoed with his white belt. In some versions of the deck, the belt is brown, which would represent him grounded in his desires and thoughts about what he is crafting. When white, it brings a pure element into his study; both his needs and ideas are driven by the act of learning the subject matter in its purity and detail. He is driven to be as good and as skilled as he can be from deep within himself, allowing a higher element into his designs and letting his intuition and imagination guide him as he works.

Both his hair and tights are orange. They show that he thinks and acts with enthusiasm, finding his study, practice and perfecting of his pentacles fun. This is not a task which he is enduring, but one he is relishing. Each morning he will run to this place to get started, full of ideas and wanting to learn as much as he can, as his work here brings his mind alive. He is not deluded about his ability and knows that each step needs to be slow and meticulous to create a perfect finished product. He wishes, one day, to make money from the skill and ability he is perfecting, and as he loves the subject and the process, he is bound to be successful. In some decks, he has brown hair, red tights and burgundy shoes. These bring the same energy: grounded thoughts, passion and ambition. In this original version of the Rider Waite Smith, his shoes are different colours. His right is orange, so, as mentioned, emotions will be excited by the work at hand. His left, brown, symbolic of grounded thoughts; he tempers his ideas with practice, doggedly, yet happily perfecting. Each shoe balances out the other so he does not run before he can walk. He wears a black apron, which is to protect him from his tools yet represents his potential and possibilities within his field and shows that he is taking care over his project. He has prospects, and here he is perfecting his wisdom, putting the finishing touches to his coins, knowing that his work and ideas are of a high standard, or soon will be. The apron is tied with three strings at the back, showing creativity, growth and happiness in his skills. He is consumed by his new skill and spends all his time either working, thinking, or planning his next coin.

He has finished five of his coins which are varied sizes, showing he has experimented with his skill, trying different approaches and methods, and is still working on the three coins left. He may still be trying to find the best way for him to work with his skills, as even having a natural talent requires practice to make it perfect. He studies his work, and as he learns, he progresses and gets better. The three coins not yet hung up on display show his creativity being utilised, as he carves each coin to the best of his abilities, improving each one.

Behind the apprentice are the walls of the city with a clear pathway and open entrance. The pathway shows us someone prepared to go out of their way to accomplish practical goals with concentration, aptitude and dedication. He has an independent outlook, as this trainee has left his comfortable home surroundings to focus without distraction. It shows a time when we need to study, practise and learn without our normal routine hindering us. He has left the hustle and bustle of the city walls to focus on his work, so sometimes we need to sacrifice to gain the experience and knowledge we seek.

This card shows the act of perfecting and learning something new, be that the utilising of natural talent or a longed-for skill, which is studied and used to its best advantage, bringing a lot of pride in what you achieve. The message within this card is of hard but satisfying work and of perfection, showing an enjoyable learning process is underway.

Numerological Value - **EIGHT** = Change, challenge, honesty and determination.

IN A NUTSHELL

Practice makes perfect, so keep doing what you are doing. Pay extra attention to the small details if you wish to progress and master a skill. You have a natural ability that is worth the time and energy, so pursue goals with the knowledge that you will have to work hard.

Do not be worried about learning something new. New jobs or that course you wish for will come your way. Stay focused on your goals, as a lesson on just how much you can achieve is on the way.

Eight of Pentacles: Upright

The Eight of Pentacles represents *a flair and talent* for a subject or profession. There will be *a natural aptitude for a subject or a strong interest in a skill* which if taken seriously will bring in an income.

This card shows the *learning and training* of new and valuable skills or the refining of existing ones. You may be starting *a new job or career* where you have no relevant experience and must *study,* even starting at the bottom as *an apprentice*. You may start a university degree, or even a home study course, but perfecting and getting to grips with a new skill will be of importance. If you are looking for a course or opening to learn from, then it will be found, even if it is a book like this one or a YouTube tutorial.

Work and/or study is a joy when this card appears, as it fires the imagination and feeds the heart. Attention is focused on detail and perfection. What you wish to learn or follow will be looked at under a microscope for every little way to make things even better.

The Eight of Pentacles brings *new and fascinating pursuits* that will be totally absorbing, and this *hard-working* card shows total *dedication*. If you can get paid for it, then enjoy doing so, as if *it is worth doing - it is worth doing well*!

If work or study is not relevant, then the card shows a time for effort to be put into life or plans, to sit down and *chisel away at things, until you find a perfect solution to ideas or issues*.

Those you meet when seeking solutions or work to be completed will be conscientious and will do a good job, give good service, or will take the time to give you the due respect and time you need.

Eight of Pentacles: Reversed

Reversed, the Eight of Pentacles shows *no satisfaction to be found in your efforts, and you will feel unsatisfied with how you are using your skills.* You will be involved in a job or set of circumstances that have *no long-term benefits*, and you will not enjoy any work or study: it bores or frustrates you, as you would rather be doing something else.

You will be putting a lot of effort into projects, ideas or situations and *getting absolutely nothing of value back in return. Attention to detail will bog you down*, leaving no room for real creativity, as you get caught up in unnecessary detail.

You will feel like you are *on a treadmill*, churning out work, favours, or effort for little reward. There can be changes with work you will dislike, leaving you with *a lack of enthusiasm or ambition.* You are left feeling *unskilled or out of your depth* and not capable of making the changes you wish for yourself.

There may also be *difficulties acquiring new skills* at work or in general. You may find the subjects hard, uninteresting, or even too easy, leaving you twiddling your thumbs or stressed as you do not wish to learn what you are being taught. Finding or affording the right course, school, or form of study may be an issue, or even, at home, finding a quiet space to practise or study in.

If the above is not an issue, you may find that you have placed time, love and energy into perfecting or learning something others do not appreciate or want. *You may find it hard to get noticed despite having practical or professional skills, qualifications and ideas.* You may feel isolated in finding a workable solution.

Those that you find to help you, with this card reversed, may not be as skilled as they portray, or not do a good job due to impatience or disliking their work and what they do.

NINE OF PENTACLES

The Nine of Pentacles shows us a relaxed, contented woman, standing in a garden surrounded by her coins.

The woman stands in her private garden. Behind her, a wooden fence and a house represent her security, safety, wealth, and emotionally rich life. The mountains are shown in the background, and here in her own space, she is wise enough to know they exist, but does not let that knowledge ruin her private time, as they are small and pose no threat. Here she is in a safe, secluded space, free from stress and hardships.

Behind her are two trees, the number of duality and balance. She stands head height and central between them, indicating her mind to be calm, balanced and peaceful. She has no conflict or tension, just a gentle energy of unity within herself. Being trees, they represent a strong foundation, and with all her luxuries, they bring a stress-free simplicity to the way she is viewing the world.

Yellow is a predominant colour within the card, showing intellect, a positive sense of well-being and personal identity. The sky is yellow, her shoes and dress are yellow, or light orange, dependent on the deck, showing us a lot of optimism, happiness and contentment.

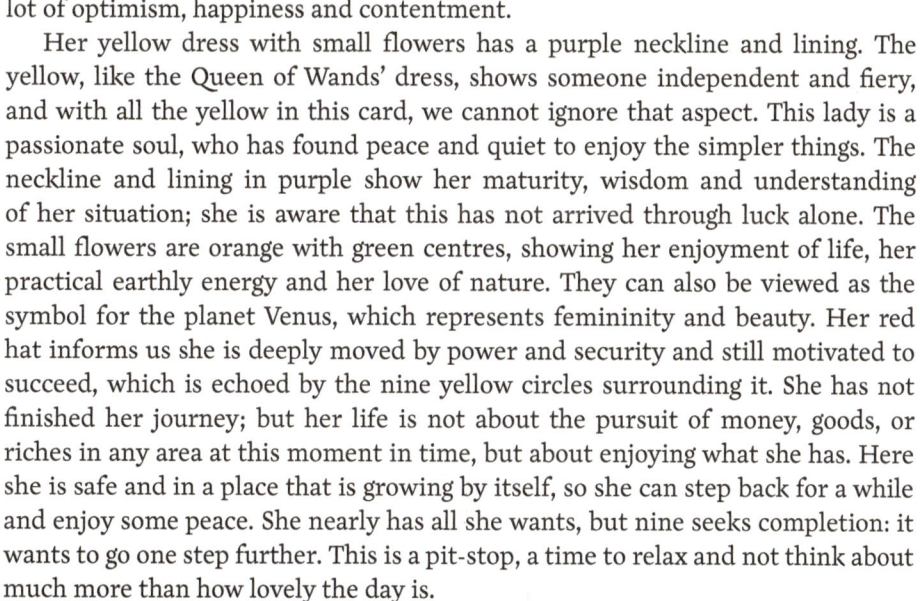

Her yellow dress with small flowers has a purple neckline and lining. The yellow, like the Queen of Wands' dress, shows someone independent and fiery, and with all the yellow in this card, we cannot ignore that aspect. This lady is a passionate soul, who has found peace and quiet to enjoy the simpler things. The neckline and lining in purple show her maturity, wisdom and understanding of her situation; she is aware that this has not arrived through luck alone. The small flowers are orange with green centres, showing her enjoyment of life, her practical earthly energy and her love of nature. They can also be viewed as the symbol for the planet Venus, which represents femininity and beauty. Her red hat informs us she is deeply moved by power and security and still motivated to succeed, which is echoed by the nine yellow circles surrounding it. She has not finished her journey; but her life is not about the pursuit of money, goods, or riches in any area at this moment in time, but about enjoying what she has. Here she is safe and in a place that is growing by itself, so she can step back for a while and enjoy some peace. She nearly has all she wants, but nine seeks completion: it wants to go one step further. This is a pit-stop, a time to relax and not think about much more than how lovely the day is.

Under her dress, she has a white top with a blue edge. Some see the motif under this blue edge as a bunch of grapes. In some depictions of the Nine of Pentacles, it's a red hexagram. Here, it looks to be another Egg of Life. Grapes, placed over her heart, would show an abundant, generous nature. When a hexagram is formed, it creates a fusion of male and female energy, bringing harmony and demonstrating someone who is at peace with herself, needing nothing but their own company. While the Egg of Life shows her potential for growth, it also represents the seven days of creation, and on the last day we rest. All these are correct. The blue trim is her faith in herself with an emotional and spiritual link, leaving her feeling connected to her surroundings on a deep level, with the white of the top adding to that simplicity. The dress flows onto the earth, connecting her to her situation and grounding any tension she may have. One yellow shoe sticks out and faces to the left of the card, so while she looks right, her body points left, as she has dreams still building within her mind, and so she will have plans to make and things to do. Right now, her mind is quiet and reflective, as she is at a stage where she can suit herself.

The hooded falcon represents her tamed mind, which she can control when she hunts for new ideas or creates new things to enjoy. Again, like the Queen of Wands, it shows her ability to direct herself rather than be led by a passion for growth, and like the Queen of Swords, as this is a bird, a creature of the air, it shows us her focus. Birds are symbolic of messages and transformation, so here she shows her patience, not just in conquering the bird but also in waiting for changes to arrive. The falcon can see things from hovering above, taking time to view ideas and circumstances, an element of air which shows she can rise above situations, ambitions and aspirations with her strong, independent will. The falcon sits on her left hand, the side of logic and thought, so she can allow it to take flight when she decides, rather than being directed by each idea or message which arises, as she has control over her life. The glove simply shows she knows when to be cautious, as impatience from the falcon would take her focus away from the garden, which may allow seeds of creation to grow in her mind at a time when she wishes not to be dealing with such things. The falcon also shows time to spend in the pursuit of self-fulfilment. Falcons do not train themselves to be tame, so she shows a time when we can indulge in hobbies and projects, as we have the financial resources, time, and skills to be able to do so.

The small snail in the bottom left of the card offers a slow and pleasurable time of being, as she is now able to travel through this stage of her life at her own pace and not at the speed or will of another. The snail is not a gardener's friend, yet she does not seem worried. She is in tune with nature and, with the mountains behind her, she knows she cannot control everything in life, so sees no reason to try. The snail is also fully contained. He has his house on his back, and can go at his speed, alone and self-sufficient, like the woman enjoying her own company, as everything she needs, she already has, enabling her to enjoy this moment in her life.

She stands on earth, which is pale green; like a lot of the cards, this is almost yellow, and in some deck editions, it is. This shows dead or dying grass, which is not in keeping with her abundant nature, so it may show that her efforts are in those things which bring her happiness. The colour of the grass could be linked to the pest element of the snail, as not everything can be given attention, so she focuses on those things she loves and what gives rewards, as a bit of grass not being full of life does not detract from her pentacle vine. It can also show that the vine itself has taken the water from the grass, leaving her happy to ignore those things that just get in the way, and which are unimportant.

The grapevines are full and heavy, showing abundance and productivity. Everything is ready for harvest, which will lead to celebrations and further enjoyment. In front of the grapes are her pentacle vines: the reward and gains from the harvest. Her right hand rests on the coins, with a grape also resting on her hand, representing her emotional attachment to her situation. She needs to be hands-on with her treasures, as she stands amongst her riches, alone, taking it all in. This results in a strong sense of individuality and contentment. It shows also that she may be enjoying a solitary phase of life, with pleasures and rewards enjoyed alone. She is often seen as someone single or enjoying alone-time away from a busy life, representing someone happy within themselves, needing no one else to complete them.

The pentacles are in two piles, one with six coins showing her liking of beauty, harmony and links to the Venus flowers, femininity, ambition and the ability to create. Like the Six of Pentacles, they can also show a benevolent personality, someone who gladly shares their wealth, ideas, love and support with others. On her other side, the three coins represent creation and further growth, as with the Three of Pentacles, her future plans which may be growing or yet to be started. Whilst she looks in their direction, her hand is on the six pentacles, as she rests and takes in all she has in her life. She is aware that enjoying what she has in life will not take away from any future wishes she has. So, she pauses, resting and enjoying the beauty about her.

This is a card which reminds us to enjoy our alone-time, the private spaces we can retreat to, our wealth in whatever way it presents within our lives, our spirituality, and our connection to what has brought us to that point, as during these times we can answer to no one. With the grounding of our issues, this earthly card opens our spiritual self, as, with a lack of stress, we can take time to tune into what we hold dear, on a spiritual or intellectual level. We can sit back and enjoy going at our own pace when this card arrives. We can take some time to look at all we have achieved and feel at peace and proud of ourselves.

Numerological Value - NINE = Inspiration, honesty and understanding.

IN A NUTSHELL

Expect good things to happen, as you will be going through a relaxed and contented phase. Inner peace and contentment will be enjoyed and push you forwards on a tide of positivity. You will find you have all you need to move forwards with issues, which brings confidence.

You will be able to look at what you have achieved, with a time to look around you, knowing you have done well. You have earned the right to take enjoyment from a situation or your life overall, and now you can relax for a while and enjoy what you have achieved.

Nine of Pentacles: Upright

The Nine of Pentacles represents *independence, self-sufficiency, self-satisfaction, and personal success.* You will be enjoying and appreciating what you have earned or achieved.

This card can place itself in any area of your life and shows someone who has found inner peace and has *self-confidence.* With the arrival of this card, *you will feel pleased with yourself.* It will be possible to take life at a pace of your choosing and you will not have to answer to another.

It indicates *a leisurely and pleasurable phase of life,* bringing happiness and feelings of *contentment.* You know that you can stand back and see what you have done, which gives the ego a boost, connecting us to our inner selves because of outer actions which give us feelings of balance.

Controlling your impulses is called for. If things are to last and stay calm, you need to know when to push for movement: and now is not the time, as *now is about enjoying what you have.*

Pampering, luxury, self-care, taking time to focus on your body, health and home are available: a time when you can go as fast or as slow as you desire. This can be a day off, or a bigger break such as a well-earned holiday, sabbatical or even retirement. It is a time when you can start to *focus on your own needs and suit yourself for a while.*

This card may also tell of *emotional independence and enjoying the single life,* or if in a relationship being independent of your partner and not relying on them totally. *Time alone can be taken, enjoyed, or given and is enjoyed fully.*

Due to the abundance of the card and everything very near to harvest, the feminine body aspect, and being an earth energy, plus a number nine, in readings, some have found this to show a full-term pregnancy with a healthy child.

Nine of Pentacles: Reversed

Reversed, the Nine of Pentacles will leave you *feeling disappointed with yourself*, and you may *feel that you have let others down* by your words or actions.

Financially, you can be left feeling inadequate by this card, as you judge yourself by others' gains, with feelings that you should have more by now. Boundaries can be pushed, spending too much, and doing things to put your longer-term security at risk.

Dependency is shown, leaving you needing to depend on others for some or all of your needs, when you really wish to be independent or free from someone or a situation that is dependent on you.

Disagreements will cause awkwardness and allow difficult situations to arise with others, due to your individuality or sense of independence. It is time to *seek balance* with your own needs if they conflict with the needs of others, by seeking a compromise. It is important to remain independent and not be railroaded by others if you are in a minority.

Any breaks, holidays or retirement plans wanted or given may not be possible, or not be as positive as wished for, due to a lack of funds or company.

The Nine of Pentacles reversed also shows *loneliness* and you seek to be with people and *feel isolated*. Due to *being overly independent,* you may be finding it hard to find or commit to personal relationships.

The pregnancy link here shows issues, and complications may arise requiring intervention in the later stages. If planning a baby, it shows a need to take care of yourself at the start of the journey or leave it a while; or if at the end, to take it easy.

TEN OF PENTACLES

The Ten of Pentacles shows a happy, contented generational family scene.

The pentacles form the Tree of Life, reflecting the possibilities of humanity to grow and reach its fullest potential; this symbolises family. The branches show how families grow and move on with their own lives, creating new branches from the main tree. It shows the growth of the family line through the generations, as well as everything being interconnected. It links also to the Kabbalah, which connects to many mystical systems. It has ten nodes, shown by the coins, linking to the number of numbered cards within each Minor Arcana. While not seen, there are twenty-two connecting lines between the nodes, the number of cards in the Major Arcana. This is the last numbered card in the deck, the accumulation of the journey through the cards, the sought-after destination. Chakras can also be represented here by the Kabbalah, showing the journey from the Base energy centre and our basic needs and drives to the Crown Chakra, the seat of our spiritual self. It symbolises a journey of personal and spiritual development, from physical needs to your own divine beliefs. A journey from our spiritual selves or our own inner minds, as we learn who we really are. A deep subject matter for those interested, yet here it shows the growth of family and the connection we have to each other now that events have reached completion.

The sky is blue, showing a calm scene, and the castle arch shows that we have arrived at a place of security and that as we go through this arch we may be starting or recognising a new stage of life for ourselves or for others. It is a welcoming sign, a doorway to life changes and a new phase beginning. Castles are symbolic of success and our own kingdoms, the place where we reign within our own lives. Inside is a courtyard surrounded by buildings showing wealth, safety, a place of retreat, comfort and the efforts of a lifetime, both ours and those who have come before us, which we have been able to build upon.

A lot of this card is taken from the elderly man's experiences, as he has built or added to the current stability of the castle; yet, of course, you can be any one of those present.

The coat of arms on the gateway indicates long-term security and the family roots we come from, our heritage. It pictures a castle surrounded by water, bringing emotional depths and safety, representing an emotionally secure situation, as the castle keeps everyone dry and safe from the pain of the outside world, and the water keeps invaders at bay. The three red markers show this was created with passion, driven by a desire to succeed. Being rectangular, they bring security, balance and, to some degree, conformity. The coat of arms can also show inheritance and the handing down of traditions, a reminder that we are all part of a bigger picture, as history is represented.

Above the old man's head are a set of scales, showing financial balance, yet being above his head, they show stability, justice and fairness, both emotionally and spiritually. This balance is also shown by the two red rectangles: his passions are now balanced and in order. His body is comfortable and so the scales show him to be content and balanced in all ways, as he can be honest with himself about how he has reached this place, with little regret.

Behind him is a plaque carved into the wall. It shows a tower on a mountain, and in front, water and flowers. This reminds him, and the others, of past troubles, old battles and the journeys of generations gone before to build what they all have, both their unified identity and possessions. This suggests that security should not be taken for granted, which is echoed by all of those in the card not making eye contact with the old man apart from the dogs. The past can easily be forgotten, and here it is asked to be remembered as it provides the foundation for their present happiness and security. In the original image shown here, you can see above two red shapes. One is a red heart, showing love, desire and sentiment when looking back on times gone by. In most decks both these red images are not shown. The second is a red and black fruit, which I cannot determine; yet could it call to the readiness of his life, the fruition of his dreams? The black and white checked border indicates he has resolved any past difficulties, leaving his past, again, balanced and in check.

Standing inside of the gateway are a man, woman and child representing the tree of life in action. They symbolise generations, family ties, community, tradition as well as the past, present and future, and the continuity of connections to those we are linked to. Each one of them will have their role to play, as each one will add their own pattern to the fabric of this family setup.

The old man sits patting and gently gazing at one of the dogs, which represent trust, faithfulness, respect and understanding, while he sits amongst the fruits of his labours. The other dog is touched by the small boy who is looking off to the right of the card, interested in something which has sparked his imagination. The boy takes us onto a new journey, back to The Fool, whereas the old man is the end of The Fool's travels through life. He takes no notice of what is taking place about him and the journey of others, as his own future adventures will be all he can dream about. A dream which will be off the back of the efforts of those around him, which will be his springboard to his possible success later in life. Together, the old man and boy show a continuing cycle: an end, and a new beginning. In some of the cards, you see the characters on a stage. Here, that stage is also shown, but at the top of the card, as opposed to the bottom being stood upon. It is upside down, showing that the future is not a stage walked on yet, as each will need to go through their own rites of passage. This is for the old man, The Fool, as he ends his journey. He has arrived at the last stage of his life, showing again the end and beginning of lives interwoven.

The old man, with his grey, well-groomed hair and beard, shows his wisdom, yet also care and respect from those about him. He sits on a seat with grapevines growing about it, showing an abundance of prosperity.

His cloak is highly decorated, and is one of the most complex items within the deck. It is embroidered or printed with magical sigils, astronomical symbols of the moon and a flower, showing the seasons, his creations, and his journey. The circles within circles show the moon or planets, yet also show life, a continuous cycle that connects to others, the movement of time and generations. The three-by-three grids show symmetry and balance; the crescent moons show the waxing and waning of events, and the stars are the means by which he has steered his own boat. In the large central image, the inner two of the four prongs are said to represent the Hebrew letter FEH/PEH whose numerological value is eighty, showing long life and wisdom. It is a letter which also shows the passing down of oral laws and history, the tales of one generation to the next. Below are what look like two towers, as found within The Moon, and by their sides, two crescent moons, waxing and waning. These tell of his struggles, his efforts in his own life, so not everything has come easily. This is his gift to the next generation, as all of what he sees in front of him is connected to the role he has played within the family tree. His cloak symbolises his security and confidence, as well as any monetary wealth, and his experience and knowledge. His cloak represents the tapestry of his life, which is his gift to the next generation to learn from.

The couple are relaxed as they stop to talk, showing peace and calmness. The man carries his own wand, held like the spear in the Six of Cups, protecting his family. His wand is black, as with The Fools, as this man is on his own journey. It has a green tip to show that he is practical, loving, and his actions are from his heart. This man's wand, and the old man's cloak, show a situation containing magic and that creation is still very present. Even in day-to-day ordinary life, magic is there for us to take hold of and utilise, and this card has it all. The man's blue cloak shows his loyalty and spiritual or psychological connection to his role within the situation. His brown tunic is his grounded and settled nature, as he is now in charge of making things happen. He is now the one in charge of any actions required to make his generation move and progress beyond what has gone before. He will be the next old man sitting, watching the world go by.

The woman is the nurturing force, the mother. The pink flowers in her hair show she can be romantic and frivolous, with a relaxing happy life. The flowers show a sentimental soul who loves her family, home and life in general. She wears a red dress, with other versions of the RWS picturing her in red and pink. Both sets of colours show her life experience, her drive for security, as well as her nurturing feminine side. Here she can care for her family, safe in the security of the castle walls.

The child is full of life in his yellow shoes. He goes where his mind flows, attracted to what shines. In some decks, again, he is dressed differently, with white shoes and orange tights: he is pure and untouched by the world outside, as he grows in safe surroundings. And with each step taken in innocence and excitement, as it should be. You can see a flash of red hair with this child, so a typical toddler, full of life and fresh new potential. The blue tunic shows he is prompted by his intuition and imagination, as he dreams of his future, or what he can enjoy next, although he is unlikely to have any knowledge of the Tree of Life. Like The Fool, he too will need to complete his journey to see the wisdom within it.

The old man is surrounded by the future, represented by the other people in the courtyard. More growth is possible from this secure situation, and there is potential for much more happiness to come. This card is not just about money: it shows happiness, contentment, safety and security with material well-being, physical comforts and progress which can be made concrete. We can secure our world for future generations or for our own potential journey. We are shown here the estate we have built and within which we can find security.

Numerological Value – **TEN** = Purpose, uniting and bringing together of energies to create a new whole.

IN A NUTSHELL

Everything comes together in the end if you stay focused on hard work. Expect everything to be going well, life is on an up.

Security is not just talked about, as it is felt. You feel part of a family, be that blood ties or otherwise, and you will feel that you belong. The long term is looked at, with the understanding that if things are cared for, they will last and grow even more. You will feel blessed, with a time to share your energy with others.

Ten of Pentacles: Upright

The Ten of Pentacles brings *material and financial well-being*. *Your home, household and financial security will be settled,* with money available. Any *financial success* will be long-term if cared for, and able to be enjoyed with whom you share your life.

This card reveals the completions of creative as well as financial projects, as *goals are reached*, greeted with success and *profit*. Commitment will have paid off, leaving you able to provide what is needed for loved ones or continued success.

It brings a time when *you feel lucky and blessed*. Even though you may have worked hard, you know it is the interaction of others which makes it all worthwhile.

Family and relationship foundations are strong and give *lasting energy* to what is asked about. *Deep roots will be formed, as the future has a solid structure to grow from*. You will have a sense of knowing that you can pass the baton down to the next generation if you stay on top of what you have, with *family traditions* also being represented.

Money, inheritances, gifts or even ideas being passed down through the generations can be relevant, and, due to your own family, you will be well cared for. Your family at large is shown, including extended family and those who have flown the nest and not just your immediate household as with the Ten of Cups. This leaves a time when *family duty* and solidarity are called into action.

In growing relationships, this card brings commitment and the linking together of families, joint accounts, weddings, engagements, with marriage being organised or even getting a pet to share. This could be anything that bonds situations in a satisfying, legal or practical way.

The Ten of Pentacles also tells of positive investments such as ***buying or selling property,*** or for that matter the buying, selling or ***investment*** of anything important which can bring large sums of money or security.

Ten of Pentacles: Reversed

Reversed, the Ten of Pentacles brings **upheavals on the home front,** especially on a financial and emotional level. It brings **a lack of personal security** with home or family, often leaving the foundations crumbling.

You may wish to break free from family constraints and traditions. You may not believe what others in your family do and wish to seek an independent path. You wish to follow your own dreams rather than those set out for you by others. ***Generational differences can cause problems,*** leaving a lack of communication and understanding within families.

Financial and other responsibilities are burdens, making you feel trapped and unhappy within your domestic arrangements. You may ***feel bored and hemmed in. You may be being misunderstood,*** which can lead to mistakes being made, jeopardising long-term security.

Family, money and respect may be taken for granted, leading to losses as attention is not given to details nor to the history of relationships, finances, community, or home life. Decisions made with no consideration for others or the bigger picture will lead you to be or feel a social outcast and unwanted by those around you.

With the buying and selling of property and businesses, there will be severe problems and difficulties, showing ***an investment to avoid or one which will go bad.*** Property and belongings may be lost, stolen, or even ***repossessed.*** Reversed, this card shows ***a loss of status,*** as it brings **bad luck** to our material security.

Branches can be torn from the family tree with divorces and separations. Feelings of rejection, abandonment and family dishonour will shake a family to its core, leaving ***disagreements with settlements and arrangements***. The passing of a loved one can cause upset due to wills and the division of property. This can create discord as ***promised or expected money, goods or gifts fail to be given or are argued about.***

Legal situations can drag on with this card, showing ***an unhappy outcome***.

— The Pentacle Family —

The Pentacle family are concerned with money, how to earn it and how to secure the future with it.

They are practical and generous by nature as well as hard-working, definitely big-hearted and enjoy being close to nature and animals. Being represented by the earth, they enjoy physical as well as material pleasures. They find it easy to earn money.

They are often found working with their hands, making money through hard and often creative work.

Astrologically, Pentacles are earth signs: Virgo, Capricorn and Taurus.

PAGE OF PENTACLES

The Page of Pentacles gives us a young boy standing in a meadow, holding and gazing at a pentacle.

Astrological Sign: Any Earth sign: Virgo, Capricorn and Taurus.

The young boy is dressed in very earthy colours, as like all the pentacle family, he is close to nature and is a down-to-earth, practical soul. His green tunic shows his connection to his environment and to patience and harmony. His clothing shows him to be a quiet individual, shown by his light brown tights, belt and sleeves. In some editions of the deck, they are orange, showing his energy and enthusiasm. Apart from his hat, his brown clothes show a calmness to this Page. Like the green of his tunic, it is a very practical colour, which links him to practicalities and a steady outlook. He will see the beauty in everything about him. His nature will be nurturing, and this Page can have a very healing energy about him. In other versions of the Rider Waite Smith deck, we can see the small white cuff of an undershirt on his right sleeve, which shows his sincere and creative thoughts about the work he wishes to do, making him an ideal student or apprentice.

His red hat and scarf show us that his mind is passionate and full of drive. Like the Page of Cups, his scarf drapes about his shoulder, not covering his throat area, so he may not be able to speak with authority on the ideas he has at this stage of his journey. His green tunic will enable him to talk with affection about his goals, as he will want to do things in a way that helps benefit everyone.

The red hat topping off his earthy-coloured clothes show he is a mix of action and inaction, displaying slow, steady energy, which also flows throughout the Pentacle family. He will think with big ideas, determination and enthusiasm, and will see the promise of those things he could create, build and grow with his coin.

His brown boots show him to be grounded, which is echoed by his meadow. He is peaceful and sensible, enjoying his learning experience with a responsible nature. He needs to feel close to the earth and the physical world, which all the Pentacle family hold dear.

His left foot points to the right of the card, with the right foot on tiptoe facing the left side of the card. This leaves him more focused on the creative side of his abilities, yet his logical side is at least touched with the toes. At this stage, he is not committed on how to do something. Rather, he is very focused on ideals, finding out how things work and the magic surrounding his dreams, as he is more interested in building within his mind.

Facing the right of the card shows the feminine elements of the suit of Pentacles. Pentacles have a need to care, germinate, cultivate and learn, with a desire and dream, nurture and grow something tangible. With the Page, this will be a dream for one day in the future, with no real goal at present.

His head is surrounded by the yellow sky, representing his confidence and enthusiasm for his subject; it is also a colour of fiery caution, which all Pentacles have. It can show the dawn or dusk, so he may have been here all day long, building castles in his head, or starting the day with a new dream of a magical creation building within his mind.

His coin is held lightly in his hands, resting on his fingertips. He does not grip the coin tightly as the other Pages hold their element, but instead, he gently balances it in his hands, as if he understands how precious it is. He studies the coin, questioning how it makes him feel and what it will be like when it grows and develops into something tangible. The Page of Pentacles is enthusiastic in his endeavours, and his desire lies in his ability to actively absorb knowledge, as learning is a fascinating part of the journey for him.

Behind him is a copse, a group of trees that are cut back yearly in a manner that allows for regrowth, benefiting future generations. It is a wonderful place for an earthly soul to play, dream and build. It represents a sign of the care pentacles can give to their environment, so that the future is provided for. Placed behind him, it shows some of the history of his past generations, the care that has gone into where he is today. Yet, he does not look at it, nor does he look at the ploughed field ready for planting, which also shows dedication from others to care about and provide for future security. Instead, his pentacle is all that he can see. He is imagining what he can grow from it and then what he can make from it. He is studying it in detail rather than engaging in the act of doing.

The ploughed field will still be there waiting once he has learnt from his studies. He can then apply what he has learnt; but now, he is not ready to plant, as he still needs to gather information. Being a Page, he may get lost in his head a little bit with the journey. Yet, being a Pentacle, he may also get lost in his heart as well.

The mountain in the distance is far away but looms over the ploughed field. However, he is not looking at what could go wrong, but more at the marvel of the coin he can make something from.

This young person is an avid student, apprentice, novice and trainee; his card can be called The Student Card. He is someone focused on understanding and grasping often practical knowledge, with the potential to gain personal and financial security one day.

IN A NUTSHELL

A time to learn something new. There will be enthusiasm, even passion, about something new in your life. It is an exciting time to absorb and take something new on board. A fact-finding mission will be beneficial if you are open to all the details and information that you find.

Try not to get distracted. Avoid extra commitments while your time is being taken up with those things which must be studied in your life in order for things to grow more efficiently.

Page of Pentacles: Upright

Personality - The Page of Pentacles is *reflective*, gentle, *hardworking and patient.* He is in the process of studying something new and absorbing, or someone who actively enjoys *learning new skills* and gaining new knowledge. This can be an individual enjoying a period of learning, representing *students of all ages and any subject.* Yet it is *a reminder not to get lost in perpetual study*, and to know when it is time to pick up, as well as put down, the books.

Dreams are examined, *studied* and considered, as *here is an enquiring mind*, which seeks to know all there is on a subject. Yet, as a Page, they may gather information which they do not or cannot use just yet.

The card can also show a time when you need to *'go back to the drawing board'.* This will allow you to see what is possible, and to focus on what direction you wish to take your creative abilities, career or work. It asks us to be realistic, as new projects are mentally and creatively created with no firm framework, so there is a need to stay focused.

He can bring a need to prepare, even at the early stages, for a situation in the future, *so if you are wanting to start something new, start reading up as much as you can on the subject now rather than later.* This Page likes to look at the mechanics of an issue and has a down-to-earth approach. He is thorough and sensible, which is called for when creating future plans.

This Page cares about environmental concerns and how others are affected by the bigger issues in life and society. These are the people who want to get out there and help others, not solely with money or sympathy, but with *practical assistance. They are often helpful, sincere individuals.*

This Page can remind us that we should make sure we can commit to anything new being considered. This is just a gentle nudge towards being realistic and making sure we are not lost in dreaming about what can be.

Message/event - With the coin in his hand, he can bring **extra income** your way. This could be a part-time job, overtime or anything which gives *a boost to your income*.

There will be a positive improvement to your current work or financial situation, as you find *financial information coming your way*.

Page of Pentacles: Reversed

Personality - The Page of Pentacles reversed shows *an individual having difficulties with study and learning or getting to grips with new financial or work ideas*.

He could represent *a child having difficulties at school*. This may be due to lessons they do not understand, or they may not bond with a teacher, are being bullied or simply dislike school for whatever reason. It can also show an unsuitable or unwanted teaching environment.

Yet it can also be an adult who is finding it difficult dealing with new ways of working, learning a new skill or even disliking a training course. There is *a lack of confidence*, a refusal to learn or a lack of ability, leaving them feeling *frustrated* and *unable to achieve* what is expected of them.

This card can show *laziness* when it comes to taking the time to learn what is needed. This stems from *a lack of interest* in what needs to be understood, and even *boredom*.

With new plans which you wish to be put into action, this Page shows you may *not have studied as much as you need* to make things work. You may be *being impatient, with a lack of commitment* to doing things right.

It can also represent *not having the funds to get things started*. An idea may need to be abandoned and left to one side, due to *not being able to get the financial help or knowledge needed*. This can leave you to abandon a dream due to a lack of basic resources, which can lead to feeling unfulfilled, upset and unhappy.

Reversed, the Page of Pentacles tells us to not turn away from what we don't understand, as we may miss learning something of value that could redirect our life or be of use later. *Take a break and come back afresh*.

Message/event - Financially, there will be a short time of *not being able to make ends meet*. If you are a student, you may not get the grades, course or school you wish. Finances and new work situations will not give you positive rewards or outcomes, bringing *a lack of progress*.

KNIGHT OF PENTACLES

The Knight of Pentacles is seated on his horse, gazing at the ploughed or sowed field just beyond his pentacle.

Astrological Sign: Virgo.

Of all the Knights, the Knight of Pentacles is the only one with a coloured sky and a static horse. The sky shows the intellectual nature of the Knight, his active mind and confidence. The sun, which is pictured in some versions of the deck, is rising or setting, showing him starting early and utilising the whole of the day to its best advantage, as he is here to work and make the best of the time given. Alternatively, he could be looking back at his hard day's work.

His large black horse is sturdy and solid, and unlike the other Knights' horses, this is a workhorse, not for show, adventuring or war. He is black as he is part of the Knight's toolbox, his blackness absorbing all colours, showing the Knight's potential. The horse is an organic machine, used to plough and work alongside the Knight, an extension of his skills and labour. The work is hard, slow and at times even boring, but energy is needed, and the horse shows his capable, strong nature. This shows that both have physical stamina and can see a job through to the end. The horse's saddle has support at the back and a blanket underneath. The support is for the comfort of the Knight, as Pentacles do like to make routine pleasurable where they can, and luxury, even if a touch, is important. In the original image here, it is black and yellow; in others it is red and black. Here, it has an almost green tinge to the yellow, showing us his comfort is found in his learned skills and in his potential, as he is supported by his mind in his ventures. Under the saddle is a blanket, which is for the horse, as this Knight values his horse's needs and comfort as much as his own. Here it is pale brown, a sincere, warm, soft colour, yet practical. In some decks, it is pictured red to match the horse's harness. This will not just be a horse from the stable, but his personal horse: a pet, a companion, and part of his daily life. He will wish to treat it with tender care like family. The horse is a sign of this Knight being a 'homebody'. Most of the Pentacles are the same, choosing to stay close to home or work solely for the benefit of home, family or community. That red harness and gear show his drive and passion, even if no rush is shown. Along the harness are eight red pentagrams, as opposed to pentacles, bringing magic to this card, a sign of creation and life made possible by a harnessed mind. It can also show the apprentice in the Eight of Pentacles, someone working hard to make things perfect. Its gear includes loin straps over the back, so this horse will be used to pull a cart or a plough. They are decorative, rather than in use, so, again, this is a Knight who is reviewing hard work done or pending, rather than doing.

On the horse's head is an acorn, symbolic of slow, steady growth, as great oaks grow from little acorns with proper care. It shows this Knight is about dedication, the long term, and the commitment to each action he takes to get there.

The stillness of the horse shows that he is not getting ready to move, restless or charging into action, as he is waiting to be directed, and that will not happen until the time is right. Timing is of value to this Knight. Nothing is rushed, as everything needs to be done at the right time, even if that means waiting. Here he waits for the correct planting times for his coin, or for the coins planted to start to grow.

The Knight is in full armour, but like the other Knights, he is not battling for love, ideas or intellect. He instead fights for a secure future, slowly taking a step at a time, as he plants his field, taking time and care while it grows. His simple tunic is an earthy, brownish red, with a red belt (orange in some RWS decks). The tunic symbolises his link to the earth, to the practical, to being hands-on and dedicated. His red belt represents the joining of his creative mind and grounding energy, giving a passion in all he does, which is also shown by the oak leaves decorating his helmet. These show him driven by a need for growth, strong roots, and propagation, with a methodical and cautious mind. Under his red tunic we see a green top, so what is kept closest to him is the generous, happy, progressive nature of this suit. His boots have spurs, symbolic of motivation and guiding. He would not use these to force the horse, but to gently nudge him to where he was needed for the best outcome. Yet the reins could also be used for that, so maybe, with the horse being an extension of himself, the spurs could be there to keep him on track if he loses focus, or, as Pentacles can be a bit slow in their approach, to speed things up. Both his hands are gloved, showing us that this Knight takes things with both hands, as he needs to handle, carefully examine and get to grips with his element as he has a manual, physical energy to him, and he plays it safe. The gloves are an earthy red-brown, so he reaches out to all his goals with a down-to-earth, sincere and purposeful nature. One gloved hand holds his Pentacle, the other the reins of the horse, both firmly controlling his situation with gentle force.

He faces the right of the card, the creative, imaginative side, showing that he has strong feelings towards his pathway and choices, with a considered and serious outlook on life.

His ploughed field is ready to be planted, or maybe it already has been, and he is checking to see if it went well or needs any attention. He stares with a stern look, taking things seriously, as a lot of effort, time and energy have gone into getting this far, along with a lot of repetitive actions and time-consuming work. He looks to see how far he can progress from his current viewpoint.

The two trees in the card show the duality of thoughts and feelings. They are placed together and towards the back of the field, so he has learned what he needs and has sorted through what knowledge is needed. This leaves him focused and skilled enough to have a balanced view of his situation. The mountains are also far in the distance, and if there are any problems present, they will have been anticipated. All angles have been studied by this Knight, who will have a backup plan already in place should those mountains cause an issue.

The Knight of Pentacles is a quiet, contemplative, naturally talented and often academic individual. He is serious in his tasks, so will not rush any plans. He employs quiet reflection and intense thought to achieve his aims. He is a Knight who wishes to master his skills.

This Knight thinks deeply about events and is thorough. He will not make any decision until he is satisfied that both he and the matter at hand are compatible. He is extremely cautious and will not move away from his current position until he has guaranteed that all is well with his choice. This Knight is a perfectionist. His progress is slow and steady but committed and assured.

IN A NUTSHELL

Now is the time for hard work, a time to be organised and methodical. Be independent of the views of others and go for what you know you can achieve. Timing is important, and you find yourself in the right place at the right time.

Be determined to finish what you have started. Be cautious: things may go slow, but you will succeed as slow and steady wins the race. Have high expectations for a happy outcome, even if it takes time.

Knight of Pentacles: Upright

Personality - The Knight of Pentacles is **an extremely patient and reliable person**, with **high expectations** of himself, who aims for **perfection** in all he does. He will look at all angles of a problem or area of work before acting. If you want a job done, he will do it well or not at all, as he would not shame himself with shoddy work. He is **confident and independent of other people's views**.

This Knight is always **organised and methodical** in his approach to life and is not afraid of **hard work**. He will stick to tradition, follow the right way of doing things and be quite conservative. **He is realistic with money,** and he often represents **steady employment** or the gaining of work.

The timing of events is important, and this card places us in **the right place at the right time**. He is **well prepared** and has **stamina,** so is well designed for the long haul, leaving **success assured in long-term goals**.

He is a **committed** soul in all that he does in life, love and work and tends to be **a quiet and calm person**. His approach to life may be viewed as **conventional** and may tend to be a bit unimaginative and **predictable**. However, he plays by the rules and is **trustworthy and honest**.

This Knight is someone who **enjoys the simple things in life** and will often be found at home or with old friends and family, enjoying simple pleasures. He is **cautious,** and likes to stick to what he knows, as he likes to work hard, but loves to be relaxed, comfortable and at ease with little fuss.

He can show boring, predictable energy, a time when we need to deal with routine, home, family and our *responsibilities,* as he is always ready to care and give his time.

This Knight tells us that we need to approach things with *proper planning and caution* when making decisions or within any other situation. He shows being in *an excellent position for long-term success*, and to just take our time.

Event - This is a positive card to have when you have money or work worries, as it points to *a regular income. A time to be busy, focused and committing to projects*, *rolling up your sleeves* to make some determined changes to your life with commitment and dedication.

Knight of Pentacles: Reversed

Personality - When the Knight of Pentacles has been laid reversed, we see someone who is *insecure and overly cautious*. He may well be *unemployed, in debt* or genuinely *concerned about how much things cost* due to financial issues, or how his skills will be seen by others. *Money or work will cause difficulties* for this person, and they will be *down on their luck*.

Timing will be off leaving projects unfinished, or *opportunities missed*. Steps may be missed, ignored, or even forgotten, leaving situations open to failure.

Due to *bad luck,* this Knight is *pessimistic and expecting the worst*. He will feel *depressed* and may react by being *lazy*, unco-operative and incredibly *hard to motivate*, as the slow and steady energy comes to a halt. This Knight can stagnate within issues, or life in general as their moods tend to infect all areas of their lives in an organic fashion.

His attitude may strike you as *irritating* and *self-pitying*, as he has become trapped in *a situation which feels impossible to change*. He will not respond kindly to criticism but will often be found to be critical of others rather than looking at his own problems.

Like all the Pentacle family, he can become *possessive* towards those things he feels he needs, loves, or is fixated on which bring him pleasure and feelings of security. To approach such matters will make him *defensive and angry*.

This Knight can warn us to *try to avoid negative thinking* and to stop being so serious about events, relax and listen to the views of others.

Event - The Knight of Pentacles reversed would show that you will suffer *a financial or personal crisis*. Financially, there will be *no improvement* in situations and may even show *unemployment*. It will be a time when you will be left with no sense of direction and stuck in your tracks.

QUEEN OF PENTACLES

The Queen of Pentacles sits on her throne within her garden and, with both hands, holds her pentacle gently.

Astrological Sign: Capricorn.

The Queen's red dress and shoes show her powerful, creative drive. She is a confident soul who has a passion for growth and security. The red connects to her practical side, her love of life, and her connection to her physical body and her environment. She has a green head-covering under her crown, showing her to think in practical, healing and nurturing terms. She will see the world through the eyes of simplicity, love, creation and compassion. Both this and her dress drape onto the ground, connecting her to the earth, as she is both mentally and physically connected to her element and again, to her environment.

Her long-sleeved white under-dress shows integrity and wholesomeness. She has no brooch like the other Queens, but a plain white neckline. The Queen of Coins could have furs and trinkets galore, but chooses a simple white neckline, as she is comfortable without displays of wealth or status. For this Queen, wealth and status come from her environment rather than from a flashy display of goods. The white also shows us her honest, sincere nature. The bar across her dress pulls her V-neck in and, with her high neckline, shows modesty. It also forms an upside-down triangle with the bar in her dress, a line through it if taken from her shoulders, which is a symbol for earth, her element, worn close to her heart. Her red shoes can be seen from under her dress, showing her passion for life. In some images of this card, the shoes are orange, showing her creative side. Each step she takes will be to make something new or to nurture something already created.

Her golden crown is different here than in younger versions of the deck. Here she has a bird at the top of her crown, which may be a dove, especially with the five purification alchemy symbols also on her crown, as both represent purity. On a golden crown, they bring purity to life with intent and love. The dove brings peace, hope, and devotion. Its wings are red, showing a desire for peace within physical life. The purity symbols show purity in action, in progress. There are five, a number of communication and curiosity, so this is a mind that talks in terms of how to make the best of who you are with a commitment to being the best you can be in the real world. Other versions of this card show a pair of red bull horns, which connects her to Taurus, which some authors and deck creators title her as, as well as Virgo. On top of her crown, horns could show a stubborn streak with this lady, who is determined.

She holds her pentacle gently in her arms as if she were cradling a baby, looking lost in thought, leading her to be reflecting on her past, present and future as well as on the value of the coin. The pentacle may be an object she has yet to create, holding it like an idea she has yet to give birth to, or conceive. Yet it may also be something she is already loving and nurturing, as she is a creator and mother, rearing her family, and possibly planning to build more within her life, based on what has gone before.

Her throne is highly decorated with pears, a symbol of affection and inner peace. They are sweet and ripe, showing generous energy and abundant optimism. At the top of the throne, a cherub watches over her from the clouds, protecting and guarding her. On the side of her throne is a fairy, known as an earth elemental, a being that is attracted to nature. They protect the earth and create a bridge from the physical to the spiritual, adding to this Queen's healing aspects. The goat on the arm of her throne is linked to her sign of Capricorn and The Devil. Next to it is a pear, which looks like a penis. If it is meant to look that way, I cannot say, yet we cannot deny her physically creative energy. She embodies sexual energy, which is also echoed by her legs being slightly apart, but unlike The Devil, this is more of an earthy sensuality, without entrapment or negativity, and she also differs from the Queen of Wands in that she does not face the front of the card, symbolising action and movement, but instead, confidence, which does not need to be flaunted. The goat represents stubborn energy, just like the bull horns on her crown in some decks mentioned above. It represents fertility, physical energy, creation, and the enjoyment of physical pleasure, as well as her protective nature toward those she loves. Her body leans away from the goat as she places her energy to the right of her throne, focusing more on nurture and love. Yet when it is time to create and build, that lively energy is there to work with. Leaning away, she may also be aware of her negative qualities, yet she knows she can be materialistic and possessive when things go wrong. The goat, to her left, shows the logical element of creation, indicating she can act with force, energy, and stubborn passion, yet she leans to the left of the card, allowing logic to mix with her loving creativity. Right now, she is simply relaxed and enjoying life and its abundance, as well as everyone and everything within it.

The rabbit in the bottom right of the card is another symbol of fertility. This Queen is the Queen of the Earth, warm and welcoming, generous and loving and shows the physical side of The Empress. It shows her connection to nature, as, like the snail in the Nine of Pentacles, the rabbit could cause damage to her garden. Yet she is wise enough not to worry, as things do not need to be perfect to be abundant. With a love of nature present within this Queen, the rabbit is a sign that there is balance, as animals tend to go where their comforts and needs can be met.

She is surrounded by earth, grass and flowers which represent an established life and continued growth. The grass about her is worn, showing a familiarity with her place in the world. She is not worried about a few brown patches of grass, as she is at ease.

About the top of her card is a red rose bush that mirrors this stability and shows love, passion and sentiment. It is also arched about her card like The Magician's, an expression of her creative physical self. As an arch, it also represents a phase of life, here the mother.

The small flowers dotted about her are orange in the original image shown, yet pink in other versions. When orange, they show vitality, energy, enthusiasm, fun and when pink, they bring romance, affection and happiness and an atmosphere that is carefree, relaxed and productive. All of which encompass this Queen, as we are introduced to an individual who represents productivity, gentleness and fruitfulness.

The calm water to her side is a bay with what I presume is a small central lush green island. It does not have the harshness of the two streams behind the Queen of Swords and so does not symbolise the same upsetting emotional separation. They flow around the small island, representing comfortable, balanced emotions, flowing, and helping her to create with an independent mind. The bay shows her collected emotions, a sign of shelter and quiet. The mountains are her distant backdrop and, as she is a practical realist, she will know they are there and what they mean, even if she does not face them.

This Queen's life is plentiful, and not just financially. She has a warm philosophy that attracts the good things in life and relationships. She has an abundance of personality and generosity, which makes her a comfort to be around.

As a member of the Pentacle family, she likes material pleasures and values comfort within her home life, but the Queen of Pentacles needs also to be surrounded by simplicity to feel contentment. She finds that riches are also to be found in love and family commitments. This Queen is not pretentious and rarely has any hidden sides. What you see is what you get.

IN A NUTSHELL

This Queen brings nurturing, love and support. She is a down-to-earth person with a firm sense of family tradition and values. She approaches situations honestly and with simple grace. Nothing is complicated, as everything is seen with a practical mindset. She shines a light on difficult issues and changes fortunes by bringing luck along with her.

She gets things done quickly, and with no fuss, as she is not elaborate but down to earth. She has a knack for turning even the worst situation into the best she can. She enjoys her surroundings and brings a smile to most situations.

Queen of Pentacles: Upright

Personality - The Queen of Pentacles' main qualities are her ***honest, loyal and big-hearted nature.*** Unlike the other Pentacles, she may not be that orderly, and not all that fussed by frills and bows regardless of any riches that she may have. With that in mind, her riches may not be financial but based on the love that she has with her ***family***. She is ***down-to-earth and generous*** with affection in a ***maternal*** way and ***likes to make sure that everyone else is happy,*** content and has what they need.

Security is important for this person, but she does not worship money, nor is she governed by it. This card often shows ***someone who is concerned for their family and security*** due to their sense of commitment being so strong.

She can be seeking a way to further secure her life, to create more for herself and her loved ones. She is ***a hard worker and*** may be able to offer help of either a financial or practical nature. This shows someone being ***sensible with money***.

The Queen of Pentacles ***likes to care for people*** and extends this even to strangers, as she is ***charitable*** and generous to those she feels may benefit from what she can give. Yet she is not gullible and dislikes those who seek to take advantage of her generosity.

She may be the Queen of Money and may enjoy nice things, but she is no snob and would buy an expensive object due to its ***practical nature*** and quality rather than its social relevance or status.

Due to her attachment to the earth element, she can be used in questions regarding ***fertility***. She is an ideal significator or representative of questions regarding such matters. She can be the mother, as well as pregnancy, or the time being right for such new beginnings, as well as the start and birth of any new creative and financial ideas.

This Queen reminds us to ***be honest and generous***, and to give help where it is needed in whatever way that is possible. ***If more security is wished for, look to the tools you have at your disposal,*** as you have all the potential you need within you to make, create and flourish.

Queen of Pentacles: Reversed

Personality - The reversed Queen of Pentacles is often *emotionally insecure*, and left *feeling lost financially* with a lack of financial status, leading to *emotional panic* and anxiety. She has lost touch with her practical energy and is *caught up in negative thought patterns* and chained to unhealthy ways of acting and thinking.

Reversed, she can be *materialistic,* which can show snobbery or greed, yet often it points to *poverty and a lack of material or emotional security.* This can be current or stemming from past experiences, making her hold onto money and status, and even hoarding items, just in case things go wrong for her again. She will be *going through a rough patch and* could be misunderstood by those around her.

She represents an individual who is suffering at the hands of bad luck, usually financial, yet can also be linked to a lack of emotional security. This could show *an individual who is concerned for their family's financial well-being*, with *a constant fear over money and making ends meet*.

This Queen will feel stressed, which may lead to *sadness and apathy*. She will need reassurance but then be critical of the advice or help offered. This Queen can demand perfection while being unrealistic, and *she can be blunt, prejudiced, aggressive and angry*.

She could willingly give her control over to those whom she feels are wiser or stronger if she thinks it will bring a solution to her issues. Sometimes this is needed, yet at other times, it is due to *a failure to take personal responsibility*.

She has lost touch with the magic of seeing the beauty in the small things in life. This can lead to *unhealthy coping mechanisms*, such as an overindulgence of food, and may have weight or body consciousness issues. Her attention to health or physical well-being will either swing between denial, with strict control of food, spending, drinking, comforts, or sex to complete overindulgence. Her nature can be untidy and even slovenly as *depression* can take hold, since she no longer sees her environment, which can also be a sign of someone *too busy* to be preoccupied with the mundane things in life.

With questions *regarding fertility or new investments for growth, her reply is negative*. The potential is there, but this Queen has lost touch with her creativity and needs to get her feet back on the ground with some realism. Her mind, body and even environment will not be in the right place, and money, or security - emotional or otherwise - may not be available.

This reversed Queen reminds us that we all go through difficult times when nothing seems to go our way and that we must *be patient, as problems will pass*. Also, to try to stay in control of our lives, and accept help from others; but *be careful whom we hand our power over to, as it can be hard to get back*.

KING OF PENTACLES

The King of Pentacles sits relaxed upon his throne, with a sceptre as a symbol of authority and power in one hand, and his pentacle is held like an orb in the other.

Astrological Sign: Taurus.

His throne is black and, like The Emperor's throne with four rams, his is decorated with four bulls, two at the top and two on the arms. In this version they are stone; in others, they can be two golden bulls at the top and two silver ones below. The bulls represent Taurus and with one on each corner, he is surrounded by practical, secure, solid earth energy. These four bulls offer stability and security, dependability and responsibility, yet also show his stubborn, cautious, unbending, committed streak. About his head, in stone or golden, they tell us about his mental approach to material wealth, or even to life in general. He does not dream: he acts and creates. He plans his way to success, organising each step and doing what needs to be done, as he is thorough and steadfast. Everything demands a firm, concrete plan of action before it is even considered. While bulls charge, they also stop to build up steam, so he is always fully evaluating his goals. The pair at the side of his throne near his feet, again stone or silver, represent his inner self, and how he approaches subjects. The golden bulls allow him to see his goal and charge at it; the silver pair make him view things intuitively, or in stone, cautiously. This balance has helped him achieve success, wealth and security. The black solid nature of his throne shows him aware of his potential and gives him security which he has absolute confidence in. Like King Midas, he knows he can make money; he is not afraid of hard work and so can rest knowing that income is always achievable. He sits, enjoying what he has already earned in life, relaxed and putting just one of his feet up. He is not ready to stop, as those bulls will still be driving him onwards.

He wears an elaborate black gown decorated with grapes and vine leaves, with the blue vines representing abundance, the fruits of his labour and his productive nature. By wearing the grapes, he shows he is the harvest, he is the work, and he is the provider. The decorative trim is a plain cream colour, orange in other versions. Cream represents a competitive aspect, and if in orange, his energetic streak. Either way, around his shoulders and over his heart he has a vibrant, striving energy and personality. He is all about security, so work or responsibility comes first. His red cowl and red hat under his crown show that he speaks and thinks with success in mind. He is passionate about his achievements and what he has built from scratch with his bare hands, patient planning and wise investments. His gown is opulent, flowing and generous, which suits this King's liking for comfort, enjoyment and satisfaction from his possessions, life and surroundings. The cowl can also serve to stop the flow of power from the crown stopping him from being egotistical about his gains, self-indulgent or stuck in the enjoyment of physical pursuits.

His golden crown has a victory wreath around it, showing his success is felt mentally. He brings this success to all he touches and is seen by others as a wealthy, prosperous soul, be it for his money or his family life. The three red flowers on the crown show that his desire to create is still present and grounded, and added to by the five golden dots about each. These represent the five points of a pentagram, showing his magically creative mind building on a physical level. The crown has either two *fleurs-de-lis* or two lilies. *Fleurs-de-lis* symbolise royalty, power, faith and honour, and lilies would show devotion. Being gold, these attributes would be relevant to the physical, practical side of life, showing someone in control of what they can create.

Under his gown, he wears a suit of armour as his left foot is shown, a sign he is mentally ready for movement and his next investment, build or goal. His foot sits on an ornamental hog, a symbol of greed, and by resting his foot upon it, he shows control over that element of earthly energies. As with money and possessions, it is all too easy to get wrapped up in greed and physical desires.

He holds a sceptre symbolising his authority and power in his right hand, so he has a deep sense of feeling for those things he creates. His left hand rests on his pentacle instead of an orb. An orb represents worldly power and God and symbolises the earth. As King of Earth, this power is within himself, and his pentacle is proof of his worldly power as he gazes at it, relaxed and content. His hard work has paid off and it has created his world. He wishes others to see that as he presents his achievements outwardly to others.

Behind his throne is a thick stone wall and below an ocean. Perhaps he is the same man who started his journey off in the Two of Wands, now mature and not needing to travel to find his happiness, security and wealth? Yet he definitely represents the end of the Ace of Wands' journey from idea to fruition. Behind him, with such a strong, solid castle wall, he will not be overly interested in deep emotions of the ocean unless they are linked to his own passions, possessions or loved ones.

The King's garden is unkempt, full of weeds more than flowers, showing a more relaxed approach to life. He loves nature, and the four small pink flowers with the hint of a fifth, which show his sentimental nature, are still there. For all his status, deep down he can be quite soft, yet as there are five, he may argue with that nature at times. Behind him is a vine with no grapes and what looks like dead wood. He has not taken the time to remove or tidy it. This may be due to being busy, enjoying too many pleasures or being lazy, yet it could also be that his cautious side may be willing to see if something can still grow and produce grapes and so leaves it there.

The background shows us his castle buildings. These represent his security and the wealth that has been amassed over time. In most versions of this card, there are two red roofs and one blue. Here, in the original, there is one red, one blue, and one purple. The red roof shows his mind, again full of drive and desire for power, wealth, security, and growth. The purple represents his wisdom and subconscious connection to his creative self. The blue shows his trust in his life, love, and himself. This roof has a flag, which is more visible on newer decks and is often blue. He flies his flag of sincerity, honesty, perseverance, and freedom, as he sits free from insecurity or financial worries. The flag is there to let people know that the King is at home, as this is where the King's focus lies, in his home life, family, surroundings, and environment.

He is proud of his money and rewards, and openly displays his wealth for all to see, yet he does not brag. As the King of Pentacles is King of the Earth, he is aware that for growth to be beneficial, nurturing is necessary for returns. He is extremely practical in his approach to all subjects, not just money or security. This King loves physical pleasure; he is relaxed about life and takes events at his own pace, and what he touches can often turn to gold.

IN A NUTSHELL

Be cautious but dedicated. Enjoy yourself, but remember to take matters of security seriously, be they financial or emotional. Pay attention to detail before you jump into anything, and do not leave any stone unturned.

Common sense guides you well, and if you do not trust your own, then another person may be a good source of clarity and grounding for you. Look to someone whom you trust to help you.

King of Pentacles: Upright

Personality - The King of Pentacles is ***good at making money*** and investing it. Yet he will only invest safely and in what he fully understands, as he ***takes money very seriously***. This man has been referred to as ***King Midas,*** as ***money easily grows*** with this person, and he is ***successful with work***. He represents ***a provider*** and a person of hard, often physical graft.

He is suited to working with his hands, performing manual labour, but copes equally well in the boardroom, although he prefers to see a finished product at the end of a day's work. He does not mind getting his hands dirty. He has ***an eye for detail*** and is methodical.

The King of Pentacles is a very committed man who is ***cautious but direct*** once he has his goal in sight. ***He views life practically,*** with a down-to-earth approach, and will try to work with what he has, what is available and what he knows when it comes to problem-solving as he likes things uncomplicated. His sentimental side will make him wish to help others or pass on his knowledge: like all the Pentacles, he has a big heart, and the help offered is often of a practical nature, even when the problem may be an emotional one.

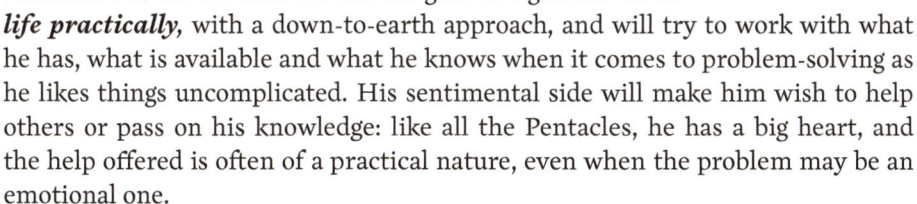

Once a decision is made on a subject, it will stay that way as ***he is practical, persevering and very stubborn.*** You will find him set in his views, and often unchangeable in such matters. Yet his whole approach to life is **honest** and based on **common sense**. He is secure and stable by nature, so can be relied upon. He knows how to enjoy life and can play as hard as he works, but only once the day's work is done.

He has a *'live and let live'*, *'each to his own'* attitude and is very relaxed with others' views if they differ. This person will not impose their views, so if you want his advice, you should ask, but be prepared for a **no-nonsense**, basic but complete answer. He will state what is obvious and is probably being missed. He also has an excellent knack for estimating the nature of others. This King tells us to be sensible, but above all, persevere and **stick to our views**.

King of Pentacles: Reversed

Personality - When reversed, the King of Pentacles shows an individual who is **arrogant and possessive**. What they have is never enough to make them happy. They can place too much importance on 'things' and by the shallow appearance, not only of material gains but also people. He is stuck in a **materialistic** rut and can **resent other's possession**, yet may not be willing to work hard or change his working life and habits to gain them himself.

He has an **uncompromising** idea of perfection and will not bend, leading us to someone frustrated, sad and often full of regret. This soul may have lost the battle, leaving others to have no confidence in him.

This King is one who, if he gets the chance, **will take advantage** and can **easily be bought and corrupted** with either flattery or money. He is **greedy**, so often will break the rules for money, or do anything which will bring pleasure.

Like the Knight reversed, this King can be lazy, allowing life to become literally or metaphorically untidy, with issues unresolved and ignored. He may leave the dead wood in place, **holding on to the past**, possessions, habits and people.

There can also be **addiction problems** as pleasure or escape is sought, whether it be drugs, alcohol, gambling, food or any other means. He is **prone to depression,** rage, anger and even violent physical outbursts, and his view of the opposite sex can often be negative, with a **chauvinistic** view of the world.

The King of Pentacles reversed can also display **physical and mental illness in an individual,** especially if they have abused their bodies and have suffered **long-term stress and negativity.**

Investments fail to grow, as there is not enough positive momentum, but rather hope that they will build themselves. There is apathy: this can lead to not trying, which limits dreams and growth and builds **resentment**.

The reversed King of Pentacles asks us to consider if we are allowing our desires to cloud our judgment, issues, and relationships.

USING YOUR TAROT DECK

Choosing and Using Your Tarot Deck

Choosing Your Tarot Deck

When you buy your first Tarot deck it can be quite a daunting task, as there are so many decks to choose from. Also, to add to the confusion, there is a lot of false information out there stating that your first (if not all) decks should be purchased by another and given as a gift. I feel you should only follow this belief if you wish by asking your gifter to get the deck that you want. You can read more about this later in the book under *Tarot Superstitions and Hearsay*.

Whether a gift or self-brought, new or second-hand, what is most important is that you pick a deck you feel drawn to. Please do not be tempted to listen to anybody else's opinion; the deck will be for your use and no one else's. What may inspire another may not inspire you.

Any superstitions should be let go of right at the start of your Tarot journey. If you cannot form a friendship with a deck suggested or gifted to you, you may never respond to them. Such decks will become keepsakes, and even some that you are drawn to may fall into this bracket. While I suggest to those new to Tarot to go for the Rider Waite Smith in its many formats and artists' impressions available, it is a very personal choice. So, follow your heart, not another's beliefs, and buy the deck you want. If you buy a Tarot deck you do not gel with, put it aside and come back to it another day. There is no limit to how many decks you have, other than that placed by your purse strings. When people started reading Tarot, they would have had a single deck which they would have used for every issue and client, which would have lasted a lifetime, so all you need is a single deck. Today, with the click of a few buttons, we can order what we wish, and some readers have different decks for different moods or issues; it is all down to your own wishes.

When you have chosen your Tarot deck, the best advice I can give is to treat them with respect, as you would a valued friend. First, count that all seventy-eight cards are present. If one is missing, a lot of publishers will send a replacement card. Shuffle them regularly, use them, study them, have fun with them and spend time with them so you build a bridge between the two of you. You will then, in time, have a well-seasoned deck of Tarot cards which you can work effectively with.

Using Your Tarot Deck

The 3 Main Ways of Using Tarot

When it comes to reading the Tarot, you have three main routes you can choose from or which may choose you – and all are perfectly wonderful!

Literally - Reading the cards as a Tarologist. This type of reader can have a great interest in the spiritual side of things, or none. They study and consider the literal, comparative and traditional meanings of the Tarot cards. (Comparative Tarot is the study of the cards, not just in relation to each other card in the layout, but also in connection to the position they are placed in within the given spread, along with the question asked.) This approach can give a reading just as full of clarity and richness as any other. A lot of readers worry about not developing their psychic or clairvoyant abilities, yet it is not needed with Tarot. While Tarot can kick-start and grow your psychic side, if for you it is missing, or not yet found, do not worry, as you can still grow with the Tarot regardless. It is worth remembering that Tarot are just pretty bits of card full of symbolic imagery; they in themselves hold no power, they are a system to master, not magic.

As a dead-set Tarot Reader, you can still work with Spirit or clairvoyantly, which can make a good mix. So do not fear that learning all the intricacies of the Tarot will diminish your intuition, as it will not do so in any way whatsoever. Following this method does not mean you leave your intuition or abilities at the door before you start. I recommend every student study the cards as thoroughly as they can.

Intuitively/Spiritually - This method is the using of your intuition or spiritual self, energy and Guides, whilst considering or even ignoring the cards' traditional comparative meanings, spreads and positions. Use the images within the cards to lead you to your answers or guidance, as a tool to open yourself up, a focal point as it were.

If you decide never to learn the Tarot card meanings, that's okay, but you will not be able to call yourself a Tarot Reader, as you will then be using the Tarot as a stepping-stone to your subconscious or spiritual self, rather than with an interest in the intricacies of the Tarot, which is what defines a Tarot Reader.

An issue with this way of approaching Tarot is that you're not learning the system of Tarot. This can present issues when your physical, emotional, mental as well as psychic energies wax and wane. When developing, it's common for energies to open, close and go awry. At such times, you may not be able to work with the Tarot as an intuitive reader, as you will not have the basic knowledge of the cards to draw from. If you wish to work professionally as a Tarot Reader, you will find that work comes to a halt. It is worth knowing that our energies shift as we grow and can shut down at times for long periods. If you work intuitively with Tarot and learn how to read them thoroughly, you will always have the system itself to fall back onto, a definite feather in your cap.

If, while you are consulting the Tarot, you find a card's traditional representation feels completely different to what you feel that it should represent, then please follow your intuition, and disregard its traditional meaning. This is true for the above method also. Once your clairvoyant intuition starts to develop, it shows that the Tarot and you are gelling, and you have started to connect to your own spiritual nature, as well as to your own creative subconscious mind where all the magic lies. By following your intuition, you will naturally and gradually open yourself to spiritual guidance and improve how you help both yourself and others with the Tarot.

Tarot Meditation – This third method involves forgetting what you have learnt and stepping into the card. This takes us into a journey that can be unrelated to the card itself or have an essence of it, and we are given the messages we need. We will look at this method later in the book in the section called *Stepping into Tarot*. With this method, often just a single card is used, yet you can use a spread.

Meditation is a natural state and one that the developed psychic works within. Whether you consider yourself on a spiritual journey or not, meditation is a part of daily life for us all; we daydream and we lose track of time. All of these are done in altered states of consciousness, but without the intent of meditation. Meditation is not a superhuman feat set aside for those who can levitate and float on clouds and is a skill worth developing on a conscious level. This method is directly aimed at psychic and clairvoyant development and is well worth the effort of mastering.

All Three – You can, happily with experience, balance all three of these together.

Do not attach yourself to a single route in fear of missing out on another. I see people adamant to just work intuitively with the Tarot and then wonder why they do not understand what the cards mean; equally, I see comparative readers battling with what they suddenly feel a card to mean if it differs from what they know. Learn the card meanings and let everything stem from there, as they are a key, a subconscious tool, nothing more.

Before we progress further, there can often be a misunderstanding between the *spiritual* and the *psychic* self.

Your *spiritual* self is who you are, a proportion of your Higher Spiritual Self – placed in your body, living life to learn what it can via your beliefs and how you are within your life. It is You. Your *psychic* abilities, be that clairvoyance, healing, intuition, etc., are separate from that, an aspect of your energy bodies. A by-product, you could say. Both are accessed via the subconscious mind, and experienced through it, as is everything we experience. While both are very linked to your spiritual selves, one is constantly present and growing, while the other changes as it develops. It tends to be that a bout of psychic growth needs time to filter through the spiritual, so we can slow down during such times. Not always; sometimes it goes unnoticed, other times not. Psychic growth promotes spiritual awareness and growth, which then enhances psychic growth, so this is a cycle worth noting.

If you wish to take psychic development seriously, take the time to learn about your spiritual body and your physical, emotional and mental self. This will help you to connect to your spiritual self, as well as to remove or resolve your own negative energy – your beliefs and unresolved issues which surround you, as it does us all. We, in ourselves, are the only people we need protection from. If you wish to work spiritually, it is beneficial if you learn about the nature of Spirit from whichever belief you're drawn to. You have greater control if you understand how it all works, or at least get a basic idea. I am not suggesting that you rush off to a mountain and get a guru; go to what you are drawn to, buy books and talk to those in the 'know', and you will soon find what fits with you. Do avoid those that have a fear-based outlook and are full of 'can't, danger, evil and shouldn't', as they will limit you.

One of the wonderful aspects of Tarot, and probably the main secret of its global reach, is that a card may symbolise one thing to me but something else to you as we view the card's traditional meaning one way or another or see the imagery in a different light. This flexibility and versatility allow us all to interpret the Tarot differently. This makes them an extremely popular tool to use for guidance and personal growth, as we can all have a very personal relationship with Tarot due to our subconscious minds being based on our own unique lives. My clairvoyant or subconscious mind will give one angle to a card, and a different one to you as we tune in to what is of value and understandable to ourselves.

There are no rights or wrongs with Tarot or any form of psychic work or ways of reading for yourself or others. You simply do what you feel is right for you. Your spiritual self knows if you wish to develop, and it will take you to where you need to be able to do so. Whatever way you approach tarot, the trick is to learn how to get out of your own way as your ego will always intervene with worries and presumptions.

People ask: *'What can the Tarot actually do and not do?'* Tarot does not in any way decide or make the future happen. Our past, present and future actions, beliefs and free will achieve that aim. Bad luck, evil or unhappy outcomes cannot be blamed on the Tarot, nor good luck attributed to them. They just simply tell of what will be in connection to our actions via the energy about us, which stems from our past and present actions, or of those about us who affect our lives.

Preparing for a Reading

Whatever your reasons for wishing to develop your Tarot reading skills, in time you will evolve your own ritual of preparation.

The word *ritual* can conjure up all sorts of ideas, but at heart, is simply a series of actions performed according to a prescribed order. For some, it is about meditation or prayer, and for others, it could be the shuffling of the cards the same way each time, or the organising of the question and what spread to use. Even those who just grab their cards and get straight to the point will find that they do it the same each time, think the same thoughts, or mentally or verbally say the same phrase.

A ritual is just a set procedure, a personal routine, that you go through to focus and to get your head in the right space. This can be as easy or as complicated as you wish, and for most, it will stem from their belief system, relating either to spiritual goals and beliefs, or practicality. Some readers' preparation routines will be for opening themselves to Spirit Guides, some will relate to their own energy or subconscious minds, their link to their cards; others will simply wish to relax and create a calm mental space. Or the ritual could be a combination of these things. As this subject is so personal, have confidence that you will find a way that suits you. Again, as an area filled with superstition: do avoid any negative or gate-keeping suggestions that it must be done a certain way.

There are no rights or wrongs with how you prepare, care for, or use your Tarot cards. (Please read that sentence again!)

My ritual or routine

When I first started with Tarot, I had no routine, no idea of what I was doing and solely thought that having them, looking at them and trying my best to learn and use them would open the psychic side of my nature, which has been brewing within me since I was a young child. Yet it did nothing other than confuse me.

I was then lucky to have what I would call a spiritual mentor, who introduced me to things linked to the Buddhist philosophy and the nature of Spirit, which came also from a Spiritualist viewpoint. The issues of mindfulness, going within, auras, Chakras and the many layers of the spiritual body, as well as the peacefulness of Spirit and being Spirit myself, clicked with me. In the same way, your beliefs and what you're drawn to will click with you. Jump into your beliefs; do not get tied by them, but let them move you towards your own evolution, and understanding of who you are.

From this I started meditating, or trying to; I learned about energy centres and energy and started to focus on my own spiritual self, aura and Chakras. Born from this was a rather long-winded ritual, as I realised that focus had been missing from my Tarot readings and practice. It acted to slow me down. Rather than just throwing the cards down in a mass of confusion, I would have my question in mind, light a candle and a joss stick. I would then leave the question to one side to go through all my main seven Chakras, cleanse and expand my aura and ask for my Guides to come and help me or the other being read for. I would then put 'chaos' (found later in the book) into my deck with the act of shuffling and the focus on the question focusing my mind further.

This, after time, gave way to just a few short breaths. I still light a candle and a joss stick, with a few quiet breaths as I focus on the question, the best spread to use or to create, I put chaos into my deck, and it relaxes me. Due to experience, I'm often in the zone the moment I think about it. As I work Clairvoyantly, with the energy about others, once in that lovely, relaxed space I give the person and issue I'm working with to the energy about me, as I know my spiritual self and subconscious are always present, and I trust my Guides are too. Often, I will just tune to the Tarot cards alone as they give a rich reading on their own. It depends on any needs at the time. All the rituals and practices we do, build up a subconscious link to help us focus on our goal. For me, thinking of a question, and picking up the deck can get me in the right place; on other occasions I need to relax more, so do more.

The act of a ritual is not just to get our 'reading hats' on, or our link to Spirit but also, and most importantly, to get our egos out of the way.

It is up to yourself what you do; others do less preparation, some do none and others more. Your ritual will be based on what you're drawn to and linked to your own spiritual leanings or way of viewing the Tarot, and how you wish to work with them. If I were to avoid my ritual, nothing bad would happen. A ritual is for achieving personal focus, a psychological tool based on subconscious programming based on repetition. If you imagine having to get to C in your mind by stringing A and B together, in time just thinking about A will get you to C in an instant as the neurons fire, as an associated link has been put in place.

For those on the path of psychic growth via the Tarot, when asking for information and insights to come forward, whether it comes from your energy connecting to theirs, your subconscious, or Guides: if you get into the habit of treating this aspect of you as a friend by talking to it as something separate to you, you will start to build a relationship, be that with yourself or those in Spirit connected to you, a bond which you can work with and build upon.

At the end of a reading, you can do what is called "closing or shutting down." A lot of people who work with Spirit or energy do this to shut the connection down and to sever the energy link. This is, on a more practical level, used to let go of the question and reason for the reading, as well as another if the reading was not for yourself. Yet it is not needed at all, which again is a personal choice to make, especially if you are working as a literal reader and something which may evolve as you progress. Some people just say thank you and goodbye, others stand up and move about as movement is a good grounding force, some use visualisation. Others put their cards away and know it is time to get on with other things. This is my route, so as soon as I scoop my cards up, I am closed, or removed from that person's issues and questions. I do not do this with fear of any energy remaining, but so that, mentally, I can close the door, as at times my concern for others, as may be the case for you, stays with me. Yet this packs it away for me. It is all down to subconscious cues. Repetition is key, as a single word or action will get you to where you wish to be via association, or you can find your mind wandering back to other people's problems. My way is just one and you will find your own. Keep it simple. None of this is done from the perspective of evil or negative energies, but more from a need to get on with daily life after your reading. Some people fear that by not opening and closing they will attract negative spirits, yet this is not the case: they will simply see or feel a reflection of their fears. We are always open. Opening is just the act of being conscious of it. Closing is just a way of turning that consciousness back off.

After a time, opening and closing become automatic. A to B = C. You will intuitively know when it is time to add to or take from your ritual, as you may feel tired and sleepy or wired, elated and buzzing. All these states are signs of psychic growth yet can also be due to the more practical element of pacing yourself, having good personal boundaries and knowing when to put the cards away. All these things also come from being totally engrossed in a reading, as the mental focus can be tiring.

Getting Ready for a Reading - Five Points to Think About

When we prepare for a Tarot reading, these five things give you structure and will form part of your own ritual, or practice.

1 - Formulate an appropriate question.

2 - Decide which spread will be used and what the position titles will be.

3 - Prepare your deck.

4 - Choose a significator if you wish one.

5 - Shuffle.

6 - Laying your tarot cards.

1 Your Question

Before a Tarot reading begins, the first thing you need is to know what you are asking about. Vague questions can get vague answers. The wording of the question is important. A clear question will get a clearer response than a fuzzy one, so do put time and effort into your question. Avoid double-barrelled questions, such as *'Will I get a new job this year and what will my love life be like?'*; stick to one question per spread unless you have a spread which gives room for two issues. In such cases, two separate readings may be best, especially if you are new to Tarot. Keep it focused.

A Tarot reading does not start the moment the cards are turned, but the very moment you sit and formulate your question. As you gain experience with Tarot you may even have the answers you seek, insights, feelings or images arising from your mind while you think about the question. Be open to everything which comes to you right from the start.

When the questions are along the lines of *'What career is best for me?'*, the Tarot do not have set cards for separate occupations, and so unless you feel something on a spiritual or clairvoyant level, a more focused question will help, such as *'What can I do to find a career that suits me?'*, or *'What is stopping me from seeing my career potential?'*, or *'How would I benefit from taking up a career in baking?'*

Wording is important, so spend time on this aspect before anything else, as it helps set the energy for the reading: be as specific as you can. This is vital, regardless of whether you are working with Tarot alone, or with the help of your Guides and clairvoyance, as it helps get you aligned with the real issue that you are asking about.

Timing in Questions

Tarot is not best for timing and the matter of time will often be of interest to the questioner or yourself. Unless you sense it clairvoyantly or find a method which works for you, it is best to be honest: say that you do not know and explain how Tarot works. To give false hope will cause disappointment and not do your reputation any good.

Timing is not an easy task and one that should not be taken lightly. I have only found one method which works outside of intuitively feeling or seeing a time reference clairvoyantly, and that is a time-framed reading. However, you can find many methods out there that you can try and test and which may work well for you.

A time-framed reading is a good way to resolve the timing problem as it assigns time limits to your Tarot spreads. Unless the questioner (yourself, or another who the reading is for) is asking a question within a time-frame, e.g. *'What can I do to find a committed relationship within the next two years?'* it is best to find a short distance of time that you feel comfortable dealing with. Doing a three-, six- or twelve-month reading can work very well, so you ask the question within the time-frame you choose, and the outcome will often be within a few weeks to a month; yet be aware that nothing can be promised with time.

If the question is, for example, *'Will I ever find love?'* first change the question, as most people do find love during their lives, and EVER is a long time. Instead, look at *'What will happen in my love life over the next month?'*, or *'Will there be any relationship changes for me in the six months?'* If a time-frame is wished for, then add it to the question.

Try not to look too far into the future, even if someone wants to know what the next ten years will bring, as the general threads that lead us there are weaker the further out that we go. The future is governed by predetermination mixed with free will, and any part of our distant future could change due to the past as well as the present. As a result, only those events that are 'set' into one's future will be visible to an experienced reader. Dealing with the next three to twelve months gives a questioner insight as to what they need to be doing to improve things within a workable time-frame.

2 Your Spread

At this stage, know what spread, sometimes called a layout, you will be using and what the title positions for the cards will be. You can use a spread from within the latter part of this book, or just take a few cards or create your own. If you're new to Tarot I do recommend a spread rather than laying cards with no focus. It is important to have this mentally in place before you start. This gives energy, mental or spiritual, and the cards an order to get in; it gives structure to your question, via the angle and perspectives it will be viewed by.

3 Preparing your Deck

Once you have your question and what layout you are going to be using, then comes preparing your deck.

Preparing your deck is different from cleansing a deck. One is for practical reasons and to remove the last shuffle order from the deck; the other is linked to someone's spiritual beliefs. Cleansing is performed as it is said that negative energy can be picked up from other people who touch the cards, or from yourself or the environment. Cleansing is commonly done with prayer, smudging, crystals, tapping on them or many other means. More about this is written later. Energy from auras can be absorbed into objects. Psychometry is the art of reading for another via picking up on absorbed energy in an object, often jewellery, owned or used by someone for a long time. The energy is not evil or positive but a view of that person's energy, a snapshot of their energy if you will, which stands even if another touches your Tarot cards. However, the energy placed on them will be slight and will not linger for long, and so any negativity will be in the mind of the card's owner. The concept of cleansing a deck can be taken however you wish, yet nothing bad will happen if you do nothing. It is another area filled with misinformation and superstition, so do avoid anything which confuses you, or causes you to feel fearful or doubtful, as Tarot should be about adventure, connection and growth.

When preparing a deck, some readers just shuffle their deck; some cut it a few times before shuffling; some like to leave any reversed cards as they are; others like to put them back upright. Some, as mentioned, will cleanse their deck, or do both a cleanse and something practical.

Chaos Method

Personally, I favour simply putting what I call 'chaos' back into the deck. I do not know where this term comes from, as I have called it that for many decades. While this is not cleansing them in the way in which others traditionally view it, it is a practical way of getting your Tarot deck back into an unshuffled order.

Chaos is simply a means of taking your deck with the images upright, and one by one placing them into two, three, or more piles. I do this for a couple of reasons. Firstly, as I go through the Tarot cards one by one, I upright any reversed cards, and secondly, it removes the last shuffle order from the deck. While I'm doing this, I also take the time to remove any dirt from a card, as it ruins the way it shuffles.

This serves to place chaos back into the Tarot deck, as it is from chaos and randomness that structure arises with the shuffle that is yet to come. I also overhand shuffle, so this method guarantees any cards from the last reading are not still together. I do this purely for practical reasons. I find the act of doing this to be rather relaxing, it's a part of my ritual, and is a very simple and practical deck preparation routine.

4 Significators

Before you start to shuffle your Tarot cards, you can use what is called a significator card from the deck, which is a card chosen by the reader.

A significator is a card which represents either the questioner or a situation and is placed either to one side of the Tarot spread or immediately under the first card. (This second is more traditional.) It is not included as part of the reading, as it is a point of focus or reference to the person or subject at hand.

It is not necessary to use a significator, and like everything in Tarot, only use them if you want to. Play with the idea and see how it works out for you: how you wish to identify individual personalities is down to you. If you use one, lay it face up in front of you from the start before shuffling.

Some readers could not proceed without a significator, as they wish to have a personal reference to the questioner in front of them, while other readers do not like to take a potentially important card from the deck. If you do not wish to use a card as a significator yet wish to have a physical representation of the person or their question, you can use their name or question written on a piece of paper or a photo if you wish. You can also take a card from an extra Tarot deck if you have one.

Court Cards as Significators and within Readings

Each Tarot deck contains sixteen court cards, four belonging to each of the four suits of the Minor Arcana.

It is possible that gender and ages can be passed between the fixed sexes of the four court cards, and Queens can represent men, and Knights and Kings vice versa, with the Pages symbolic of either sex. The court cards can symbolise extensions of your own personality and the influence of others who have been, are, or will be involved in, or relevant to the problem or situation raised by the Tarot reading.

The court card used as a significator, or laid within a Tarot spread, will tell which area of an individual's personality you will be faced or dealing with, or a general summary of a person, depending on how you choose one. It would be rare that any one person would strictly be solely represented by just one card. For example, the main aspects of your personality may be that of the King of Wands, striving and rising to meet the next challenge but who are you when your pride is hurt? Maybe you will continue to act the same, or react like the Page of Wands reversed, feeling insecure, or even like the Queen of Swords by putting on a brave, strong face, having learned a valuable lesson.

The side of your personality shown to your partner will be different to that you show to a friend, which will be different to that which you portray to a colleague, etc. We are all many different personalities at different times and under different circumstances, as we are all multi-faceted. As you learn about your own nature, you will see aspects of both yourself and others in all the court cards, upright as well as reversed. While the court cards represent personalities, they also reflect people's feelings and reactions, and how they are affected by the situations they find themselves in. This can also give you a handy tool to understand the court cards. Look at those around you and aspects of their personalities, their reactions and inactions, and see which one of the court cards they remind you of. This can help them stick in your mind, as the court cards can cause issues for many when studying.

When a court card appears in a reading it can often not represent a person and instead show how we should deal with and approach issues, so energies which we need to embody.

Traditional Court Card Depictions

Pages usually represent the young or the immature, but they are also messengers. They represent young children or single young females up to mid-teens.

Knights represent not only individuals but also situations or circumstances. They represent young or single males in their mid-teens to mid-thirties.

Kings and Queens solely represent individuals who are mature and can be used for those who are married/in committed relationships.

For quick reference, next are the astrological signs and with a mix of the relevant, traditional, and non-traditional, colouring of the court cards.

You may also wish to use whichever colourings or references you find in your own Tarot deck if it differs, or, make up your own if you wish to use significators.

There are several points to consider when choosing a significator. You can choose a card that represents the astrological sign of the questioner, personality, age, marital status, or hair and/or eye colouring.

You could also use the card that represents their question: for instance, a woman wanting a financial reading could have the Queen of Pentacles, while a man wishing to know about his work could have the King of Wands; and so on.

You can also use the other cards in the deck as significators - for legal matters, you could use Justice, Lovers for relationships or even the Ace of Pentacles for finance, etc. But remember, this will also take a potentially important card from the deck.

Astrological Signs and Colouring

Wands - Fire

Sagittarius (November 22nd to December 21st) = Knight
Leo (July 23rd till August 22nd) = Queen
Aries (March 21st till April 19th) = King

Or presents with. Hair: fiery colours, brown, ginger, red, auburn, strawberry blond(e), brunette. **Skin:** fair to medium. **Eyes:** brown, green, hazel.

Cups - Water

Scorpio (October 23rd till November 21st) = Knight
Cancer (June 21st till July 22nd) = Queen
Pisces (February 19th till March 20th) = King

Or presents with. Hair: pastel colours, pale ginger, pale light blond(e)
Skin: fair **Eyes:** blue, brown, hazel.

Swords - Air

Gemini (May 21st till June 20th) = Knight
Libra (September 23rd till October 22nd) = Queen
Aquarius (January 20th to February 18th) = King

Or presents with. Hair: pale and sharp colours, black, grey.
Skin: dark. **Eyes:** dark brown, striking blue.

Pentacles - Earth

Virgo (August 23rd till September 22nd) = Knight
Capricorn (December 22nd till January 19th) = Queen
Taurus (April 20th till May 20th) = King

Or presents with. Hair: earthy colours, light, or dark brown, dark blond(e).
Skin: dark or tanned. **Eyes:** dark eyes, brown, green, hazel.

5 Shuffling

A lot of new Tarot students get confused about how to shuffle and when to stop shuffling. Like all things Tarot, this is down to your intuition. At times, stopping shuffling can cause panic due to a fear of not getting it right or getting the wrong answer. This is often a sign of being too emotionally invested in the question asked of the cards and a worry about hearing unwelcome news. If you find that you are really finding it hard to define a stopping moment, give yourself a certain number of shuffles and then stop.

When shuffling your Tarot cards, it is important to relax. Clear your mind as much as possible and start to think about the subject that you wish to gain insight into, your question and your spread. By shuffling, you are placing order back into the deck, which stems from the question you are asking. Without a firm question, you must be willing to not always see a clear reply or know instantly what area of your life the cards are relating to. Be firm, direct and try to avoid open-ended questions or multi-questions if you wish to gain clear advice; be direct in your approach to the situation you wish guidance on.

If you read for another and they shuffle the Tarot deck themselves, you can clairvoyantly pick up advice or direction from the small temporary residue of their aura that is left on the deck by the handling of the cards. As mentioned before, this is called Psychometry and is a reason why you may want to allow others to shuffle for themselves. Some readers will not allow anyone else to touch their cards, some do. That is your choice.

How to Shuffle your Tarot Deck

I have been asked many times if you should shuffle the cards with the backs of the cards or the pictures facing you. Both are okay: I prefer the backs as it keeps my mind clear, yet my way may not suit you, so try both.

1. **Overhand Shuffle.** The traditional shuffle performed with playing cards.

2. **The Riffle-Shuffle.** Also called the Dovetail Shuffle. For this method, you divide your deck into two piles, and riffle-shuffle them into each other by letting the corners of one pile fall onto the corners of the other, as if you were shuffling before gambling. Personally, I am no good at this method. My cards tend to go flying off, *Alice in Wonderland* style. This method of shuffling will also slightly bend your cards, so it is not for everyone.

3. **Cutting the Deck.** Yet you can cut the deck into piles and keep doing that until you're happy. Yet this will rarely give a good shuffle to your cards.

4. **Wash or Wax Shuffle.** Put your Tarot cards on a flat surface and messily swirl them about before putting the deck back together. If you do not want reversed cards, this method may not be suited to you.

5. **Intuitive Shuffling.** This is more a method for the advanced reader, especially someone who is at ease with their own routine and ritual. If you are connected to yourself and relaxed, and with your question already set, you may get answers of images appearing within your mind as you shuffle, or even as you hold your cards. Close your eyes if it helps. If you find images, insights or messages arising, however they come to you, just stop shuffling, keep hold of your cards and listen. If you are drawn to take a Tarot card, scan the back of the cards and take the one which you are drawn to, or from a cut of the deck, or shuffle stop. Whichever you choose, just go with what you feel. This method can leave a single card being of value, yet two to four can be okay. More than that and this method tends to get lost.

6. **A mixture of the methods above.** If it makes you happy, flow with it.

After shuffling, with your chosen method, you can then cut the deck if you wish. You can cut your Tarot deck into two piles, or even three or four, or more and place the one you or your questioner feels drawn to on top of the Tarot deck to take the cards for the reading from.

Reversed Cards

Should you wish to use reversed cards, here are many ways to get them into your deck and a decision to make prior to starting shuffling.

1. You can cut the Tarot deck into two, three or more piles and turn one of them upside down before shuffling. If you use this method, make sure that you shuffle the deck well so that the cards are evenly distributed.

2. Lay all the cards face down on a smooth surface and jumble them about with the Wash or Wax method, before putting the deck back together. You can shuffle more once the deck is back together if you wish.

3. Reverse random cards as you shuffle with the Overhanded Shuffle. I use this method myself. When shuffling my prepared deck, I reverse the cards that are at the end of most overhanded shuffle movements, or any cards which stick out. This gives me a slight percentage of reversed cards. I find this gives me a balanced reading.

Jumper Cards

On occasion during shuffling, you will find that a card or cards jump from the deck, or start to poke out. These are commonly called Jumpers. Although you can ignore Jumpers if you wish, you can at times find that these odd individual cards are relevant, if not to the present, then to the outcome, answer, or advice to the question asked. Jumpers can be viewed from the perspective that everything occurs for a reason and sometimes the whole reading can stem from and be resolved by a single card. You can put them to one side or take no notice of them: as with all things Tarot, experiment and see what works best for you.

If a lot of cards fall out, that is just a case of butterfingers, but if it is one or two, they may hold a message for you to consider.

I have seen an increasing number of readers who only read Jumpers or those cards which start to slide out. With this method, you could wait a long time to get enough cards for a spread. Traditionally, Jumpers were cards which you ignored, and put back, yet now they are seen as cards which may hold value to some. So if you wish to use this method, a rough, fast overhand shuffle is needed, with the cards held loosely.

6 Laying Your Cards

After shuffling, you can then cut the deck if you wish into two piles, or even three or four, or more and place the one you, or your questioner if reading for another, feels drawn to on top of the Tarot deck to take the cards for the reading from. Yet, you can also fan your cards out face down to be able to pick the ones you're drawn to.

You can now lay your cards in your pre-chosen spread as your Tarot deck is now ready. Lay the cards, if using a spread in the order given, so Card One will go to Position One, etc. If a spread has no numbers, decide before you start which order you will lay the cards in.

Putting Your Cards Away

Storage of Your Tarot Deck When Not in Use

When your Tarot cards are not in use, keep them in a box and they will remain undamaged and last you for many decades. This is for practical reasons, as once a single card gets bent it interferes with the smooth shuffling of the deck. Pets or children can easily damage a much-loved Tarot deck if it is left unattended, as can decks which are wrapped solely in cloth in a place where they can be damaged.

Be practical about the care of your Tarot cards. Keeping them wrapped in silk with a crystal will no more benefit them than keeping them in the box they came in. It is the relationship that you build with them that will aid you. You are the magic, not the cards themselves.

Yet, if you wish to wrap your Tarot cards in silk, or anything else, do that and follow your heart: if you are happy, then you will be more relaxed and open to hearing their messages to you.

TRADITIONAL TAROT SPREADS

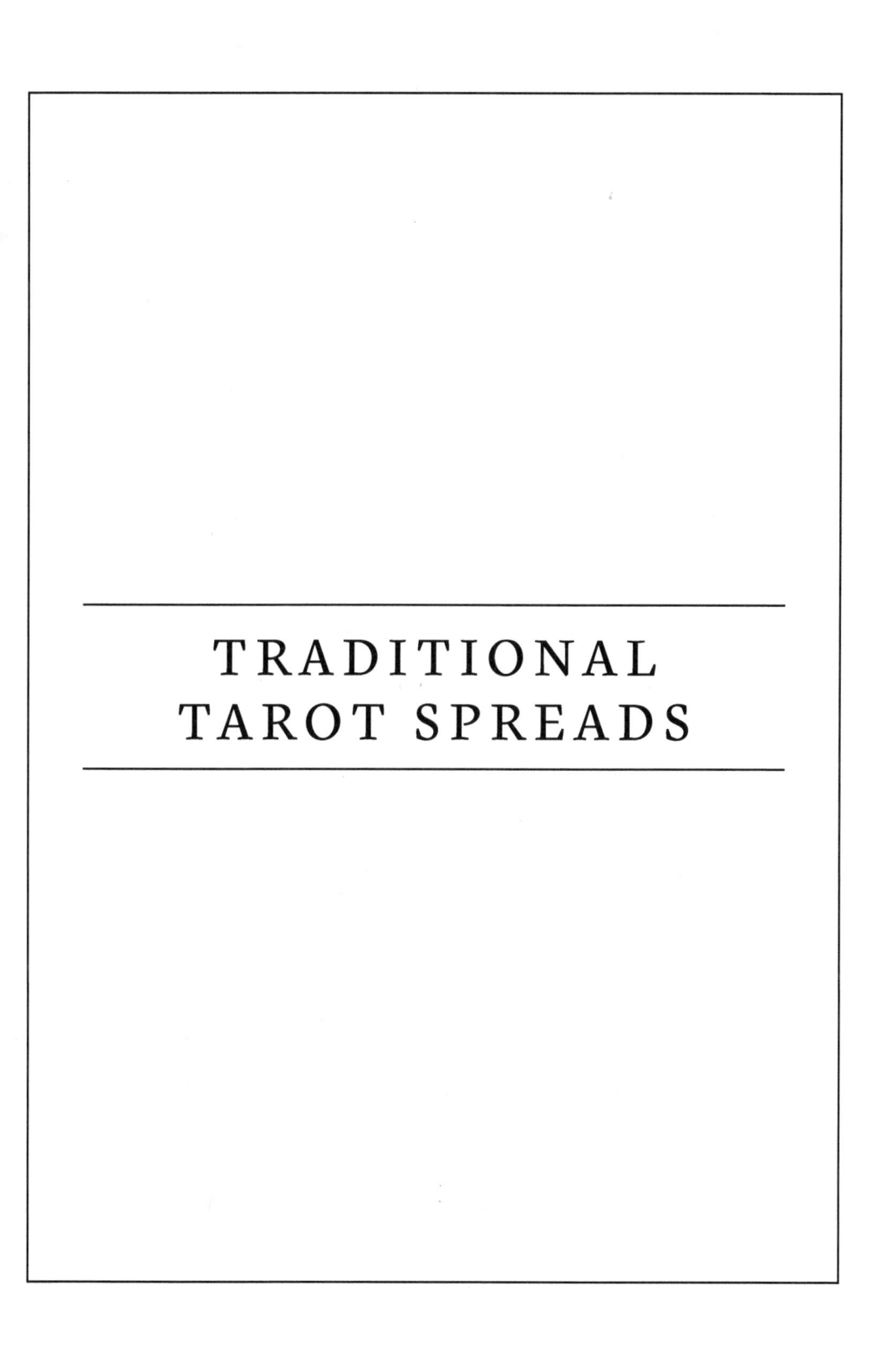

Using and Creating Tarot Spreads

Here we will talk about using Tarot spreads. A Tarot spread is a set format for laying the cards with titled positions such as Past, Present or Future. Each position title will govern what perspective any card is read from. A Tarot layout with its positions will show you many aspects of a situation, which can be wonderful for seeing the bigger picture and unexplored perspectives.

Spreads can be complex, or straightforward. If you are just setting out with Tarot, a ten card Celtic Cross may not be best spread to use, as it can confuse those new to the subject. The Celtic Cross can confuse an experienced reader if they are not focused, let alone some of the larger spreads you can find or create. Often a large number of cards are not needed to answer a question, so starting with a smaller spread will not limit you in any way. The more you understand the symbolic nature of each card, the easier you can read larger spreads. You will see the interlinking energies and meanings between the cards individually and together, combined with the position they are in within the spread, leading to an understanding of Comparative Tarot.

Can I create my own spreads?

A lot of people ask if they can make their own layouts and the answer is yes. You can also take an existing spread and change it to suit your situation.

You may find if you create a simple layout which fits all your questions, that you can change the position titles when needed. Imagination is key to understanding what side of a situation you wish to have insight into. Every layout within this book, with some imagination, can be changed to suit your own needs, as well as creating new ones which serve you.

With all the presented Tarot spreads here in this book, relax with them, change them if you want to, play, and find what works for you. Prepare for them well and you will connect to them better.

Do I lay my cards face down or face up?

When you lay your cards, a lot of students ask if they should be laid face down or face up. I advise that you give both a go. Some people like to lay the whole spread face down, picture side to the table or surface, and to then view each card as it's turned to slowly build up what is being seen and then look at the whole layout. Others like to see it all in one go and lay each card face up before looking at it in detail. You can even lay each card face up, giving it some thought before laying the next.

Clarifier cards

A Clarifier card is an extra card laid to give more insight into the spread as a whole, or to clarify a single placed card within a spread. I have added details here as they are only relevant once a spread has been laid as a clarifying card is aimed at helping you see more depth, detail, or context.

If you use them, as you gain more experience with the Tarot, you may find you do not need a Clarifier card as much as you did at the start. If you find that you need them with every reading and for each card laid, it is a sign that you have not prepared yourself, have used a spread which is too large, or a spread which has no positions, or simply do not yet have enough Tarot wisdom to draw from. At times, a Clarifier, or a whole bundle of them, just adds extra confusion to what you already do not understand.

To get your Clarifier card, you can obtain it by taking the top card of the remaining deck or cutting the deck at a point you feel drawn to, or reshuffle, cut, and taking the card from the top. You can even shuffle until one comes loose from the deck.

Spreads: Some General Timing Insights

When preparing for a reading, the timing of issues can be added to your question as mentioned. While time cannot be guaranteed, you can focus on a time-frame. Such as *'How will my relationship be over the next 4 weeks/6 months/year?'*, *'Why am I feeling this way today?'*, *'What has gone on at work over the last two months?'* These give past, present and future time-frames.

I was taught that without a time-frame added to the question a Tarot reading gave a six-month to a year outlook. So do consider time when you're preparing for a reading. If not, have a general presumption that all spreads, or time-relevant positions, will have a generalised time-frame, as then it is incorporated in your preparation and mindset when preparing for a reading.

In general, where no time-frames are presented, such as, Near Future, common time-based positions can mean the following, so it can be good to have a prearranged set of time frames, an understanding in mind, to work by.

Any Past positions show the energy; the actions which have led to your current position/Present. When it comes to the past, it can pick up on what happened years ago regardless of the time frames used, as it can show what has happened to create the present, and the time frame can be very fluid.

Past: Unless otherwise stated or chosen, when referring to a Past card position, this can be decades ago, or even just a few days, or even an energy just leaving.

Recent Past: If this position is in a spread, it will refer to anytime from the time of the reading to the last three to six months. Yet of course can be longer, especially if nothing has occurred within that time-frame to impact the situation being asked about.

Any cards in a Past position will be relevant to your situation and question and can still be present.

Present: This is the here and now. Yet at times it can be energy just entering your life or situation, or even just leaving.

Future: The same goes for any Future position cards: the energy can already be with you, just coming in or be weeks, years, or decades away.

Near Future: Near Future: If you do not set time-frames and Near Future is stated as a position, this often refers to any time between the time of the reading to three to the next six months.

Long-Term Future: This position often refers to anything over six months, to a year or longer unless you pre-prepare mentally for it to be otherwise. This position is in the same vein as a standard Future position. Of course, times are not concrete, as we are working with energy and human emotions which are very changeable, but this gives you a guideline to work within.

Future positions will show what is coming, based on the energy you have at the time of the reading, or even with outside actions beyond your own knowledge or control which will impact the situation.

ONE CARD READING

One card can hold all the answers that you need and should never be dismissed as 'not enough'.

Choose one of the reading methods at a time (literal/intuitive/meditation). Practise what method suits you for now; see where your strengths and weaknesses lie. Remember not to get stuck on or within your current level of ability, as it will change as you progress with your knowledge of the Tarot, as well as your psychic growth if you wish that path.

If you wish to use a Significator, with this or any other spread, remember to place it to one side or under the first card or beside the first card.

With a single card, word your question very clearly as it does not have the benefit of other card positions. 'Yes' and 'No' questions can be a problem if you are inexperienced or get a card which does not show an outright answer, which can occur in any reading where a 'Yes' or 'No' is asked for.

THREE CARD SPREAD

The three card Tarot spread is very versatile as well as easy for those new to Tarot, and even for those more experienced. It can often be a go-to spread as it can give you all that you need.

As with all the spreads within this book, there are different versions for you to enjoy. Always lay the cards in numerical order and if you cannot remember the titles of the positions, write them down on a piece of paper and place them next to the cards.

Here are a few ideas:

1 Past	2 Present	3 Future

1 Me	2 Him / Her / Them	3 Advice

1 Situation	2 Action needed	3 Outcome

1 Present	2 Happening next	3 Advice

1 Problem	2 Advice	3 Outcome

SIX CARD SPREAD

The six card Tarot spread is one of my favourites as it is quite detailed and forms the cross of the Celtic Cross. Here we start to look at Main and Root Energies, which show us a lot more about a situation.

At its heart, the Main Energy positions point to the energy which we are aware of, or in some cases, is all about us, yet we cannot really see as we are too caught up in our situation. The foundation or Root Energy is what is underpinning the Main Energy. At times, we may not know what this is, yet this card can often be the driving force for the problem at hand, as it encompasses the energy which your question is built upon.

Six Card Spread 1

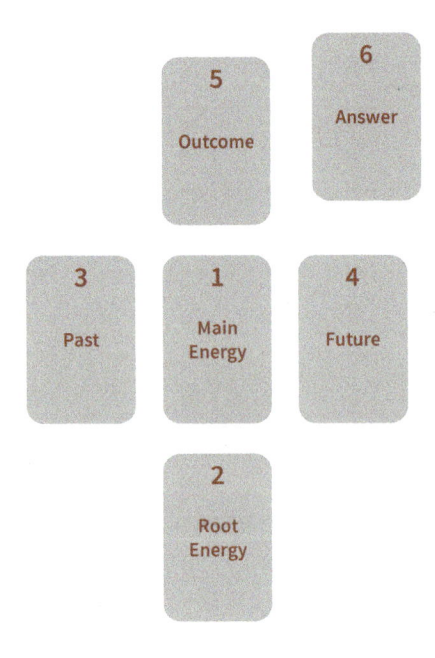

```
              ┌─────────┐  ┌─────────┐
              │    5    │  │    6    │
              │ Outcome │  │ Answer  │
              └─────────┘  └─────────┘

┌─────────┐  ┌─────────┐  ┌─────────┐
│    3    │  │    1    │  │    4    │
│  Past   │  │  Main   │  │ Future  │
│         │  │ Energy  │  │         │
└─────────┘  └─────────┘  └─────────┘

              ┌─────────┐
              │    2    │
              │  Root   │
              │ Energy  │
              └─────────┘
```

Six Card Spread 2

In the second version of this layout, the title Outer Energy refers to the energy surrounding you and the situation, which at times you may not be aware of as it can involve others.

The Leaving Energy position refers to what is on its way out within your life or situation yet can still be affecting you. The Coming Energy position can show what is yet to arrive, what is flowing your way, yet can also be already present within your situation. You will notice, the cards are laid in a different order than the Six Card Spread 1.

Please also choose beforehand if card Six will be for Advice or your Answer.

```
              3              6
           Outer          Answer
           Energy         Or Advice

    4         1              5
  Leaving    Main          Coming
  Energy    Energy         Energy

              2
            Root
            Energy
```

THE CELTIC CROSS

The Celtic Cross is one of the most popular Tarot spreads known, and for those new to Tarot, this can be one of the hardest. Like a lot of Tarot readers, who started pre-internet, I had access to a few books, and this was the go-to spread. For those new to Tarot, I would personally advise leaving it until you are more confident. If the cards confuse you, then placing them into an equally confusing spread is not a good teaching tool. I never really started to grasp the cards until I ditched the Celtic Cross in favour of simpler spreads in those early days of my Tarot journey.

You will find as you study this that there are many versions of it. If someone says they will be using a Celtic Cross Tarot spread, ask what position placements they have, as it could give you a new layout to use if you like to collect spreads. Like all layouts, it can be changed to suit your own needs or preferences, and when you find a version you like, you will probably stick to it.

The spread contains ten Tarot cards and is made from a cross of six cards with a column, sometimes called a pillar, which consists of four cards. Like all Tarot layouts, you can use this spread for an overall look at the energy about you or a situation or aim it at a specific question.

If you wish to use a Significator, as before, place it to one side or slightly under the first card face up. Do this from the start before you start to shuffle, as this is the layout where Significators are mostly used. Within a Celtic Cross, if you wish to be traditional, the Significator card is meant to be laid directly under the first card, which leaves it unseen once the cards are laid.

A Significator is said to be meant to be facing front, or to the future, yet as you have noticed with the court cards, not all the characters face you head on. When using a Significator with the traditional Celtic Cross, or any Tarot spread where the cards to the right and left of the cross are for Past and Future, you can, if you wish, swap positions Five and Six around if you use a Significator which faces the wrong way. Let's say you wish to use a Significator and have chosen one on your astrological sign of Sagittarius, which is the Knight of Wands who faces the left of the card. In the traditional Celtic Cross layout, he faces the 'What is Behind You' position, which is the Past, so swap card Five with card Six 'What is Before You' so he is facing the future. You may find other views on this issue, yet I am adding it here to show another aspect. Like all things Tarot, you only need to do this if you wish, as it will not change your reading in any way.

The Traditional Celtic Cross

The Celtic Cross was made popular by Arthur Edward Waite in his published book, *The Pictorial Key to the Tarot* (1911). While the position titles in a more modern Celtic Cross may be easier to understand, this one can confuse if you are not familiar with the wording, so let us look at the positions in this version.

The Cross

In this traditional layout, you can view cards one to four as the emotional and mental aspects of the self.

Card 1 - What Covers You. This card represents the person who the reading is for, the Querant (a word used to describe the questioner), and refers to the heart of the matter. This can show elements of how you are connected to your situation and what is affecting you. It is phrased as *What Covers You* or traditionally *This Covers Him/Her* as it is meant to be placed directly over the Significator, leaving the Significator obscured: hence, it covers you.

Card 2 - What Crosses You. This position can also have the title of *What Crosses Him/Her* in this traditional version, and refers to what is helping or hindering you, and so can show a problem energy or an assisting one. Card 2 is traditionally placed on its side, yet of course you can place it upright if you wish.

Card 3 - What Crowns You. This is the conscious mind, showing where you are mentally with the issue at hand. Often, it can also refer to the direction your issue can take, as it reflects your own movement within your problem if your mind and actions stay the same.

Card 4 - What is Beneath You. This position shows your subconscious, which consists of those things you may not be aware of, yet are driving you, or alternately an outer force propelling the situation. It will be where the situation stems from, the foundation of your issue.

Card 5 - What is Behind You. The past which is affecting the present.

Card 6 - What is Before You. The future. This can in part show the outcome, yet more reflects the coming energy, what is next within your situation.

The Column (starting from the base upwards)

Card 7 - Yourself. Your role in your problem or situation.

Card 8 - Your House. This position refers to your Environment, which you will find in many versions of the Celtic Cross. It refers to others within your life or situation, and those who can affect the outcome. It represents those things beyond your control, outside of yourself.

Card 9 - Your Hopes, Fears or Expectations. This line shows your deeper feelings about your question and what you are wanting or worrying the outcome to be.

10 - What is Coming. Quite like an outcome card, this can be read with Card 6, What is Before You. Yet Card 10 will trump that card as it caps the questions with the ultimate direction in which your issue is travelling.

The Traditional Rider Waite Celtic Cross 1

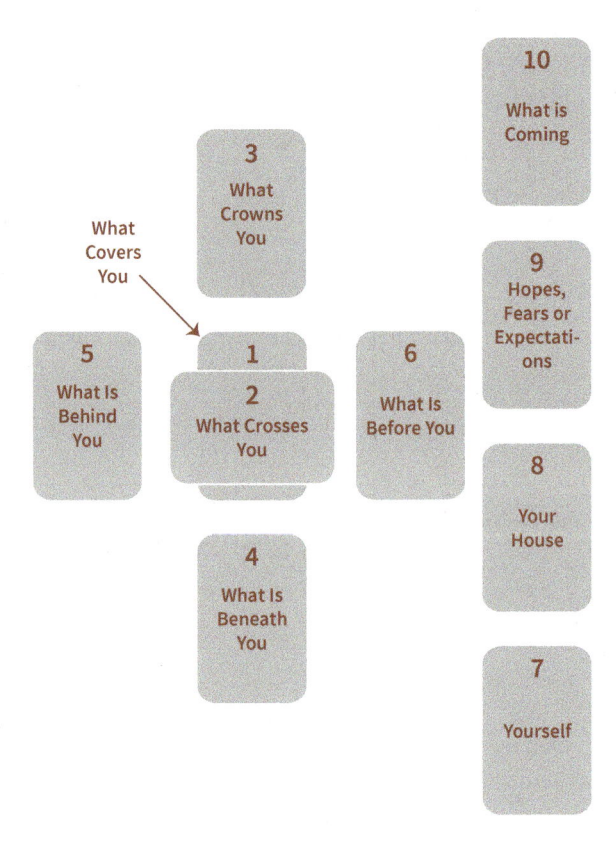

```
                                                    10
                                                    What is
                                                    Coming
                              3
                              What
                              Crowns
              What            You
              Covers
              You                                   9
                   ↘                                Hopes,
                                                    Fears or
                                                    Expectati-
        5           1            6                  ons
        What Is     2            What Is
        Behind      What Crosses Before You
        You         You
                                                    8
                                                    Your
                                                    House
                              4
                              What Is
                              Beneath
                              You
                                                    7
                                                    Yourself
```

398   UNDERSTANDING TAROT

Alternate Celtic Cross 2

This layout is like the original, yet with more modern position titles. It looks at the short- as well as long-term aspects of your issue. In Tarot, the short term, Near Future, usually refers to days, weeks and often no more than three to six months, with the long term being anything from six months plus, unless you change those time-frames prior to your reading within your question.

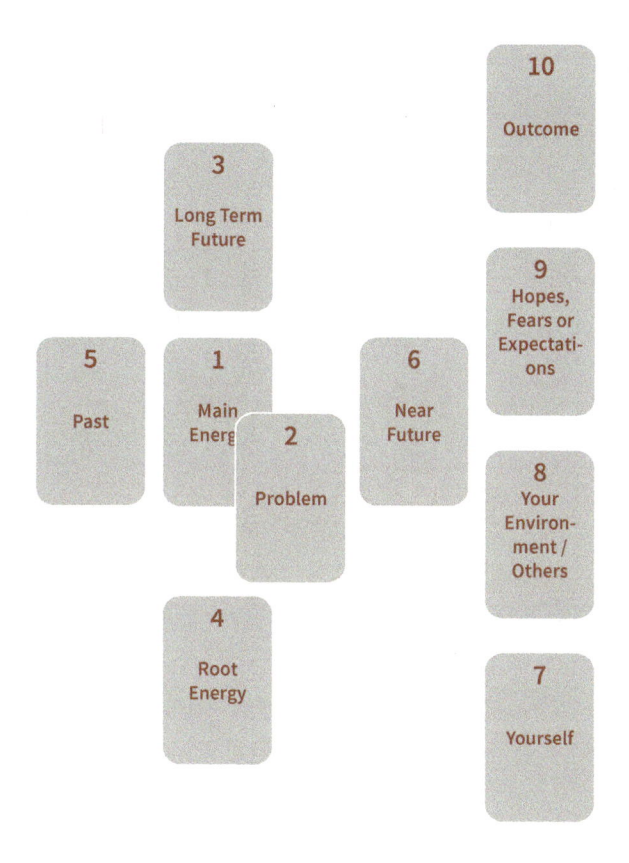

Position	Meaning
1	Main Energy
2	Problem
3	Long Term Future
4	Root Energy
5	Past
6	Near Future
7	Yourself
8	Your Environment / Others
9	Hopes, Fears or Expectations
10	Outcome

Alternate Celtic Cross 3

This is a good layout for looking at where aspects of your life are in the present. If you wish, you can also use the column to look at those areas within a time-frame, for example, 3 months or a year. To do this use a single time-frame to cover all four positions.

```
                                                    10
                                                  Work &
                                                  Finances
                    3
                  Outer
                  Energy
                                                    9
                                                  Love &
                                                  Relation-
       5           1           6                   ships
     Leaving                 Coming
     Energy     You          Energy
                    2                               8
                  Problem                         House,
                                                  Home &
                                                  Family
                    4
                  Root                              7
                  Energy
                                                  Yourself
```

Alternate Celtic Cross 4

This is my version of the Celtic Cross, the one I use for myself or others. I do not like the Crossing card, yet I always value an Advice card, as that can help greatly when looking at issues. It gives an angle of help and can shine a light on those things which you can change.

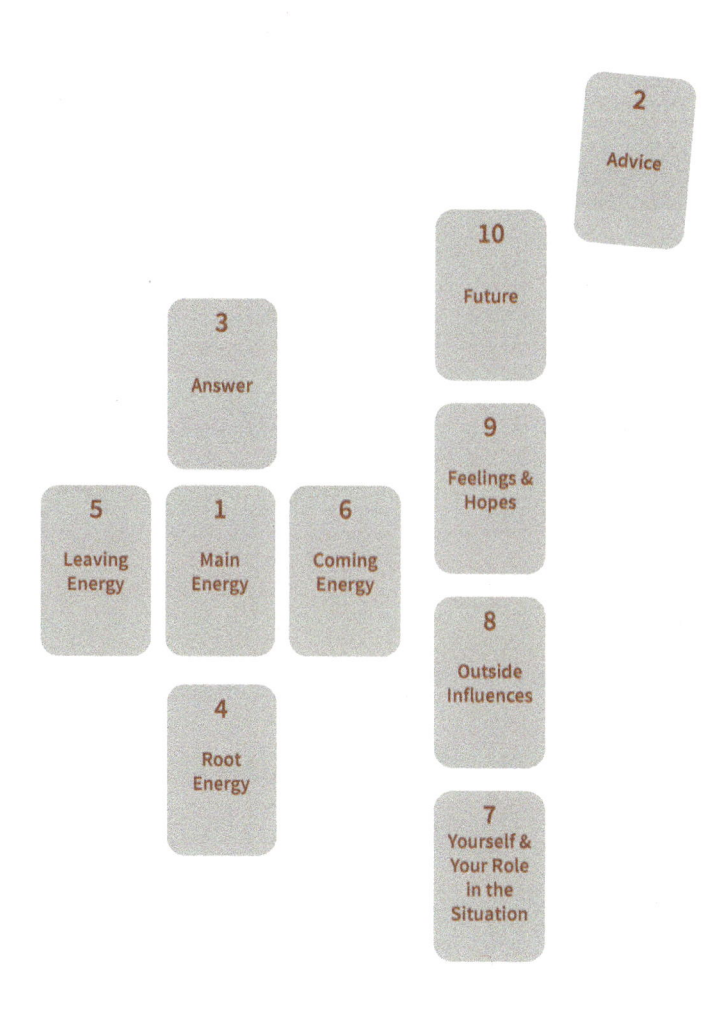

```
                                              2
                                            Advice

                                    10
                                   Future

                3
              Answer
                                    9
                                Feelings &
                                  Hopes
     5          1          6
  Leaving     Main      Coming
  Energy     Energy     Energy
                                    8
                                 Outside
                                Influences
                4
              Root
             Energy
                                    7
                                Yourself &
                                Your Role
                                  in the
                                Situation
```

THE CELTIC CROSS

The 26 Card Celtic Cross, or the Super-Duper Celtic Cross!

This layout is not for the novice, but fun for those who wish to try it and have a grasp of the cards.

This cross can be done with both the Major and Minor Arcana together as one deck, though you can also separate the two decks. To do this, remove the Major Arcana from the deck, and instead of preparing one deck, you will be preparing two. Once you have done all you need to do and are ready to lay your cards, use the Major deck for the first cross and column, cards one to ten. With your Minor deck, lay out the rest of the cards as they are numbered. The Minor cards are an addition to the Majors, placed upon them within the cross, or alongside them up the column.

The preparation time for this is naturally longer, which can focus the mind, yet it can also give you more Major cards than you may otherwise get, so try it with both, a single mixed deck, and the two separated decks. It gives you two cards to describe positions 1-5, and four cards for each of the columns.

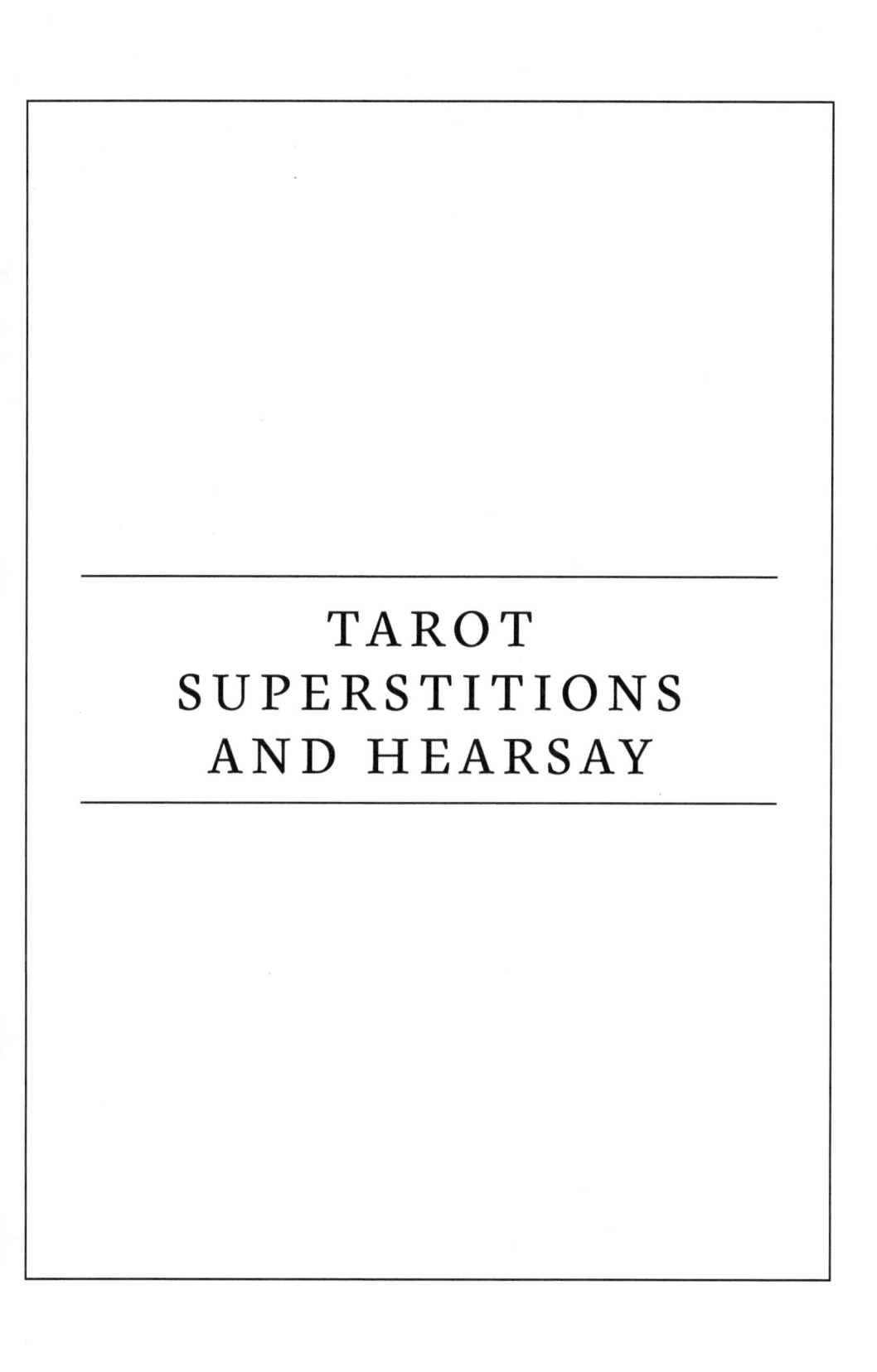

TAROT SUPERSTITIONS AND HEARSAY

Superstitions, Hearsay and Negative Presumptions on the Tarot

There are a lot of superstitions about Tarot and Psychic Development. I will try to broach some of the main ones here. If, as you journey with Tarot, anyone mentions that you cannot do this or that, look at it logically. Challenge the beliefs and reasons of the person giving you the fear-based advice, and yourself also.

A superstition is an irrational belief, which often dictates that if something is not done in a set way, something bad will occur. Anyone being superstitious may not see it as such, as to them it is fact or the truth. With this in mind, if anything you think or feel about Tarot scares or worries you, look at it as a false belief needing to be rationalised.

When asking for guidance from your Tarot deck, do not attempt to do so if you feel nervous or fearful, as any information will be tainted by it. If you are not open or relaxed, answers will come from your ego, bypassing the higher part of you which you may wish to be in contact with, be that your subconscious self, energy or spirit.

The only negativity you will meet will be your own gremlins, deep-seated fears and subconscious concerns which have been ingrained into you. To think otherwise means Tarot or spiritual and psychic development may not be for you, as it will distract you too much.

Create a down-to-earth approach. To be worried about evil is to not trust yourself and the army of Spirit Guides around you. Some of the most spiritual people I have met are also some of the most practical, filled with common sense over their spiritual work. However, Tarot does not require any spiritual beliefs, and any negativity seen in the cards is simply a reflection of your mind.

Some Common Superstitions and Myths

'You should not read Tarot for yourself.'

This myth has some basis in fact. When we read for ourselves, we can often see what we fear and wish for. It can take time to be able to put ourselves to one side and read the Tarot as we would for another, and see honesty rather than fiction from our own spreads. Yet only experience can lead us to be able to open to our own truths, and Tarot is a wonderful tool to enable that. No harm will come from reading for yourself, but you may see confusion and negativity in the cards, or even hopes highlighted when your mind is not in a good place. If you have trouble reading for yourself, it can be good to treat yourself as a friend. For example, I will ask, *'How will this situation affect Pam?',* etc.

'You are not allowed to buy your own Tarot deck.'

This myth stems from the first Tarot cards originally being hand-painted, often with gold edges and leaf, and quite expensive to commission. They were not on general sale as they are today. These were treated as valued possessions, not just due to their artwork, as even with the invention of the printing press, they still would not have been readily available to the average person. They would have been handed down, in most cases, through the family line, thus gifted to the inheritor. This also throws out the superstition about second-hand decks being bad luck, as by nature, these decks would only ever have one original owner. A lot of readers would never get started on their Tarot journey if they waited to be gifted a deck of new cards; I know I wouldn't have. Go to the cards you are drawn to and buy them yourself if you wish.

'You are not allowed to let others touch your Tarot deck.'

This links to the myth above. As decks were such precious items, you did not wish someone else to ruin them with dirty hands. It made sense not to allow others to touch them, to preserve them for longer. When you start reading Tarot for others, you will be aware, even with the ease of being able to replace a deck nowadays, that it pains you to see a loved deck get dirty, bent, or damaged by someone else shuffling them. This is a personal choice issue. Some Tarot readers like the sitter to connect with the cards energetically by shuffling them. Other readers prefer to shuffle the cards themselves, allowing the sitter to pick a pile from a deck which has been divided into two or three piles, and some for the questioner to have no contact with them at all. Do it your way.

There can also be a fear of the negative energy of others being absorbed into a deck, yet as mentioned elsewhere in this book, which is not a concern to pay any focus to, and can be something that can enhance your readings.

'You cannot use the Tarot unless you know how to.'

This superstition always confuses me, as a chicken-and-egg scenario is created. No reader has ever come pre-loaded with Tarot instructions. Every Tarot student must learn how to read the cards, and for that, you need to use them when they are a mass of unknown confusion to you.

'You need to sleep with the deck under your pillow.'

Apart from being uncomfortable and risking damaging your Tarot deck, placing them under or even near your pillow is meant to allow the cards to enhance your third eye (Brow Chakra), and even vice versa. Or, also for their knowledge to sink into your subconscious mind. However, only studying them will do that. Psychic development comes from dedication, practice and patience. I have placed this here as it can cause tension in those who try it and find that they are not enjoying any development, or a deeper understanding of their Tarot cards, or any psychic growth.

'You must interview a new Tarot deck.'

To 'interview' a Tarot deck is a new concept and performed via a Tarot spread designed for such a meeting. This is something that is not a must, yet if it is done, two things need to be considered.

The first is that the Tarot cards are not an entity, they work via your energy and subconscious mind. With this in mind, they reflect your own self, and how you are responding to the Tarot deck at that time. Secondly, if you are new to Tarot, any messages the reading gives may not be understood, as you do not have a grasp of the cards themselves.

'You must not cross your legs when you read Tarot.'

Crossing your legs is said to 'stop your energies from grounding into the earth via your Base Chakra found at the base of your spine, by stopping the flow of energy between Spirit and the earth'.

Please note that even with both feet off the floor, we are still grounded. Grounding connects our Spiritual Self to our physical body and our physical body to the earth. If we're alive, we're grounded. It is usually illness, stress, tiredness, depression, and anxiety that cause grounding issues, not the positions of our legs or feet. So, please do not worry about how you are sitting.

'Tarot cards are evil and attract negative energies.'

Nothing in this world is evil in itself: even a humble carrot could be seen as evil if it had poison added to it. Yet, it would be the intent of the person giving you the meal with the carrot who would be to blame. Any evil, any negativity, as mentioned, stems from within your mind. Remember, Tarot cards are just printed card stock, and even if you work with spirit, or energy, they are love, and, again, any negative experiences stem from within.

'Pregnant women should not use Tarot.'

This superstition arises from a fear of the foetus being taken over by an evil spirit, or even the mother. The only way pregnancy can affect a Tarot reading is via the energy of the reader or the pregnant client. Some Tarot readers will be more energetic whilst pregnant and drawn more to the Tarot, others may have their interest turned off. To those readers who work with energy, it can cause confusion or mixed messages, as there are two energies present within the client, their own and the babies. To be a pregnant questioner or a reader of the Tarot will not cause harm in any way.

'It is a gift from God, so you should not charge to read for another.'

Tarot readers come in all shapes and sizes. Some are atheist or agnostic, and some see the Tarot solely as a subconscious tool. There is no pre-set faith assigned to those on a spiritual pathway, nor to those who read Tarot for Tarot's sake or perform any kind of reading or spiritual service.

The statement that it is a gift from God brings two things to consider.

Firstly, if you view your development, psychic, spiritual or with the Tarot as a gift, it can limit you. A gift suggests it is something you have been given and therefore something you cannot control, direct or be independent with. This can leave you relying on a higher power and the beliefs you have attached to it, which can be limiting, and fear-based. Rather than seeing it as a gift, it can benefit some people to see it as an ability. If you have no faith, then it is from you that any ability lies. If you see yourself as a spiritual being, being a Spirit in a body means you are simply tapping into yourself, which is something you can take full control of.

Secondly, your time is precious, so guard it well. A reading, with or without a spiritual element, is your time being implemented. You will never get that back. Value your time, and your commitment to your growth. Never be scared to charge for the service you provide, as it is simply an exchange of energy between reader and questioner. When you are still trying to work it all out, you may happily gift it to people for feedback, but there may come a time when it becomes a more serious element of your life.

Others who feel your services should be free and who do so due to their own religious beliefs, can be reminded that that if you were a priest, monk, or a nun doing God's work, you would be given a roof over your head. No one works for free in an official capacity for God, and even faith-based charity workers do so as they know they have their basic needs being met elsewhere. If you called a plumber out, you would be charged, it's no different, as your time is just as valuable.

'Tarot must be tapped three times before you use your Tarot cards.'

This is done in the belief that it will either open a door to your Guides in Spirit, ward off negative energies with the noise, like the banging of pots and pans on New Year or open the reader to friendly energies.

Smudging, Moonlight, and Crystals

I have placed these together as new tarot students get stuck on the issue of cleansing their deck. While you can smudge, use moonlight, bury the cards in the earth, or salt and place crystals with or on them, it will only make a difference if you believe it does. To do or not do any of these things will not bring you any bad luck, nor affect your relationship with your deck as that is a psychological matter.

Smudging is often done with sage, as it is said to remove negative energies from things, places and people. In itself, sage is antimicrobial (viruses and fungus) and antibacterial and so literally cleans the air.

Moonlight is said to charge crystals and Tarot cards. Using this would be a part of your belief system, so again this is a personal choice, as to not do it would not cause any issues or a lack of energy to your cards, as that all stems from the reader.

Crystals resonate with their own vibrations, and people choose certain crystals for certain issues, illnesses, or goals. The chosen crystal is meant to be kept with the Tarot deck to keep it charged or clear from negative energy. If you are drawn to crystals, use what you are drawn to, yet know it is not a necessity. As with all things, it will not affect your development with the Tarot.

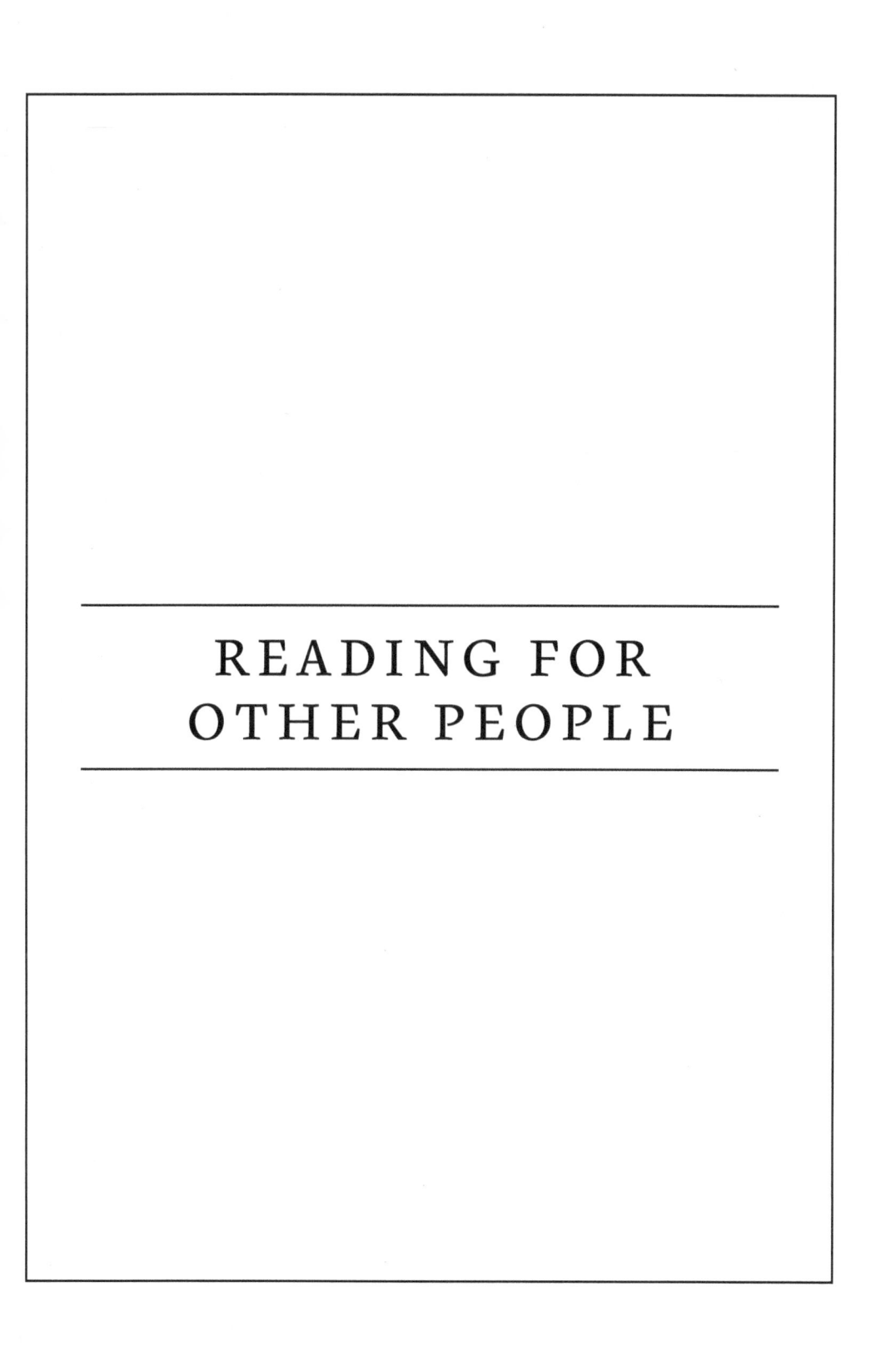

READING FOR OTHER PEOPLE

Reading for Others

In time, you will lay your cards for someone other than yourself. While this may be fun, or nerve-racking to comprehend, it does come with responsibility.

When you interpret the Tarot cards for another, remember, whether that individual is open-minded or sceptical, that a responsible approach is needed, as you will be dealing with their emotions. Being flippant in response to their questions or imposing your own opinion is irresponsible. If you give an opinion, make sure the individual knows it is from you and not from the Tarot cards, Spirit or clairvoyance. If that person is a stranger, ask if they want your opinion first. The face that a questioner may present to you may not hold truths, what they feel may not be what they show, so never presume how they may feel deep down, or how they will feel once they have left you. When you use the Tarot to assist others or yourself, you are given the keys to hidden fears, wishes and feelings, so use this responsibility wisely.

Do not be tempted to please someone, or yourself, by continuing to lay more cards until you get an appealing answer: trust the cards that are laid. A single clarifier card is one thing, but two or three, or more readings on the same issue show a lack of faith in the original Tarot cards laid, and your ability to understand them.

Whatever area of a client's or friend's life needs guidance, never feel afraid or embarrassed to admit you cannot find an answer, as wanting knowledge is not a guarantee to receiving it. You may be tired, they might be confused or there may be no answer to be had at that moment in time, or the truths within the cards may be being avoided. Do not be tempted to create an answer where one cannot be found; be honest with them and leave the reading for another day.

When you read for another, even if they think it light-hearted fun, you are still delving into their private life as well as those with whom they are connected to. What happens between you and a client, paying or non-paying, is private and no judgement should be passed. Confidentiality and non-judgement are king: if you cannot be confidential and love to pass judgement, it will hurt you professionally.

If someone who fears Tarot cards, or any spiritual ability, wishes a reading, it can be best to decline until they see such things in a more productive and positive light. Such people will often blame you or the cards for creating an outcome they do not like or wish. So, try to educate people who wish guidance, but are visibly or verbally scared of any form of divination.

To avoid tiredness, restrict a reading from one to three questions and try to stick within a time-frame of about an hour, or preferably less. It is easy to waffle or be badgered by the questioner into giving as much as you can. This can be draining so be nice to yourself, polite to the questioner and respect your own time and ability.

When you read for another, it is worth noting that they have not come to see you as a person, but you as a phone line, a link, a guide, and so ego is pointless, even though it is you who has spent time and energy studying Tarot, or is a psychic, developing your abilities. Learning the art of putting yourself to one side takes time, as when it comes to a reading, you are not the important one in the room. So, relax when starting to read for others. Take time to be with the person in their entirety by allowing your mind to reach out for what is needed. Open yourself up to everything and leave your ego outside of the reading. Your Spirit Guide, higher self, or Tarot wisdom will direct you to where you need to go to assist them; you are there to shine a light on what they cannot see within themselves.

Readings for or about Others without Their Knowledge or Permission

At some stage, you will probably wish to investigate another person's life, thoughts or feelings without their knowledge, or someone will want you to do so. For a lot of readers, this is the bulk of the questions they will present to their Tarot deck, and others will request of them. While there are no real rules to Tarot, there is an element of personal responsibility and ethics. If you wish to look at someone else to be nosy, for fun, or to find out their secrets, then not only may you be disappointed, but you need to ask if you would like it done to you? Often such situations arise out of spite, anger, jealousy, immaturity, fear, desire, desperation or a need for gossip, yet at times also out of genuine love, and in most cases, from a lack of communication.

When you lay cards to spy on another person, often you will see a reflection of yourself; you will read the cards to suit your own narrative, seeing what you wish or fear. Look to your intent when a reading involves another, and in all readings you do. Often you cannot confirm what you are being given if it is an eavesdropping reading on an unsuspecting person, which can lead you astray and to presumptions.

Just look at how that person will affect you.

You will find you can easily see how any individual impacts your life and the connection they have to you. This allows you to see the links between you both, which are there to pick up on and known either consciously or subconsciously, to either the individual or known about within the situation using the Tarot alone. Tarot reflects the self, so you may see what you already know, even if it is at a deeper level. Added to this, the energy links which connect us can be seen and reflected in the cards, which can show how that person will continue to affect you as time progresses.

During a reading, it is natural that other people will impact situations, and your reading may even be about your relationship with them, or a situation affected by them. This is okay and is quite natural. What you will be seeing will be how that person will react, interact and respond to you or the joint issue and situation, the side of them you will be dealing with and how they and you will, are or have progressed together. In such a reading, while you are asking about your connection to someone, the reading is still about your own life.

Focus on your own life, or that of an enquiring friend or client, by asking how those relevant to the situation at hand will affect you and how they wish to interact with you. Then everything you are looking at is within your energy, directly affects you, is your business and is easier to confirm.

THE FUTURE

The Future?

When I am asked if events in the future can be changed, the answer I give is, 'Both Yes and No'. Yet, Tarot tends to deal with the present in a greater way than people think, which is where the future stems from.

The Major Arcana represents strong and meaningful influences which shape and develop our lives. In doing so, they cannot in the long term be changed as they depict what is, what underpins a situation, or the foundation energy and what is relevant to the individual's situation. This is akin to the process of destiny or karma, or the energy which has built up and has created the situations we find ourselves in.

The energies that the Major Arcana represent are concentrated, hard to avoid and are largely unchangeable but not totally unavoidable. The Majors will tell of what is to be, and karma cannot be avoided, just maybe temporarily bypassed, or dealt with better. If you go for the bypass, you will find that what has been avoided will come around again sooner or later, and possibly worse.

The Minor Arcana can be changed, if you change your outlook and understand that *being forewarned is being forearmed* and take notice of where the spotlight is shining. The Minors indicate how we react to both the energies and events governed by the Majors. They fill in the details of the Majors' energies with the hows and whys. You can change and restructure the outcome to future events by changing your views, i.e. if the resulting position of the spread being used shows you reacting negatively to the situation at hand or an outcome you do not wish for, then by being prepared for it either physically, mentally or emotionally, you can change your reactions to it when it arrives, allowing you to work with it rather than against it.

Probable Outcomes

Once you have laid your chosen Tarot spread, it will inform you of the probable outcome. Tarot is all about probable outcomes, as a simple act of free will can change everything. That is not just free will from the questioner, but anyone connected to the situation, and even those on the outskirts of it, as ripples go out in ever-increasing circles.

The real magic of the Tarot lies in the NOW. Most people view the Tarot as a means to see the future, yet they are far more than that. Tarot, if used wisely, can shine a light on who you are, what you need to be doing and how you can best move forwards. You may well find, as you progress with the Tarot, that while seeing the future may be your concern, it is the here and now which your readings focus upon, on the reactions, feelings and actions which you are having or are being restricted by. It is by changing these things as you meet them which will direct you and where your real power lies. Tarot can help you recognise those things which you need to challenge about yourself and your life.

Free Will

We can all use free will, and we do so with every action and thought that we make. With the use of our free will, we can direct and mould our futures. As such, everything we do results from using our own personal free will and never abiding by the will of another (which if we do would still be the result of directing our own free will, as we have chosen to do so). As a direct consequence of free will, we can choose or aim for our future goals. Unfortunately, there is a lack of understanding of the principle of free will, and so most individuals do not consider the possibility of changing or purposefully directing their life's pathway. While I may have made it sound easy, breaking free of our belief systems can be hard to do, so please do not feel downhearted if you are struggling with such issues.

A Tarot reading will only show one's future possibilities if one is to stay on the same path mentally and/or emotionally from the time of the reading. So, by implementing free will, can events be subtly or drastically altered?

Yes, they can. However, strength will probably be required by the questioner to be able to deal with the events in a manner that they may not be used to. While we may not be able to change the actions of others who appear within our lives, we can control our own. While changing views or differing responses to avoid a situation may be a sign you have learnt from an event, it may also show avoidance. If that is the case, whatever you may have failed to learn will appear again, maybe under a different scenario, but it will return all the same.

To see or try to understand how events can be changed, ask for specific questions such as *'How can I ...?'* or *'What can I do to improve...?'*, instead of just accepting the given outcome that will result if your present views stay the same.

Just remember that Majors' influences are in existence until they have worn away naturally, and their energy has been used up. The action of the combined Minor and the Major decks form a loop. Minor Arcana cards bring about the influences of the Major Arcana, while the same is true in reverse, that the Majors bring about the effect of the Minors. When trying to redirect your future, the solution lies within your reaction to the 'Magical Minors', as they hold the key to our responses to the apparently immovable energies that the 'Majestic Majors' bring.

If you have laid a Tarot spread with either a majority of Major or Minor cards, whichever one of the two decks is predominant would have the upper hand. A majority of Major Arcana would indicate that events are not under your control and that destiny is playing its part, whereas a predominantly Minor Arcana spread would suggest that you have more control over the outcome of events.

TAROT MEDITATIONS FOR PSYCHIC DEVELOPMENT OR SUBCONSCIOUS CONNECTION

Stepping into Tarot

Most people who start to use the Tarot wish to develop their psychic and clairvoyant abilities. If you see these things as abilities rather than gifts, you will subconsciously find them easier to relate to, as mentioned before. As a Spiritual Being, you are naturally psychic, yet some have a more natural skill than others, and even those who do have a natural inclination still need to hone and practise to develop their connection. If you see it as a gift, you may hold yourself back, thinking you cannot, should not or are not good enough, when it is already within you, a part of you just waiting to be accessed.

When we study Tarot, the images and what we personally feel for the card will be what determines what each card means to us outside, or alongside their traditional meanings. There is no 'one size fits all' way of using Tarot, as we form our own relationship with the Tarot cards. In time, you will find that certain cards, while they contain a lot of information, mean just one or two things to you. A lot of the symbolic imagery is universally recognised and resonates with our subconscious minds to mean one or a few things based on our own life experiences. More symbolic knowledge gained from studying the cards will enhance what your subconscious mind already has programmed within it, so a lot of insight can come from the inner mind alone. This is why Tarot can be used so very well without any spiritual ability.

At times, it can be hard to see the subtle line between insights between reading energy or the subconscious. As for spiritual energy to speak to us, be that energy about a person, Guides, or your own Spiritual Self, it comes via our subconscious mind and the language of imagery, feelings and sensations we have pre-set in there. To learn more about a subject makes that language dictionary larger and more detailed, and why spiritual development is not needed with Tarot yet can often occur. The imagination is key, to visualise is part of the magic, not to control the images but to interact and just watch. At times, you will still get mixed messages, especially if you fear the reply, as egos can always lead us astray however experienced we are.

Psychic development is a large topic. Here I will give the basics as clearly as I can to give you a framework to start from and try to clear up any initial confusions you have. Spiritual titles can be confusing, as there is a lot of disagreement out there as to what each one means.

I will be using the terms *Psychic*, *Clairvoyant*, and *subconscious mind* to mean the following things:

Psychic: The word *psyche* refers to the mind, spirit and soul. The word describes the act or ability to draw information and energy down into the conscious self, and yet covers a lot of different things in practice. If someone says they are 'Psychic', it is best not to presume in what way, as it could represent or entail many different abilities. It is an umbrella term used to describe spiritual abilities and refers to those things beyond our conscious recognition. It is the act of connecting and bringing energy down to yourself, or others, which you may be aware or unaware of. These may include: healing energy, channelling Guides to write or create, guidance, insights, information, connecting to your own Higher Spiritual Self/Higher Mind. This can also include your subconscious mind, as it is something which we are not consciously aware of in the normal course of events.

Clairvoyant: This is a French word meaning 'clear sight' or 'clear vision', and within this field what we are reading is energy. That energy is taken in via your energy centres from yourself, another person or situation and translated into images or feelings which you can understand based on your own subconscious and conscious knowledge. Clairvoyance allows us to see or sense the past, present and future by being able to tune into the energy surrounding an object, individual or situation. This energy is seen in the form of pictures, which can be moving or still images, ideas, metaphors, words, symbols, colours, strong feelings, sounds or smells. It can be broken down into quite a few ways of receiving information, and with all of them, you can still call yourself a Clairvoyant. You may find that to have one Clairvoyant ability will mean you may well, at times, experience others. Here is a list of common Clairvoyant abilities:

Clairvoyance - to see within the mind's eye.

Clairsentience - to feel.

Claircognisance - to know.

Clairalience - to smell as if it were a fragrance present and about you, or the memory of a smell.

Clairgustance - to taste, as with smell.

Clairaudiance - to hear as if you were hearing it with your physical ears.

One Clairvoyant's symbol, sound, feeling, etc., for a situation, emotion or event will be different from another Clairvoyant's. Each one will be linked to their own life experiences, wisdom, understandings and symbolic knowledge, which is drawn upon, and through which the energy linked to is filtered. This gives you your own unique language, as energy is converted into a symbol in whatever form you would personally understand it. For example, for someone waiting for an event to occur, you may see a set of traffic lights stuck on red each time it is picked up from someone. For someone in love, you may see the colour pink or a snapshot of your past which encapsulates that. Also, with Tarot symbolism embedded inside your mind, you may get a whole card pop into your head, or a tiny aspect of one to give you the information you need, or you may just 'know'.

People can confuse Clairvoyance with Mediumship or being a Medium, yet they are different. A Clairvoyant works with energy; a Medium is someone who gives proof of the survival of a person's spirit after death. Yet, Mediumship can be conveyed clairvoyantly, communicating via our Guides or energy where our own clairvoyant language is used, and is called Mental Mediumship. Being a Clairvoyant does not mean you will be a Medium. To be a Medium does not mean you will be Clairvoyant; one ability does not mean you will have others, yet you can also be multi-skilled and have them all. A Medium can just be a Medium but can also be Clairvoyant, and vice versa. Yet they are all Psychic. Where your natural abilities lie will often not be something you can choose, as it is something based on your own Higher Self, vibration, and life lessons.

Subconscious mind: Your subconscious mind controls all that you are: from your psychological responses to your unknown quirky reactions to things which you do not understand. It can be seen as a massive computer with billions of files containing all of who you are, with each thing you have ever experienced recorded. These files of information link to your individual clairvoyant language. Our subconscious minds are aware of everything about us, and when energy is focused on an issue or situation or picked up, our subconscious will connect to something known within one of those files which means something to you. A bit like a subconscious filter taking news to a file that will recognise it, and which then informs you with imagery or by clairvoyant means, giving the energy form which can then be 'read' by you. This allows for a stronger connection to your Guides, even if you are not aware of them and a stronger connection to your spiritual self. This can also, in time, lead you to be able to work without Tarot cards if you wish.

The subconscious mind is the inner doorway to your Higher Spiritual Self and your connection to Spirit, and so are very linked. As a spiritual being, you are the energy you are wishing to use: it is all about you, as well as present from those you connect to. Imagination is the gateway to psychic awareness and the main key to successful psychic development.

You may feel that imagination is the place of the unreal, of vague impressions and daydreams, but it opens doors in development and will give you the first experiences of your psychic potential. The imagination is not to be neglected or pushed to one side if you wish to develop, as it is of the utmost importance. We are brought up to ignore our imaginations; it is for childhood and dreams. But it is from the foundation of the imagination that psychic growth starts. It is here that we can picture in our minds what does not exist outside of us. It is from here that we create. We all can imagine. In some, it may be a bit rusty, but it is still there. If I ask you to imagine a green fish, what do you see or know inside your head? Or a yellow tree, a blue dog, a hand-sized whale. They all conjure up an image or a sense of an image, feeling or knowing. The imagination is a real force, one that can help you to develop clairvoyantly, as you start to work with symbols, feelings and images, pictures playing in your head. A strong imagination helps with this. Your subconscious mind gives you images, symbols and pictorial references all the time, you just need to start recognising them. Tarot is an excellent way to get the imagination going.

Stepping into Tarot - Getting to Know a Card

Here we will learn a method which I call 'Stepping into Tarot', a method used to build a relationship with an individual card. You can use this with each card, or just those cards you find hard to gel with or grasp. Use the card upright, as within that, you can ask about its reversed energy if you wish. Of course, with no rules, you can focus on the reversed card, yet the mind may find it hard to work with a reversed image, as we are used to seeing the world about us upright.

With the Tarot card you wish to meditate on, study it, absorb as much as you can about it. Leave it a day before you do this meditation to allow for some of what you have learned to settle into your mind, as you are trying here to get your subconscious mind to speak to you in a way you can grasp on a personal level. So, give your mind food for thought.

- *Have a pen and paper handy if you wish to jot down any ideas or thoughts that come to mind. Some may prefer to put down notes after, as it means not having to go in and out of the card, especially at the start when it may be hard to do. If you have a 'Tarot Journal' (a notebook used to write down your insights about Tarot), this is an excellent place to write your findings down.*

- *To begin, you do not need to shuffle your Tarot deck, unless you wish a random card: just take out the card you wish to focus on and place it face down for a moment. Do not lie down, sit upright, and place your Tarot card in front of you in a place easy for you to see without straining your neck or body.*

- *Meditation is about feeling, not thinking, so light a candle if it helps with relaxation, as this is a wonderful tool for focus. If you are struggling, losing focus, getting frustrated or anything which makes you feel disconnected from the card, just take time away from the image to gaze at the flame, or focus on your breathing, or even to a blank space on the wall, and focus on relaxing your breathing.*

- *Close your eyes and take a few deep breaths; focus on relaxing your body for a minute or two, then just rest with your breathing for a few more minutes. When you feel ready, open your eyes. If you wish, gaze at the candle for a while and visualise the flame in your mind's eye, or just breathe and imagine your breaths coming in and out of you in any way you are given by your mind. Do not control any images you get. All of this helps give you some space between normal life and meditating on, or journeying into, your chosen Tarot card. It is a time to separate your stress from your mind and centre yourself. If you wish to develop your psychic self, it will start you off with a ritual which shows the mind that now is Tarot Time. This triggers the subconscious queues which you can benefit from. By visualising your breath or the flame in your mind, you are starting to use your visualisation skills and strengthening a muscle.*

- *You can stay like this for as long as you like. Try to aim for a few minutes, even five or ten if you feel stressed. However, we are not here for meditation's sake, but to create a state of mind open to the imagery within your chosen Tarot card and how your own mind perceives those messages.*

- *Turn your Tarot card over.*

- *Look at your card, see the edges of the card as an open door into the world shown. Look at it as if this were the world outside of your front door which you have just opened and are viewing for the first time. But stay on the threshold unless you are drawn in at this stage.*

- *Try to picture the card in your mind after a time of gazing at it. If you find this hard, do your best, as it will get easier. At the start, you may find you can only hold a small bit of the card's imagery in your mind if you close your eyes, and that's okay. If keeping your eyes open helps, then do that, yet you will not cancel out all the other visual stimuli about you. You may need to use the Tarot card like the candle if you're struggling, by opening your eyes and just recapturing the card once again in your mind.*

- *As you take the card in, you may even be pulled to a certain aspect of the card. If you are, you can go straight to that point or just start to look at the world about you, as you now imagine that you're standing on the threshold of this doorway.*

- *Take some time to hear the sounds and noises which the scene inside your Tarot card would possess, the smells, the air temperature, any wind or breezes. Then step in and allow it to be all about you.*

- *You can move, walk, talk and see everything. You are here to see what this card means to you, to gel with it, so be curious. Talk to those within the card as if you had just met them, introduce yourself. If you wish to touch something, ask as you would in real life. No response or even a look given can hold a lot of insight. Sense what you are feeling, relax and notice if anything is shown in your mind's eye. Talk to the characters with simple direct questions such as 'What do you represent?' or 'What do you give to the world?', or 'What is your role?'*

- *If you start to struggle at any stage, go back to your candle or breathing and leave the card for a few seconds or a minute and go back.*

- *You may enjoy deep conversations, lots of feelings and insights. You may be taken somewhere else as your mind, Spirit or clairvoyance passes you information. You may smell, hear, taste, touch or feel within your mind a sense which seems very real, or you may get a single word or feeling which tells you everything, or nothing at all.*

- *If nothing comes, do not worry, it can take time to learn a new skill. No one can pick up a musical instrument and play it perfectly in one day. Sometimes the answers may come later when you are not stressed about your experience or practice. At other times, you will need to let go of your expectations, give it more time and try again another day.*

- *When you feel 'done', just say your goodbyes to anyone within the card and open your eyes.*

A lot of the time when this meditation is done, you will be working with your subconscious mind. It holds far more insights than you could ever know. It is a treasure chest of information which we are not consciously aware of, a bit like the Arcana's, a chest in which treasure is stored. Within it will be millions of symbols and images which are universal, and while you may not grasp what something means, your subconscious probably will, so ask it.

I have mentioned before that your clairvoyant self, which is often a mix of imagery, feelings and just knowing, is linked to your subconscious mind, using it to give messages substance which you as an individual will then understand. While examining your Tarot card, this side of you can be working, you may not be able to tell the difference, yet that does not matter. Just get to know the cards you are stuck on or wishing to meet for now.

Try not to do one or two cards a day, as you may find that you tire as you are learning new skills. It is easy to get confused, frustrated, or worn out as those new neurons start to connect. Sometimes we need to sleep on our findings, so what we have seen makes more sense.

The more you do this exercise, the easier it will become, so if you struggle with it, come back to it. If you are new to meditation, focusing or using your imagination, then it's a method that once learnt will help you further your psychic and spiritual development, as well as the link to your own mind and inner self. At this stage, as well as in the future, when you sit with each card and ask the card to talk to you, it will welcome you to view its secrets. You will develop your own personal understanding of the individual cards in a deeper manner when you meditate upon them. Go slow, as you cannot rush development, nor relationships and you have seventy-eight relationships to form. Do take patience along with you as a travelling partner as you build your relationship with the Tarot. All knowledge gained is information learned.

Stepping into Tarot – Personal Answers

The technique is similar to the Getting to Know a Card Method. Yet your card's traditional meaning can still be considered at first glance while you are open to what messages the card holds for you, as it can help you to be able to step into it.

Make sure you are seated comfortably. Create your question, word it clearly and be ready to hear some truths. If you fear your answer, you will not listen or see what is given, and this can cause confusion and blocks.

- *Get a pen and paper if you wish, and if you wish, light a candle to focus and relax with.*

- *Shuffle and prepare your deck, thinking about your question. Once you are happy with your shuffle, take a card and do not look at it at this stage. Place it face down somewhere you can see it with ease.*

- *As with the above method, take time to relax, close your eyes and let go of your question, focusing on your body and the candle flame, or your body relaxing and your breath. Visualising either of them in your mind's eye.*

- *Be open to the guidance you seek, be open to your Spiritual Self or mind, whichever you choose. Ask for guidance, such as 'What is happening within my relationship with John?' If you wish, you can take a few breaths and visualise your energy, your aura (a light made of seven energy layers that surround your physical self), expanded as far as your mind's eye can see, feel safe, happy and relaxed. Or use the personal beliefs you feel comfortable with. If you lose focus while you are opening, just relax by going back to the flame or your breath.*

- *When you are feeling ready, gently think about your question, let go of any expectations, open your eyes, turn the card and gently scan it.*

- *Don't be shocked or put off if it isn't a happy Tarot card, as here the card's traditional meaning can be noted, but it is what you will find within the card that is of importance, and life is not all about the happy cards. You may find the card's actual meaning gives you what you need, and you may still wish to step in and journey, or it may not speak to you at all. For now, just move your eyes gently over the card and hold the card's image in your mind's eye as best you can.*

- *As before, treat the card as a doorway. If you are drawn to something, go straight to it, if not, step in and relax a bit more. Look about you, you can even go round the corners of the card to the bits unseen, walk over horizons, put your feet into the sea, touch the trees, just follow what you feel you should do. Always allow for things to organically evolve rather than forcing anything, do not try to change anything you see or feel. Ask your question again if you are not connecting to anything, and give it all some time, as you can easily get in your own way. Sometimes you may find yourself transported somewhere else in your mind, even to things which seem completely unlinked to the card and that's okay. Your mind or Spirit is just helping you to find your answer. Just let it happen. Aspects of the card's imagery may be highlighted, leading you to an answer. If you do not understand, ask 'What do you mean?', and it may show you something else, in many of the different ways in which energy can be seen or felt.*

- *When you feel you have found your answers or wish to leave the Tarot card, simply open your eyes, and come back. If you wish, you can close down by saying thank you, blowing out your candle, or taking in a deep breath and imagining the expanded energy about you shrinking to a few feet or a metre about you. Trust that your Spiritual Self will regulate your energy as needed, so do not worry about doing it right or wrong. You have an army of Guides in Spirit about you who will take care of you if you are worried about anything negative, as anything negative will solely be in your mind.*

In time, you will find that you can use this method with a larger spread if you wish. Yet one card can give you all you need if used well.

A couple of simple examples: I once drew the Three of Pentacles to a love question, I was taken to the plans the architect holds and told to 'stick to my original plans', which was simple, brief but correct. A more complicated visit to a card was for a friend over a work issue and I drew the Knight of Pentacles. The Knight got off his horse and to the right of him my friend's company fell to the floor, only to be rebuilt again; the number two was shown to me, which turned out to be two months. They showed she would return to work but to be careful of going back to this company as it was a 'dying industry'. The company had shut down; after two months it reopened, and she went back, but now the whole business is literally demolished and gone. The meditation showed moving and still colour images; I knew or felt the words used rather than heard them, plus had thoughts and feelings with this journey. In others, I have entered the card and been taken to other scenes completely alien to the Tarot card chosen.

As you learn more about what each Tarot card and its imagery means, you will have a greater language for Spirit and energy to communicate to you with. This is the beginning of using your natural intuition and clairvoyant abilities. Don't worry if no messages or impressions come through. Just relax and leave it for another day. In time, you will know whether it is your ego, fear or expectations talking, as equally as if your own higher mind or Guides are talking to you, as once experienced they have a different feel to them.

How Often Should I Meditate upon a Card?

If you can try to do at least one card a day, make it a routine part of your life, even if each day your question is *'What messages do you have for me today?'*

Live Tarot, although step away if you get too confused and come back later. Daily connections to your cards, or even psychic self will help you to build your Spiritual or subconscious imaginative muscles. But please remember that it cannot be rushed, and everyone will develop as fast as their mind or Spirit will allow.